I N S I D E T H E M I N D S

Telecommunications Client Strategies

Leading Lawyers on Negotiating Agreements, Facilitating Transactions, and Resolving Disputes

ASPATORE

Mat #40756110

BOOK & ARTICLE IDEA SUBMISSIONS

If you are a C-Level executive, senior lawyer, or venture capitalist interested in submitting a book or article idea to the Aspatore editorial board for review, please e-mail TLR.AspatoreAuthors@thomson.com. Aspatore is especially looking for highly specific ideas that would have a direct financial impact on behalf of a reader. Completed publications can range from 2 to 2,000 pages. Include your book/article idea, biography, and any additional pertinent information.

Inside the Minds Project Manager, Merissa Kraham; edited by Michaela Falls; proofread by Melanie Zimmerman

Aspatore books may be purchased for educational, business, or sales promotional use. For information, please e-mail West.customer.service@thomson.com.

ISBN 978-0-314-19512-8

For corrections, updates, comments or any other inquiries please e-mail TLR.AspatoreEditorial@thomson.com.

First Printing, 2008

10 9 8 7 6 5 4 3 2 1

Praise for *Inside the Minds*

"Need-to-read inside information and analysis that will improve your bottom line - the best source in the business." – Daniel J. Moore, Member, Harris Beach LLP

"The Inside the Minds series is a valuable probe into the thought, perspectives, and techniques of accomplished professionals…" – Chuck Birenbaum, Partner, Thelen Reid & Priest

"Aspatore has tapped into a gold mine of knowledge and expertise ignored by other publishing houses." – Jack Barsky, Managing Director, Information Technology & Chief Information Officer, ConEdison *Solutions*

"Unlike any other publisher – actual authors that are on the front-lines of what is happening in industry." – Paul A. Sellers, Executive Director, National Sales, Fleet and Remarketing, Hyundai Motor America

"A snapshot of everything you need..." – Charles Koob, Co-Head of Litigation Department, Simpson Thacher & Bartlet

"Everything good books should be - honest, informative, inspiring, and incredibly well-written." – Patti D. Hill, President, BlabberMouth PR

"Great information for both novices and experts." – Patrick Ennis, Partner, ARCH Venture Partners

"A rare peek behind the curtains and into the minds of the industry's best." – Brandon Baum, Partner, Cooley Godward

"Intensely personal, practical advice from seasoned dealmakers." – Mary Ann Jorgenson, Coordinator of Business Practice Area, Squire, Sanders & Dempsey

"Great practical advice and thoughtful insights." – Mark Gruhin, Partner, Schmeltzer, Aptaker & Shepard, PC

"Reading about real-world strategies from real working people beats the typical business book hands down." - Andrew Ceccon, Chief Marketing Officer, OnlineBenefits Inc.

"Books of this publisher are syntheses of actual experiences of real-life, hands-on, front-line leaders--no academic or theoretical nonsense here. Comprehensive, tightly organized, yet nonetheless motivational!" - Lac V. Tran, Sr. Vice President, CIO and Associate Dean Rush University Medical Center

"Aspatore is unlike other publishers…books feature cutting-edge information provided by top executives working on the front-line of an industry." - Debra Reisenthel, President and CEO, Novasys Medical Inc

ASPATORE

www.Aspatore.com

Aspatore Books, a Thomson Reuters business, is the largest and most exclusive publisher of C-level executives (CEO, CFO, CTO, CMO, partner) from the world's most respected companies and law firms. Aspatore annually publishes a select group of C-level executives from the Global 1,000, top 250 law firms (partners and chairs), and other leading companies of all sizes. C-Level Business Intelligence™, as conceptualized and developed by Aspatore Books, provides professionals of all levels with proven business intelligence from industry insiders—direct and unfiltered insight from those who know it best—as opposed to third-party accounts offered by unknown authors and analysts. Aspatore Books is committed to publishing an innovative line of business and legal books, those which lay forth principles and offer insights that, when employed, can have a direct financial impact on the reader's business objectives, whatever they may be. In essence, Aspatore publishes critical tools—need-to-read as opposed to nice-to-read books—for all business professionals.

Inside the Minds

The critically acclaimed *Inside the Minds* series provides readers of all levels with proven business intelligence from C-level executives (CEO, CFO, CTO, CMO, partner) from the world's most respected companies. Each chapter is comparable to a white paper or essay and is a future-oriented look at where an industry/profession/topic is heading and the most important issues for future success. Each author has been carefully chosen through an exhaustive selection process by the *Inside the Minds* editorial board to write a chapter for this book. *Inside the Minds* was conceived in order to give readers actual insights into the leading minds of business executives worldwide. Because so few books or other publications are actually written by executives in industry, *Inside the Minds* presents an unprecedented look at various industries and professions never before available.

CONTENTS

Preliminary Considerations for Developing Successful Strategies in Telecom Disputes

Shira R. Yoshor

Partner

Baker Botts LLP

ASPATORE

Taking on New Clients and Avoiding the Pitfalls of Conflicts

Before meeting with a new client on a telecom matter for the first time, it is critical to understand the nature of the company and its operations, where it operates and how it is regulated, and what issues are at stake. This information is particularly important for initial strategy planning. Perhaps even more importantly, you must have this information before the first meeting to make sure that the new client is one you can comfortably represent from the perspective of conflicts.

Indeed, even if there is not any ethical bar to the representation, it is important to consider the potential business or issue conflict that may arise. For example, if a new telecom client is a competitive local exchange carrier (CLEC), will the matter at issue cause you to take a position that may be detrimental to your incumbent local exchange carrier (ILEC) client? Historically, ILECs have owned the majority of the telecommunications infrastructure. ILECs have specific restrictions that do not apply to CLECs or companies that provide telecommunication services only through the Internet. Your ILEC client wants to protect its infrastructure from competitors as much as legally possible, and that may put it at odds with the new CLEC that wants to hire you. Before you agree to represent the CLEC, you have to know how that representation will possibly affect your ILEC client. Additionally, as in most industries, some telecom clients are particularly sensitive to the representation of other telecom clients that could be viewed as competitors or potential adversaries. Understanding the players will allow you to reassure the client that you have considered the potential challenge in this arena and have plans to resolve or avoid such a challenge.

It is also critical for you to understand the nature of the proceeding at issue and how it is connected to other matters for the prospective client. Is the issue related to any matters pending before a regulatory agency, and if so, to what stage has the regulatory proceeding advanced? Will a new rule or decision at the regulatory agency impede your ability to move forward with your new case? Is there any way to protect the current issue from being decided in the other forum? Understanding the range of potential implications of regulatory activity on your case is essential to a telecommunications matter.

By obtaining this information in advance, you can immediately begin to discuss the parameters of the anticipated representation. It is important to understand how and where the telecom client is regulated so that you can represent them with a well-coordinated approach. Sometimes you will have to learn about related activities at the local, state, and federal level to make sure that the client is taking consistent positions. Doing some initial research to find out what has occurred in these various arenas will allow your client to introduce you to the right people within the company who are working on related issues, or the same issue in a different forum. Additionally, by making sure you understand the nature of the issue and the players, you will gain the necessary comfort that you are not running into a conflict situation with this new client.

For example, your telecom client may approach you about representing it with respect to a dispute over billing. Billing issues are frequently addressed by the state regulatory agency that oversees telecommunications issues, and in some jurisdictions, telephone bills are vetted through the state agency. In some jurisdictions, even the wording on bills must be approved in advance. The Federal Communications Commission may also be examining the same issues. Your representation of the client in the billing dispute has to be informed and must consider the activities in each of these other arenas. If your client has worked with each of these agencies to try to combat billing problems, your client may have a strong defense against attempts by consumers to challenge billing that these agencies approved.

Formulating Client Strategy

When you first meet with a client, it is important to understand the context for the issue, including the factual background; the client's goal with respect to the matter (i.e., what is the preferred resolution); historic practice (how the client has dealt with similar situations in the past); key contacts and decision makers for the case; the opponent; and the preferred method of communication. This information is important when beginning work on any new case—not just a case for a telecom client—because these are the tools that will craft your strategy for the case. It is essential to understand and confirm the client's needs and wants before you embark on any strategy.

This information, in addition to the information obtained before the first meeting, will set the tone for the strategy going forward. In virtually every case, especially at the beginning, there are several potential approaches. Choosing the right approach requires discussion up front in order to figure out what has happened to date—i.e., how the client has handled similar situations in the past—so that you can either continue with the same approach, or jointly decide that a new approach is necessary.

To formulate a client strategy in a telecom matter, you must also know the client's desired endgame. What is the result that would make it happiest? If necessary, what would its next choice be? To reach that result, what constraints will it face? You need information about the client's budget; authority; prior practice; how it interfaces with the regulatory agency or agencies; political opposition or opposition on policy grounds; internal organizational challenges; applicable statutes, rules or ordinances; and any applicable deadlines. Before you can formulate a strategy, you must have at least a preliminary understanding of most, if not each, of these issues.

Indeed, you cannot plan a viable strategy without considering these factors at a minimum. In almost every circumstance, achieving the client's objective should also be your objective. By considering these factors, you and your client can develop a plan to address the issue at hand in a practical way.

Protecting the Client's Interests

Any lawyer representing a client involved in a telecom dispute should aim to protect the client's interests as best as possible. Achieving that goal depends heavily on the situation at issue. For example, many telecom providers are heavily regulated by local, state, and federal agencies. You must be familiar with the statutory and regulatory framework in which your client operates. My main goal is to make sure that the advice I provide is well coordinated with other parts of the client's business so that the strategy does not negatively affect other positions that the client is taking or would like to take in a different forum.

I have found this approach critical to my representation of telecom clients, in order to ensure that they do not win the battle, but subsequently lose the war. If you consider the dispute you are handling in isolation, you may achieve a successful resolution in that dispute, but create problems in other areas.

For example, your client may aim to protect itself from a dispute in state court involving an issue under examination by the state regulatory agency. You must advise your client with knowledge of the proceedings before the state regulatory agency. If you are not well informed about the ongoing regulatory proceeding, you may take an inconsistent position in the court case unwittingly. Likewise, if you represent the client before the regulatory agency, you should learn as much as possible about related court cases so that you will be able to consider the best way to frame the issues in your regulatory filings.

Coordination between different parts of the company and between different geographic regions, if applicable, can often be beneficial to all involved. When a legal strategy has been well coordinated, important and unexpected benefits can often be achieved within various segments of the client organization. For example, a well-coordinated approach between the regulatory and litigation staff can be used to defeat a court action and preserve the company's interests in the regulatory sphere. A successful outcome in another jurisdiction may provide helpful insights to others dealing with the same issue in another region of the country, even if the first decision is not binding on the other jurisdiction. Of course, if a telecom client operates in a limited market or focuses on a very specific aspect of the business, this coordination process is much simpler. If you represent a small cooperative telephone company that operates in a very limited market, you will not likely have to coordinate among too many various parts of a company or many outside agencies.

Key Questions

There are five key questions that I will typically ask of a client in order to determine the best strategy in a telecom matter/dispute:

1. Can you describe the historical practice with respect to this issue within the company?
2. Are there any tariffs that apply or potentially apply to the dispute?
3. Are there any related proceedings within any other geographic region and in any forum?

4. What is the result that you aim to achieve, or what would you consider a successful outcome to this dispute?
5. What is the anticipated budget in terms of both time and resources for this dispute?

The purpose of these questions is to glean a better understanding of potential claims and defenses that may be relevant to the dispute. Also, the answers to these questions will guide initial strategy and recommendations to the client, and help me better understand the limitations for handling the dispute. Essentially, the answers to these questions guide the approach for moving forward.

Important Documentation

When working on behalf of a client that is involved in a telecom dispute, it is critical to receive documentation such as any applicable tariffs (or even arguably relevant tariffs) or applicable agreements. If end users are involved, it is helpful to receive information about the relationship with those end users. It is also very important to receive copies of any written communication, including electronic communications with the other party to the dispute, and the internal communications relating to the dispute.

This documentation is important because it provides the factual background and the legal context to frame the case. This documentation will help you to better understand your case—although it may not necessarily be helpful; indeed, you may discover some evidence or legal issue that will limit your claims or defenses. You may learn that the claims asserted against your client are explicitly covered in the tariff, and that your client did not comply with the requirements set forth in the tariff. It is much better to learn that information sooner, rather than later, so that you can consider some negotiated resolution to the dispute, or at least understand and explain to the client how this information may affect the case.

The Client-Attorney Relationship

Communication is critical in establishing a positive client-attorney relationship in a telecom matter, much as it is in other legal contexts. Communicating difficult news may be unpleasant, but it cannot be ignored.

In addition, listening to the client and understanding the client's preferences on strategy is very important. The attorney must also be sensitive to the organizational issues surrounding the client and the dispute in question. Sometimes there may be miscommunication or misunderstanding between the business organization and the attorneys who are responsible for that organization. Communicating the issues requires discretion and an understanding to avoid unwarranted blame on one individual or an organization.

Responsiveness is also essential to developing a good client-attorney relationship. You must make it clear that you care about the client and understand the client's business, and that your interests are aligned in reaching the desired outcome. Focusing on the client's objectives is key. In fact, it is difficult to be successful if you focus on your definition of success, rather than listening to the client.

A good attorney-client relationship is primarily based on trust—and developing a good rapport with the client is the only way to gain the client's trust. By listening, the attorney understands the larger context for the dispute, and can mold the strategy for handling the dispute with those considerations in mind. Ultimately, your ability to develop a strong client-attorney relationship makes it much more likely that you will be able to achieve the desired result on behalf of the client.

Understanding the Client's Goals/Managing Expectations

I learn my client's ultimate goals in a telecom matter by talking with them and listening to them—both to what they say, and equally to what they do not say. If there is something that appears obvious to someone who approaches the matter more objectively, there may be a reason that the client has not addressed that particular element of the case squarely with you. Perhaps the client's direct supervisor is responsible for the decision that is now under attack. The situation is even more challenging when others recognize a potential problem, but the person who created the situation does not.

You also need to ask questions to learn what the client's ultimate goals are for that particular matter. Start with the obvious: what do you want to achieve? What would you consider a winning result? If the client wants to make a change from prior practice, why? Practically, how easy or difficult would it be for the client to change its approach? What are some of the impediments? If the matter is critical to the client, the attorney has to make it a matter of first priority, or adjust the client's expectations about the matter. A client's belief that its matter is of the highest importance will likely spur quicker action on my part than would be the case should the client call about something that is not pressing. If a client calls with an inquiry stemming from an issue that is not imminent, that is important to know so that the timing of the response can be adjusted accordingly.

When I think that the client's goals in a telecom matter or dispute are unrealistic, the actions that I take will depend on the client. With some clients, especially those with whom I have already established a rapport, it is easier to point out the dangers in their assumptions, and why their goals are not realistic. It is often helpful to have other real-life examples to illustrate your point and show why the client's goals are unlikely to be obtained.

For example, in order to help clients understand the realities of their case, it is helpful to point to applicable authority, cases, or administrative opinions that addressed a similar issue, and then describe the outcome of those cases. When precedents involving the same or analogous issues are not available, or other factors make the case challenging (i.e., potentially damaging evidence or a bad witness), it is useful to communicate those hurdles to the client very soon after you are aware of them. In the world of telecommunications, clients frequently deal with issues that have never been tested before. The outcome from these situations may be particularly difficult to predict. To the extent you can draw from similar types of situations, you can develop and create successful strategies. But you have to anticipate the challenges and risks along the way. Clients generally do not like to be surprised, especially when such information could have been disclosed sooner.

These strategies are helpful in telecom disputes and other types of cases because, in most instances, clients will need to report information on the status of the case and expected results to their managers. If they are not well informed or appear to be unprepared or unfocused, your advice may come into question. Good attorneys enable their clients to be well prepared and well informed on the issues in the dispute.

Developing Case Theory

The first step in developing a theory of a telecom case is to find out how the client has handled similar matters in the past. You should also investigate the facts and begin your legal research by educating yourself on the regulatory and statutory authority that may be appropriate, as well as case law and applicable tariffs.

The client should always be involved in discussions concerning historical practice. The client is also a helpful resource to comment on the pros and cons of the previous strategy. Additionally, the client may have information about similar issues and how they are being handled in another region or business department of the company. Indeed, I believe that it is very important to work in partnership with your client in these matters. A telecom client may have knowledge of internal information, detailed information about certain technology at issue or information about another project internally that is relevant to the dispute—information that you would not otherwise be able to access. Sometimes the client does not think to coordinate with other business units until recommended by the attorney. By involving the client, you get closer to achieving the coordination that is critical, especially with large telecom clients.

For example, if the client is poised to embark on a large scale effort to take certain action with respect to its end user customers and does not realize the effect such action could have on another aspect of its business, your involvement could be key to make sure that the action is accomplished in a way that comports with its other business strategies and legal obligations. You will also further develop a rapport with the client that helps direct you to the desired outcome.

To Settle or to Litigate

If a telecom client is unwilling to settle a dispute, you may wish to consider more creative ways of asserting or defending the claim, but you need to explain to the client the risks attendant to proceeding with the litigation. If the client is willing to settle, you should conserve the amount of resources you expend on the litigation, if possible, so that the settlement remains financially advantageous to the client.

It is very hard to say whether telecom clients are more or less likely to settle than clients in other practice areas. In my experience, telecom clients will settle occasionally; however, the likelihood of settlement largely depends on the issue and the client. In some cases, the client may choose to fight on principle to create a precedent that will guide them going forward, even if the amount at stake in that particular case is not substantial.

Consideration of Business Impact from Resolution of a Telecom Matter

The non-legal ramifications of a telecom matter are very important. In addition to the legal ramifications that may affect the businesspeople involved in the dispute, such as preservation of enormous amounts of data or dedication of substantial support to assist the legal team, it is important to consider the business and organizational ramifications of a dispute. For example, sometimes a proposed settlement will result in a change to the business practices, not just a new contract provision. The attorney must understand the practical difficulties that may arise from implementing these changes. The lawyer should be prepared to explain why they are necessary, and definitely, the attorney should understand in advance the time and effort that will be required to implement the change. Understanding the practical business effects of a proposed resolution may affect the strategy to propose such a resolution in the first place.

Sometimes the optimal business solution is very different from winning the legal issues in a dispute. For example, the marketing organization may be focused on using specific materials that it has generated through years of research, but to avoid major litigation, the legal team aims to change those materials substantially. Explaining the need for the changes and working to keep as much as the materials as possible will help to alleviate the tension between the two groups.

Additionally, an attorney must be sensitive to perceptions and perspectives, especially in potentially assigning fault or laying blame within the organization, regardless of the fact that those issues probably will not have legal ramifications. If the attorney intends to build a long-standing relationship with the client, he or she must have the trust and confidence of the individuals involved in the litigation, whether they are attorneys or businesspeople.

When advising a client, I try to consider more than the immediate problem that gives rise to the discussion or request for advice. Learning about the client's business enables the attorney to anticipate challenges that may arise from a legal strategy that has negative business implications. Creating a solution that addresses both the legal and business issues, short and longer term, is key.

Mistakes to Avoid

In a worst-case scenario, if you follow an improper legal strategy in a telecom matter, and do not realize it until it is too late, you may lose the case, and create wider problems for the client in other areas—i.e., in pending cases; in the regulatory arena; and with other business customers.

You can avoid following the wrong path by coordinating with others in the client organization. It is important for a telecom law attorney to understand the impact of its legal strategy on the client's business, as well as how it affects other matters the client is facing. Ultimately, the attorney must understand how the legal strategy in his or her client's case could affect issues pending in a variety of other areas.

Final Thoughts

When representing a client in a telecom dispute, it is essential to:

- Listen to the client carefully.
- Learn the client's business.
- Understand the major challenges to the client.
- Learn the client's definition of success.
- Determine whether the client has cost sensitivities.
- Coordinate with others within the organization to make sure that the client is taking a consistent position that will not be undermined by or will not undermine other proceedings.

This information is important because these are the basic ingredients necessary for successful representation in the complex and changing environment that telecommunications clients face. The technology in the world of telecommunications is developing at an unbelievable fast pace. As new technologies emerge, the legal community faces new challenges, and the law must adapt as well. Courts and regulatory agencies address these new technologies, but frequently, the situations created in this fast-paced environment are so new and unprecedented that the attorneys who deal with them may not have any clear guidelines. These novel issues present great opportunities and challenges for attorneys practicing in the world of telecommunications.

Shira R. Yoshor grew up in Charleston, South Carolina, and now lives and works in Houston, Texas. She graduated from Yeshiva University's Stern College for Women summa cum laude, serves as vice chair of the board of directors for Stern College for Women, and is a member of the Strategic Planning Committee for Yeshiva University. Ms. Yoshor graduated from the University of Chicago as a member of the Law Review. *She is a partner at Baker Botts LLP, an international law firm of more than 750 lawyers recognized for its creative approach to the legal and business issues facing its clients. Ms. Yoshor was named a "Texas Rising Star" and "Texas Super Lawyer" by* Texas Monthly *and* Law & Politics *magazine in 2004.*

During her fifteen years of practice, she has represented clients in commercial trial and appellate matters as well as arbitrations. She has done work regularly for major telecommunications, energy, and media companies in various courts throughout Texas and the United States.

Dedication: *To Daniel Yoshor, for supporting me in every way.*

Representing Telecom Clients: Looking for Opportunities Amidst Rapid Change

Stephen R. Clark

Partner

Husch Blackwell Sanders LLP

ASPATORE

Introduction

As an attorney who specializes in telecommunications law, I keep a close watch on this rapidly changing industry so that I can help my clients exploit business opportunities. Of course, clear communication and responsiveness, and a clear understanding of the client's objectives, are essential. This is a growing and evolving industry, with new and competing technologies constantly emerging. We now have the ability to make long distance calls over what is called voice-over-Internet protocol (VoIP), and for a flat fee you can make long distance calls over your computer with Skype and another emerging service called Ooma, an Internet-based phone service that promises to eliminate your phone bills.

Indeed, this is an evolving environment, and the evolution of telecommunications technology occurs much more rapidly than the evolution of the surrounding legal and regulatory environment. An attorney representing telecommunications companies must be mindful of that fact at all times because the changing technological environment may provide advantages to the telecom client. Telecom industry business cycles are also much faster than the legal and regulatory environment cycles, and that can create opportunities for clients as well.

For example, when first available on the market, new technologies such as Skype or Ooma may not be regulated by state public utility commissions (PUCs). This is so because the laws giving PUCs authority may be specific to landline technology, for example, and therefore do not extend to other technologies. Being free of regulation allows the telecom company to set its prices competitively without the burden and expense of PUC regulation; it also allows telecom companies to change prices quickly and change their service offerings in reaction to competition.

The often-slow pace of lawmaking gives opportunities to new entrants into the telecom market. As state laws are enacted to regulate last year's technology, new technologies can be developed that are not covered by those laws. Keeping close watch on technological and legal developments allows the attorney to see opportunities for clients to get ahead of the competition.

Regulatory Trends

The telecom industry has seen several trends in recent years, such as attempts by state legislatures to increase regulation of the wireless industry by state PUCs. In Nebraska, for example, the legislature has attempted to give its PUC more authority over wireless companies. LB 815 (2008). State legislatures have waged "war" on VoIP, in one author's view, by trying to regulate it. *See* G. Sopkin; State Revanchism: Can the Latest Efforts to Regulate Voice Over Internet Protocol be Stopped? 3/20/08, available at http://www.fed-soc.org/publications/pubID.698/pub_detail.asp. There have also been many complaints in recent times regarding service contract issues such as early termination fees; and the level of service and contract terms, which ties into the regulatory trends at a couple of levels. Missouri legislators have attempted to limit early termination fees in cell phone contracts. HB593 (2007)

Landline telephone services are regulated such that a provider of landline service has to guarantee a certain level and availability of service in most states, but wireless providers generally do not have similar regulations. For example, you may sometimes pick up your cell phone and you will not have a signal, which will very rarely happen when you pick up your landline, simply because that level of landline service is mandated by state PUCs. Years ago, monopolies provided landline phone service, and since you did not have an alternative, the state required that the level of landline service be "ultra optimal" or essentially always available. To ensure that level of service, landline monopolies spent millions of dollars building redundancy into the landline system; if one piece of the system collapses, another piece, or a redundant piece, can pick up and eliminate the gap in service. That level of redundancy is not required on the cell phone network, and whatever redundancy exists is generally not regulated. In some cases, quality of service is driven by business factors—cell phone providers advertise the reliability of their networks to get more customers. If you do not like the service that one wireless company is providing, you can get your service from another company because you have a number of alternatives.

Simply put, an entirely different regulatory environment exists for landline companies than for wireless companies, and state legislatures and PUCs are now trying to expand their regulatory reach to more aspects of the telecommunications industry, such as the efforts to regulate VoIP. *See* MO HB1779 (2008). I believe that trend will continue over the next several years, and it will be up to the individual participants in the wireless industry to decide how much they want to fight. However, I believe that as more states try to regulate various telecommunications technologies, the federal government will start to push back on that trend, and the industry is likely to go to Congress to seek legislation that prevents the states from regulating more aspects of its business—indeed, some of that legislation in already in place. The Telecom Act of 1996 prohibits many state attempts to regulate wireless service by imposing ultra redundancies, for example.

Another major trend that is affecting this industry is telecom taxation. Telecom is one of the most heavily taxed services in our country, according to CTIA, the wireless industry association. *See* www.ctia.org/advocacy/policy_topics/topic.cfm/TID/27; *see also* S. Mackey, Excessive Taxes and Fees on Wireless Service: Recent Trends, *State Tax Notes*, 2/18/2008 (available at www.ctia.org). Telecom providers are hit with much higher business license taxes than retailers—as high as 11 percent in Missouri, for example, which means 11 cents of every dollar that you spend on your wireless or landline service in that state is taxes. Municipal governments are always hungry for tax dollars, and they have historically tended to tax the industry heavily: " 'Our customers are tired of having state and local governments treating them like ATM machines, so we are fighting on their behalf,' said John Taylor, a Sprint spokesman, who says the average Sprint customer pays 17 percent of the bill in taxes." *Missouri Case Could Ring up Cellphone Taxes*, *Wall Street Journal*, Aug. 22, 2007, at B1.

Looking ahead, however, I believe that we are going to see changes in the rules regarding taxation of telecom companies, because ultimately the customer pays those taxes—for example, a calling plan with a price of $39.99 a month ultimately costs almost $47 because of all the taxes that are added, and I believe there is going to be more push back from consumers in that area.

In terms of pending decisions in this area, the Supreme Court has declined to take on a case involving the ability of wireless telecom companies to pass on taxes to their customers. A decision by the 11th Circuit Court of Appeals in *Sprint Nextel Corp. v. National Association of State Utility Consumer Advocates,*

457 F.3d 1238 (11th Cir. 2006), cert. denied 128 S.Ct. 1119 (2008) upheld a law that prevents telecom companies from passing taxes on to their customers, or from identifying them as state taxes or surcharges; industry watchers will need to keep an eye on possible congressional action to overturn the case.

Speaking of the congressional side, a great deal of attention has been paid to the whole issue of telecom company immunity with respect to wiretapping, a national security issue that is currently being closely watched. Shortly after 9/11, telecom companies cooperated with the federal government in providing cell phone records of suspected terrorists. Now, Congress is debating whether to grant immunity to those telecom companies. S2248. The immunity is important to the telecom companies that fear class action lawsuits over the companies' cooperation with the government.

Preliminary Client Meetings

Before my first meeting with a new telecom client, I always want to know what specific business segment the company is in—telecom is a very broad field that can include landline, wireless companies, and broadband; providers of communication services or resellers of communications services; equipment manufacturers or software providers. I need to know whether the client is a carrier—i.e., does the client actually provide the service?—or whether the client is a vendor providing support to telecommunication companies—i.e., a company that provides switching gear or fiber optic cable, or software or system design. It is important to know what business segment the client is in, and where its products or services fall within the entire rubric of telecom.

If the client has a specific issue or problem that has prompted them to hire me, I want to know as much as possible about that issue as well. If the client has documentation with respect to the issue, I want to review it before the meeting, and I will try to talk with key people involved first so that I can understand the issues, and if need be, do a little more research or due diligence on my end.

Most importantly, I want to assess the client's business objectives and what the client would define as a successful outcome, whether it is a litigation matter or some other type of matter. I then identify as many alternative ways of achieving those objectives as possible.

Key Questions and Issues

When discussing the client's objectives in a litigation matter, I want to know how the client prioritizes them. It is also important to know whether we are in litigation with a competitor; a potential competitor; a vendor; a party that the client wants to have a long-term, ongoing relationship with; or whether the client is looking to end the relationship. Are there business-sensitive reasons beyond the specific issues of the litigation that might lead us to handle the dispute in one way versus another? For example, some years ago I represented a company that was considering buying the company that had sued my client—it was also possible that the other company might buy my client—and as a result, we took a different approach to the litigation than we might otherwise have taken. We looked for common ground early on and tried to get in front of the top executives of our opponent as soon as possible.

Broadly speaking, I do not take a "one size fits all" approach to litigation in this practice area—the attorney has to fully assess the client's position; look at the strengths and weaknesses; and determine what leverage points she has. A client that is in litigation with a big customer has very different leverage than a client that is a big customer of an opponent in litigation. A client that is in litigation with a company that is the only supplier of a component essential to making its telecommunications systems operate properly is in a very different position from a client that can get that component elsewhere quite readily.

Telecom clients also need to consider where the rest of the industry stands on a given issue—i.e., is this issue specific to this client such as a dispute with a vendor, or is it an issue that would be very important to the industry in general, such as a taxation issue? In some cases, the disputing parties may find that they can work together to bring about a resolution of the issues through a trade association, or through actions taken in the state legislature, Congress, or even at the local level, rather than in litigation. There is always more than one way to skin a cat, and litigation is not the only alternative for resolving a dispute, particularly a broad-based dispute that would affect the entire telecommunications industry, as opposed to a dispute between two parties. For example, legislation can be used to resolve statewide telecom disputes.

Developing Case Theory

If you represent the plaintiff in a litigation matter, your client is seeking something. From a defendant's perspective, you are defending your client against a claim; therefore, you have to consider whether your client has any counterclaims to assert so that you are not only in a defensive posture, and so that you can have some offensive weapons in your arsenal. For example, a vendor sues your client for payment under a contract. Did the vendor fully and properly perform? If not, your client may have a counterclaim for breach of contract.

In either case, to develop a litigation strategy it is important to determine what is at stake for your business, from the macro-perspective of the industry or from the micro-perspective of your individual company. It is also important to determine the total dollars at stake, and the dollars in relation to the size of the company. For example, a million dollar dispute may be a "bet the farm" case for a small company, whereas that would not be the case for a large company. In some cases, the dollars that are at stake may not be as important as the business principles that might apply to the dispute, or the client's business objectives, short term and long term, for example if the outcome of the dispute would shape tax policy for years to come.

Most importantly, the attorney must determine what an ideal outcome might be from the client's perspective—and what a realistic outcome might be. That analysis helps you to formulate an effective litigation plan, and helps you to understand what the client's expectations are, and whether they are reasonable.

When analyzing the client's goals in relation to their dispute, I determine whether the dispute is an industry-wide type of dispute, and what the realistic outcomes might be, as I earlier noted. I will also analyze whether we could develop a legislative strategy that would avoid or circumvent litigation—i.e., can we reasonably advocate for a change in the law? If so, what is the best venue for the change—can we advocate for that change in court or in the legislature? Is the existing law clear or unclear with respect to this issue? Indeed, has this issue been decided before, or is this a new issue—i.e., are we charting new territory? In that case, we must be more open to looking at alternative ways for resolving the issue.

Key Documentation in Telecom Disputes

When representing a telecom client in a litigation matter, I need to see any contracts, and any communications relating to those contracts. E-mails and other electronic documentation are critically important these days. It is important to examine any billing statements that are at issue, and any regulatory documents that might apply. For example, if the client is a regulated company that provides landline service, are there any tariffs on file with the PUC? Are any other regulatory filings or regulatory proceedings that occurred in which documents such as position statement have been filed? Even if the client is not a landline provider, the client may have filed documents with the FCC, and if a publicly traded company, you would need to look at its annual reports, proxy statements, and 10Qs, if the dispute may potentially involve any information that may be found in those documents.

Typically, publicly filed documents are signed under oath or with some sort of affirmation that it is the official statement of the company. Look in those publicly filed documents for positions that are inconsistent with the position your opponent now takes in litigation.

Dealing with Bad Facts

Indeed, in addition to knowing about the strengths of your client's case, you need to be aware of your potential weaknesses, and figure out how to deal with them to avoid surprises during litigation.

I always want to know the "bad" facts in relation to my client's case before the other side does; once I know what they are, I can then manage them much better than if they turn up as "surprises" later in the case. For example, if I know in advance about bad facts that exist in relation to a client's case, I can discuss them beforehand with the witnesses who are going to give depositions, and we can determine whether they are truly bad facts, or facts that can be minimized when put into context, or through some other strategy.

The Attorney-Client Relationship

Having a positive working relationship with the client is critical in this practice area, as in most, and such a relationship must be based on trust, confidence, and most importantly, competence—if you are not competent at what you are doing, you will not be able to establish or hold the trust and confidence of your client.

Conversely, even if you are competent, you will not automatically gain the trust and confidence of your client; therefore, you have to demonstrate and earn your client's trust at every step of the way. It is very difficult to be an effective attorney if your client does not trust you, or you do not trust your client. The expression that your reputation is like a brick wall—built one brick at a time—and can come crashing down all at once, holds true. Similarly, trust and confidence in a client relationship is built one brick at a time, but it can come crashing down if you do one thing to violate the trust that a client places in you.

Certain boundaries are a necessary part of an attorney-client relationship; however, the client pays me, not the other way around, and therefore, if the client wants to contact me at odd hours, that is the client's prerogative—you have to be responsive to the client's needs. One set of boundaries relates to acting honestly and ethically—an ethical, honest attorney will not do something unethical, even if her largest client asks her to do so.

Given the fact that an attorney-client relationship should be based on trust and confidence, if you suspect at any time that your client is not giving you the whole story, you have to assess whether that is because the client is being evasive, or because you have not built up a level of trust to the point where the client feels comfortable providing all of the information that you need.

Part of my job is to analyze whether the client's goals are obtainable, keeping in mind that I cannot set their goals for them—I can only help them to understand the possible outcomes of a given dispute, and what the likelihood of a set of given outcomes is, within broad parameters. At the same time, I think that if you are anything other than forthright with your client about the possibility of various outcomes, then you are sowing the seeds of trouble. If you over-promise and under-deliver, you will have harmed the attorney-client relationship; you will have violated or breached that trust with the client, and it will then be difficult for the client to place confidence in you down the road. I look to have long-term relationships with my clients; therefore, I look well beyond the particular situation when it comes to advising the client. If I promise the client an outcome that is unattainable or unrealistic, then I have done the client a great disservice—and I have done myself a great disservice because I am unlikely to have a long-term relationship with the client.

Learning Your Client's Motivations and Goals: Dealing with Key Decision Makers

To learn the client's motivations in a telecom dispute, the attorney should look at any documents that provide an historical record of the dispute—i.e., what happened to get us to this point; what were all the steps in the process; what position was the client taking during those steps—and is that position consistent or inconsistent with what the client is now saying?

In addition, it is important to talk to the key people at the client company, as well as any other people who may be involved in the dispute. At a big company, that may be as many as ten, twenty, or even more people, while at a small company, maybe just one or two. You have to find out who the decision makers are—the people who are setting the objectives—as opposed to those who are carrying out those objectives. In some cases, I will find that the people who set the objectives have very positive attitudes, whereas the down-the-line people do not have the same attitude as the decision makers, and that will often affect the level of cooperation I'll get from the down-the-line people as we proceed. An employee who disagrees with management's directives may undermine the work the attorney does. It is important to assess each individual's personality and his or her sensitivities, including "hot-button" issues.

If you are having difficulty in obtaining information from certain departments with a client company, or you need help in gathering historical data or getting access to archives, you may have to go up the chain within the company to try to move your project up the priority list within a certain department. However, you need to remember that your role as attorney is to represent the company—and not the other way around. In some cases, if you are not getting what you need from the company, it may be that people are busy working on the business objectives of their day-to-day jobs, and litigation tends to be an interruption of those activities. Therefore, a good lawyer has to set realistic deadlines for clients with respect to responsiveness to document requests, or providing other information.

To Settle or to Litigate: Considering Alternatives

The determination of whether to settle or litigate a telecom industry dispute often goes back to the client's business objectives—i.e., what is the desired outcome for the client? Litigation is very expensive; therefore, a cost-benefit analysis should be made because some disputes may be very small in dollars but very large in business principles, and you have to assess if the client is willing to spend a lot of money on these business principles.

I think nearly every lawyer who has been practicing for any length of time has heard a client say, "This case is critically important to me, and I will never settle—I will litigate to the death." Whenever I hear a client say that, I know that I have to take those words with a grain of salt; clients may talk tough up front, but at the end of the day, litigation may not be what is really best for their business. If the client is emotionally entangled in a particular dispute, you may have to let the emotions play out over time, and eventually get back to finding a business resolution. That is a situation where the term "counselor" really comes into play.

The old saying, "begin with the end in mind" is true in litigation; it is my job to obtain up front the best understanding of what the client's desired outcomes are in a particular dispute, and then I work with the client to identify and select the best alternative strategies for getting there. Indeed, litigation often involves a constant re-evaluation of your original strategy in light of current developments and the evolution of the client's business. Litigation is often like a road trip; if there is an accident you can sit in traffic for six hours while it is cleared, or you can look at the map and take an alternate route to bypass the situation. You have to continually re-evaluate your client's case in light of the changing and evolving circumstances that occur during litigation—new facts or new documents may come to light; a witness for your client may leave the company; and the same things may happen to your opponent. Therefore, in order to be an effective advocate for your client, the attorney needs to evaluate developing facts; evaluate the current environment and situation; and then project forward by identifying what changes may occur down the road—and then be prepared to deal with those changes.

Non-Legal Ramifications of Telecom Disputes

Indeed, a good attorney will consider how what she is doing in the course of litigation affects the client's business. Attorneys sometimes take a position in litigation that may seem to be correct; but if it affects the client's business in a negative way, then the attorney has done the client a disservice. You have to look at your client's total business environment in order to determine the key issues and their ramifications.

For example, if your client is a telecommunications company that has customers who use cell phone services, and you are taking a position in litigation that ultimately hurts your client's ability to serve those customers because it will put more restrictions on their business, or make doing business with their customers more cumbersome, then you have not really helped your client—you may have won the battle, but lost the war. My role as litigator/advocate for the client is to resolve the dispute, but I need to keep in mind that the client's business is going to go on after the resolution; and if I have done something that negatively affects the client's ability to do business, then I have done a disservice to the client—in fact, I need to look out for opportunities to make the client's ability to do business much easier.

Client Ambivalence and Conflicting Viewpoints

In some instances, a client who was initially very energized and motivated with respect to litigation becomes ambivalent, and in such cases, you have to adapt and assess why this is so. If it is because the client has other business priorities, you have to re-evaluate where you are, where you are going, and how you plan to get there. In some cases, the end game may have changed for the client as the result of other business transactions. For example, I once had a client that had sold one of its business lines, and it was sued with respect to one of the products that it had stopped manufacturing. In order to resolve that dispute, the client licensed its rights to that product to our opponent so that the opponent could then manufacture and produce the product, which was a win-win situation for both parties.

If a client wants to follow a strategy that I think is not in the client's best interest, I keep in mind that I do not know the client's business nearly as well as the client does. That said, I may run into a situation where I think a client's emotions or entanglement in the issues is causing the client to want to act contrary to its long-term interests. In those cases, if I have been able to build a relationship of confidence and trust with the client, I can talk very frankly in terms of letting the client know what I think, based on what my experience and my judgment tells me. At the end of the day, a client hires attorneys for their good judgment; therefore, in every client relationship, I try to bring to the table the judgment that comes from the experience that I have developed over the years. Therefore, when a client is doing something that I think represents bad business judgment, it is my job to speak up—but I can only do that if I have a relationship with the client that consists of a certain level of trust and confidence. The client may or may not take my advice, but I am doing my client a disservice if I keep my mouth shut—I believe that I providing the client with the value that they are hiring me for when I provide them with my judgment.

Final Thoughts

The biggest mistake that an attorney can make in this field is to not understand her client's business. If you do not understand the client's business, you minimize the ability to effectively represent your client and help achieve its business objectives through litigation, legislation, or otherwise. Therefore, the better you understand the client's business and their industry in general, as well as the specific technology that is involved in the dispute and how it operates, the better able you are to represent your client and develop strategies to advocate for your client's interests. I believe that it is incumbent upon me as an attorney to understand the client's business, and I do not expect the client to educate me—I expect to educate myself—and the better educated I am on the client's industry or issue, the better an advocate I can be for my client.

Knowing the industry allows the attorney to see opportunities for telecom clients. Seeing those opportunities gives the attorney a competitive edge by providing value added service to the client. The attorney who adds value brings a winning strategy to the table.

Stephen R. Clark, a partner at Husch Blackwell Sanders LLP, represents clients across the country in more than twenty federal district courts, four federal courts of appeal, and the courts of nine states. He is currently lead counsel for a national telecommunications company in a number of state tax disputes, including a class action and several other state and federal lawsuits. He has tried a number of jury and bench trials in state and federal courts and has argued several appeals. Mr. Clark has developed and executed legislative strategies, including testifying before the Missouri legislature on several occasions and negotiating and drafting parts of groundbreaking legislation. He served as lead defense counsel in a number of class actions in state and federal court, and regularly represents a national company known as a pioneer in arbitrating employment disputes and often is called on by clients to enforce arbitration agreements.

Mr. Clark is AV rated by Martindale Hubbell. He was named a "Super Lawyer" by Missouri & Kansas Super Lawyers 2005 *magazine as the top 5 percent of attorneys chosen by their peers and through the independent research* of Law & Politics. *Mr. Clark received his J.D. from Saint Louis University in 1991 and his B.A. from the University of Notre Dame in 1988.*

Responding to the Needs of the Telecommunication Client

Robert B. Kelly

Partner

Squire, Sanders & Dempsey LLP

ASPATORE

The Role of the Telecom Lawyer

As a telecom lawyer, I become involved in all aspects of legal issues that telecom companies must address. This includes regulatory issues before the Federal Communications Commission (FCC), the National Telecommunications and Information Administration (NTIA) of the Department of Commerce, and various state utilities and corporation authorities. I also advise telecom companies on transactional matters, including mergers and acquisitions, carrier to carrier agreements, and specialized telecom business relationships. I am also involved in a certain amount of litigation, mainly on the appellate side, such as in court reviews of FCC decisions. I have done a significant amount of strategic counseling for companies in the telecom industry, including counseling foreign companies that are looking to break into the U.S. telecom market and assisting existing U.S. companies to expand into other lines of business within the telecom industry.

The most important element a telecom lawyer can bring to the table is the integration of an understanding of telecommunications markets with an understanding of the legal issues facing those markets. This integration enables a telecom lawyer to understand his or her client's business objectives and to focus their representation appropriately. In the telecom industry, many public companies face issues with securities, regulations, foreign investments, anti-trust, competition, and FCC requirements. These issues may translate into conditions on approvals that can require divestitures or other limitations on a merged company's ability to do business. In short, we distinguish ourselves from traditional M&A counsel by offering an understanding of the specific needs of telecommunications clients.

Understanding the Market

The legal issues facing the telecom industry have analogs across many traditional legal practices. We handle litigation, transactions, and regulatory issues on both the domestic and international level. We are also involved in standard corporate matters such as raising capital and equity. There are unique aspects of the telecommunications market that must be taken into account when working with a telecom client.

Obviously, companies entering a telecom marketplace must understand that any transaction should be subject to extensive due diligence. Due diligence is comprised of business components, financial components, and legal components, all of which are frequently intermixed. Understanding where the transactional risks lie goes beyond merely understanding underlying risks or gaps in contracts or similar issues; it is also critical to understand where the markets are headed, who the key players are, and where the target stands in terms of competition and market opportunity.

We add value for our clients through an understanding of the integrated body of risks and opportunities in a target transaction. We also identify issues that clients may not otherwise recognize without the benefit of telecom counsel. Many state and federal proceedings can have a significant impact on our clients, such as the definition of privacy and data transfer, investment issues, capital formation, and venture capital practices.

There are a number of areas in telecommunications that present pitfalls for our clients. One area in which we have seen a great deal of trouble is for companies whose main line of business is not in telecommunications. Very often, these companies fail to consider the technical concerns of non-telecom transactions, such as whether there are FCC licensed properties involved in the acquisition. Oftentimes there are a number of regulatory approvals (usually FCC) that must be obtained before a transaction can be closed. While every telecom practice deals with these issues on a regular basis, they can be easy to miss for companies outside the telecom realm.

In addition, the area of information protection—including privacy and data issues—is currently in flux, and the laws governing this protection are increasingly complex. Companies facing issues regarding how they handle and transfer data, both internally and externally, can glean particular benefits from legal advice. We help these clients identify the holes that exist in their programs, steer them away from unnecessary risk, and manage unavoidable risks. While we are operating in a specialized field, we also offer expertise across a broad range within that field.

Working with the Telecom Client: Keys to Success

In working with telecom clients, I start with a top-down approach. I first consider the client's market, considering both geographical and service areas, as well as the competition within that market. Furthermore, I analyze the market structure and direction. It is equally important to understand the company's business strategy and goals, assessing how the company defines itself and its path into the future. Putting these pieces into place helps to bring the client's situation into greater focus, allowing the lawyer to drill into the legal issues on an as-needed basis.

A good working relationship with the company is primarily founded on open, healthy communication. In many cases, this is a matter of working with the right people internally at the company, thus ensuring that the information flow between counsel and client is both bi-directional and robust. The best way to understand a company is to understand its management, which is best accomplished through direct discussion.

An attorney in this field may also expand his or her knowledge through standard participation in bar events and industry conferences. The Federal Communications Bar Association is highly active and offers a great deal of educational opportunities for its members. In addition to conferences, there are a number of legal and industry trade publications that must be followed. Finally, maintaining regular interaction with key clients who are facing current issues will help an attorney to stay current with the law.

The Negotiation Game

Negotiation is an art, not a science. Consequently, there is no one correct way to approach the negotiation table. Instinct and intuition are two key tools that can make or break a negotiation, and one must define a personal approach based on those instincts. Some lawyers are natural deal makers, while others are natural litigators. My personal approach involves understanding the client and its goals, while at the same time minimizing the impact of individual personality on the result. A lawyer should never become the issue in a negotiation. All too often negotiations become a matter of pride, and strong personalities among the parties at the bargaining table can become barriers to a deal. Negotiations will always involve a certain number of surprises; success lies in how one reacts to those surprises through good communication, flexibility, and a constant eye on the client's goals.

My role in any negotiation is to accomplish my client's objectives. In some cases, it may be necessary to help the client define those objectives in a way that will both meet the client's needs and maintain sensitivity to the legal issues at hand. It is the attorney's duty to alert the client to legal signposts, staying within the bounds of what is reasonable and productive while working toward the common goal.

There are a number of parties who may become involved in the negotiation process, depending on the specific situation. I have participated in negotiations in which bankers or venture capital representatives have been involved alongside legal counsel, particularly in the case of technology start-up companies. Principals may also be present at the negotiation table, as well as other kinds of business counsel and advisers. However, the key player across the table is the opposing counsel, who is often the best source of information on the opposing party's stance. Counsel is also usually the best channel for communicating clearly the objectives and positions of your client in the negotiations.

As with any legal proceeding, negotiation requires preparation. One must understand the documents at hand, the client's position on the issues, and the limitations of each player in the room. It is also important to have a good sense of who is sitting on your side of the table; a CEO will have the power to commit to much more than a representative lower down in the company. In my experience, it is critical to keep a clear understanding among all parties to the negotiation of where the issues stand and who holds the decisive power. Even if a certain path of action seems like the best course, it may need to be approved by higher-ups in the company not otherwise in the negotiation in order to prevent misunderstandings that may later poison the negotiation. There is nothing that will create ill will between parties in a negotiation faster than having to withdraw an offer or compromise that may not have been fully cleared by the client. It is counsel's responsibility to prevent this from occurring.

The Sticking Points

Across all industries, the single most negotiated point is price. In the telecom industry specifically, however, regulatory approvals are another key item of negotiation. These approvals can become very complicated in larger deals, such as in the recent XM/Sirius merger, which brought up hugely complex and sensitive issues over how approvals should be managed through the Department of Justice and the FCC. Similarly, telecom negotiations must consider the particular authorizations held by the company in question, including any risks that may cloud or compromise the company value. Those risks must be identified and apportioned in the transaction. Competing claims and pending license renewals can become extremely important in apportioning risk for telecom businesses. Finally, one must consider the specific market and its effect on the transaction, particularly in the case of mergers.

The apportioning of risk has the greatest potential for obstructing a telecommunications deal. However, regulatory approvals can be equally hard to bridge, and there have been several recent examples—including a recent merger between DIRECTV and the Dish Network—that fail to gain the necessary approval. In other cases, conditions placed upon the transaction may not be survivable. For instance, when similar assets are merging, the FCC often requires a divestiture in certain markets to prevent undue concentration. Depending on the specifics of the deal, such a divestiture may not be acceptable, or may substantially alter the benefits of the transaction.

Overall, however, telecom negotiations do not differ greatly from negotiations in other areas of the law. Large companies face the same problems across industries in terms of pension, employee, and environmental concerns. The greatest difference lies in the treatment of competition, technology transfers, and foreign investment, all of which are more sensitive in the telecommunications area than in many other fields. The Exon-Florio statute, for instance, is often implicated in telecom transactions and the parties may elect for review of foreign investment in technology-related ventures by the Committee on Foreign Investment in the U.S. (CFIUS).

At minimum, a successful negotiation is one that achieves the client's objectives. However, negotiations typically must achieve the objectives of both sides in order to enjoy true success and forestall problems arising in the consummation of the transaction or even after closing. This is particularly true in the case of a merger, in which both sides will have an ongoing working relationship. Even if the negotiation fails, however, the client may ultimately come out on top; many deals fall through because there is simply too much risk involved, or the objectives are unachievable.

Pursuing Settlement: Key Considerations for a Successful Outcome

Litigation can be a very damaging process for all parties involved. Naturally, litigation is expensive, but more to the point, it distracts companies and their management. A company can only afford so much, and in many cases, settlement may be a preferable option. A lawyer must always consider the indirect costs of litigation on his or her client.

Approaching settlement requires certain key considerations. From a defense standpoint, one must honestly weigh the legitimacy of the claim and the merits of the defense against the cost and length of the proceeding. Litigation is not only a distraction to key management—it may become a shareholder issue and even a press issue. There is no universal set of conditions under which it is the "right time" to settle, but I generally do not encourage my clients to pursue litigation unless the case is strong.

The plaintiff's bar sometimes brings class actions against telecommunications carriers on specific consumer issues, and depending on the claims involved, these sometimes large suits tend to end in settlement. That being said, telecommunications companies have frequently been sued on a number of points, including labor issues, corporate issues, employment issues, pension issues, and environmental issues. Telecom litigation tends to focus on how the company conducts its business and provides customer service, although there are instances of litigation between carriers over settlements of revenue.

As a lawyer, I must consider the potential exposure of the client before deciding whether to pursue litigation or settlement. It is extremely important to understand the objectives of the client's business; for public companies, this means knowing how they serve their shareholders today and where the company is looking to go in the future. It is critical to ensure that whatever decision is reached, it is the client's decision and not the attorney's. Furthermore, one must consider the costs to the business. If the CEO must conduct two weeks of depositions, it can ultimately be more costly than a judgment. Finally, one must ensure that the client does not suffer from any surprises. The client must be provided with the best possible information in order to make the best possible decision about whether to settle.

In order to get the best deal for the client, it is important not to appear overly eager to settle. An overabundance of enthusiasm will drive up the cost of any settlement. In general, I prefer that the settlement discussion be initiated by the other side whenever possible. However, one of the most important issues in settlement is the timing, and it may not always be possible to control the specifics of when or where settlement discussions are opened.

Ultimately, the key to settlements and negotiations is to know what you are trying to achieve. The objective of a business is not to merge with another company or to settle a litigation; rather, it is to improve the business opportunities and maintain a strategic vision for the future. The telecom attorney must not only respect the client's objectives, he or she must also build a thorough understanding of the client's business and future directives in order to assess the best options available to that client. Lastly, it is critical to understand the telecommunications market, including the scope and scale of the market and the barriers that exist within it. True success is achieved when the issue is extinguished not only for the time being, but also in perpetuity.

Robert B. Kelly, a partner at Squire, Sanders & Dempsey LLP, has practiced telecommunications and emerging technology law since 1981. He negotiates major transactions involving acquisitions in the telecommunications industry and advises U.S. and international interests regarding transactional, legislative, and regulatory matters, often appearing before U.S. regulatory authorities.

Mr. Kelly has extensive experience in the area of wireless communications and spectrum-related services. He represents wireless service providers and equipment manufacturers in matters relating to spectrum policy, allocation, and assignment, and is a coauthor of the

Spectrum Regulation Handbook. *Mr. Kelly has advised publicly traded and privately held clients with respect to their participation in spectrum auctions and their acquisition and consolidation of major spectrum holdings.*

In his capacity as general counsel of the 800 MHz Transition Administrator, Mr. Kelly has overseen the development of polices and processes to administer the reconfiguration of the 800 MHz band in the United States. He has the primary responsibility of coordinating the Transition Administrator's responsibilities with the U.S. Federal Communications Commission and has extensive experience in working in public/private partnerships and other cooperative relationships with government authorities. He also serves as a member of the Transition Administrator's Leadership Committee.

Mr. Kelly has served as counsel to the principal trade association for intelligent transportation systems (ITS) in the United States since 1992 and has advised the ITS industry on a wide array of issues involving the deployment of emerging technologies. He served as chairman of ITS America Task Forces on Privacy and e-Commerce. Mr. Kelly is a columnist on ITS legal issues for Thinking Highways, *a bi-monthly publication, and is a frequent speaker on legal issues associated with ITS deployment.*

Mr. Kelly received his J.D. from Duke University in 1981, and his A.B. from Duke University, magna cum laude, Phi Beta Kappa, in 1978.

The Role of the Attorney in the Telecommunications Industry Today

Thomas H. Jackson

Partner

Smith, Gambrell & Russell

ASPATORE

Service Provider Aims

Telecommunication service providers are primarily interested in providing up-to-date services that are protected by their own IP, or by the IP of their suppliers. In negotiating with suppliers—which can be manufacturers of components, or whole systems of telecommunication networks—the telecommunications service provider may come up with a new service idea or other new patentable subject matter that relates to a new service: for example, the ability to provide a widescreen TV set in the back of a car for receiving and displaying movies on demand via radio frequency. When discussing these ideas with suppliers, the first order of business the service provider is interested in is obtaining patents in order to be in a negotiating position with suppliers. Suppliers to service providers are in turn in a negotiating position with their suppliers, and there is a hierarchical chain, for example, from service provider to manufacturer to assembler to chip manufacturer. In many instances, the product itself may be manufactured abroad, perhaps in China.

If a component product to such a new idea manufactured abroad is a microchip, for example, then the law surrounding the importation of these chips is extremely important to consider. There are two major bodies of law in the U.S. that protect the service provider's provision of new goods and services. One is the body of law associated with the importation of potentially infringing goods at the border, which body of law is under the jurisdiction of the International Trade Commission and Section 337 of its laws. 19 U.S.C. § 1337 (2004). Under this section, one is entitled to request the initiation of an investigation and to further request adjudication based on an infringed United States patent in the U.S. International Trade Commission before an administrative law judge. The outcome can prevent the goods in question from entering the U.S. at the border.

Important Laws

In the U.S., there is a separate body of law under the 35 USC § 281 that relates to remedies for infringement of patents by domestic infringers. Within this body of law, one is able to enjoin or obtain damages for the manufacture, use, and/or sale of any infringing product within the U.S. Using the patent system to advantage, one would typically want to obtain patents for themselves and to actively seek cross licenses among members of the hierarchical chain, chip manufacturer, to assemblers, to manufacturers of whole systems, to service providers again. These cross-licensing agreements promote the use of new technology as well as the opportunity for new services to the public.

Unfortunately, disputes will frequently erupt during these processes—especially between certain chip manufacturers. Most recently, there has been a dispute in the ITC and the federal district courts between Broadcom and Qualcomm over implementation of a standard wireless protocol. The result in the ITC has been a ban on importation for new fourth generation wireless technology entering the country. This means that consumers are presently limited to older technology, and that the United States will not be able to move into new technologies to the extent that we are dependent on sourcing outside of the U.S., which is prohibited.

The Role of the Attorney

As an attorney in this field, I bring value to my clients by assisting with licensing negotiations between members of the telecommunications chain and with the preparation and prosecution of new patent applications for new ideas. We also have an important role in the defense of telecommunications manufacturers and service providers from those whose interests may be adverse to the expansion of technology without first paying what may be perceived as a toll for its use. The entities that would extract such tolls have become known as "trolls" but, while known once for their failure to develop technology of their own, are now initiating their own research and development programs and seeking patent protection for developments. Nevertheless, a cross-licensing agreement or other agreement is typically not the objective of a serious troll. Rather, the objective of a true troll is to seek as much money as possible for their investors and themselves. Whether this objective is beneficial to the patent system and to the provision of new services as a whole is debatable; many side with the interests of the trolls as they frequently provide access for the small inventor to the court system to enforce their patents.

Consequently, the role of the attorney is to assist the telecommunications entity to promote a strong defensive posture by building a valuable patent portfolio and assist in the promotion of joint defense groups against the onslaught of a troll and, at the same time, to promote a strong offensive posture by assisting the telecommunications entity to assert their patents through letter campaigns, opinion counseling, and negotiation.

Obtaining Key Information

Prior to meeting with a new client, I need to carry out a basic level of initial research. Google is typically a sufficient starting point for learning about a given telecommunications entity and its products and competitors. This foundational information helps me to be in a better position to serve my clients and to fulfill their interests. Of course, when you meet with the client, cooperation and interactive communication are always the best tools, and will get you information that is not necessarily on any Web site.

The alternatives you can present to a client are either licensing, or putting their patent in a safe, precluding others from making, using, or selling the claimed subject matter. The latter strategy has worked many times before in the past. The idea is to preserve a unique feature for a service provider or equipment manufacturer, so that no other equipment manufacturer can use it. On the other hand, in order to promote a new telecommunications standard and serve as a participant in standards making, it is necessary to disclose one's patents to the standards making organization under, for example, non-discriminatory terms and at reasonable royalty rates.

The two entities most involved in fairness in standards setting are the Department of Justice and the Federal Trade Commission, which have published joint guidelines for anyone interested in participating in standards setting. For example, what was once prohibited patent-pooling is now acceptable behavior (not violating antitrust laws), for example, as demonstrated by the availability of fair and reasonable terms from the Motion Pictures Engineering Group located in Los Angeles, promoting digital television standardization.

Another question I ask clients is whether they are interested in obtaining patents to use outside the realm of their business, for example, as the above described troll is interested in making money on its patents. If they are interested, then they become almost a troll themselves. I have attended troll conferences where an entity will stand up and say they intentionally issue patents for something that is not necessarily in their field, but since that patent can generate money in a different field, they go ahead and use it to do so. For example, if someone is working for a telecommunications entity, and the entity invents a new garage door opener, they would patent it and hope to sell it to an overhead garage door company. The entity is encouraged to identify patents it owns which are not in its field of endeavor and form a licensing organization to do so.

Necessary Documentation

The most important piece of documentation to assist a patent attorney to obtain a patent is typically called the invention disclosure. In this document, the inventor sets forth his interpretation of an invention. When you have an inventor interview, you want to draw that inventor out to determine who the competitors are, how the invention will be used, acquired, built, and whom the components will be built by. The invention disclosure compiles these aspects together as one piece. From there it is possible to break the disclosed subject matter down into smaller pieces, and maybe, if it is worth such treatment, file several different patent applications based on the single invention disclosure statement. You would not want to take this course with every disclosure, as every patent is very expensive. It is a $10,000 investment just in a patent application alone, and another $10,000 to prosecute in the U.S. to issue. Filing patent applications in other countries is particularly expensive. A patent, including maintenance fees over its life, can cost millions of dollars if obtained in several foreign countries. Thus, there are important choices to be made as to what an entity patents, why and where. These decisions are typically left to a patent committee who filters the valuable invention disclosures from the not so valuable. Many entities would rather file patent applications on as many potential inventions as possible and develop large patent portfolios, having many with marginal value and a few with great value.

This strategy, however, is becoming more difficult to follow after the Supreme Court decision in *KSR v. Teleflex*, 127 S. Ct. 1727 (2007). The U.S.P.T.O. has followed on the heels of the decision by publishing guidelines and policies for use by examiners. At the appeal board level, the trend between fiscal year 2006 and 2007 is toward affirming rejections of applications based on obviousness. In other words, it appears to be becoming more and more difficult to obtain a patent, making the decision to file a patent application for a given invention disclosure more difficult to make.

Strategic Considerations

I provide excellent services to clients by visiting as often as possible, telephoning them frequently, and by keeping in general contact. It is also important to keep up on the news, whether through business news sources or other various Web-based sources.

Keeping up with the news is important because the areas of telecommunications, patent law, and technology can change at any time. Presently, we patent attorneys are faced with potential immediate changes either through actions of the Supreme Court, our Congress or at the United States Patent Office. There is, also, a lot of overlap with the FCC decisions that are made on allocation of spectrum and interstate rates and state corporation commissions on allocation of local rates for services, and so on. There is also a constant change in telecommunications technology, which has resulted in a convergence between what used to be entirely separate industries. For example, today, a telecommunications consumer may obtain practically free voice-over-internet telephony capabilities where you can have a telephone conversation with someone in Kenya over the Internet. Just a few years ago, one needed an international carrier to connect you for probably a $75 telephone call. The allocation of spectrum, on the other hand, is important to the capabilities of wireless versus wired telephony and promoting a balance between the services provided by each. I think that it is fair to say that there may even be a trend away from wire telephony—that many consumers may not even have a wired telephone anymore with the passage of time.

When a client becomes involved in a dispute, a strategy needs to be developed. The idea is to balance the interests on both sides, and hopefully, to enter into a dialogue in order to accomplish a desirable outcome where both sides are able to prosper from whatever negotiation occurs. You also still want to leave yourself open to potential new developments or changes that will occur over a three to seven-year period in the future. No negotiation should occur without both sides making a reasonable assessment of the future for the technology in question. For example, the cost of a new cellular telephone will be expected to go down and yet, at the same time, provide greater memory for storing data (in effect becoming a small personal computer) and, at the same time, provide more and more enhanced services such as the downloading of music, computer software, movies, and games. Adding a dollar to the cost of a cellular telephone should bring more than a dollar's worth of enhancements to the telephone itself. The issue in a negotiation can be what is a fair and reasonable royalty rate for the claimed subject matter of a given patent in dispute.

Patents are important, and entirely necessary. I once worked with an entity that was not interested in patents. They were patent-adverse, in fact, until they were sued and came to realize how useful crucial patents are in a defense. At some point in time, every client will appreciate the importance of having a patent portfolio. Even if one does not appear to be interested in patents at first, they will eventually come to appreciate the benefits a portfolio provides.

Mistakes to Avoid

Several codified prohibitions exist under current patent laws. These include prohibitions on publishing an invention more than one year prior to filing for a patent application, and on publicly using or demonstrating your invention more than one year prior to filing. Breaking either prohibition is a mistake that clients can easily make, and the result can be a nightmare for the involved patent attorney. The invention disclosure forms the inventors fill out should delve into these issues, asking exactly when did the inventor conceive of this invention and when they first published on it, or disclosed it outside of the company. Under the proposed patent harmonization policies promoted with the yet-to-pass Patent Reform Act, the United States will move from a first-inventor-to-file nation to a first-to-file system, for example, as is available in Japan. In the meanwhile, like Alexander Graham Bell who allegedly conceived the telephone before Elisha Gray, inventors today should maintain laboratory notebooks documenting with witnesses the conception dates of their inventions and significant milestones toward reduction to practice.

Attorneys can easily make mistakes in this field as well. For example, going to a consumer electronics show with the new Apple telephone, without having adequately protected it by filing a patent application first, would certainly be a mistake. There are also problems tied in with taking the direction of an already established standard in the industry. Sony versus Blu-Ray DVDs would be an example of this. Also, the two major service providers in the U.S.—Verizon and AT&T—follow different standards in the wireless sector. The problem is, if you go down one path, it becomes very difficult to reverse course and go down the other when it turns out to be the path of choice internationally.

Obtaining Patents

The practice of telecommunications patent law has not experienced any major shifts until recent times. The law is changing in important ways (in the courts, in Congress, and through the United States Patent Office promoting its own changes). However, attorneys in this area are having difficulties currently due to the recent *KSR v. Teleflex Supreme Court* decision. Also, certain proposed changes in rules at the U.S. Patent Office regarding limitations on the number of continuation applications one may file, the number of claims in a given application, requirements for prior art searched, appellate rules, so-called KSR guidelines for the examining corps at the U.S.P.T.O., and other factors are making it harder and more costly for telecommunication entities to obtain patents. As a result, the choices telecommunication entities make have to be more carefully thought out and well documented. Ten to twenty years ago, the focus was on getting as many patents as possible rather than sifting for quality patents. Today it is more fundamental that quality patents are secured.

Thus, every entity preparing and filing patent applications will require more and more security as to the patent's future value. This is because the expenses demanded in filing a patent application, and in prosecuting it to issue, are becoming increasingly steep. While many entities now have patent committees within their organization who are responsible for weighing the value of different inventions, the processes they follow and guidance the attorney can provide have had to change.

That decision-making process is one that I, as outside counsel, do not usually get to participate in. Yet, it is an important process for in-house counsel to become involved with, and it is absolutely necessary that patent counsel be present at committee meetings. Quality counsel can ensure the decisions are judicious, and not overly influenced by the inventor who makes the most noise. A knowledgeable attorney serves to temper clashing thought processes, to weigh all the inventions fairly, and keep the committee on an even keel, so that most significant inventions are the ones that do indeed become patented.

Industry Convergence

Companies want to be as friendly and cooperative with one another to the most extent possible, although there are frequent disagreements between them. Today, another factor influencing this arena is convergence. Convergence describes the phenomenon of telecommunications converging with satellite communications, cable TV, and the Internet services. As a result, major entities increasingly are sharing greater portions of what used to be called the wire telecommunications arena. Due to convergence, there is more serious competition among the broader group of members of this consolidating group.

Patent Trolls

The patent troll has already been mentioned. Another notable change can be seen in what is called "the troll," some would say the thrust of the Patent Reform Act pending in Congress. This is not an entity that is a manufacturer, member of the telecommunications chain, or in the process of convergence—rather, it is an entity that buys or exclusively licenses patents for the sake of asserting the patent rights solely for making as much money as possible from patent ownership. There is no good way to defend against the troll, because they do not care about the industry they are affecting. For this reason, there are movements underway within Congress, the U.S. Patent and Trademark Office, and in the courts to limit the opportunities of the troll. The most powerful weapon they have held thus far has been the injunction. The best defense against the troll is a strong joint defense group formed by defendants or potential defendants of the troll who may share information among them about strategies, prior art and the like under a common interest privilege.

International Patent Laws

One important development happening right now concerns the harmonization of patent laws internationally, an alleged feature of the Patent Reform Act of 2007 (S. 1145 and H.R. 1908) which is pending before Congress and is expected to reach the Senate floor for a vote by the summer of 2008. The House version has already passed. One of the included proposals will require harmonizing patent laws throughout and across the law. Yet even with this patent reform act in place, there would continue to be considerable differences in the patent prosecution existing between many large countries and continents. The European Patent Office, our own U.S. Patent Office, and the Japanese Patent Office are three examples of extremely important markets and different processes of preparing patent applications, filing them, and obtaining patents.

The only thing that will actually be "harmonized" by the Patent Reform Act of 2007 is the fact that we are all going toward a first-to-file environment. This is what is alleged to be the harmonization aspect of the patent reform act—that the first to file a patent application at the United States Patent Office will win among different applicants for an invention on the same subject matter. This may help to harmonize us with Europe or Japan, which are first to file rather than first to conceive and reduce to practice. First to conceive and reduce to practice has been the law in the U.S. for more than one hundred years.

Thomas H. Jackson is partner in the Intellectual Property Section of Smith, Gambrell & Russell LLP. Before joining Smith, Gambrell & Russell, Mr. Jackson was with the intellectual property law firm of Banner & Witcoff, Ltd. in their Washington, D.C. office and earlier served as in-house patent counsel at Siemens AG in Iselin, New Jersey, and at AT&T Bell Laboratories.

Mr. Jackson has written and prosecuted hundreds of patents to issue in the electrical, electronic, and computer arts including specialties in medical device, optical device, telecommunications, and converging television technologies. He is also an experienced litigator serving as counsel to both patent owners and in defense of patent litigation.

Mr. Jackson received his B.S. in electrical engineering from the University of Pennsylvania, where he was a member of the Hexagon Honors Society. He received his

Masters in engineering administration from George Washington University. He earned his J.D. degree from Seton Hall University. Mr. Jackson is a member of the District of Columbia and New Jersey Bars and conversational in French and German.

Assisting Telecom Clients as Creditors in Bankruptcy Proceedings

Robert D. Towey
Member

Vincent A. D'Agostino
Member

Lowenstein Sandler PC

ASPATORE

Bankruptcy Litigation Trends in the Telecom Realm

Less than a decade ago, there was a high degree of resignation to the bankruptcy process by critical service suppliers, including telecom companies. Telecom service providers were forced into recognizing the importance of dealing with the bankruptcy filings of their commercial customers because of the magnitude of bankruptcy filings that occurred starting in 2000, when the telecom bubble burst, which affected the industry and crippled many telecom providers.

Not knowing how to react to these cases could have been a potential deathblow to even the most solvent and solid telecommunication companies. In the past, many telecom companies were resolved to accept the worst when a customer filed for bankruptcy protection. Typically, this included writing off past amounts owed by customers in bankruptcy, continuing to provide services without adequate assurance of payment, and to add insult to injury, paying money *to* the customer when faced with bankruptcy preference claims for having received payments from the customer within ninety days of the bankruptcy filing.

However, a much more informed and aggressive approach is now being taken with respect to bankruptcy cases—not only on the part of telecom clients, but also on the part of other suppliers of critical goods and services. Rather than accepting a customer's bankruptcy filing with resignation and simply writing off the pre-petition amounts that are owed to them, telecom clients are discarding that thinking and taking a very proactive approach to bankruptcy cases. These days, it is advisable for counsel to jump in early in order to be seen, heard, and get our client's position out there. This approach has been very successful.

Pre-Petition Strategies – Obtaining Key Information

Signs of trouble with a telecom customer are often apparent—bills are not paid or are paid out of time. It is important for a telecom company to recognize these signs and to deal with the customer promptly. Pre-bankruptcy planning includes identifying financially distressed customers; implementing pre-payment or cash on delivery (COD) terms; gathering information about the customer; meeting with the customer to obtain information about the customer's financial condition; and entering forbearance agreements that address modification of payment terms and the release of claims against the telecom company.

Key Questions

The following types of questions help determine the best pre- and post-bankruptcy filing strategy:

a) What is the extent and magnitude of the relationship with the customer and do the parties want to continue the relationship?
b) What was the payment history of the customer for the year before bankruptcy filing?
c) Does the client want to continue the relationship with the customer (what is the balance of interests between the sales and credit collection departments)?
d) Does the customer have intellectual property belonging to the telecom client?

These questions are designed to elicit information about the mindset of the telecom client and the financially distressed customer in terms of the continued business relationship; to assess the likelihood of a cooperative relationship with the customer during the bankruptcy case; and to assess potential pressure points (against both the customer and the telecom client).

For example, if there is a desire to continue the business relationship by both the telecom client and a customer in Chapter 11, a scaled-down litigation approach designed to get the attention of the debtor's counsel with respect to adequate assurance of payment for services provided during the bankruptcy case and the assumption of executory contracts may be effective. On the other hand, where the relationship between the telecom client and the customer deteriorated before the bankruptcy filing, and in instances where there is intellectual property at risk, a more aggressive litigation strategy is more likely to be successful in terms of protecting the telecom client's interest. In these instances, a persistent presence in the case and the filing of appropriate motions and adversary proceedings to protect contract rights and seeking the return of intellectual property is essential.

Challenges of Working with Telecom Clients

Perhaps the most challenging aspect of representing a telecom company as a creditor and service provider to a customer in Chapter 11 is the identification of all services and applicable business units of the telecom company that are involved in the relationship. Because there are often multiple layers of contractual relationships between a telecom company and its business customers, it is important for counsel to obtain a full understanding of all aspects of the relationship including all services that are provided; all business units that are involved; and the business objective of each unit in terms of collection and ongoing relationships.

An elevated level of due diligence is often required when representing a telecom client in a bankruptcy case, as opposed to a sole source provider of equipment or goods. The failure to understand all aspects of the business relationship can result in missed opportunities, or worse, disastrous results such as the unsuspecting waiver or release of rights of the telecom client.

Key Players in the Client Organization

Typically, there are two levels of critical client contacts—in-house attorneys and business contacts. Although communications are usually through the client's in-house attorneys, whenever possible, it is important to have direct access to business clients who are responsible for the collection aspect of the bankruptcy process (i.e., monitoring accounts receivable and filing the appropriate claims), the account team/sales group (responsible for the ongoing relationship with the customer), and the credit department (responsible for determining what deposits or security is needed to provide services).

Determining Strategy

It is important to assess the client's expectations in terms of severing or continuing the relationship with a customer in bankruptcy. While the initial approach may be the same in terms of seeking the court's assistance to protect the telecom client's interests, a valued customer relationship may be saved and the telecom client's interests protected through the negotiation process. Such negotiations are often multifaceted and can be used to reach a "global resolution" of such issues as payment terms; the assumption of executory contracts pursuant to Section 365 of the Bankruptcy Code; and the negotiation or elimination of liability for potential preference claims.

If a customer of a telecom client files a bankruptcy case, it is important to treat the case as a litigation matter. Although the bankruptcy process requires artful negotiations, the willingness to litigate over issues often postures the case for a more favorable outcome for the client. Certainly, there are times when a client's financial status impacts strategy because of budgetary constraints. In such cases, counsel can temper the litigation approach and seek early avenues for negotiation and alternative dispute resolution when appropriate. Additionally, the magnitude of exposure in a bankruptcy case can heighten the need for an aggressive strategy where the client's financial status is threatened.

The bottom line is that information and preparedness is a telecom client's most important weapon. Counsel is well advised to take a "first strike" approach in terms of participating in the "first day" hearings in a bankruptcy case where such critical issues as deposits and adequate assurance of payment for future services and goods are typically dealt with. There is truth to the adage that the squeaky wheel gets the most oil in a bankruptcy case.

Managing Client Expectations

When a telecom company is faced with a customer's bankruptcy filing, expectations are nearly always set at the worst possible outcome—especially in situations where the chances of recovering amounts owed before the bankruptcy are slim, and/or where the landscape is uncertain as to what the contractual relationship will be like following the bankruptcy proceedings. The good news is that taking the right approach to a bankruptcy case often results in an outcome that exceeds the client's expectations in terms of recovering monies that are owed to the client, protecting contract rights, and limiting liability for potential bankruptcy preference claims.

Balancing the Client's Interests

Balancing the need to take a more aggressive approach to bankruptcy litigation while leaving the door open to continue the business relationship with the customer sometimes requires using a "fist in a velvet glove" strategy. In the initial days after the commencement of a bankruptcy case, counsel frequently needs to educate adverse bankruptcy counsel as to the issues impacting the telecom client. This may be accomplished by filing motions to force the customer to assume or reject an executory contract and/or motions to compel the turnover of intellectual property. Such attention-getting steps are often necessary in the early stages of a bankruptcy proceeding, and are often the steps that lead by natural progression to negotiations. Counsel should be mindful of the fact that these steps are not necessarily mutually exclusive.

Of course, there are also situations where the telecom company and its customer are in communication, and are working together before and during the bankruptcy case. In those instances, all parties have their eyes open—the customer recognizes that they need to deal with your client, and can take a more tempered approach to litigation.

Negotiation Strategies

Whether counsel takes a cooperative or aggressive approach to negotiations depends on various factors—i.e., the client's overall desired approach; the dynamics with adverse counsel; the relationship between client and debtor; and the types of issues involved. The general philosophy overriding almost all bankruptcy cases is that better resolutions are the result of negotiation rather than litigation. Bankruptcy counsel tend to look at a bankruptcy case as an opportunity to negotiate resolutions that are favorable to both sides. Negotiations on behalf of telecom clients in bankruptcy cases generally involve obtaining the greatest recovery for the clients relative to their claims as well as a focus on the continued relationship between the telecom clients and the bankrupt customer.

In a bankruptcy liquidation where the debtor is closing its doors, counsel must be particularly vigilant to make sure that any services provided post-bankruptcy will be paid, and intellectual property returned before the debtor ceases its business.

Protecting the Telecom Client's Contractual Rights

An important role in representing telecom clients in bankruptcy proceedings is protecting their contractual rights after a debtor has filed for bankruptcy. For example, there are instances when telecom clients are considered "utilities" pursuant to Section 366 of Bankruptcy Code. In these instances, telecom clients are required to continue to provide services to the debtor after the bankruptcy filing under the current terms of their contract so long as the debtor provides some form of adequate assurance to the telecom client. The type and amount of adequate assurance is negotiated between the debtor and the utility provider. Adequate assurance can include security deposits, prepayments, and letters of credits. Under the amendments to the Bankruptcy Code, which took effect in 2005, prepetition payment history, or the fact that a utility provider held a prepetition security deposit, are not factors in determining the form or extent of adequate assurance provided to utility providers by debtors.

In addition, it is important to know the debtor's intentions relative to the contractual relationship with the telecom client after the bankruptcy filing. Pursuant to Section 365 of the Bankruptcy Code, debtors have the ability to assume or reject their agreements with non-debtor parties to contracts after the filing of their bankruptcy case. If a debtor assumes its agreement with the telecom client, it intends to continue the contractual relationship through the end of the agreement term. If this occurs, the debtor must "cure" all prepetition and post-petition monetary and non-monetary defaults under the contract. As such, all prepetition claims must be paid in full. In addition, an assumption will typically serve to insulate the non-debtor parties to contracts from any preference exposure pursuant to Section 547 of the Bankruptcy Code. Negotiations play a very important role in the assumption of the agreements between the debtor and the client as well as the payment of cure amounts associated with the assumption.

Conversely, if a debtor rejects its agreement with the telecom client, it terminates the contractual relationship. There are claims that arise from such a rejection and it is important to calculate the claims and meet all deadlines relative to filing such claims in a timely manner.

Protecting the Telecom Client's Intellectual Property

Customarily, telecom companies that supply telecommunications equipment enter into agreements with their customers that include licenses of software and firmware (the "licensed materials") which are required for the operation of the equipment. Pursuant to such agreements, the telecom company normally retains title to the licensed materials and the licenses are "perpetual, non-exclusive, and non-transferable." The customer only has the right to use the licensed materials pursuant to the license agreements. However, the customer in Chapter 11 may seek to sell its assets, including the telecommunications equipment in which the licensed materials are imbedded. Likewise, the Chapter 11 customer may also seek to assign executory contracts to third parties. In either situation, it is incumbent upon the telecom company to be vigilant as to its rights in protecting its intellectual property in the context of a bankruptcy proceeding. The failure to object may result in the transfer of intellectual property despite the restrictions on transferability in the license agreement.

Licensed materials that are "personal, non-transferable or non-exclusive licenses" of intellectual property cannot be assumed or assumed and assigned without the express consent of the telecom client pursuant to Section 365(c)(1) of the Bankruptcy Code. That section provides that a debtor "may not assume or assign any executory contract or unexpired lease of the debtor" if applicable non-bankruptcy law precludes assignment. It is well established that the "applicable law" referred to in Section 365(c)(1) includes patent and copyright law and the non-exclusive licenses of patents and copyrights are not generally assumable or assignable without the licensor's consent. Often, Chapter 11 customers file voluminous pleadings in a bankruptcy case in which contracts that the customer seeks to assume and assign are identified in a lengthy schedule. The failure to object to a motion to assume or assign a contract will typically be construed as "consent" by the bankruptcy court. Further, despite the fact that Section 365(b)(1)(A) of the Bankruptcy Code requires that all prepetition amounts owed be "cured" (i.e., paid in full) in connection with the assumption and/or assumption and assignment of an executory contract, oftentimes the

Chapter 11 customer will identify the cure amount as "zero," thus, placing the telecom client at risk should they fail to object to the assumption and/or assignment and/or the cure amount. Again, the failure to do so can result in the forfeiture of any rights to object to the assumption and assignment and to the establishment of the cure amount as zero.

Because of the many potential land mines associated with protecting intellectual property rights, counsel should consider an aggressive approach to representing clients' interests in this regard. Despite the fact that the bankruptcy code entitles the Chapter 11 customer to reserve decision on which contract should be assumed and/or assumed and assigned until its plan of reorganization, the filing of a motion early in the case to compel assumption or rejection of the license agreement is often advisable on the basis that the customer needs the telecom communications equipment, but is not entitled to a free ride on the licensed materials without assuming its obligations under the license agreement and paying all amounts owed. Although bankruptcy courts typically allow a debtor time to decide whether to assume or reject a license agreement, once the issue is raised, it must be dealt with by the customer in Chapter 11.

Conclusion

Protecting the interests of telecom companies that are in contractual relationships with financially distressed customers presents various challenges. Pre-bankruptcy planning with the telecom company provides a distinct advantage in terms of identifying customers in financial difficulty; implementing favorable payment terms for services and for amounts owed and appropriately documenting same; and gathering information about the customer, its financial problems, and the extent and nature of the relationship with the telecom client. Further, upon the filing for bankruptcy protection by a customer of a telecom client, counsel is well advised to actively and aggressively engage in the bankruptcy at the commencement of the case and to proactively take steps to secure adequate assurance of performance for future services provided by the telecom client; protect the telecom client's contractual rights; reduce potential liability for exposure to bankruptcy avoidance actions, including preference claims; and protect intellectual property. Extreme diligence is required by counsel to ensure that opportunities are not missed to protect the telecom client's rights in connection with critical filings in the bankruptcy case, especially with respect to the first day utility motions dealing with adequate assurance issues; assumption or rejection of contracts; the establishment of cure amounts for assumed contracts; proof of claim bar dates; and plans of reorganization. A well-organized approach to the representation of the telecom client can maximize the financial return to the client and minimize potential risk and liability.

Robert D. Towey *is the chair of the Commercial and Business Litigation Practice of Lowenstein Sandler in Roseland, New Jersey. He represents clients in complex litigation involving a wide range of corporate and commercial matters. Mr. Towey has experience in all phases of litigation, both at the trial and appellate levels, in federal district, bankruptcy courts throughout the United States, as well as in arbitration tribunals. He has tried numerous jury and non-jury cases.*

Mr. Towey has represented a broad spectrum of clients, both as plaintiffs and defendants, cases involving breach of contract, fraud, trade name disputes, breach of fiduciary duty, interference, consumer fraud class actions, creditors rights disputes, public contract bidding protests, toxic torts, product liability, and franchise relationships.

Mr. Towey is listed in the 2007 and 2008 editions of New Jersey Super Lawyers. *He graduated from Seton Hall University School of Law (J.D., 1984), cum laude, and was the business editor of the* Seton Hall Law Review. *Mr. Towey completed his undergraduate studies at Drew University (B.A., 1981), and graduated summa cum laude and Phi Beta Kappa.*

Vincent A. D'Agostino *is a member of the Bankruptcy, Financial Reorganization & Creditors' Rights Group at Lowenstein Sandler. Mr. D'Agostino's practice focuses primarily on creditors' rights, where he represents large creditors in bankruptcy cases. He attended Rutgers, the State University of New Jersey (B.A., 1989), and New York Law School (J.D., 1993), and is admitted to practice in New Jersey.*

Enabling Successful Negotiations with Overseas Telecom Partners

Sallye Clark

Partner

Arent Fox LLP

ASPATORE

Introduction: An Historical Perspective

Currently, my practice focuses on international satellite regulatory work. I started out in this area when mobile satellite telecommunications were initially emerging, working for the company Iridium. In the beginning, Iridium had a new satellite phone service they wanted to roll out in every country in the world on the same day. My job was to work with local regulators and telecom partners in every country in Asia where they were needed in order to work with the local regulator to develop a regulatory environment that would allow for licensing of the Iridium system. I wrote model regulations and I would negotiate with the local regulators to adopt those regulations. I also wrote model licenses and negotiated those. In most countries, we had to work with local telcos to secure market access and licensing.

After Iridium, I went to work with Teledesic. Their plan was to have broadband Internet via satellite available across the globe. Here too, I negotiated with local governments and partners, only this time I had global responsibilities and an international team to work with. From there I went to PanAmSat, an established satellite company, where I had to negotiate regulatory access with local regulators and service agreements with potential local partners.

I have since left that company, and now work with satellite operators, defense contractors, the U.S. government, and system integrators. On behalf of the U.S. military, I have negotiated with foreign governments to allow the military to operate satellite networks locally. I also do similar work on behalf of the U.S. State Department to allow use of their Embassy telecom networks around the world. This is generally a diplomatic negotiation. I also work on projects such as securing orbital slots for new satellites, negotiating landing rights for satellites, and securing authorizations for new telecom networks for end users in countries around the world.

Overall Negotiation Strategies

Although my practice is somewhat specialized in terms of the negotiations I take part in, many key elements apply to all negotiations involving telecommunications entities. The first thing one has to do is to think about the strategy on each side of the negotiation, and to determine where you have common goals, as well as where common goals are lacking. It is crucial to know as early as possible what an acceptable solution to both sides will be in order to work toward that goal with both sides being taken into consideration. In many cases, this is especially important because my clients often have to negotiate market access with monopoly carriers that control access to the local market, and without their agreement and cooperation access is impossible.

Quite often, there may be security concerns about your client's telecom equipment being used in the country without local controls, so you have to determine whether the client's equipment can be tracked or monitored by the local partner. The idea here would be to share information in real time with local partners, if that is possible and does not violate privacy concerns. Another concern that needs to be addressed is fees. Every company, of course, wants to pay the smallest possible amount of fees to the local partner that controls the market, and of course the local partner wants the highest amount of revenue they can get, though, and these two conflicting perspectives can prove problematic in coming to a fair and equitable revenue split. Some factors that you take into account in coming to a fair revenue split are to try to determine what the usual revenue split is, or what the revenue split is in similar sized markets.

Client Background Research

The first step in negotiations, from my end, is to research local regulations to determine if there are foreign ownership restrictions. If there are, you want to know if forming a local subsidiary is necessary, and if so how much ownership does the other party need to have, and how much of that can be foreign ownership. Sometimes there are other barriers that are not immediately obvious from reading the regulations that you can only understand by discussing the market access situation with local advisers.

It can be very helpful to talk with the local sources (local experts, advisers, your national embassy, and anyone they may recommend) to determine what kind of information you can get from them (e.g., if there are new regulations in the works, or if the situation is different than it appears on paper). For instance, there might be multiple potential partners for your client, but really only one partner that will be effective in the market. From there you have to determine whether your competitors are also partners with these local companies, and how that will affect your client. You need to determine if there is something unique about your client's service that will be attractive to this local partner as a differentiator and potential killer application.

It is also important if you are bringing your client for the first round of meetings with potential partners in the country to make sure you are meeting officials at the proper level. Clients become irritated when they are meeting unnecessarily with lower level people. Thus, you need to confirm that they are meeting with the equivalents at the prospective partner company.

You also need to determine if you are going to need local counsel, if the situation is such that you cannot handle everything from the U.S., and a local person will be necessary to make filings or set up meetings. Also, you need to know if an interpreter will be necessary.

To know the background of a client, you also need to find past agreements that the company has signed with other types of partners. This helps you determine if you would have a similar deal, and whether that deal would be acceptable to the client.

I have also found you need to have a level of respect for everyone you are working with. Many Americans will go into negotiations wanting to achieve immediate resolution, not at the same pace as the people in the other country, trying to resolve major issues at the first meeting. You do not want to be impatient. Part of a successful negotiation is offering the opposite side a fair deal that does not insult them. This way, if they do take the deal later on, there will not be bad feelings that could poison the working arrangement between the companies.

Initial Client Meeting Strategies

When first meeting with a partner you want to explain who you are, why you are there, and what you want to do. Generally, it is a good idea to bring a presentation that is tailored to the meeting, which includes what you know are going to be the hot-button issues and any unique characteristics of your client's product that would appeal to your foreign partner. It always makes people more comfortable to know about the other people you have as partners in the region and in the world. With the presentation, you need to anticipate what the prospective partner wants to know. At the same time, you have to realize that if it is a high-level meeting, you might not be able to give a two-hour long presentation. The presentation has to be concise and relatively quick. If there is a lot of information, it may be better to leave the details in a separate document.

In many countries, it is helpful to get to know the people you are working with on a personal level. You can give yourself an opportunity to do this by socializing, usually at lunch or dinner. Clients are not going to be as invested in doing business with you if they do not know you. Thus, they need to have a level of trust with you so that they will be more likely to be honest and to candidly tell you their concerns. Also, if you only hold a meeting it can be difficult to get their attention later on. As a lawyer, there is a good chance you are going to be working with a respective partner not only for your current client, but for future clients as well.

Prepping the Client for Meetings

It is important to ensure that clients understand local market access conditions, that they understand what prospective partners are available, and that they understand the local regulations and laws that will affect their plans. They also need to know about any political situation that might affect these elements. If there is going to be elections and a change in government, it is always important to prep them about what is important to the prospective client, and if there are things they should not talk about. For these reasons, it is helpful to read the bios of the people you are meeting with, if they are available. Biographies can help you to find anything you might have in common, or can simply help you to understand their background and where they are headed.

Timing and Task Completion

Timing is always an important issue. How long processes will take is often unpredictable, and always a question that your client is going to have.

Giving them a reasonable estimate is necessary. It is always better to under-promise and over-deliver, and so you do not want to be overly optimistic from the outset. Clients want to know about expenses along with time estimates, as they want to make sure they are getting the right value for their money. They should feel like once you conclude the negotiation, the relationship has not ended; you have to keep that partner happy afterwards, and going forward. They have to understand what kind of infrastructure and personnel they are going to have to put in place after the agreement is reached in order to manage the relationship.

It is possible to speed up the negotiating process. You do not want to be a pest, but you do want to make sure things keep moving. Checking in on a regular basis is a good idea. I generally come out of initial negotiations with a to-do list (e.g., I will prepare the non-disclosure agreement, you will take a look at my service agreement, and we will both provide comments on the memo of understanding). You want to complete this list as quickly as possible after the initial meeting, because if you fail to set the pace at the beginning you will probably fall behind. You have to show you are serious by doing what you promised to do at the outset in a timely manner.

You also need to make sure that you met with the right people, and find out if there are any other meetings you need to have with others in the company, or if there is someone who needs to understand the product or deal before you can proceed. If there is a key person who needs to sign off on a deal, especially before you leave the country, then you certainly need to meet them. It is always a good idea when doing a foreign negotiation to visit the local embassy. The staffs at embassies can often provide key information, or if they hear relevant rumors, they will tell you those as well.

Client Expectations

To manage client expectations, I always find it is a good idea to provide regular status reports to the client, even if there is not very much to tell them. It is important that the client knows you are still working on the issue, and are not off on the next project. Keeping the client in the loop means giving them regular weekly or bi-monthly updates. Of course, when there is any new development it is important that you immediately talk to the client about whatever that may be. It is important to strategize with them as well. It is always reassuring to clients if you spend time making sure they understand how the process works from beginning to end, along with what steps will be taken in between.

The Client's Role in Negotiations

The extent to which clients participate in negotiations depends on the client's knowledge in a particular area. For instance, I am currently working with one client who wants to enter the Chinese market, but the general counsel I work with is in the U.S., and he has never worked on any projects in China. Clearly, he needs a lot more prepping in order to understand the details of how Chinese negotiations generally proceed—how many days you would have to be there, who would you meet with, as well as the types of meetings and agreements you need, and the terms the Chinese like to use in negotiating. On the other hand, the same company has a regional VP who speaks Mandarin Chinese, and who has negotiated many contracts in China. He is more like a peer to the Chinese client, and has a level of experience in China that presumably exceeds that of anyone else in his company.

Clients will let you take the lead once you make everyone feel comfortable and at ease. There is a lot of pressure on the client in these situations because the negotiation could very well be a make-or-break deal for the company. For this reason, you need to understand the pressures involved, and have the full picture of the circumstances. When you look at negotiations, you have to realize what is important to your client, and what they are most sensitive about. Do they have to have that service in place in six months? If they do, you have to push the other side and make sure they understand there is a target date. In order to get that date done you have to give them a reason why they would want to do it as well. Again, the process requires making sure both parties have a stake in the deal as well as a mutual interest in getting the deal done.

Negotiating Financial Aspects

Finances are always a key factor in negotiations. To prepare for this aspect, you want to understand as much as possible about the company—if it is a negotiation with a foreign company what is acceptable, what is the usual revenue split, what have other companies agreed to, and so on. If you agree to 20 percent of revenues, and then you find out everyone else gives 2 percent, then your client will be upset. Thus, understanding precedents is crucial to protecting your client's interests. There will be a lot of issues related to costs—such as who is bearing what costs, what is the location of personnel—and so you must make sure that the business plan is compatible with both companies. Understanding the roles and responsibilities of both companies is key to feeling comfortable with a negotiation and whatever terms end up arising out of discussions.

Determining who owns the customer can often be a significant issue. When you are negotiating this type of agreement, the foreign company will sometimes want to have all the information about your client's customers. This is usually proprietary, and even if it is not, you want to make sure that as much information as possible about your client's customer stays with you. Oftentimes the battle is over who gets information about the end user customer, and how much of that is proprietary, and how much are both companies willing to share about their mutual customers. Much of this information is quite sensitive, and nobody wants to reveal their customers, so these circumstances pose a challenge to levels of trust as well.

Regulations in Negotiation

The regulatory aspect of a business negotiation can often be a mystery to both sides. In the U.S., the FCC has a transparent and open process, including public notices whenever there is a new regulation the FCC is considering. In other countries, however, the regulations may be virtually nonexistent. It might even be the case that there will be no existing regulations if it is a new technology. If your local partner is tasked with getting the regulatory approvals they might not be able to do that if there are too many regulatory barriers, and quite often regulatory uncertainty can be what delays the entire transaction.

Defining Success

I define a successful negotiation as when both parties feel like they have won, and they both walk away looking forward to working with each other and the prospect of building their businesses with one another. A winning negotiation has to be a win for both parties. There has to be a foundation of mutual trust for negotiations to benefit each company.

Successful negotiators will be able to anticipate the other party's concerns and desires. They also need to understand the client's business plan along with the objectives of the negotiation. Over the years, I have found that those who are unsuccessful in negotiations generally lack the adequate amount of cultural sensitivity. They do not look at the concerns from the other side, they are not flexible in understanding how the local process unfolds, and they want to do everything their way. One needs to understand that there is a middle ground and that they have to be flexible in order to find that place. Respect is also crucial. Every once in a while I hear stories about people marching in and making demands, and not treating potential partners as partners, but more like employees. This approach obviously does facilitate successful outcomes. Parties involved in a negotiation need to be respectful, and should consider the long-term effects of their meeting.

Sallye Clark, a partner at Arent Fox LLP, has extensive experience in international market access and government relations for the telecommunications industry. Her background includes negotiating and securing authorizations and license agreements for telecommunications projects from foreign governments around the world. Ms. Clark has advised corporations and governments on legal, trade, and market access issues in her representation of their interests in regulatory proceedings in the United States and abroad. Ms. Clark has negotiated and drafted sales, operating and service agreements with commercial and government entities globally. In addition, she has developed and executed successful legislative strategies to improve market access and federal procurement of telecommunications services. On behalf of the U.S. government, Ms. Clark regularly negotiates Host Nation Agreements (HNAs) with foreign governments to allow U.S. military and government networks to be used in-country.

Prior to joining Arent Fox, Ms. Clark was the senior counsel for international affairs for PanAmSat Corporation. Based in PanAmSat's Washington, D.C., office, she managed the company's domestic and international government affairs and ensured that PanAmSat services were available and authorized throughout the world. Previously, Ms. Clark was the executive director for international affairs for Teledesic LLC, a Bill Gates/Craig McCaw "Internet in the Sky" broadband project, and headed up ICO Global's international regulatory effort for McCaw. Ms. Clark also worked for Iridium

LLC as the senior manager and attorney for regulatory matters, and clerked at the Federal Communications Commission's International Bureau.

Ms. Clark was chair of the Satellite Industry Association's Trade Working Group where she worked on market access issues with regulators around the world on behalf of the satellite industry. Ms. Clark is an industry representative on the president's National Security Telecommunications Advisory Committee (NSTAC), focusing on emergency communications and interoperability issues. She has also given seminars to the U.S. Department of Defense (DoD) and at various military conferences on HNAs and foreign licensing of DoD networks. Ms. Clark was elected to the Pacific Telecommunications Council's Advisory Council and is on the steering committee of the Global Telecom Women's Network. She has also been a guest lecturer on international business and law at Johns Hopkins School of Advanced International Studies and Catholic University Law School. Ms. Clark frequently speaks about regulatory and licensing issues at various industry events around the world and is a member of the Federal Communications Bar Association (FCBA).

Ms. Clark has been published in Space News *and other newspapers,* APT Journal, FCBA International Law Journal *and in various seminars and conference proceedings. She received her J.D. from Catholic University of America, Columbus School of Law, and her B.A. from University of Maryland.*

Structuring and Negotiating a Telecommunications Deal

Owen D. Kurtin

Founder and Principal

The Vinland Group LLC

ASPATORE

Introduction

As a telecommunications lawyer, I counsel telecommunications and electronic media operators, service providers, equipment manufacturers, and their enterprise-level customers on a variety of transactions involving telecommunications and media services and products. The principal industry subsectors are telephony (wireline telephone communications); broadcast; cable; wireless; satellite; undersea cable; digital media rights acquisition, distribution and management; and broadband and internet protocol (IP) communications. In addition, when the cross-border provision of telecommunications goods or services is involved, there is a substantial overlay of other country law and regulation (and also European Union law and regulation, where applicable) and international telecommunications law and regulation, generally pursuant to the International Telecommunications Union, an agency of the United Nations.

Each of these subsectors has its own industry, technology, and regulatory peculiarities, which change rapidly over time, and it is of course very important for me to maintain a firm grip on those evolving distinctions to serve my clients effectively. I do that through reading, attending conferences and trade shows, and, above all, listening to the creative, technical, and businesspeople in the industry—they are the primary source for cutting-edge and coming trends; what is likely to take hold and what is not; and what business, legal, and regulatory impediments to telecommunications business development have arisen. I need to know the state of the industry to be able to think of solutions for its problems.

I believe that I add the greatest value for my clients by being able to incorporate an in-depth and up-to-date knowledge of the industry, technology, and regulatory aspects of each telecommunications subsector to my transactional advice and deal making. This added value comes into play in surprising and subtle ways. As an example, it frequently occurs that I am able to make an apparently valuable concession in a negotiation with the other party in exchange for a concession urgently needed by my client because I know what the other party and its counsel do not—that some evolving industrial, technological, or regulatory consideration has made my proffered concession moot and of far less value to the other party than it believes it to be. The other party, incorrectly believing it has obtained a concession of great value, frequently gives my client the concession that it needs.

Structuring the Transaction

Telecommunications transactions may fall into the general merger and acquisitions (M&A) categories of stock purchases, asset purchases, and statutory mergers. Joint venture structures are also common, with joint ventures embodied in commercial agreements or in juridical entities such as corporations, partnerships, limited partnerships (LPs), and limited liability companies (LLCs). Strategic alliances, which generally are looser relationships, are common as well. Telecommunications transactions that do not involve combinations or formal partnering of companies may take the form of strategic investments (by companies vertically or horizontally aligned with the investment target), financial investments (by individual investors, private equity firms, or divisions of larger financial institutions), or other private or public offerings of equity and debt securities. Finally, telecommunications services and equipment may be procured or outsourced through commercial arrangements.

Mergers and Acquisitions

M&A is a catch-all term used collectively to refer to a variety of transactions by which one business entity (the purchaser) acquires all or the majority of the stock or assets of another (the target). Negotiated (as opposed to hostile) acquisitions are essentially contractual arrangements, involving an acquisition agreement that routinely contains certain elements. Among these are a description of the basic transaction contemplated by the agreement; the acquisition consideration or purchase price and ways in which it may be adjusted; conditions to closing, the failure of which to be satisfied relieves the beneficiary party from its obligations to close; representations and warranties by target and purchaser that a certain state of affairs exists as of the date of the agreement's signing, as of the date of the transaction's closing, and in some cases, for a defined period of time after closing; and affirmative and negative covenants, promises by target and purchaser either to do something or refrain from doing something in order to produce or preserve a certain state of affairs. There are also generally termination provisions, choice-of-law provisions, and dispute resolution provisions, among others.

A leveraged buyout (LBO) involves the purchase of a business by a private equity firm purchaser that itself offers a relatively low percentage of the purchase price in the form of equity and the balance in the form of debt, which is secured and to be serviced by target's own expected revenues. Because of the low equity/high leverage model pursued by LBO firms, successful LBOs can produce very large returns for purchaser. However, the model leaves the target burdened by a heavy debt load. Frequently, the LBO plan is to restructure the target and sell non-core or less profitable businesses in which it is engaged, in order to retire some of the debt. At times, the LBO firm acts in concert with a group of the target's managers, funding them in their takeover of the target in exchange for some of the equity, the consideration for which is their expertise in running the target and indispensability post-acquisition. This form is called a management buyout (MBO).

A stock acquisition is ostensibly the simplest transaction form. It can be accomplished as simply as by the purchaser's executing one stock purchase agreement with the target's shareholders. The target is generally not a party to the agreement. Complications arise when there are multiple target shareholders that do not all agree to the transaction. In such cases, state corporation statutes provide for squeeze-out rights and appraisal remedies. Following the transaction, the target becomes a subsidiary of the purchaser. All other things being equal, the target shareholders generally prefer the stock purchase form because the purchaser succeeds to all of the target's assets and liabilities. By contrast, purchasers generally do not prefer stock purchases for the same reasons and because they receive no tax "step-up" of assets, even if the fair market value of those assets is usually greater than the target's basis in them.

In an asset acquisition, the transaction is usually directly between the purchaser and the target. The target does not become a subsidiary of the purchaser; it continues to be owned by its current owners, who do not directly receive the acquisition consideration in the absence of a target dividend or liquidation. In general, the asset acquisition is a preferred structure for a purchaser, because it can pick and choose among the target's assets rather than take (and pay for) assets and assume liabilities it may not want, as it does in a stock acquisition. Targets generally do not prefer asset sales, for the same reasons and because of tax considerations.

By contrast, mergers are a transaction form created and governed by state corporation statutes such as the Delaware General Corporation Law (DGCL). The use of a statutory merger provides both ease and established legal certainty. When the certificate of merger is filed with the Secretary of State of the state of incorporation, one company merges into the other, the first company's legal existence ends, and title to its assets (and liabilities) transfer automatically to the surviving company. Dissident shareholders are bound by the transaction, although, as in stock acquisitions, they may receive a better price than selling shareholders through squeeze-out rights and appraisal remedies. In a "forward" merger, the target merges directly into the purchaser; the purchaser is the surviving entity, and the target ceases to exist. In a "reverse" merger, the purchaser merges into the target and it is the purchaser that ceases legally to exist.

In a "triangular merger," the purchaser forms a shell subsidiary (subsidiary) (or a pre-existing one is used) in order to serve as a vehicle for the merger, resulting in the "triangle" of purchaser, target, and subsidiary. In a "forward triangular merger," the target merges into the subsidiary, leaving the subsidiary as the surviving entity and subsidiary of the purchaser.

In the case of a "reverse triangular merger," subsidiary merges into the target, and the target is the surviving entity, becoming a subsidiary of the purchaser. The reverse triangular merger form allows the purchaser to remain separate from, and structurally unaffected by, the core transaction, while allowing the target, which is generally not a shell company like the subsidiary, to become an intact operating subsidiary of the purchaser. The reverse triangular merger form also often permits the purchaser to take control of the target without triggering anti-assignment provisions in third-party contracts to which the target may be bound. The need to obtain third-party consents and the assignment clauses of agreements to which the target is a party can be a significant factor. Some third-party agreements can represent so much of the target's value that a failure to obtain the third-party consent could derail the transaction. Obviously, the obtaining of such consents is a critical condition to closing for the purchaser and review of material third-party agreements and their assignment clauses is a critical due diligence item.

The merger consideration can be composed of cash, equity, and/or debt (convertible or not) securities or a combination thereof. In a "cash election" merger, the target's shareholders are given the option of receiving cash, stock, or a combination of cash and stock for their shares. Where not all the merger consideration is cash, parties also allocate risk through adjustable pricing formulas. In a "fixed-exchange" ratio, each of the target's shares is converted into a fixed number of the purchaser's shares based on a negotiated "exchange ratio." Fixed-exchange ratios are most common in "merger of equals" transactions, since both parties equally share the risk of movement in the purchaser's share price. The formula is also common in the telecommunications sector, based on perceived sector volatility and the purchaser's resulting position that volatility risk in its stock price should be shared.

In a "fixed-value" transaction, it is the exchange ratio that floats. The formula usually provides for measuring the purchaser's stock price during a negotiated period of days or weeks prior to closing or meeting of target's stockholders to approve the transaction. A fixed-value pricing formula is used to insulate the target's shareholders from market risk prior to closing. The formula is used when one party is clearly the purchaser and the other clearly the target, rather than in "merger of equals" contexts. Also, hostile bidders use fixed-value structures because they have more appeal for target shareholders. In either the fixed-exchange or fixed-value scenario, the party bearing the risk of a decrease in stock price may seek to limit its risk through use of collars, caps, and floors that limit the transaction's potential volatility.

Joint Ventures

Joint ventures generally are formed when two or more parties have a limited but continuing business purpose that justifies a formal mechanism of cooperation, but does not justify a full business combination. As with mergers and acquisitions, the term is a catch-all for a variety of transactions. A joint venture can be as simple as a contract to collaborate, with no new business entity formed. An example might be an agreement to pool resources for the joint distribution of each company's products, including the renting of warehouse space, employment of personnel, engagement of accountants, and other attendant details.

More classically, though, joint ventures involve the formation of a new business entity, sometimes a corporation, but often an LP or an LLC, in order to take advantage of pass-through taxation rules and avoid taxation at the joint venture level. Because joint ventures are so common in telecommunications transactions, and because the form is less familiar than standard stock and asset acquisitions and mergers, a sample (and simple) joint venture structure is presented here.

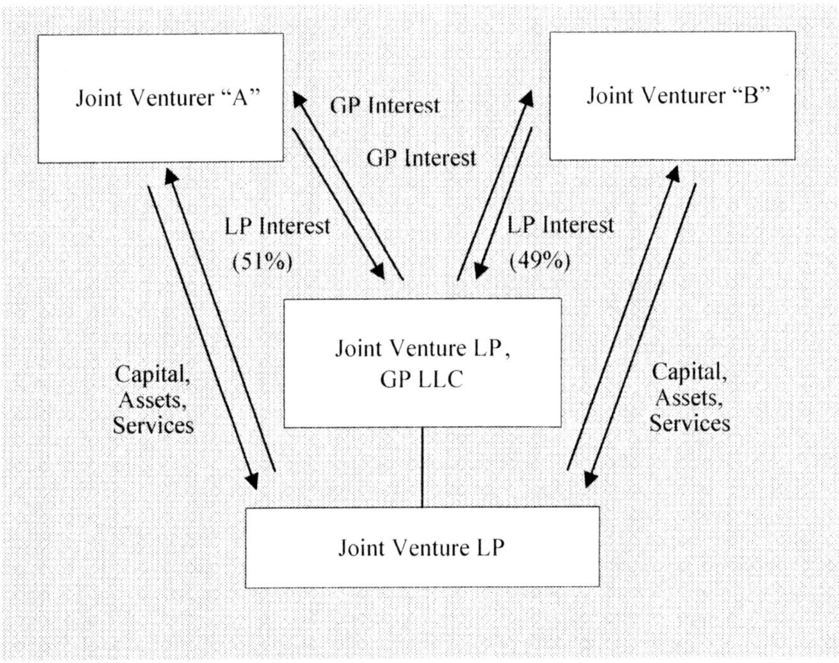

In this joint venture structure, the two joint venturers, "A" and "B," have formed a joint venture by creating an LP through the execution of an LP agreement and the filing of a certificate with the Secretary of State of the state under whose law the LP is formed. A and B receive "limited partnership interests," much like shares in a corporation.

An LLC formed under the same or another state's law will serve as the necessary general partner (GP) of the LP and the sole entity with both day-to-day managerial power over the LP's affairs and unlimited liability for the LP's liabilities. A and B will have limited liability in respect of their LP interests, just as though they were shareholders in a corporation. However, unlike in the case of a corporation, under Internal Revenue Code "check-the-box" rules the joint venture will not be taxed at the entity level—that is, the LP level—and tax income and losses will flow through directly to the limited partner level. The form not only allows the joint venturers to avoid entity level tax but to take advantage of early stage losses to offset against profits of other business operations and thereby reduce taxes.

Although A holds a majority interest in the LP, A and B can negotiate to protect B's minority interests by providing "super-majority" or unanimity vote requirements for specified partnership actions in the LP agreement and the GP operating agreement and by side agreements that provide for ancillary obligations of A and B to provide services, goods, or capital to the joint venture or to each other under specified circumstances.

Strategic and Financial Investments

Strategic and financial investments play a significant role in the incubation of early stage telecommunications service providers, equipment manufacturers, and applications developers. A strategic investment denotes a minority investment (hence, not an acquisition) in a company's stock by another company that is vertically or horizontally integrated in a target's supply chain. For example, an equipment manufacturer might invest in the manufacturer of, or holder of intellectual property rights to, a component strategically important to the investor's own products. While a return on investment may be a goal, the real driver of the investment is the investor's desire to take a proprietary interest in the target for strategic reasons. This may be motivated by the desire to assure supply or preferential pricing of target's products or to prevent competitors from having such access. In such cases, the strategic investment may be the prelude to a full acquisition further down the road.

By contrast, a financial investment also denotes a minority investment, but in this case by a company not in target's business or in any other business other than investing. These are so-called "private equity" firms, including venture capital funds, mezzanine lenders, buyout firms, and "hedge funds," an ill-defined group employing a wide variety of investment strategies. Financial investors seek return on investment only (although an investor's other holdings in an industry or perception of that industry can imbue a given investment with "strategic investment" attributes), and generally focus upon the "exit" event, generally either an initial public offering (IPO) or a sale to another company. Occasionally, a private equity firm for a time pursues a "buy-and-hold" strategy, whereby some of the expected return on investment is obtained from the target's operating profits.

Strategic and financial investments are often made through the use of preferred stock, which provides liquidation preferences, pre-emptive (antidilution), and other rights; convertible preferred stock, which converts to common stock at a specified conversion rate upon certain events, such as an initial public offering; and convertible debt instruments, that pay interest which is tax deductible for the issuer, but which also converts to stock upon the occurrence of specified events. Representation on target's board, rights upon registration of target's stock and other issues are dealt with in shareholders' agreements, registration rights agreements, voting agreements, and other ancillary documents.

Regulatory issues as well as business or economic considerations can influence the decision of what investment instrument to use. For example, the foreign ownership restrictions of the Communications Act of 1934, as amended by the Telecommunications Act of 1996, generally prohibit a non-U.S. entity's investment in a target broadcast or common carrier radio licensee above certain limits. However, the Federal Communications Commission generally has treated convertible debt instruments as not activating the statutory limits as would an equivalent equity stake, even if the investment, on an as-converted basis, would breach the statute.

Telecommunications Service and Outsourcing Agreements

Telecommunications services are provided by a carrier or a service provider to a "customer," which may be an end user subscriber, such as a business enterprise, another carrier, or other telecommunications provider, such as a cable operator that wants to offer VoIP service to its subscribers. Depending upon the range and complexity of the services being provided, such arrangements may be denominated as "outsourcing" transactions. If more than one service is offered, or additional services during the life of the agreement are contemplated, the arrangement may be structured as a master services agreement providing general terms with schedules annexed to it setting forth specified services.

Issues often highly negotiated include pricing and payment terms; MAC or MARC clauses (minimum annual commitment or minimum annual revenue commitment, by which the customer agrees to pay a specified amount for service each year of the agreement's term) and the penalties for a MAC or MARC "shortfall;" adjustments to the MAC or MARC, such as in the case of a business downtown for customer or technological change; service outages and credits for them; installation and uninstallation charges; service level agreements that establish specific metrics that the service provider must meet and associated financial penalties that are triggered if the metric is not met; warranty, indemnification, and limitation of liability provisions; and termination rights.

Negotiating the Transaction

Though it may sound cliché, negotiation really is an art. It is not so much that the art is different in telecommunications transactions, but that the technical and rapidly evolving nature of telecommunications means that the "state of the deal" changes rapidly, and things that were routinely taken for granted in last year's deals will not necessarily continue to be. Because there are so many kinds of telecommunications transactions, it is critical to keep the client's business goals always uppermost in mind, so as not to become consumed, and distracted, by the process of deal making itself to the client's detriment. As I mentioned earlier, in many cases, in-depth technical, industry, and regulatory knowledge permits me to make apparently valuable concessions in negotiation in exchange for a consideration of real value to my client, when those technical, industry, or regulatory considerations actually make my concession far less valuable than it appears. When I negotiate, I start by framing the discussion as a business transaction that both parties wish to conclude to their mutual benefit. When a party on the other side of the deal is obdurate about a deal point that is troubling for my client and me, and where we do not understand the other party's concern, I will sometimes just ask the party to leave aside the language and tell me straight out what business interest it is trying to protect. If the other party can satisfactorily explain its position, and we can accept the issue, finding the right language to memorialize it is usually less of a problem. However, if the other party cannot or will not explain its concern, it becomes fair game to suggest that its issue is not a real one, and that it should drop its position.

Part of not becoming lost in process is making sure that the client principals are engaged in the negotiation and aware of its status. Principals often have their eye on the ball—the business goal—better than do their lawyers. The way in which I prepare is to sit down with the client, analyze the transaction, determine and prioritize our hierarchy of business points from those we most want or need to achieve, and which may be "deal breakers" if we do not get, to those which are subsidiary or ancillary points for us. We then attempt to guess the same hierarchy for the other side.

To give an example, in a telecommunications services procurement or outsourcing, the MAC or MARC thresholds referred to earlier are often key, as are provisos for technical change and business downturn. In a joint venture, distribution of profits and losses, termination rights, and rights of one joint venturer to buy out the other are often critical. In an M&A transaction, purchase price adjustments, the conditions to closing, representations and warranties, and covenants, and their respective "carve-outs," or exceptions, are often critical. As useful as it is to try to estimate the other side's key concerns, it is important not to assume too much. What the other side turns out to be critically concerned with is often a surprise, and sometimes the revealed concern is a rational, but unanticipated, one (sometimes because the issues underlying the concern were not known to us) and sometimes it is an irrational one, that could not have been anticipated even with knowledge of all the facts, but which must be addressed nevertheless.

Conclusion

A negotiation is a success when a client gets the deal it fundamentally wanted. If that goal is achieved, then success is not measured by the concessions made to get that deal. Failure occurs when concessions necessary to achieve the deal make it a fundamentally different deal from the deal the client wanted, whether by way of what is obtained, its cost, or other considerations. While a broken or withdrawn deal is not a success, it is not necessarily failure, either. Real failure is a client closing a bad deal, either because of failure in negotiation, due diligence, inadvertence or—in a dynamic familiar to all transactional lawyers—because the client just felt itself to be too far down the road to withdraw, even when the transaction's deficiencies became apparent. When that dynamic comes into play, the lawyer has a critical role in reminding the client of the original business goal and the pitfalls newly appearing. Of course, the decision of whether to proceed or withdraw is always the client's, but with thoughtful and diligent counsel, that decision is most likely to be informed and justified.

In the appendix section are several documents illustrating a few of the transactional paradigms we have discussed. Appendix A is a cable operator system asset purchase agreement, Appendix B is a cable service VoIP outsourcing agreement and Appendix C is a cellular service resale agreement.

Owen D. Kurtin is a founder and principal of private investment firm The Vinland Group LLC. He is also a practicing lawyer in New York City, specializing in mergers and acquisitions, corporate finance, and corporate/commercial representation in the telecommunications and media, satellites and space, and information technologies sectors. He may be reached at okurtin@vinlandgroup.com.

Working as a Team with Clients to Achieve Success in Telecom Matters

Pantelis Michalopoulos

Partner

Steptoe & Johnson LLP

ASPATORE

Adding the Most Value for Clients with Respect to Telecom Matters

It is said that there are two kinds of clients: the ones who ask, "Can I do what I want?" and the ones who ask, "*How* can I do what I want?" Under that theory, the first kind of client values the lawyer who can help steer clear of illegality, fines, and prison. The second kind of client values the lawyer who can help steer around the law's prohibitions. This is a misleading distinction, because it is based on an outmoded perception of the law. It assumes that the law is a number of "don'ts." While these "don'ts" are still an important part of the law, today, far more than in the past, the law also creates opportunities. The federal government can grant licenses, exclusive rights, and privileges. It can impose conditions on a competitor's rights. Further, it can require a company to give new competitors access to its pipes or to its programming. It has delegated to the Federal Communications Commission agency for the telecommunications area the power to make rules regarding the public resources; in this case, these rules apply to such issues as electromagnetic frequencies, orbital slots, and rights of way.

In my view, the area where I can add the most value for the client is by suggesting ways to take advantage of a law, regulation, or rule to the client's advantage. Sound judgment from a relative outsider is also valuable. This can be illustrated anecdotally; for example, my wife and I display better judgment when one of us counsels the other about the other's problem than when handling the problem ourselves. This is another way of saying that a fool is his own lawyer. This type of help, in the form of providing an objective third-party opinion, is more valuable than telling the client, "You cannot do this under the law." It can be even more valuable than telling the client, "Here is another way to do this."

Major Telecom Related Issues with Which Clients Need Help

Most telecom-related issues arise as a function of the law of scarcity. There is only so much spectrum and so many orbital slots to go around, and usually only one company can use a frequency or a slot; otherwise, providers would jam each other and Americans would be throwing objects at their TV sets for getting no picture and slamming down their cell phones for getting no sound, or no Internet access. In the area of multichannel video, only some programs are must-have; these are the ones Americans simply must have, meaning your cable and satellite distributors must provide them if they are to compete effectively. There are only so many "pipes" through which a consumer can have broadband access to his or her home or PDA. Thus, the law of scarcity defines the issues with which I help clients, which include: licenses to use the spectrum or orbital slots on terms that are as favorable to the client as possible in order to provide satellite television, cell phone service, terrestrial high-speed access or other services; access of television distributors to must-have programming; access of programmers to dominant television platforms, as when a start-up network seeks to be carried by cable; fighting discrimination, as when a popular cable network favors an affiliated distributor over a competitor; and defending the consumers' right to those TV programs over the Internet when doing so does not infringe on one's copyright.

The Different Components of Telecom Law

Telecom law covers "plain old telephone service," wireless service, such as cell phone voice or broadband, satellite television, broadcast television and radio, cable television, Internet access, voice and video over Internet protocol and other information services.

With respect to each of these components, we provide a number of services to help clients. We help satellite television companies compete on a par with cable operators. We help them secure access to popular programming and so they are not forced to carry programming that no one aside from Washington lobbyists want to see. We have helped programmers in their efforts to secure carriage on cable systems. We have helped consumers secure the ability to make legitimate copies of high-definition television programs. Further, we have helped telecom companies obtain cost-effective—or even free—access to the spectrum that is their lifeblood. We have helped private equity firms buy telecom companies. We have helped Internet companies with online advertising, child protection, and gambling issues. These are just a few examples of the many services an attorney focusing on telecommunications can provide for clients in this industry.

The Financial Implications of Telecom Law

In some cases, the value of the services that telecommunications lawyers provide their clients is easy to ascertain. The value of the electromagnetic spectrum can be inferred by looking at the dozens of spectrum auctions that the FCC has conducted. This helps put an approximate tag on the opportunities that counsel can open up for the client. In other cases, the value added by outside and indeed in-house legal counsel is substantial but more difficult to quantify.

Common Mistakes with Respect to Telecom Law

As a general matter, clients are no more prone to making mistakes than are their outside lawyers. I do not approach client problems from any presumption of infallibility. However, in general, the worst mistake a telecom company can make is a lack of candor in its dealings with the Federal Communications Commission or any other government agency. Most other lapses or rule violations are solvable. Lack of candor undermines the regulator's confidence and can be fatal. I always advise clients that truth is their best ally, and I am happy to report that this advice has consistently been followed, at least to my knowledge.

On a tactical level, I sometimes find that clients are reluctant to make concessions early on, such as accepting conditions to a deal, accommodating a regulator's concerns, or addressing a legislator's pet issue. Usually, clients are concerned that they would be "giving away the shop." They prefer to defer concessions for later, if it becomes necessary. There is much to be said for this, but sometimes later is too late. A concession that would have saved the day has been stripped of its power. The timing of concessions is easy to miss-time. Without pretending to have the right answer—there frequently is none—I often urge clients to consider a flexible strategy where they are not backed into the corner of foreclosing concessions.

On the attorneys' side, the biggest mistakes stem from the views that the lawyer knows better than the client does and is supposed to manage the client, as well as the idea that playing favorites or politics within a client's organization is a good idea. The best way to avoid making these mistakes is to avoid these views completely and approach each client as a team member who deserves and requires respect and has the right to make his or her own decisions. It is the attorney's job to ensure that clients are making informed and ethical decisions; but the outside counsel should not attempt to control or manage clients in any way and should focus instead on truly listening to and communicating with them.

Achieving Success as a Telecommunications Attorney with Respect to Clients

While I cannot say that I have personally developed anything as grand as master strategies, I have found my general approach to clients to be useful. Generally, I advise clients that having a license allowing them to conduct their business is much safer than striking a deal with the person who has that license. I also often point out that an over-abundance of spectrum has seldom hurt a telecom company. In briefing a case, I advise that three arguments are better than seven are. Basic tactics such as this have served both my clients and me well over the years.

One of the worst mistakes a lawyer can make is to think he or she is better than other lawyers, including clients and competitors. Washington, as well as the nation as a whole, abounds with excellent lawyers. Excellent work quality is a must, but many others can provide it. Victory helps, but victories in the regulatory world usually come in shades of gray. In my view, success means to apply good judgment and creativity in helping clients accomplish their business objectives.

Another important component to achieving success in this field is an attorney's ability to stay on top of his or her knowledge in this industry. My method of achieving this includes regularly reading the trade press and the FCC decisions on areas of my interest. I try to stay at the bleeding edge of advances in telecommunications and technology regulation, an ability that has become increasingly important as the speed of news dissemination increases. Anything of which you do not apprise clients yourself immediately becomes something that they find out another way. It is critical in this role to be able to keep your clients informed, and emerging information that is relevant to their telecom matters should preferably come from their attorney.

Preliminary Information and Research to Obtain Prior to a First Meeting with a New Client on a Telecom Matter

Before the initial meeting with a client regarding a new telecom matter, I want to find out everything I can about the client, including who they are, what they do, what their issues are, and information of which they should be apprised and perhaps counseled about. In this way, I can avoid taking the client's time with questions that could be answered on the Web. To prepare I thus try to glean information from securities disclosures, if the client is a public company, as well as from Google, Nexis, and other publicly available resources. I also assemble pleadings that the client has filed in the FCC or in the courts to get a sense of the legal/policy issues that matter to the client. A diary reports that in President Clinton's view, the emphasis in politics has shifted from achievements to future promise. It is the same in legal practice. Clients are not indifferent to the achievements of the attorneys they want to hire; they have a unique problem, and they are interested more in that problem. A first meeting with the client will more usefully focus more on the problem at hand than on my background, regardless of whether the client has already decided to hire me or not.

Formulating a Client Strategy and Approach in a Telecom Matter

The main factor in determining strategy is how the client's goals coincide or intersect with the public interest—the standard that the FCC, like other agencies, applies in its deliberations. Another factor is whether the client's objective can be accomplished by an aggressive interpretation of existing rules or whether a new rule is required.

It is difficult to generalize on an approach one takes when representing a client involved in a telecom dispute. The approach varies depending, among other factors, on the competitive posture of the client. Is the client an incumbent or new entrant? Is it interested in cementing its established position or in the necessary conditions for establishing itself as a serious player in the market?

If the client is a new entrant, the themes available to us are more about competition and the public benefits deriving from it—lower prices, more diverse and high-quality services. If the client is an incumbent, the more attractive arguments are different. It becomes important to point to the essential benefits that the client provides, such as service to underserved communities, and to the risk that these benefits will be exposed if certain protections are withdrawn.

The questions that I will ask a client with respect to determining strategy in a telecom matter vary greatly depending on the project. Some basic questions include:

How will consumers benefit from your business objectives?
To what extent do you think you compete with the company you are trying to acquire?
How can we reassure the FCC that higher prices are unlikely?
Are the terms of a transaction with an affiliate or investor comparable to the terms of any arm's-length transaction?
Why are the other side's objections invalid?

Depending on the project, the answers to these questions help me formulate a public interest rationale in support of the client's position and anticipate objections such as concerns about competition.

As a rule, I normally do not need to ask particularly incisive questions. Clients generally have a brilliant grasp of their own businesses. As a result, they therefore tend to have a strong understanding of what they want to achieve and what the facts relevant to their goals are.

With respect to important documentation to receive from clients regarding their telecom disputes, all relevant agreements, talking points, and presentations to the board are critical. Investment bank presentations are particularly important as they shed a candid light on the business objectives and the ways in which the parties hope to benefit from the transaction. These documents can either be helpful to the argument that the transaction will generate efficiencies or damaging to the argument that prices will not increase. In either case, the documents will play an important role.

Establishing a Positive Client Relationship in a Telecom Matter

Because no lawyer is smarter than his or her competitors, the relationship with the client is all-important. You have to persuade the client that the rapport, the mutual confidence you have built, your understanding of the client's business, and the application of your judgment to the client's unique problems are likely to produce a better result than the use of another competent lawyer. To do this, it is essential to project oneself as the service provider, not as some sort of Delphic oracle whose pronouncements are the last word on a matter. I also dislike the concept of "managing the client," on which many outside lawyers pride themselves. Some even pride themselves on their ability to do it well. In my view, outside counsel serves the client, and their role is not to manage the client. To establish a positive relationship with a client, I forthrightly give my advice, even if the client does not want to hear it. If the client decides to disregard my advice and decides in favor of a different course of action, I have to accept and implement that decision, except in the highly unusual case where the course of action would be illegal and it would be unethical to continue with the representation.

Learning Clients' Ultimate Goals in a Telecom Matter

I learn my client's ultimate goals by directly asking the client. Clients are generally candid with their lawyers, especially if they are assured that the lawyer takes the privilege seriously. It is important not to overpromise, and I try not to. I do not assure the client it is likely to prevail in a particular dispute unless I am confident of that likelihood. I find most clients realistic. Even when a client entertains over-rosy expectations, sometimes they are meant as a rallying-the-troops technique and almost always they are moderated after a rational exchange of views.

The possible negative consequences associated with developing and following an improper strategy include failure to win approval or timely approval, a court defeat that hampers the client's business objectives, and enforcement proceedings. As long as the client does not lapse in its unremitting candor with the government, many enforcement issues can be avoided or ameliorated. The way to achieve damage control in the enforcement area is first to ascertain that a clear-cut violation exists—that there are no gray areas and no colorable argument that the rules were complied with. You do not want to be visiting the regulator in order to confess to sins that may not have been sins in the first place. Having concluded that there was indeed a lapse, early and full disclosure and concrete measures to avoid recurrence are the answer in a broad range of situations and before many regulatory agencies.

Similarly, when clients reveal "bad facts" in connection with their telecom dispute, I tell them that voluntary disclosure of bad facts is almost always preferable to failing to disclose them. This approach allows the client to put the best light on those facts (for example, present all mitigating circumstances or counter-arguments to neutralize them), and it avoids the regulator's displeasure if the facts come to light in another manner.

When developing the theory of the case in a telecom dispute, it is more appropriate to say that the client involves me in the process than that I involve him or her. I do not like the idea of lawyers who assume the mantle of grand strategists, formulate theories, and sometimes deign to involve the client in their deliberations. This approach is a feature of a bygone era, and working together as a team is a far more effective approach.

Considering the Non-legal Ramifications of a Client's Telecom Matter

Policy ramifications are important in Washington. A course of action that is justified based on the interpretation of existing law may nevertheless not be advisable because it may attract undue controversy or cause the client's executives to be dragged to a cngressional hearing. An effort to require the agency to do something (by filing a petition for a writ of mandamus in the Court of Appeals) or pressing the agency to act within a strict deadline is often counterproductive, even if legally justified. Often what you get is a quick defeat.

The Impact of Client Attitude on Strategy

When a client is determined to follow a strategy that I deem not to be in his or her interest, my approach is to advise forthrightly. However, as I have already said, I will generally accept the client's decision not to follow my advice, unless doing so were not ethically appropriate. I do not like to repeat my advice after it has been rejected, and I can tell you that clients detest such repetition. But this does not mean I will not engage in a spirited exchange of views with the client in support of my advice and try to discern the appropriate moment at which to stop. In fact, as a general rule, I never establish boundaries with my client as a threshold matter. Such a discussion would be appropriate only if I thought my client is contemplating a course of action that is outright illegal.

I represent all my clients zealously. While the tone of the advocacy may depend on the client's attitude (for example, it could be more or less aggressive, or the prose could be more or less hard-hitting), the differences are ones of nuance. However, a client's willingness to settle does affect my approach, and the willingness to settle before it is too late matters even more. As I have mentioned, I have found some clients are inclined to defer concessions for longer than is advisable. I fully understand the client's view, especially since the pound of flesh being extracted is the client's, not mine, but I do think this is an issue worth sensitizing clients to.

The Impact of a Client's Financial Status on Strategy

The client's financial status per se does not have an impact on the strategy, except in specialized circumstances, such as when the client needs to demonstrate its financial qualifications to complete a project. As mentioned, the status of the client as a large versus a small company, or as an incumbent versus a new entrant, does matter. It affects both the tone of the advocacy and the substance of the arguments.

Regardless of a client's specific situation, a lawyer always needs to remain open to alternatives. It is foolish to insist that there is only one appropriate course of action, because there rarely is only one. It is dangerous both for the client and attorney to decry the approach recommended by another lawyer as doomed to failure, because if it is chosen, it just might succeed. Also, the discussion of alternatives often results in a synthesis, yielding a third way that is beneficial to the client. Such instances truly emphasize the importance of good communication in any legal matter, and I feel that frequent, honest discussions with clients are one of the most effective tools an attorney has at his or her disposal.

Pantelis Michalopoulos is a partner with the Washington office of Steptoe & Johnson LLP. His practice covers the entire span of telecommunications law and regulation.

Mr. Michalopoulos practices before the Federal Communications Commission and has represented telecommunications companies in numerous licensing, rulemaking, and complaint proceedings before the FCC, as well as appellate proceedings. He has also assisted clients in telecommunications matters handled by other agencies such as the Copyright Office. Representing the consumers and the American Libraries Association, he argued in the Court of Appeals for the D.C. Circuit against the FCC's "broadcast flag" requirement, which would have prevented the Internet redistribution of high definition television content. The court struck this rule down in 2005. He has also represented satellite carriers and private equity funds in a number of high-profile transactions. He has written a number of articles about regulated industries, and has authored the legal thriller The War of Art *under the pseudonym Philip Blackpeat.*

Transactional Work in the Telecommunications Arena

Barry A. Friedman

Partner

Rachel Gagnebin Talay

Of Counsel

Thompson Hine LLP

ASPATORE

Introduction

All types of companies look to us for assistance with a broad range of telecommunications matters. For the purpose of this chapter we are narrowing our focus to the broadcasting industry and, more particularly, to the following general (yet overlapping) areas in which our telecommunications clients are regularly involved: M&A work, contract negotiations, day-to-day telecommunications issues, regulatory compliance work, and legislative affairs.

M&A Work – Let's Buy a Station

Clients retain us to assist them with M&A work including, among other things, the acquisition and divestiture of broadcast stations and other media ventures. If, for instance, a client comes to us to assist them in purchasing a station, we begin by understanding what the client wishes to accomplish and what the client expects the acquired business to look like, from a corporate and regulatory perspective, following consummation of the transaction. Sometimes our client will have already entered into a non-binding term sheet or letter of intent. If no such preliminary agreement exists, we consider whether this sort of a non-binding agreement would be beneficial to our client, taking into consideration the framing of issues and the timing of the transaction. Often, where there is uncertainty as to the parties' mutual understanding, it is better to have an initial written document memorializing what has been agreed to so the parties know they are on the same page before they invest significant amounts of time and money to conduct due diligence or negotiate a purchase agreement.

The parties will usually enter into a confidentiality agreement or a non-disclosure agreement at this stage as a precondition to the deal moving forward. Both parties will usually want to keep confidential the fact that they are in discussions for a potential transaction but their interests vary with respect to information about the station. On the one hand, a buyer will need access to all of the information of the seller relating to the business and operation of the station during this due diligence stage. Seller, on the other hand, wants to protect all of the information that it is providing to the buyer. Accordingly, confidentiality agreements must generally protect the seller and the seller's information while at the same time ensuring that buyer is receiving adequate information about the station and that buyer is free to share such information with its officers, directors, employees, counsel, accountants, engineers, lenders, potential lenders, and affiliates as well as any governmental authorities if required to do so.

Many parties shy away from negotiating a complex agreement at this stage of the transaction. A short confidentiality agreement can still provide adequate protection. We caution clients about including confidentiality provisions in the letter of intent or non-binding term sheet without careful consideration. Confidentiality provisions are intended to be binding on the parties and are supposed to survive even if the transaction does not. Including these types of binding provisions in a non-binding term sheet can be troublesome.

At this point, we have already started learning more about the station and the assets being purchased. We highlight issues, risks, or other concerns to the client before the client becomes invested in the transaction. Truly understanding the station and the assets being transferred can help the client reduce the likelihood of disputes and the need for settlements down the road. The client should simultaneously be conducting diligence of its own, including working with engineers, business and financial advisers, lenders, accountants, tax advisers, and consultants.

The licenses, authorizations, and approvals issued by the Federal Communications Commission (FCC) are often the most valuable assets in these types of deals so the regulatory diligence is very important. Our research frequently turns up issues to be resolved between buyer and seller—maybe through a reduction in the purchase price or an agreement to file joint applications with the FCC. We conduct due diligence to ascertain whether the station is compliant with Federal Aviation Administration regulations and that there are not any border issues involving Mexico or Canada. We also help the client identify environmental, tax, intellectual property, real estate, employment, and Internet related issues that all tend to play a role in the acquisition of a station.

There are so many important elements of any due diligence process for a telecommunications transaction including, but not limited to, making sure that all issues related to the assets of the station are identified, and that, at closing, the client is acquiring all the assets that the client wants and/or needs. The client needs to be aware of any issues in these areas. Beyond the issues that could arise in connection with the FCC licenses, we must also consider, among others, environmental, tax, intellectual property, real estate, employment, and Internet related issues. If the client will not end up obtaining title to some intellectual property related to the station that the client wants, then that is clearly an issue. If there are some environmental issues related to the real property then the client might decide not to go forward with the deal, have the seller remedy the issue, or restructure the deal. When the parties arrive at the closing, the client needs to know that, among other assets, the licenses, intellectual property, real estate, employees, and Web sites the client wants to assume are being properly and fully transferred to the buyer without any unknown or unwanted liabilities and without violating any applicable laws or regulations.

If the parties opt to continue moving forward with the transaction after this initial due diligence, then we start negotiating a deal that will enable our client to realize its goals. The parties determine early on whether the buyer will be permitted to continue conducting due diligence after a purchase agreement has been signed. If this is the case, it is important that the buyer has an easy way to terminate the purchase agreement without any liability and without losing any earnest money deposits made by buyer in the event that buyer decides not to move forward. These types of provisions need to be clear and precise so that disputes do not arise. Sellers do not like to see buyers walking away so it is easy to understand how disputes could arise under these circumstances. Properly drafted agreements can help prevent disputes or the need for settlements in the event the buyer uncovers issues that result in the buyer reconsidering its commitment to the transaction.

It is always important that the principal agreements for any deal clearly and concisely set forth the terms and conditions of the transaction. Some of the key considerations that we take into account in drafting and negotiating the principal agreements include:

- Ensuring that our client is purchasing all the assets that the client wants and/or needs to operate the station, and assuming only those obligations and liabilities that the client intends to acquire, if any. We don't want any surprises for the client in this area because surprises are what often leads to disputes. We make sure that the client is protected after the closing of the transaction—we don't want the seller seeking to assign liabilities or obligations that our client didn't agree to assume; we don't want our client left with assets that don't work; and we don't want our client to be missing any assets that it needs to run the station. We avoid disputes and the need for settlements by properly drafting provisions that provide for the deal that the parties envision. Negotiations at this stage of the transaction tend to take place among the businesspeople as well as among the lawyers.

- We also remain current on FCC and legal market conditions to ensure that we are negotiating the best deal possible for our client. Provisions in agreements that, as they say, are "market" are continually changing. It is important to stay current in the telecommunications area as well as transactional law generally. This is an important aspect of our practice and is discussed in more detail below.
- We make sure that the client does not have any unexpected obligations after the closing. Certain deals may require limited post-closing obligations but we endeavor to keep post-closing obligations to a minimum.
- We include provisions in the purchase agreement that will enable the client to be in the best position in the event a dispute arises. We consider, among other things, jurisdiction, venue, jury trials, litigation, arbitration, mediation, other dispute resolution options, and costs/expenses.
- Where appropriate, we help the client get non-compete agreements that will protect the client's business going forward.
- We work with the FCC to obtain consent to assign the licenses, authorizations, approvals, applications, and registrations of the station. We always work toward the timelines proposed by the client but in normal cases, you might expect to receive consent within 130 days of filing an application for consent to assign the station license with the FCC. However, there are situations where FCC consent could take longer or be denied.
- If the FCC has granted its consent to assign the licenses, authorization, approvals, applications, and registrations of the

station but the consummation of the deal has been delayed, we also work with the FCC to extend the time within which the deal was required to close.

- We notify the FCC once the deal closes. For clients who purchase stations, we then provide assistance with contract negotiations, day-to-day telecommunications issues, and regulatory compliance for that station going forward as described below.

From time to time, the parties will find themselves in a dispute at some point during this process. This could be a dispute that arises leading up to the closing, or a dispute that comes up after the closing. In either event, we help our client weigh its options and negotiate the best settlement possible as discussed below.

Contract Negotiations

We assist clients in negotiating various types of contracts including, among other things, programming agreements, leases, affiliation agreements, employment agreements, advertising agreements, and leases. This area overlaps with our transactional work as described above.

Day-To-Day Telecommunications Issues

We assist clients with day-to-day telecommunications issues like contests, collections, and advertising. We also help clients comply with the regulations governing contests and sweepstakes. These laws are complex and vary by state. For clients that hold contests in many states, this means that the rules governing a contest must comply with the rules of each such state. We are able to assist clients with broadcasts issues such as defamation, slander, and obscene and indecent speech, and political broadcasting questions. Clients also look to us to help determine the types of advertising that can be broadcast. Advertising cannot be broadcast if, for example, it is false or misleading or contains obscene, indecent, or profane language. Finally, we offer training to help clients understand their regulatory obligations and to help all employees of the client learn how to broadcast responsibly.

Regulatory Compliance Work

We oversee the regulatory aspects of our clients' businesses to keep the clients in compliance with state and federal telecommunications regulations. This type of work includes complying with digital broadcasting requirements, securing license renewals and construction permits and modifications, filing ownership reports and otherwise helping clients stay current and in compliance with the applicable regulations.

Legislative Affairs

Clients can look to us to keep them apprised of regulations that might affect their business or industry. We can help our clients get the attention of key congressional representatives when proposed or pending regulations or other governmental activities are of particular importance to our clients. We have counseled clients on securing legislative assistance, including communicating with federal agencies and supporting legislative initiatives.

Adding Value

Everything that we do for the client is geared toward adding value to our clients' businesses. We aim to help our clients increase their viewers and/or listeners while at the same time avoiding costly expenses, liabilities, and fines.

In helping clients increase their listeners and achieve greater advertiser loyalty, we assist the clients in effectuating some of their business strategies whether they include maintaining their size, growing, or downsizing. We make sure that the clients' business-side understanding is accurately reflected in the legal documents prepared for the transaction, and that the clients' goals are achieved as quickly and efficiently as possible. Our clients rely on us to make certain that a business deal does not run afoul of applicable telecommunications laws.

Additionally, we make sure that our clients comply with applicable telecommunications regulations. Clients want to spend their time focused on their listeners and advertisers and not worrying about filings that they need to make with the FCC. To this end, we do help clients become aware of, and comply with, day-to-day regulations that affect their business and operations. The telecommunications regulations are constantly changing. We feel that it is our job to help clients stay current with these changing regulations and thereby stay in compliance. The last thing a client wants to do is monitor changing regulations. Clients value our assistance because we can do the monitoring for them. Additionally, by helping our clients steer clear of regulatory enforcement proceedings and lawsuits, we save them legal fees, regulatory fines, and civil damage awards, which can be quite substantial.

Other ways we add value include:

- If a client wants to acquire a number of stations in the same market then we work to figure out how best to achieve the client's goal.
- We work with clients to find potential buyers and sellers of broadcast stations.
- We also work with clients to help them determine if there are opportunities to increase the power of their station or move their station to locations allowing for more coverage in the client's targeted area.
- We offer training and guidance to encourage responsible broadcasting.
- We assist clients in navigating the potential traps that can arise from indemnification, assumed liabilities and related aspects of any deal.
- We educate our clients on the different types of insurance available to broadcasters.

Negotiations

There is obviously a large regulatory focus to all telecommunications deals, more so than in many other types of deals. In purchasing a broadcast station, the most important asset being transferred is heavily regulated by telecommunications laws. So the negotiations in a telecommunications transaction may focus on different issues or topics but the goals and strategies should be the same as in any transaction.

The art of negotiation with respect to any sort of transaction is all about being prepared. Negotiations entail knowing as much as possible about your client, the parties with whom you are negotiating, the industry in which the parties participate, and the type of transaction the parties are envisioning.

You need to know your client, your client's strategy, and how much your client wants or needs to do the deal. Could the client easily find another deal with another party? Is this the client's only option? Does the client need this for its business? Does the transaction need to be completed quickly? You also need to understand the other parties to the transaction. You should do some preliminary research on the other parties to the transaction so you have some background knowledge going into the negotiations. All of this will help you determine what will be the standard for reasonable in the negotiations.

You will also need to understand the subject of your negotiations. This entails more than just knowing that the parties are negotiating, for instance, the transfer of a broadcast station. This means knowing about all of the assets that are being sold with the radio station. This includes knowing about, among other things, the intellectual property, the real property, the environmental issues, the personal property, the contracts, the employees, and the finances. You should do due diligence on the assets before going into a negotiation about the transaction. Having more information about the assets being transferred will help you understand when you can hold strong, how far you can push the other side, and how many concessions your client is willing to make.

There is another important element of the "art" of the negotiation. Too many times the lawyers are trying to "negotiate" an issue or a transaction by e-mail or by sending marked up documents back and forth. These steps, of course, are helpful and certainly have their place in any transaction. However, at some point the negotiations need to be in person or on the phone. The parties need to be able to make proposals and receive immediate feedback. The parties need to be talking with each other in real time to get to the root of the issue, which cannot happen if the parties are not meeting in person or talking on the phone. In addition, too often misunderstandings are created and grow because of e-mail communications.

Parties are more likely to be reasonable on the phone or in person. A phone call or a face-to-face meeting is an essential element of a successful negotiation.

Negotiation Strategy

Our negotiation strategy is simply to provide the best services to our client as possible; this means different things in different situations and it is our job to understand those differences. In the event that parties reach an impasse in negotiations, it may help to take a break and come back in a few minutes, or to move on to other issues or negotiations on which agreement may be reached more easily. It is also always important to keep in mind and sometimes even discuss the concerns and needs of the other side to better understand each side's positions. Redirecting the focus to the needs of the parties as opposed to the disputed issue itself can help to move the negotiations forward.

The Role of the Attorney in Negotiations

Attorneys represent the interests of their clients in the negotiations. Our goal is to make sure that our client is happy, profitable, protected, and in compliance with telecommunications laws at the end of the day. A lot of the time, we take on the role of working out some of the more controversial issues and raising sensitive topics with the other side's lawyer so that we look like the bad guys; this helps the business people maintain a better relationship during and after the transaction.

Key Players

Negotiations tend to start with the businesspeople and then move to the lawyers who document the deal agreed to by the businesspeople, as well as point out issues and inconsistencies with the business deal. The lawyers generally go back and forth as each side is working to best protect their client. The focus then turns back to the businesspeople for some clarification as to the terms of the agreed upon deal. This back and forth continues until the lawyers confirm that the parties have reached agreement and that it is accurately and fully depicted in the documents.

Negotiating Specific Items

No two transactions are the same, so the issues tend to be very different as well. If we are just looking at the sale of a broadcast station, then parties often tend to heavily negotiate provisions dealing with the price and how it is paid, the assumption of liabilities, conditions to closing, and indemnification.

The businesspeople may not have focused on these issues in their preliminary discussions. It is up to the lawyers to bring these issues to the attention of the businesspeople as in many cases it is a business decision as opposed to a legal issue.

Pricing

One would assume that the pricing of a deal is easy—agree upon a number and pay it. However, pricing can be an art itself and involves different forms including cash, promissory notes, non-compete agreements, leases, etc. Not only does each of these terms have to be structured, but also there have to be decisions made as to timing, interest rates, and security. Counsel must also be sensitive to the tax considerations that may affect the treatment of the investment or amount the client earns.

Assumption of Liabilities

No buyer wants to assume liabilities and no seller wants to be stuck holding liabilities after the closing. Here, it is important that the buyer has done due diligence so that the buyer has an idea as to the liabilities that are outstanding. It is still, however, imperative that buyer's counsel protect buyer against any unwanted liabilities of seller, whether they are known or unknown.

Conditions to Closing

There are often situations where one party will want to close but another party wants certain milestones to have occurred prior to closing. The buyer wants more conditions to closing. The buyer wants everything settled before the closing, including having all of the assets in good repair and working condition, all security interests released, and all consents secured prior to paying the purchase price to the seller. The seller, on the other hand, wants the purchase price from the buyer as soon as possible.

Indemnification

Not many sellers are willing to provide indemnification for long periods of time after closing but lots of buyers will look to the seller to provide as much indemnification as possible. Many buyers look for indefinite indemnification in areas such as title, taxes, and authority. Sellers, on the other hand, also like to include provisions that limit the amount of indemnification. These provisions are important and can become extremely complicated with terms and conditions providing for time limitations, thresholds, and caps, all of which will often require input from the business side.

Deal Breakers

Sometimes telecommunications deals fall apart because the buyer uncovers some issues regarding the assets in the due diligence process. Or, perhaps there are financial issues that arise on the buyer's side. Other times the parties cannot reach agreement on the purchase price. We are now starting to see deals that fall apart because there are financing and potential bankruptcy issues on the seller's side.

In general, these deals are falling apart on the business side and not on the legal side. The lawyers should not be destroying a deal if the legal issues have been identified and the businesspeople are in agreement.

When to Settle

Settlement is best when the client prefers to avoid the cost, publicity, and time of a trial or ADR, but does not want to, or is not able to, walk away from the deal entirely. Of course, there are times when claims are brought to our clients that are, simply put, ridiculous. In these cases, it probably does not make sense for the client to negotiate or settle. In these cases, we do not focus on anything other than getting the complainant to go away. We ultimately look to the client to make the decision as to whether to proceed to court. It is clear that any client would prefer to avoid litigation if they could achieve the same result through a settlement.

Recent Trends and Developments

In the past year, the FCC cracked down on some of their deadlines and issued record-breaking fines which overall seemed to evidence more aggressive enforcement efforts by the FCC. For the most part, this seems to be continuing into 2008. Among other things, the FCC:

- Issued fines for FM translator renewals that were not filed on time.
- Entered into consent decrees with four broadcast companies (which admitted no guilt) with voluntary contributions totaling $12.5 million with respect to claims that the companies engaged in payola practices. The broadcast companies are required to track and record all gifts (valued at $25 or greater) received by station employees from music labels. The FCC is permitted to inspect these records upon request. These consent decrees should help provide some guidance to licensees going forward with respect to rules relating to payola and sponsorship identification.
- Released a number of Notices of Apparent Liability for Forfeiture relating to contents run by stations. Stations need to be aware of the FCC's scrutiny in this area and should take special care to make sure that contests are well planned to comply with applicable rules and regulations, and executed along those same lines.

Digital Television Transition

The FCC also adopted measures with respect to the upcoming digital television transition: for example, the importation and interstate shipment of analog-only televisions was banned, but retailers are permitted to sell equipment from their existing inventory. However, effective May 25, 2007, retailers were required to post warnings on or close to analog-only televisions to notify consumers that the television will not receive broadcast signals after the transition on February 17, 2009 without a separate digital-to-analog converter box. 47 C.F.R. §15.117(k) (2007). Hundreds of retailers were cited within a month of the order for failing to post such notices in violation of Section 302(b) of the Communications Act of 1934, as amended, 47 U.S.C. §302a(b), and Section 15.117(k) of the FCC's Rules, 47 C.F.R. §15.117(k). This will continue to be a big issue for television stations, and retailers as well, in 2008 and 2009. On April 10th, 2008 the FCC issued Notices of Apparent Liability for Forfeiture to Wal-Mart Stores Inc. and Sam's West Inc. ($992,000), Target Corporation ($296,000), Sears Holdings and Kmart Corporation ($1,096,000), Fry's Electronics Inc. ($384,000), CompUSA Inc. ($168,000), Circuit City Stores Inc. ($712,000), and Best Buy Co. ($280,000) Inc., for failing to place the required Consumer Alert label with respect to television receiving equipment that contains an analog broadcast television tuner but not a digital broadcast television tuner. Fines were issued in the amounts noted above. In addition, on that same day, Syntax-Brillian Corporation received a fine of $1,266,100 for the importation and interstate shipment of television receivers that do not comply with the FCC's rules regarding digital television reception capability with an additional $11,000 for providing to the FCC during the course of an investigation information that was incorrect without a reasonable basis for believing the information was correct. And finally, also on April 10th, the FCC fined Precor Incorporated in the amount of $357,900 for the same violation of importation and interstate shipment of television receivers that do not comply with the FCC's rules regarding digital television reception capability.

Violence on Television

The FCC also grappled with the issue of violence on television. The FCC issued a report to Congress stating that research shows that a child's exposure to violence on television can increase aggressive behavior in that child. The report recommends restrictions on the time of day that violence can be aired on television and notes that an *a la carte* channel option would allow consumers to purchase programming with limited violent content. The FCC also suggested that Congress should develop a definition of excessively violent programming. We expect to see this addressed throughout 2008.

Indecent Speech

The FCC's policy with respect to treating fleeting expletives as indecent speech was vacated by the U.S. Court of Appeals for the Second Circuit on

June 4, 2007. *Fox Television Stations Inc. v. FCC*, No. 06-1760, slip op. (2d. Cir. June 5, 2007). This will most likely also develop throughout 2008.

Media Cross-Ownership

The FCC continued to address the media cross-ownership rules. At the end of 2007, the FCC voted to end the absolute ban on the ability of a company owning a newspaper to also own television and radio stations. Federal Communications Commission, Cross-Ownership of Broadcast Stations and Newspapers, Report and Order and Order on Reconsideration, MM Dkt. No. 01-235 (Adopted December 18, 2007; Released February 4, 2008). There are still limitations but this would allow companies owning a newspaper to also own one television station or one radio station in the twenty largest markets in the United States. It seems that there are some, including members of Congress, who are not happy with this change so we expect to hear more about this in 2008.

Strategies for 2008 and Beyond

With the economy the way it is, it is more important than ever to make sure that clients are not incurring unnecessary costs and expenses. FCC fees or fines would definitely fall within the unnecessary category.

The current market conditions will affect the telecommunications industry in a number of ways. We are already seeing deals put together for financial reasons—in many cases the seller needs capital quickly and is accordingly selling its assets. Sometimes the seller is already in bankruptcy. There are some great deals out there for potential buyers that have available capital.

We are also seeing companies that are struggling to comply with the digital transition rules. This is turning out to be a financial burden for some companies, especially in this economy. This means that potential buyers need to be aware of whether the seller is in compliance with the transition schedule, and whether the seller has started purchasing the equipment needed for such transition in the event the buyer is considering a possible acquisition of a television station.

Because of these issues and concerns, we are focused on making sure that our clients are protected from the other parties' financial problems. We are also still focused on making sure that our clients are in compliance with all rules and regulations so as to avoid unnecessary regulatory enforcement proceedings.

Additionally, when advising a client in a negotiation or litigation type situation, we are likely to continue to request information about the digital transition. We may also request more information from the seller regarding its financial position and security interests securing the assets.

Upcoming Hurdles for Clients

Financial Hurdles

We anticipate financial hurdles for sellers who are being required by their lenders or financial situations to sell, and buyers who wish to acquire but cannot secure financing. The changing market has created many financial hurdles for companies. Some companies are in financial distress, while other companies are putting all of their capital to work to buy distressed companies. Either way, companies are facing different financial challenges.

Regulatory Hurdles

This is the same hurdle our clients have faced in previous years, although the regulatory issues themselves are changing. The challenge is to stay current with all rules and regulations.

Compliance Hurdles

Compliance hurdles aren't really new hurdles either. Clients have faced these in the past and will continue to face them in the future. It is important that the clients understand the current climate.

Mistakes to Avoid

Common areas where we see clients getting into trouble in the telecommunications area include:

- Not staying current with telecommunications regulations – It is important that clients stay current with the changing regulations.
- Irresponsible broadcasting – Broadcasting programs or commercials that do not comply with telecommunications regulations related to defamation and slander, or indecent or obscene speech; or holding contests that violate laws.
- Setting up broadcast stations in a manner that is not easily transferable or assignable – For example, the client intends to sell a radio station in a few years but the client has entered into many station contracts that are not assignable to a buyer.
- Agreeing to buy a station before conducting sufficient diligence – There are often issues on the FCC side that need to be identified before the parties can reach a final agreement.

Conclusion

In closing, we simply note that the most important aspect of any transaction is knowing the business of your client. Only then will you be able to provide the highest quality counsel to your client.

Barry A. Friedman *is a partner in Thompson Hine LLP's Telecommunications practice group. He focuses his practice on the representation of broadcasters, common carriers, telecommunications users engaged in enterprise contracting, communications lenders, broadcast talent, and television program producers. Mr. Friedman is experienced in a broad range of telecommunications issues including new technologies, telephone service agreements, acquisitions and divestitures, and debtor/creditor rights involving telecommunications ventures.*

Rachel Gagnebin Talay *is of counsel in Thompson Hine LLP's Telecommunications practice group. She is also a member of the firm's Corporate Transactions & Securities practice group as well as the Competition and Antitrust & White-Collar Crime practice group. Ms. Talay focuses her practice on advising clients on a broad range of corporate, telecommunications and antitrust matters. In the telecommunications area, she represents clients on acquisitions and divestitures of broadcast stations and has significant involvement with other issues facing broadcasters.*

Appendices

APPENDIX A

CABLE OPERATOR SYSTEM ASSET PURCHASE AGREEMENT

ASSET PURCHASE AGREEMENT, dated as of [ ] (this **"Agreement"**), between **"Seller"**, and **"Buyer"**.

RECITALS

A. The Seller, through the subsidiaries described on Schedule 1 of the Disclosure Schedules (each, a **"Subsidiary"** and collectively, the **"Subsidiaries"**), owns and operates Cable Systems (as defined in the Communications Act) as described on Schedule 1 of the Disclosure Schedules(the **"Systems"**).

B. The Seller has agreed to cause the Subsidiaries to convey, as appropriate, to the Buyer the Transferred Assets, including the Shares, upon the terms and conditions set forth in this Agreement.

C. The Buyer has agreed to assume the Assumed Liabilities upon the terms and conditions set forth in this Agreement.

AGREEMENT

In consideration of the foregoing and the mutual covenants and agreements herein contained, and intending to be legally bound hereby, the parties agree as follows:

ARTICLE I
DEFINITIONS

Section 1.1 Certain Defined Terms. For purposes of this Agreement:

"Action" means any claim, action, suit, arbitration or proceeding by or before any Governmental Authority.

"Active Customer" means a subscriber of the applicable service from a Subsidiary, but excluding (i) any subscriber who has a past due balance in excess of $10 in the aggregate for more than 60 days from the first day of the billing period to which a bill relates, (ii) any subscriber who has not paid at least one full month's payment for services in an amount at least equal to the standard rate for Basic Services in the applicable Franchise Area, (iii) any subscriber, with respect to a service, which service is pending disconnection for any reason, and (iv) any subscriber who was obtained after the date hereof by offers, promotions or marketing practices other than those set forth on Schedule 1.1(a) of the Disclosure Schedules or as otherwise approved in writing by the Buyer.

"Affiliate" means: (i) with respect to the Seller or any Subsidiary, or any Person directly or indirectly controlled by [ ], (ii) with respect to the Buyer, [ ] or any other Person directly or indirectly controlled by the Buyer or [ ], and (iii) with respect to any other Person, any other Person that directly, or indirectly through one or more intermediaries, controls, is controlled by, or is under common control with, such Person.

"Ancillary Agreements" means the Bill of Sale, the Assumption Agreement, the Transition Services Agreement, the Digital Transport Agreement, deeds with respect to each parcel of Owned Real Property in the forms (as applicable) included herein on Exhibit A (each, a **"Deed"**), duly endorsed stock certificates representing the Shares, Retained Franchise Management Agreements (if any), the Escrow Agreement, endorsed vehicle titles, FIRPTA certificates and all other instruments and documents necessary for the Subsidiaries to transfer the Transferred Assets or for the Buyer to assume the Assumed Liabilities.

"Antitrust Division" means the Antitrust Division of the United States Department of Justice.

"Assumption Agreement" means an assignment and assumption agreement in the form of that attached hereto as Exhibit B, pursuant to which the Subsidiaries shall assign to the Buyer all of the intangible personal property included in the Transferred Assets and the Buyer shall assume the Assumed Liabilities.

"Basic Services" means the lowest tier of cable television programming sold to subscribers as a package, including broadcast and satellite service programming for which a subscriber pays a fixed monthly fee to a Subsidiary, but not including Pay TV.

"**Basic Subscribers**" means, as of any date and for each System, all Active Customers of Basic Services of such System who are individually billed for Basic Services.

"**Bill of Sale**" means a bill of sale in the form of that attached hereto as Exhibit C, pursuant to which the Subsidiaries, as applicable, shall transfer to the Buyer all of the Transferred Assets that are transferable pursuant to a bill of sale.

"**Business**" means the business of providing customers with Basic Services, Expanded Basic Services, Pay TV, Digital Services, High-Speed Internet Services and other services conducted by the Subsidiaries, on the date of this Agreement, through the Systems.

"**Business Day**" means any day that is not a Saturday, a Sunday or other day on which banks are required or authorized by Law to be closed in either The City of New York, New York or St. Louis, Missouri.

"**Business Employees**" means, as of any date, all individuals employed by Affiliates of the Seller as of such date (including those on approved leaves of absence), whose duties relate primarily to the operations of the Business, regardless of the company payroll on which such individuals are listed.

"**Buyer Material Adverse Effect**" means any event, change, circumstance, effect or state of facts that is materially adverse to the ability of the Buyer to perform its obligations under this Agreement or the Ancillary Agreements or to consummate the transactions contemplated hereby or thereby.

"**Buyer's Knowledge**" means the actual (but not constructive or imputed) knowledge of David Bach, Regional Vice President, Atlantic Region, as of the relevant date, without any implication of verification or investigation concerning such knowledge.

"**Cable Act**" means Title VI of the Communications Act, the Cable Communications Policy Act of 1984, the Cable Television Consumer Protection and Competition Act of 1992 and the provisions of the

Telecommunications Act of 1996 amending Title VI of the Communications Act, in each case as amended and in effect from time to time.

“[ ] means [ ].

“[ ] means [ ].

“C-Corporations” means **“[ ]”** means [ ] limited liability company.

“Closing Time” means 12:01 a.m. (local time with respect to each System) on the Closing Date.

“Code” means the Internal Revenue Code of 1986, as amended through the date hereof.

“Communications Act” means the Communications Act of 1934, as amended, 47 U.S.C. Sections 151 et seq., including amendments by the Cable Communications Policy Act of 1984, the Cable Television Consumer Protection and Competition Act of 1992, and the Telecommunications Act of 1996, and as may be further amended, and the rules and regulations and published decisions of the FCC thereunder, as in effect from time to time.

“control”, including the terms **“controlled by”** and **“under common control with”**, means the possession, directly or indirectly, of the power to direct or cause the direction of the management and policies of a Person, whether through the ownership of voting securities, as trustee or executor, as general partner or managing member, by contract or otherwise.

“[ ] Assets” means substantially all of the assets to be acquired under that certain Asset Purchase Agreement dated October 31, 2005, by and among [ ] Communications, Inc. and certain of its affiliates on the one hand, and the Buyer on the other hand.

“**CPA Firm**” means Deloitte & Touche LLP, or such other firm of independent certified public accountants as to which the Seller and the Buyer shall mutually agree.

"**Current Assets**" means the following current assets of the Business:

(i) all prepaid expenses (other than inventory) and credits (including prepaid real and personal property Taxes to the extent attributable to any periods or portions thereof beginning on or after the Closing Date, copyright fees, FCC regulatory fees, and Franchise or License fees or charges);

(ii) petty cash at the business offices located within the Systems

(iii) all customer and advertising accounts receivable related to the Business; provided, however, that:

(A) only 98% of accounts receivable resulting from customer accounts of which more than $10 is past due more than 30 and up to and including 60 days as of the Closing Date are included as "Current Assets";

(B) only 90% of (1) accounts receivable resulting from customer accounts of which more than $10 is past due more than 60 and up to and including 90 days as of the Closing Date and (2) accounts receivable resulting from advertising sales of which any portion is past due more than 90 and up to and including 120 days from the date of invoice as of the Closing Date are included as "Current Assets"; and

(C) none of (1) any accounts receivable resulting from customer accounts of which more than $10 is past due more than 90 days as of the Closing Date or (2) any accounts receivable resulting from advertising sales of which any portion is past due more than 120 days from the date of invoice as of the Closing Date are included as "Current Assets";

For purposes of making "past due" calculations for customer accounts pursuant to this clause (iii), the billing statements of a System will be deemed to be due and payable on the first day of the period during which the service to which such billing statements relates is provided and will be deemed to be past due if any portion of the customer account in excess of the $10 amounts referred to in this clause (iii) is past due; and

(iv) all deposits relating to the Business and operations of the Systems that are held by third parties as of the Closing Time for the account of the Subsidiaries and that relate to the Systems or as security for any Subsidiary's performance of its obligations, including deposits on leases and deposits for utilities.

"**Current Liabilities**" means the following current liabilities of the Business:

(i) all advance payments to, or funds of third parties on deposit with, the Subsidiaries as of the Closing Time and relating to the Business, including advance payments and deposits (including any accrued interest on such deposits) by subscribers served by the Business for converters, encoders, decoders, cable television service and related sales and services;

(ii) the economic value of all accrued and unused vacation leave that the Buyer credits to the Transferred Employees in accordance with Section 5.5(f), where economic value is the amount equal to the cash compensation that would be payable to each such employee at his or her level of compensation on the Closing Date for a period equal to such accrued and unused vacation leave;

(iii) the amount, if any, equal to the monetary obligations contemplated by clauses (a), (b) and (d)(i) of the definition of Permitted Encumbrances; and

(iv) the prorated amount of certain obligations, including Franchise fees, pole rental fees and copyright fees for any period prior to the Closing Date not to be paid by the Seller by the Closing Date.

"**Digital Services**" means an optional tier of digital video services offered by the Systems to their customers.

"**EBUs**" (or Equivalent Basic Units) means, as of any date and for each System, the number derived by dividing (a) the total monthly billings for sales of Basic Services by the System during the most recent month ended prior to the date of calculation to commercial bulk billed Active Customers of the System that do not take Expanded Basic Services and other such Active Customer accounts of the System that do not take Expanded Basic Services not billed by individual units, whether on a discounted or undiscounted basis (but excluding billings in excess of a single month's charges for any account), by (b) the standard monthly rate (without discount of any kind) charged by the System to single family households for Basic Services sold by the System then in effect; and adding to such quotient the number derived by dividing (c) the total monthly billings for sales of Basic Services plus Expanded Basic Services by the System during the most recent month ended prior to the date of calculation to commercial bulk billed Active Customers that take Expanded Basic Services and other such Active Customer accounts of the System that take Expanded Basic Services not billed by individual units, whether on a discounted or undiscounted basis (but excluding billings in excess of a single month's charges for any account), by (d) the standard monthly rate (without discount of any kind) charged by the System to single family households for Basic Services plus Expanded Basic Services sold by the System then in effect. For purposes of the foregoing, excluded are that portion of the billings to each bulk billed account representing an installation or other non-recurring charge, a charge for equipment or for any additional outlet, a charge for any tiered service (whether or not included within Pay TV), or a pass-through charge for sales taxes, line-itemized franchise fees and charges and the like.

"**Employee Plans**" means all "employee benefit plans" within the meaning of Section 3(3) of ERISA, all formal written plans and all other compensation and benefit plans, contracts, policies, programs and arrangements of the Seller or any of its ERISA Affiliates (other than routine administrative procedures) in connection with the Business in effect as of the date hereof, including all pension, profit sharing, savings and thrift, bonus, stock bonus, stock option or other cash or equity-based incentive or deferred compensation, severance pay and medical and life insurance plans in which any of the Business Employees or their dependents participate.

"**Encumbrance**" means any charge, claim, mortgage, lien, option, pledge, security interest or other restriction of any kind.

"**Environmental Laws**" mean any Laws of any Governmental Authority in effect as of the date hereof: (i) related to releases or threatened releases to soil, surface water, groundwater, air or any other environmental media of any substance, hazardous material or other substance or compound regulated under Laws relating to such releases, including petroleum or any refined product or fraction or derivative thereof (**"Hazardous Substances"**); (ii) governing the use, treatment, storage, disposal, transport or handling of Hazardous Substances; or (iii) related to the protection of the environment and human health. Such Environmental Laws shall include the Resource Conservation and Recovery Act, the Comprehensive Environmental Response, Compensation and Liability Act, the Emergency Planning and Community Right-to-Know Act, the Clean Air Act, the Clean Water Act, the Safe Drinking Water Act and the Toxic Substances Control Act.

"**Equity Sponsors**" means GS Capital Partners V Fund, L.P., Par Investment Partners, L.P. and OCM Principal Opportunities Fund II, L.P.

"**Equipment**" means electronic devices, trunk and distribution coaxial and optical fiber cable, amplifiers, drops, power supplies, conduit, vaults and pedestals, grounding and pole hardware, subscriber devices (including converters, encoders, transformers behind television sets and fittings), headend hardware (including origination, earth stations, transmission and distribution systems), test equipment and any other equipment used or held for use in the Business.

"**ERISA**" means the Employee Retirement Income Security Act of 1974, as amended, and the rules and regulations thereunder, as in effect from time to time.

"**ERISA Affiliates**" means, with respect to the Seller, (i) any corporation which at any time on or before the Closing Date is or was a member of the same controlled group of corporations (within the meaning of Section

414(b) of the Code) as the Seller; (ii) any partnership, trade or business (whether or not incorporated) which at any time on or before the Closing Date is or was under common control (within the meaning of Section 414(c) of the Code) with the Seller; (iii) any entity, which at any time on or before the Closing Date is or was a member of the same affiliated service group (within the meaning or Section 414(m) of the Code) as the Seller, any corporation described in clause (i) above or any partnership, trade or business described in clause (ii) above; and (iv) any entity which at any time on or before the Closing Date is or was required to be aggregated with the Seller under Section 414(o) of the Code.

"**Escrow Agreement**" means an escrow agreement in the form of that attached hereto as Exhibit D, to be executed by the Seller, the Buyer and the Escrow Agent on the date hereof and pursuant to which the Seller, the Buyer and the Escrow Agent shall provide for the management of the Escrow Fund.

"**Expanded Basic Services**" means an optional tier of video services offered by each System to its customers other than Basic Services, a la carte tiers, premium services, Digital Services, any new product tier, Pay TV, and High Speed Internet Services.

"**FCC**" means the Federal Communications Commission.

"**Final Net Asset Value**" means (x) the total Current Assets shown on the Final Working Capital Statement, minus (y) the total Current Liabilities shown on the Final Working Capital Statement.

"**Final RGU Purchase Price Adjustment**" shall be determined as follows:

(i) if, at the Closing, the Purchase Price was decreased pursuant to Section 2.9(b)(ii), and if the number of RGUs set forth in the Final RGU Statement is greater than the number of RGUs as set forth in the Pre-Closing RGU Statement, then the Final RGU Purchase Price Adjustment (which, for the avoidance of doubt, will increase the Purchase Price) shall be an amount equal to (1) the number of RGUs set forth in the Final RGU Statement less the number of RGUs used in calculating the

Pre-Closing RGU Adjustment, multiplied by (2) the Price Per RGU, provided, however, that such amount shall not exceed the amount by which the Purchase Price was reduced pursuant to Section 2.9(b); or

(ii) if, at the Closing, whether or not the Purchase Price was decreased pursuant to Section 2.9(b)(ii), the number of RGUs set forth in the Final RGU Statement is less than the number of RGUs set forth in the Pre-Closing RGU Statement, and is also less than the Lower RGU Limit, then the Final RGU Purchase Price Adjustment (which, for the avoidance of doubt, will decrease the Purchase Price) shall be an amount equal to (1) the Price Per RGU multiplied by (2) the number of RGUs (as set forth in the Final RGU Statement) less the Lower RGU Limit.

"Final RGU Statement" means the RGU statement that sets forth the average of the number of RGUs (including any RGUs related to the Retained Franchises, if any) as of the last day of the month for each of the six months prior to (and including) the Closing Date, prepared, or caused to be prepared, by the Buyer in accordance with Section 2.9(e) hereof and, in the event of a Seller RGU Objection, as adjusted by agreement of the Buyer and the Seller, or by the CPA Firm, acting pursuant to Section 2.9(f).

"Final Working Capital Adjustment Amount" equals (i) the Final Net Asset Value minus (ii) the Pre-Closing Net Asset Value (as amended pursuant to Section 2.9(c)).

"Final Working Capital Statement" means the net working capital statement that sets forth the Current Assets and the Current Liabilities (including the Current Assets and the Current Liabilities related to the Retained Franchises, if any) as of the Closing Time, prepared, or caused to be prepared, by the Buyer in accordance with Section 2.9(d) hereof and, in the event of a Seller's Working Capital Objection, as adjusted by agreement "of the Buyer and the Seller, or by the CPA Firm, acting pursuant to Section 2.9(f).

"**Franchise**" means each franchise (as such term is defined in the Communications Act) granted by a Governmental Authority authorizing the construction, upgrade, maintenance and operation of any part of the Systems.

"**Franchise Area**" means, with respect to any Franchise, the geographic area in which any Subsidiary is authorized to operate the Systems related to such Franchise.

"**FTC**" means the Federal Trade Commission.

"**GAAP**" means United States generally accepted accounting principles as in effect on the date of the Financial Statement to which it relates.

"**Governmental Authority**" means any United States federal, state or local governmental, regulatory or administrative authority, agency or commission or any judicial or arbitral body.

"**High Speed Internet Services**" means Internet service provider and backbone connectivity services offered by the Systems to their customers through a cable modem and cable modem termination system.

"**HSI Subscribers**" means, as of any date and for each System, all Active Customers of High Speed Internet Services of such System.

"**HSR Act**" means the Hart-Scott-Rodino Antitrust Improvements Act of 1976, as amended.

"**Indentures**" means the indentures governing the debt securities issued by [ ] Communications Holdings, LLC and its subsidiaries.

"**Intellectual Property**" means all (i) trade names, trademarks and service marks (registered and unregistered), domain names, trade dress and similar rights and applications to register any of the foregoing; (ii) patents and patent applications and rights in respect of utility models or industrial designs; (iii) copyrights and registrations and applications therefor; and (iv) know-how, inventions, discoveries, methods, and processes (whether or not patentable).

"**Knowledge**", with respect to the Seller, means the actual (but not constructive or imputed) knowledge of the persons listed on Schedule 1.1(b) of the Disclosure Schedules with respect to the System(s) identified with respect to such persons on such Schedule as of the relevant date, without any implication of verification or investigation concerning such knowledge.

"**Law**" means any statute, law, ordinance, regulation, rule, code, injunction, judgment, decree or order of any Governmental Authority.

"**LFA Approvals**" means all consents, approvals or waivers required to be obtained from any Governmental Authority with respect to the transfer or change in control of any Franchise in connection with the transactions contemplated hereby.

"**License**" means any license, permit or other authorization (other than a Franchise) issued by any Governmental Authority, including the FCC, used in the operation of the Business, including TV translator station licenses and microwave licenses, cable television relay services and television receive only earth station registrations.

"**Lower RGU Limit**" means 312,992 RGUs.

"**Material Adverse Effect**" means any event, change, circumstance, effect or state of facts that (i) is or could reasonably be expected to be materially adverse to the business, financial condition, operations, assets, liabilities or results of operations of the Business, taken as a whole; provided, however, that "Material Adverse Effect" under this clause (i) shall not include the effect of any circumstance, change, development, event or state of facts arising out of or attributable to any of the following, either alone or in combination: (1) matters affecting the multi-channel video programming distribution or High Speed Internet Services industries generally, or competition in or to those industries, (2) general national, regional or international economic or financial conditions or markets that do not affect the Systems disproportionately as compared to other similarly situated participants in the cable industry, (3) changes in technology, (4) the public announcement of this Agreement or of the consummation of the transactions contemplated hereby or (5) any changes in federal or state Laws that do not affect the Systems disproportionately as compared to other similarly situated participants in the cable industry or (ii) has prevented, materially impaired or materially delayed, or could reasonably be expected to prevent, materially impair or materially delay, the ability of the Seller or any Subsidiary to perform its obligations under this Agreement or the Ancillary Agreements to which it will be a party or to consummate the transactions contemplated hereby or thereby.

"**Material Real Property**" means any parcel of Real Property used as a headend or primary hub site.

"**Operating Cash Flow**" means (i) revenue less (ii) operating expenses (including programming, ad sales and service, and excluding depreciation and amortization) and selling, general and administrative expenses (including marketing).

"**Pay TV**" means for each System, premium programming services selected by and sold to subscribers on an a la carte basis for monthly fees in addition to the fee for Basic Services.

"**Permitted Encumbrances**" means (a) statutory liens for current Taxes not yet due or delinquent (or which may be paid without interest or penalties) or the validity or amount of which is being contested in good faith by appropriate proceedings, (b) mechanics', carriers', workers', repairers' and other similar liens arising or incurred in the ordinary course of business relating to obligations as to which there is no default on the part of the Seller for a period greater than 60 days, or the validity or amount of which is being contested in good faith by appropriate proceedings, or pledges, deposits or other liens securing the performance of bids, trade contracts, leases or statutory obligations (including workers' compensation, unemployment insurance or other social security legislation), (c) with respect to Real Property, zoning, entitlement, conservation restriction and other land use and environmental regulations by any Governmental Authority that do not materially interfere with the use of the Real Property or any buildings or structures thereon as currently being used, (d) in the case of any Leased Real Property, (i) landlords' liens for sums not yet due or which are being contested in good-faith by appropriate proceedings, (ii) the rights of any lessor and (iii) any Encumbrances granted by any lessor of such Leased Real Property or any such lessor's predecessors in title, (e) any severed mineral or oil and gas estates, or mineral or oil and gas leasehold estates, or rights of a proprietor of a vein or lode to extract or remove his ore, in each instance that do not materially interfere with the use of the Real Property or any buildings or structures thereon as currently being used, (f) those Encumbrances described as "**Permitted Encumbrances**" on Schedule 1.1(c) of the Disclosure Schedules, (g) any Encumbrances created in connection with or pursuant to an Assumed Liability and (h) with respect to Real Property, all exceptions, restrictions, easements, imperfections of title, charges, rights-of-way and other Encumbrances, discrepancies and conflicts in boundary lines, shortages in area, encroachments, and any fact that a correct survey and inspection of the property would disclose, and that does not materially interfere with the use of the Transferred Assets as currently being used.

"**Person**" means an individual, corporation, partnership, limited liability company, limited liability partnership, syndicate, person, trust, association, organization or other entity, including any Governmental Authority, and including any successor, by merger or otherwise, of any of the foregoing.

"**Pre-Closing Net Asset Value**" means (x) the total Current Assets shown on the Pre-Closing Working Capital Statement, minus (y) the total Current Liabilities shown on the Pre-Closing Working Capital Statement (as amended pursuant to Section 2.9(c)).

"**Pre-Closing Tax Period**" means all Tax periods ending before the Closing Date and the portion of any Straddle Period ending on (and including) the day before the Closing Date.

"**Pre-Closing RGU Adjustment**" means the decrease, if any, in the Base Purchase Price determined pursuant to Section 2.9(b) hereof.

"**Pre-Closing RGU Statement**" means the statement that sets forth the average number of RGUs (including the RGUs related to the Retained Franchises, if any) as of the last day of the month for each of the last six full months for which System Reports are available prior to delivery of such statement, prepared or caused to be prepared, and as may be revised, by the Seller in accordance with Section 2.9(b) hereof.

"**Pre-Closing Working Capital Statement**" means the net working capital statement that sets forth the estimated Current Assets and Current Liabilities (including the Current Assets and Current Liabilities related to the Retained Franchises, if any) as of the Closing Time, prepared, or caused to be prepared, and as may be revised, by the Seller in accordance with Section 2.9(a) hereof.

"**Price Per RGU**" means $2,403.89.

"**Required Consents**" means any authorization, approval or consent of any Governmental Authority or other Person under any License, Franchise, agreement or other instrument that by law or by its terms requires a third party's consent as a condition for the Seller or the Subsidiaries to transfer, assign or engage in a transaction that results in a change of control over, such License, Franchise, agreement or other instrument to the Buyer.

"**Retained Franchise Management Agreement**" means an agreement, substantially in the form of Exhibit E, whereby the Seller or any Subsidiary shall transfer to the Buyer, to the extent practicable, the benefits and burdens of any Franchise not transferred to the Buyer pursuant to Section 2.1.

"**RGUs**" means the sum of Basic Subscribers, EBUs and HSI Subscribers.

"**Seller Objections**" means the Seller Working Capital Objection and/or the Seller RGU Objection.

"**Shares**" means all of the issued and outstanding equity of the C-Corporations.

"**Straddle Periods**" means all Tax periods beginning before and ending on or after the Closing Date.

"**Subscribers**" means all Basic Subscribers and EBUs.

"**System Reports**" means the unaudited, internal, monthly reports showing revenues and expenses and individual basic subscribers, digital subscribers, equivalent basic units for bulk and commercial subscribers and high-speed Internet subscribers for the Business.

"**Tax**" or "**Taxes**" means, with respect to any Person, any federal, state, local or foreign net income, gross income, gross receipts, sales, use, ad valorem, value-added, capital, unitary, intangible, franchise, profits, license, withholding, payroll, employment, excise, severance, stamp, transfer, occupation, premium, property or windfall profit tax, custom, duty or other tax, governmental fee or other like assessment or charge of any kind whatsoever, together with any interest or penalty, addition to tax or additional amount imposed by any jurisdiction or other taxing authority, on such Person.

"**Tax Benefit Adjustment**" means the net present value of the tax benefit the Buyer would receive if it were to purchase the assets and assume the liabilities of the C-Corporations, which the parties hereby agree shall be $10,000,000 for all purposes related to this Agreement and the Ancillary Agreements and the transactions contemplated hereby and thereby.

"**Tax Return**" means any return, declaration, report, claim for refund, or information return or statement relating to Taxes, including any schedule or attachment thereto, and including any amendment thereof.

Section 1.2 Table of Definitions. The following terms have the meanings set forth in the Sections referenced below:

Definition	Location
1060 Form	2.10
Agreement	Preamble
Allocation Schedule	2.10
Assumed Liabilities	2.3
Audited Financial Statements	5.22(a)(i)
Balance Sheet	3.5
Base Purchase Price	2.6
Books and Records	2.1(g)
Business Permits	2.1(f)
Buyer	Preamble
Buyer Indemnified Parties	7.2
Buyer Welfare Benefit Plans	5.5(e)(i)

Qualified Intermediary	9.12
Real Property	2.1(b)
Representatives	5.2(a)
Retained Assets	2.5(b)
Retained Employees	5.5(a)
Retained Franchise	2.5(b)
Retained Shares	2.5(b)
Securities Act	4.9
Seller	Preamble
Seller Indemnified Parties	7.3
Seller RGU Objection	2.9(e)(ii)
Seller Working Capital Objection	2.9(d)(ii)
Seller's Required Consent Letter	5.7(c)(i)
Straddle Period Fraction	5.19(f)
Subsidiaries	Recitals
Systems	Recitals
Tangible Personal Property	2.1(e)
Termination Date	8.1(c)
Third Party Claim	7.4(a)
Transfer Tax Returns	5.19(b)
Transfer Taxes	5.19(a)
Transferred Assets	2.1
Transferred Employee	5.5(a)
Transition Services	5.15(b)
Transition Services Agreement	5.15(b)
WARN Act	5.5(g)

ARTICLE II

PURCHASE AND SALE

Section 2.1 Purchase and Sale of Transferred Assets. Upon the terms and subject to the conditions of this Agreement, at the Closing, (i) the Seller shall cause the Subsidiaries (other than the C-Corporations) to, sell, assign, transfer, convey and deliver to the Buyer the Transferred Assets (other than the Shares) free and clear of all Encumbrances other than Permitted Encumbrances, and (ii) the Seller shall cause the C-Corporation Parent Company to sell, assign, transfer, convey and deliver to the Buyer the Shares free and clear of all Encumbrances other than Encumbrances created by the Buyer, and the Buyer shall purchase, acquire, accept and pay for the Transferred Assets and the Shares and assume the Assumed Liabilities. **"Transferred Assets"** means (A) the Shares and (B) all of the assets, properties and rights (wherever located), whether tangible or intangible or real or personal, that are located within any of the Franchise Areas that are owned, leased, used or held for use in the operation of the Business or the Systems or, if located elsewhere, that are used or held for use primarily in the operation of the Business or the Systems (other than the Excluded Assets), as they exist on the date hereof, with such changes (with respect to both assets being transferred and condition of those assets) therein as are permitted by this Agreement, including the assets, properties and rights referred to below:

(a) subject to Section 5.26, all contracts and agreements to which the Subsidiaries are a party or by which the Subsidiaries are bound that are used in the Business, including the Material Contracts, other than those contracts that constitute Excluded Assets (the **"Contracts"**);

(b) all real property, leaseholds and other interests in real property owned or leased by the Subsidiaries that are located within any of the Franchise Areas and used or held for use in the operation of the Business or the Systems or, if located elsewhere, that are used or held for use primarily in the operation of the Business or the Systems, together with the Subsidiaries' right, title and interest in, to and under all structures, facilities or improvements currently or as of the Closing Time located thereon, all fixtures, systems, equipment and other items of personal property attached or appurtenant thereto and all easements, licenses, rights and appurtenances relating to the foregoing (the **"Real Property"**);

(c) all assets as of the Closing Time that are Current Assets;

(d) all accounts receivable, notes receivable and other receivables due to the Subsidiaries in connection with the Business, together with any unpaid interest or fees accrued thereon or other amounts due with respect thereto;

(e) all machinery, Equipment, advertising insertion equipment, furniture, furnishings, inventory, parts, spare parts, vehicles (including the vehicles listed on Schedule 2.1(e) of the Disclosure Schedules) and other tangible personal property owned by the Subsidiaries located within any of the Franchise Areas and used or held for use in the operation of the Business or the Systems or, if located elsewhere, that are used or held for use primarily in the operation of the Business or the Systems (the **"Tangible Personal Property"**);

(f) all Permits used or held for use primarily in the Business (the **"Business Permits"**);

(g) all books of account, general, financial and accounting records, files (including the originals of the Contracts and the Permits, where available), invoices, customers and suppliers lists, other distribution lists, billing records, engineering records, drawings, blueprints, schematics, copyright, FCC and other regulatory records, manuals and customer and supplier correspondence owned by the Seller and the Subsidiaries, but only to the extent relating primarily to the Business and corporate records of the C-Corporations (including the minute books and stock books thereof) (the **"Books and Records"**); provided, however, that the Books and Records shall not include personnel records relating to the Business Employees;

(h) all rights to causes of action, lawsuits, judgments, claims and demands of any nature in favor of the Subsidiaries to the extent relating to the Business, the Transferred Assets or the Assumed Liabilities;

(i) all guarantees, warranties, indemnities and similar rights in favor of the Subsidiaries to the extent transferable and related to the Transferred Assets;

(j) petty cash at the business offices located within the Systems;

(k) all Internet protocol addresses that have been assigned to all elements included in the Transferred Assets, including Internet protocol addresses that have been assigned to (i) end-users, (ii) network elements, (iii) local area network and billing elements, (iv) telephony elements, (v) data and video transport elements, (vi) digital controllers, (vii) digital customer premises equipment and (viii) switches and routers (**"IP Addresses"**); and

(l) all software described on Schedule 2.1(l) of the Disclosure Schedules.

Section 2.2 Excluded Assets. Notwithstanding anything contained in Section 2.1 to the contrary, the Seller and the Subsidiaries are not selling, and the Buyer is not purchasing, any of the following assets of the Seller, the Subsidiaries or their Affiliates, all of which shall be retained by the Seller, the Subsidiaries or their Affiliates, respectively (collectively, the **"Excluded Assets"**):

(a) any real property or tangible personal property located outside any of the Franchise Areas that are not used or held for use primarily in the operation of the Business or the Systems;

(b) programming contracts (including music programming contracts and retransmission consent agreements) and cable guide contracts;

(c) all billing contracts and related equipment that is not owned by the Seller, the Subsidiaries or their Affiliates;

(d) the Permits set forth on Schedule 2.2(d) of the Disclosure Schedules and all Permits that are not transferable and are not material to the Business taken as a whole;

(e) all state and federal telecommunications Licenses and authorities for non-cable services (except any such Licenses that are held by the C-Corporations);

(f) contracts (including those for management and consulting services) with any Affiliates of the Subsidiaries;

(g) intercompany receivables owing to the Subsidiaries by any of their Affiliates;

(h) any of the Subsidiaries' cash and cash equivalents (other than the petty cash included in the Transferred Assets);

(i) other than such books, records and papers of the C-Corporations, the Subsidiaries' corporate books and records of internal corporate proceedings, tax records, work papers, personnel records relating to the Business Employees and books and records that the Subsidiaries are required by Law to retain, provided that the Seller agrees to make copies of such books and records available, to the extent permitted by Law, to the Buyer in accordance with Section 5.2 of this Agreement;

(j) any Intellectual Property, other than the IP Addresses and other than as set forth on Schedule 2.1(l) of the Disclosure Schedules;

(k) all of the Subsidiaries' bank accounts (other than the C-Corporations);

(l) all accounting records of the Subsidiaries (other than the C-Corporations) (including records relating to Taxes, but excluding records relating to subscribers) and internal reports relating to the business activities of the Subsidiaries that are not Transferred Assets;

(m) any interest in or right to any refund of Taxes relating to the Business, the Transferred Assets or the Assumed Liabilities for, or applicable to, any taxable period (or portion thereof) ending on or prior to the Closing Time, other than to the extent such Taxes were included in Assumed Liabilities; provided, however, that the portion of any such interest or right equal to the amount necessary to satisfy any actual Tax liability resulting from the receipt of such refunds shall be Transferred Assets and shall not be Excluded Assets;

(n) any insurance policies and rights, claims or causes of action thereunder;

(o) except as specifically provided in Section 5.5, any assets relating to any Employee Plan;

(p) all rights, claims and causes of action relating to any Excluded Asset or any Excluded Liability;

(q) all contracts to which any Subsidiary and/or one or more Affiliates of the Seller are parties that relate to any System as well as one or more cable systems of [ ] and its subsidiaries that are not included in the Systems, including (i) master contracts for retransmission consent, advertising sales, tower leases, master multiple dwelling units and (ii) the other master contracts listed on Schedule 2.2(r) of the Disclosure Schedules, which for all contracts under this Section 2.2(q) includes such contracts that would, but for the fact that they relate to one or more cable systems of [ ] and its subsidiaries that are not included in the Systems, be required to be disclosed on Schedule 3.15 of the Disclosure Schedules (but not including any subordinate tower lease or multiple dwelling unit contracts that incorporate the terms of such master contracts by reference), other than those listed on Schedule 3.15 of the Disclosure Schedules;

(r) the assets listed in Schedule 2.2(r) of the Disclosure Schedules;

(s) all rights of the Seller and the Subsidiaries under this Agreement and the Ancillary Agreements; and

(t) all capital leases and vehicle leases, provided that at the Closing, the Seller shall cause any such vehicle or other equipment to be transferred as provided in Section 5.18.

Section 2.3 Assumed Liabilities. In connection with the purchase and sale of the Transferred Assets pursuant to this Agreement, at the Closing, the Buyer shall assume and agrees to pay, discharge, perform or otherwise satisfy the following liabilities and obligations of the Subsidiaries relating to the Business (the "**Assumed Liabilities**"):

(a) all liabilities as of the Closing Time that are reflected in the amount of Current Liabilities determined in accordance with Section 2.9;

(b) all liabilities accruing or otherwise arising out of the conduct or operation of the Business or the ownership or use of the Transferred Assets from and after the Closing Time;

(c) any Taxes to be paid by the Buyer pursuant to this Agreement;

(d) all obligations and liabilities of the Subsidiaries under the Contracts and the Business Permits in respect of periods following the Closing Time;

(e) any liability arising pursuant to Section 5.17, related to telecommunications certificates obtained by the Buyer or the failure of the Buyer to obtain the same; and

(f) all liabilities expressly assumed by the Buyer pursuant to Section 5.5.

Section 2.4 Excluded Liabilities. Notwithstanding any other provision of this Agreement to the contrary, the Buyer is not assuming, and the Seller or the Subsidiaries (other than the C-Corporations) shall pay, perform or otherwise satisfy, every liability or obligation of the Seller and its Affiliates (including the C-Corporations) other than Assumed Liabilities, including the following liabilities and obligations (the "**Excluded Liabilities**"):

(a) all Taxes (i) now or hereafter owed by the Seller or any of its Affiliates including Taxes of any C-Corporation for a Pre-Closing Tax Period (including all Taxes allocable to the Seller pursuant to this Agreement) and (ii) arising from or with respect to the Transferred Assets or the operation of the Business that are incurred in or attributable to any period, or any portion of any period, ending on or prior to the Closing Time (except as otherwise provided in this Agreement);

(b) any liability not assumed by the Buyer pursuant to Section 5.5 arising in respect of or relating to the Business Employees or any Employee Plan;

(c) any liability or obligation accruing under the Contracts or otherwise arising out of the conduct or operation of the Business or ownership or use of the Transferred Assets prior to the Closing Time (including all liabilities related to all litigation scheduled on Schedule 3.8 of the Disclosure Schedules) unless and to the extent assumed by the Buyer under Section 2.3;

(d) any indebtedness of the Seller or the Subsidiaries for borrowed money or guarantees thereof outstanding as of the Closing Time, other than Current Liabilities included in the Assumed Liabilities; and

(e) any liability or obligation relating to an Excluded Asset.

Section 2.5 Consents to Certain Assignments.

(a) The Buyer agrees that, other than with respect to the breach of any obligation hereunder, neither the Seller nor the Subsidiaries shall have any liability to the Buyer arising out of or relating to the failure to obtain any consent, including as set forth in Section 2.5(b), that may be required in connection with the transactions contemplated by this Agreement or the Ancillary Agreements or because of any circumstances resulting therefrom.

(b) If the LFA Approval with respect to any Franchise is not obtained prior to Closing, then such Franchise (each, a "**Retained Franchise**") and any assets required to be held by the franchisee pursuant to such Franchise (the "**Retained Assets**"), shall not be transferred to the Buyer at Closing, and the Seller and the Buyer shall execute a Retained Franchise Management Agreement with respect to each Retained Franchise. At the Closing, if LFA Approvals representing at least 65% of the individually-billed subscribers of the Systems owned by any C-Corporation are obtained, the Seller shall transfer the Shares related to such C-Corporation to the Buyer. If LFA Approvals representing at least 65% of the individually-billed subscribers of the Systems owned by any C-Corporation have not been obtained at the Closing, (1) the Shares relating to such C-Corporation (the "**Retained Shares**") will not be transferred at the Closing and will be retained by the Seller until the earlier of 10 days after LFA Approvals representing at least 65% of individually-billed subscribers of the Systems owned by such C-Corporation are received, six months following the Closing or the termination of the respective Retained Franchise Management Agreement and (2) the Franchises owned by such C-Corporation will be treated as "Retained Franchises". Each Retained Franchise Management Agreement shall provide that the Buyer shall manage such Retained Franchise on behalf of the appropriate Subsidiary, subject to the following: (A) the Buyer shall bear all expenses relating to the Retained Franchise and the operation thereof after the Closing and shall receive the cash flow from the Systems served under the Retained Franchise as its management fee and (B) such management shall continue with respect to such Retained Franchise until such time as such Retained Franchise is assigned and transferred (or in the case of the Retained Shares, until such time that such shares are transferred) to the Buyer in accordance with this Agreement is revoked or the Retained Franchise Management Agreement is terminated pursuant to its terms. The Seller shall cause the Subsidiaries to transfer, at no additional cost to the Buyer, each Retained Franchise and the related Retained Assets to the Buyer within 10 days after the LFA Approval for such transfer is received, or six months following the Closing or the termination of the respective Retained Franchise Management Agreement, whichever is sooner (except with respect to those Retained Franchises held by a C-Corporation which will be transferred with any Retained Shares). In the event the Retained Franchise is revoked or the Retained Franchise Management Agreement is terminated pursuant to its terms, the Seller shall cause the appropriate Subsidiary promptly thereafter to assign to the Buyer any right such Subsidiary may have with respect thereto and transfer the related Retained Assets to the Buyer. In the event that the Buyer is legally prohibited from managing any Retained Franchise, the Buyer and the Seller shall negotiate in good faith to resolve the management thereof to preserve the purpose and intent of this Section 2.5(b). Except as the parties shall agree as set forth in Section 2.5(c), the Base Purchase Price shall not be reduced in respect of any Franchise or Shares not transferred at the Closing, and any adjustments to the Base Purchase Price pursuant to this Agreement shall be made as of the Closing Time as if the Retained Franchises, Retained Assets and the Retained Shares were transferred at the Closing. In addition, the Buyer shall become liable for the Assumed Liabilities with respect to the Retained Franchises, Retained Assets and Retained Shares as of the Closing Time, and all representations and warranties (except as to those Required Consents that have not been obtained) made in connection with the Retained Franchises, Retained Assets and Retained Shares shall (I) be made as of the Closing Date rather than any subsequent transfer date and (II) survive as if such transfers occurred on the Closing Date. The Buyer and the Seller shall cooperate with respect to, and shall equally share the expenses of defending any legal challenges alleging the premature, unlawful or invalid transfer of any of the Franchises, including reasonable attorneys' fees and consultants' fees as well as the actual amount of any judgments obtained by a Governmental Authority resulting from (i) the transfer of any such Franchise without proper consent, or (ii) any action taken by the Buyer as manager and any amounts paid to reinstate any such Franchise revoked. If a Retained Franchise is revoked for any reason, there shall be no compensation or other remuneration paid by any party to another party as a result of such revocation. Solely for purposes of determining the applicable percentage of individually-billed subscribers under this Section 2.5(b), Section 6.2(c) and Section 6.3(c), the parties shall use the number of subscribers in the Systems set forth on Schedule 6.3(c) of the Disclosure Schedules.

(c) If any Governmental Authority exercises its right of first refusal under any Franchise and the applicable Subsidiary is thereby required to transfer any of the Transferred Assets to such Governmental Authority or its designee, then the parties shall negotiate in good faith to resolve the treatment of such Franchise (and corresponding subscribers) and equitably adjust the Purchase Price and other terms of the Agreement in a manner that preserves the purpose and intent of this Agreement as if such Franchise was never a part of this transaction.

Section 2.6 Consideration. In full consideration for the sale, assignment, transfer, conveyance and delivery (including pursuant to Section 2.5(b)) of the Transferred Assets to the Buyer, at the Closing, the Buyer shall (a) pay to or as directed by the Seller, by wire transfer to a bank account or accounts designated in writing by the Seller to the Buyer at least two Business Days prior to the Closing Date, an amount equal to $770,000,000 (the "**Base Purchase Price**", and as adjusted in accordance with this Agreement, the "**Purchase Price**"), less (i) the Tax Benefit Adjustment and (ii) the Escrow Fund, in immediately available funds in

United States dollars and (b) assume the Assumed Liabilities. The Purchase Price shall be subject to adjustment as provided in Section 2.9.

Section 2.7 Purchase Price Deposit. Within 5 days after the execution and delivery of this Agreement, the Buyer shall deposit a portion of the Purchase Price in the amount of $11,550,000 (together with any additional amount paid pursuant to Section 2.7(iv) below, if any, the **"Deposit"**) in immediately available funds in United States dollars in escrow with the St Louis, Missouri branch of US Bank, N.A. (the **"Escrow Agent"**), to be held by the Escrow Agent in accordance with the terms and conditions of the Escrow Agreement (the Deposit, together with any interest earned thereon, is referred to herein as the **"Escrow Fund"**). By the close of business on May 15, 2006, (i) the [ ] Assets shall have been acquired by the Buyer, (ii) the [ ] Assets shall have been acquired by an entity under common control with the Buyer (or a permitted assignee of the Buyer) and the equity financing for the acquisition of the [ ] Assets shall have been contributed by a parent company of such Person, (iii) either (A) the Seller shall have failed to furnish to the Buyer the Audited Financial Statements in the form required by Section 5.22(a) on or before April 3, 2006 (or such other date as the parties shall reasonably agree that does not impact the Buyer's financing of the acquisition of the [ ] Assets or the financing contemplated by the Financing Commitments) or (B) the Seller shall have failed to comply, in all material respects, with Section 5.24(b) or (iv) the Buyer shall have deposited an additional $11,550,000 in the Escrow Fund (each a **"Liquidity Transaction"**). At the Closing, the Escrow Agent shall disburse the amounts held in the Escrow Fund to the Seller. In the event that this Agreement is terminated prior to the Closing, the Escrow Agent shall disburse the Escrow Fund in accordance with Section 8.3.

Section 2.8 Closing.

(a) The sale and purchase of the Transferred Assets and the assumption of the Assumed Liabilities contemplated by this Agreement shall take place at a closing (the **"Closing"**) to be held at the offices of Gibson, Dunn & Crutcher LLP, 200 Park Avenue, New York, NY, at 10:00 A.M. New York City time, on the third Business Day after all conditions to the obligations of the parties set forth in Article VI (other than such conditions as may, by their terms, be satisfied only at the Closing or on the Closing Date), have been satisfied or to the extent permitted by applicable Law, waived (or at such other place, date, or time as may be agreed by the parties). The day on which the Closing takes place is referred to herein as the **"Closing Date"**.

(b) At the Closing, the Seller shall cause to be delivered to the Buyer the following documents:

(i) duly executed copies of each of the Ancillary Agreements;

(ii) a duly executed certificate of the secretary of the Seller and each of the Subsidiaries as to (x) incumbency and specimen signatures of officers of the Seller and/or such of the Subsidiaries executing this Agreement and/or the Ancillary Agreements and (y) the resolutions of the appropriate governing body of each such entity authorizing the execution, delivery and performance of this Agreement and/or the Ancillary Agreements;

(iii) a duly executed certificate of an officer of the Seller pursuant to Section 6.3(a);

(iv) the originals or, if not readily available, copies of all Required Consents received on or before the Closing;

(v) all Books and Records (which, other than the corporate records of the C-Corporations, the parties agree are deemed delivered to the extent they exist at the Systems);

(vi) duly endorsed stock certificates representing the Shares;

(vii) evidence of the release of the liens set forth on Schedule 3.4 of the Disclosure Schedules together with any other liens of record on the Closing Date (other than Permitted Encumbrances); and

(viii) the resignations of the directors and officers of the C-Corporations.

(c) At the Closing, the Buyer shall deliver or cause to be delivered to the Seller the following documents:

(i) duly executed copies of each of the Ancillary Agreements;

(ii) a duly executed certificate of the secretary of the Buyer as to (x) incumbency and specimen signatures of officers of the Buyer executing this Agreement and the Ancillary Agreements and (y) the resolutions of the appropriate governing body of the Buyer authorizing the execution, delivery and performance of this Agreement and the Ancillary Agreements; and

(iii) a duly executed certificate of an officer of the Buyer pursuant to Section 6.2(a).

Section 2.9 Adjustment of Purchase Price.

(a) Closing Date Working Capital Adjustment.

(i) Not later than 15 days prior to the Closing, the Seller shall prepare, or cause to be prepared, and deliver, together with reasonable supporting documentation, to the Buyer the Pre-Closing Working Capital Statement, which shall set forth the Seller's good-faith estimate of the Current Assets, the Current Liabilities and the Pre-Closing Net Asset Value of the Business as of the Closing Time. The Current Assets and the Current Liabilities reflected in the Pre-Closing Working Capital Statement shall be prepared in a manner consistent with the Seller's accounting methods, policies, practices and procedures used in the preparation of the Balance Sheet.

Not less than seven days prior to the Closing, the Buyer shall provide the Seller with any good-faith objections to the Pre-Closing Working Capital Statement in writing. After considering the Buyer's objections, the Seller, in good faith, shall make such revisions with which it agrees to the Pre-Closing Working Capital Statement not less than three days prior to the Closing, and the Pre-Closing Net Asset Value shall be based upon the amount set forth in the Seller's revised Pre-Closing Working Capital Statement. Any disagreements that may continue to exist with respect to the Pre-Closing Working Capital Statement shall be resolved in connection with the Final Working Capital Statement pursuant to Sections 2.9(d) and (f).

(ii) At the Closing, the Base Purchase Price shall be: (A) increased by the amount the Pre-Closing Net Asset Value (as amended pursuant to Section 2.9(c))is greater than $0.00 or (B) decreased by the amount the Pre-Closing Net Asset Value (as amended pursuant to Section 2.9(c)) is less than $0.00.

(b) Closing Date RGU Adjustment.

(i) Not later than 15 days prior to the Closing, the Seller shall in good-faith prepare, or cause to be prepared, and deliver to the Buyer the Pre-Closing RGU Statement, together with reasonable supporting documentation. The Pre-Closing RGU Statement shall be prepared in a manner consistent with the Seller's accounting methods, policies, practices and procedures used in the preparation of the System Reports (as adjusted to conform with the definition of "RGU" as set forth in this Agreement). Not less than seven days prior to the Closing, the Buyer shall provide the Seller with any good faith objections to the Pre-Closing RGU Statement in writing. After considering the Buyer's objections, the Seller, in good faith, shall make such revisions with which it agrees to the Pre-Closing RGU Statement and shall deliver a revised Pre-Closing RGU Statement not less than three days prior to the Closing. The RGU adjustment referred to in clause 2.9(b)(ii) shall be based upon the number of RGUs set forth in the revised Pre-Closing RGU Statement. Any disagreements that may continue to exist with respect to the Pre-Closing RGU Statement will be resolved in connection with the Final RGU Statement pursuant to Sections 2.9(e) and (f).

(ii) At the Closing, the Base Purchase Price shall be decreased, if the number of RGUs (as set forth in the Pre-Closing RGU Statement) is less than the Lower RGU Limit, by an amount equal to: (1) the Price Per RGU multiplied by (2) the Lower RGU Limit less the number of RGUs (as set forth in the Pre-Closing RGU Statement); provided, however, that adjustments made pursuant to this Section 2.9(b)(ii) shall not reduce the Purchase Price paid at the Closing by more than 10% of the Base Purchase Price.

(c) Closing Date Adjustment for Buyer's Objections. If, after the Seller considers the Buyer's objections with respect thereto, the aggregate amount of disagreements with respect to the Pre-Closing Working Capital Statement and Pre-Closing RGU Statement exceed $3,000,000, then at the Closing, the Pre-Closing Net Asset Value shall be decreased by the amount of such excess over $3,000,000 and the amounts in dispute will be resolved pursuant to Section 2.9(f).

(d) Final Working Capital Adjustment.

(i) Not more than 120 days following the Closing, the Buyer shall prepare, or cause to be prepared, and deliver to the Seller the Final Working Capital Statement, which shall set forth the Current Assets and the Current Liabilities of the Business as of the Closing Time. The Current Assets and the Current Liabilities reflected in the Final Working Capital Statement shall be prepared in a manner consistent with the Seller's accounting methods, policies, practices and procedures used in the preparation of the Balance Sheet. The Buyer shall derive the Final Net Asset Value from the Final Working Capital Statement, and shall deliver such calculation and the Final Working Capital Statement to the Seller.

(ii) The Seller shall complete its review of the Final Working Capital Statement and the Buyer's calculation of the Final Net Asset Value within 30 days after delivery thereof. In the event that the Seller determines that the Final Working Capital Statement has not been prepared on the basis set forth in Section 2.9(d)(i), the Seller may, on or before the last day of such 30-day period, so inform the Buyer in writing (the **"Seller Working Capital Objection"**), setting forth a specific description of the basis for the Seller's determination and the adjustments to the Final Working Capital Statement and the corresponding adjustments to the Final Net Asset Value that the Seller believes should be made. If no Seller Working Capital Objection is received by the Buyer on or before the last day of such 30-day period, then the Final Net Asset Value, as set forth on the Final Working Capital Statement delivered by the Buyer, shall be final. The Buyer shall have 30 days from its receipt of the Seller Working Capital Objection to review and respond to the Seller Working Capital Objection.

(e) Final RGU Adjustment.

(i) Not more than 120 days following the Closing, the Buyer shall prepare, or cause to be prepared, and deliver to the Seller the Final RGU Statement. The Final RGU Statement shall be prepared in a manner consistent with the Seller's accounting methods, policies, practices and procedures used in the preparation of the System Reports (as adjusted to conform with the definition of "RGU" as set forth in this Agreement).

(ii) The Seller shall complete its review of the Final RGU Statement within 30 days after delivery thereof. In the event that the Seller determines that the Final RGU Statement has not been prepared on the basis set forth in Section 2.9(e)(i), the Seller may, on or before the last day of such 30-day period, so inform the Buyer in writing (the "**Seller RGU Objection**") setting forth a specific description of the basis for the Seller's determination and the adjustments to the Final RGU Statement and the corresponding adjustments to the Final RGU Purchase Price Adjustment that the Seller believes should be made. If no Seller RGU Objection is received by the Buyer on or before the last day of such 30-day period, then the Final RGU Purchase Price Adjustment, as set forth on the Final RGU Statement delivered by the Buyer, shall be final. The Buyer shall have 30 days from the receipt of the Seller RGU Objection to review and respond to the Seller RGU Objection.

(f) Resolution of the Seller Objections. If the Seller and the Buyer are unable to resolve all of their disagreements with respect to the proposed adjustments set forth in the Seller Objections within 15 days following the completion of the Buyer's review of the Seller Objections, they shall refer any remaining disagreements with respect to the Seller Objections to the CPA Firm that, acting as experts and not as arbitrators, shall determine, on the basis set forth in and in accordance with Sections 2.9(d) and 2.9(e), and only with respect to the remaining differences so submitted, whether and to what extent, if any, the (i) Final Working Capital Statement or (ii) Final RGU Statement, as the case may be, require adjustment. The Buyer and the Seller shall instruct the CPA Firm to deliver its written determination to the Seller and the Buyer no later than 90 days after the remaining differences underlying the Seller Objections are referred to the CPA Firm. The CPA Firm's determination shall be conclusive and binding upon the Seller, the Buyer and their respective Affiliates and may not be challenged or appealed in any tribunal by any party. The Buyer and the Seller shall make readily available to the CPA Firm all relevant books and records and any work papers (including those of the parties' respective accountants, to the extent permitted by such accountants) relating to the Final Working Capital Statement, the Final RGU Statement and the Seller Objections and all other items reasonably requested by the CPA Firm in connection therewith. If either party fails to reasonably cooperate with the CPA Firm or provide supporting information requested by the CPA Firm within 30 days after such request, then such party shall be in breach of this Agreement, which may be remedied in accordance with Section 9.13(b) relating to enforcement. The fees and disbursements of the CPA Firm shall be borne by the Seller and the Buyer in proportion to the CPA Firm's determination, as determined by the CPA Firm in accordance with this Section 2.9(f), provided, however, that if either party seeks to enforce this provision in accordance with Section 9.13, and such relief is granted, then the other party will bear all additional fees and costs in connection with such enforcement, including all court costs and attorney's fees.

(g) Access to Information. Each party shall provide to the other full access to the books and records of the Business and to any other information, including work papers of its accountants (to the extent permitted by such accountants), and to any employees during regular business hours and on reasonable advance notice, to the extent necessary for the preparation of or response to the Final Working Capital Statement and the Final RGU Statement or any objections thereto, and to prepare materials for presentation to the CPA Firm in connection with Section 2.9(f).

(h) Final Purchase Price Adjustment.

(i) Following the Closing, the Purchase Price shall be adjusted by the Final Purchase Price Adjustment Amount. The **"Final Purchase Price Adjustment Amount"** shall be equal to the amount determined by netting the Final Working Capital Adjustment Amount and the Final RGU Purchase Price Adjustment, if any, as payable to the Seller or the Buyer, as the case may be.

(ii) If the Final Purchase Price Adjustment Amount is positive, the Buyer shall promptly (and in any event within five Business Days) after the final determination thereof pay to the Seller the Final Purchase Price Adjustment Amount, plus interest from the Closing Date to, but not including, the date of payment at LIBOR calculated on a 365-day basis, in U.S. Dollars by wire transfer of immediately available funds to an account or accounts designated by the Seller.

(iii) If the Final Purchase Price Adjustment Amount is negative, the Seller shall promptly (and in any event within five Business Days) after the final determination thereof pay to the Buyer the Final Purchase Price Adjustment Amount, plus interest from the Closing Date to, but not including, the date of payment at LIBOR calculated on a 365-day basis, in U.S. Dollars by wire transfer of immediately available funds to an account or accounts designated by the Buyer.

Section 2.10 Allocation of Purchase Price. The Buyer and the Seller agree that the Purchase Price and the amount of Assumed Liabilities that are liabilities for income tax purposes shall be allocated for federal income tax purposes among the Transferred Assets as shall be determined by the parties in accordance with this Agreement (the **"Allocation Schedule"**). The Allocation Schedule shall be prepared in accordance with Section 1060 of the Code. The Buyer shall deliver a draft of the Allocation Schedule at least 30 days prior to the Closing Date for approval and consent, and the Buyer and the Seller shall use their commercially reasonable efforts to agree upon the Allocation Schedule prior to the Closing Date. Neither the Buyer nor the Seller shall unreasonably withhold its approval and consent with respect to the Allocation Schedule. The Buyer and the Seller agree that the Allocation Schedule shall be amended to reflect adjustments to the Base Purchase Price made pursuant to this Agreement. If the parties are unable to agree on the final Allocation Schedule within 90 days after the Closing Date, a third-party appraiser selected by the Buyer, and reasonably acceptable to the Seller, the fees of which shall be borne equally by the Buyer and the Seller, shall resolve the allocation of the consideration to any items with respect to which there is a dispute between the parties. Unless otherwise required by applicable Law, the Buyer and the Seller agree to act, and cause their respective Affiliates to act, in accordance with the computations and allocations contained in the Allocation Schedule in any relevant Tax Returns or similar filings (including any forms or reports required to be filed pursuant to Section 1060 of the Code (the **"1060 Forms"**)), to cooperate in the preparation of any 1060 Forms, to file such 1060 Forms in the manner required by applicable Law, to update such 1060 Forms in accordance with the method used in making the allocation to the extent necessary to reflect purchase price adjustments and to not take any position inconsistent with such Allocation Schedule upon examination of any Tax Returns, in any litigation or otherwise. For the purposes of this Section 2.10, the covenant contained in Section 5.21 shall be included in the Transferred Assets.

ARTICLE III

REPRESENTATIONS AND WARRANTIES OF THE SELLER

Except as set forth in the Disclosure Schedules attached hereto (collectively, the **"Disclosure Schedules"**), the Seller hereby represents and warrants to the Buyer that the statements contained in this Article III are true, correct and complete as of the date of this Agreement and will be true, correct and complete as of the Closing Date, except in each case to the extent that such statements are expressly made only as of a specified date, in which case the Seller represents and warrants that such statements are true, correct and complete as of such specified date.

Section 3.1 Organization and Qualification. The Seller and each Subsidiary is an entity validly existing and in good standing in the state set forth opposite its name on Schedule 3.1 of the Disclosure Schedules and has all necessary corporate, limited liability company or partnership power and authority, as the case may be, to own, lease and operate the Transferred Assets and to carry on the Business as it is now being conducted. Each Subsidiary is a direct or indirect wholly-owned subsidiary of the Seller. Each Subsidiary is duly qualified or licensed as a foreign corporation to do business, and in good standing, in each jurisdiction set forth opposite its name on Schedule 3.1 of the Disclosure Schedules.

Section 3.2 Authority. The Seller and each Subsidiary has full corporate, limited liability company or partnership power and authority, as the case may be, to execute and deliver this Agreement and each of the Ancillary Agreements to which they will be a party, to perform their obligations hereunder and thereunder and to consummate the transactions contemplated hereby and thereby. The execution and delivery by the Seller of this Agreement and by the Seller and each Subsidiary of each of the Ancillary Agreements to which they will be a party and the consummation by the Seller and the Subsidiaries of the transactions contemplated hereby and thereby have been duly and validly authorized by all necessary corporate, limited liability company or partnership action, as the case may be. This Agreement has been, and upon their execution each of the Ancillary Agreements to which the Seller and the Subsidiaries will be a party will have been, duly executed and delivered by the Seller and the Subsidiaries, as the case may be. This Agreement constitutes, and upon their execution each of the Ancillary Agreements to which the Seller and the Subsidiaries will be a party will constitute, the legal, valid and binding obligations of the Seller and the Subsidiaries, as the case may be, enforceable against the Seller and the Subsidiaries in accordance with their respective terms, except as enforcement may be limited by applicable bankruptcy, insolvency, reorganization, moratorium or similar laws affecting creditors' rights generally and by general principles of equity (regardless of whether considered in a proceeding in equity or at law).

Section 3.3 No Conflict; Required Filings and Consents.

(a) Except for the Required Consents set forth on Schedule 3.3 of the Disclosure Schedules, and all consents required for the transfer of agreements related to multiple dwelling units which serve 200 or less units or commercial establishments, the execution, delivery and performance by the Seller of this Agreement, and by the Seller and the Subsidiaries of each of the Ancillary Agreements to which the Seller and the Subsidiaries will be a party, and the consummation of the transactions contemplated hereby and thereby, do not and will not:

(i) conflict with or violate the organizational documents (such as the certificates of formation or limited liability company agreements) of the Seller or any Subsidiary;

(ii) conflict with or violate any Law applicable to the Seller or the Subsidiaries, the Business or any of the Transferred Assets or by which the Seller or the Subsidiaries, the Business or any of the Transferred Assets may be bound or affected;

(iii) conflict with, result in any breach of, constitute a default (or an event that, with notice or lapse of time or both, would become a default) under, require any consent of or notice to or any filing with, any Person pursuant to, or give to others any rights to modify, amend, terminate, accelerate or cancel, any (A) Material Contract or Permit, (B) leases for Material Real Property or (C) retransmission consent, or otherwise to materially impair the ability of the Buyer to own and operate the Systems after the Closing in the manner operated by the Subsidiaries prior to the Closing;

(iv) give rise to any right to acquire any of the Systems or Transferred Assets pursuant to any right of first refusal or similar right; or

(v) result in the creation upon any of the Transferred Assets of any Encumbrance (other than a Permitted Encumbrance);

except, in the case of clause (ii), for any such conflicts or violations that would not, individually or in the aggregate, reasonably be expected to have a Material Adverse Effect or that arise as a result of any facts or circumstances relating to the Buyer or any of its Affiliates.

(b) Neither the Seller nor the Subsidiaries are required to file, seek or obtain any notice, authorization, approval, order, permit or consent of or with any Governmental Authority in connection with the execution, delivery and performance by the Seller of this Agreement and by the Seller and the Subsidiaries of each of the Ancillary Agreements to which the Seller and the Subsidiaries will be a party or the consummation of the transactions contemplated hereby or thereby or in order to prevent the termination of any right, privilege, license or qualification of the Business, except (i) for any filings required to be made under the HSR Act, or (ii) for any Required Consents set forth on Schedule 3.3 of the Disclosure Schedules.

Section 3.4 Transferred Assets. Upon consummation of the transactions contemplated by this Agreement and receipt of all necessary consents, the Subsidiaries will have, directly or indirectly, assigned, transferred and conveyed to the Buyer, title to all of the Transferred Assets, free and clear of all Encumbrances except Permitted Encumbrances. Schedule 3.4 of the Disclosure Schedules sets forth those Encumbrances, other than the Permitted Encumbrances, that exist as of the date hereof, which Encumbrances will be terminated, released or waived, as appropriate, at or prior to the Closing Date. Except as described on Schedule 3.4 of the Disclosure Schedules, the Transferred Assets and the Excluded Assets comprise all the assets, properties or rights used or held for use by the Seller or the Subsidiaries or any Affiliate thereof in the operation of the Business or the Systems.

Section 3.5 Financial Statements. True and complete copies of the unaudited consolidated balance sheet of the Business as of December 31, 2004 and 2005, (the balance sheet as of December 31, 2005 is referred to herein as the **"Balance Sheet"**) and the related unaudited consolidated statements of results of operations and cash flows of the Business for the three years ended December 31, 2005, (collectively referred to as the **"Financial Statements"**) and the System Reports as of the end of each month from January 1, 2004, through December 31, 2005, are attached hereto as Schedule 3.5 of the Disclosure Schedules. The Financial Statements (i) have been prepared based on the books and records of the Seller and the Subsidiaries pertaining to the Business (except as may be indicated in any notes thereto); (ii) have been prepared in accordance with GAAP applied on a consistent basis throughout the periods indicated (except as may be indicated in any notes thereto) and (iii) fairly present, in all material respects, the consolidated financial position, results of operations and cash flows of the Business as at the date thereof and for the respective periods indicated therein, except as otherwise noted therein. The

System Reports have been and will be prepared in a manner consistent with the Seller's accounting methods, policies, practices and procedures used in the preparation of the Financial Statements. Since December 31, 2005, the Seller and the Subsidiaries have not changed, in any material manner, any accounting methods, policies, practices or procedures, unless required by GAAP, and no change has materially impacted the calculation of Operating Cash Flow.

Section 3.6 Absence of Certain Changes or Events. Except as disclosed in Schedule 3.6 of the Disclosure Schedules, as of the date of this Agreement and since the date of the Balance Sheet, the Seller and the Subsidiaries have conducted the Business, in all material respects, in the ordinary course of business consistent with past practice and there has not occurred any Material Adverse Effect.

Section 3.7 Compliance with Law.

(a) The Seller and the Subsidiaries have complied in all material respects with all Laws applicable to them in connection with the conduct or operation of the Business and the ownership or use of the Transferred Assets. Except as disclosed in Schedule 3.7(a) of the Disclosure Schedules, neither the Seller nor any Subsidiary has, since January 1, 2004, received any notice of any claims of any Governmental Authority with respect to the failure to comply in any material respect with any such Laws.

(b) Schedule 3.7(b) of the Disclosure Schedules sets forth a list of all Franchises and Licenses related to the Business, all of which are held by the Subsidiaries. Except as set forth in Schedule 3.7(b) of the Disclosure Schedules, all permits, Licenses, Franchises, approvals, certificates, consents, waivers, concessions, exemptions, orders, registrations, notices or other authorizations of any Governmental Authority necessary for the Subsidiaries to operate the Business (the "**Permits**") are held by the Seller and the Subsidiaries and are in full force and effect and constitute the valid, legal, binding and enforceable obligation of each Subsidiary that is a party thereto, except where the failure to have, or the suspension or cancellation of, any of the Permits would not, individually or in the aggregate, reasonably be expected to have a Material

Adverse Effect. The Subsidiaries are in compliance in all material respects with the Permits and no suspension or cancellation of any of the Permits is pending or, to the Knowledge of the Seller, threatened. True and correct copies of each Permit listed on Schedule 3.7(b) of the Disclosure Schedules have been delivered to or made available to the Buyer.

(c) Except as set forth in Schedule 3.7(c) of the Disclosure Schedules, a written request for renewal has been timely filed pursuant to Section 626(a) of the Cable Act with the proper Governmental Authority with respect to any Franchise expiring within 30 months after the date of this Agreement. Schedule 3.7(c) also lists (i) any Franchise Areas in which the Subsidiaries maintain material operations within the public right-of-way without a written Franchise and (ii) any areas in which the Subsidiaries maintain material operations within the public right-of-way without a Franchise.

Section 3.8 Litigation. Except as set forth on Schedule 3.8 of the Disclosure Schedules and except for routine claims in the ordinary course of business which are not individually or in the aggregate material (and which do not relate to the C-Corporations), as of the date hereof, (a) there is no Action by or against the Seller or any Subsidiary in connection with the Business pending, or to the Knowledge of the Seller, threatened in writing; and (b) there is not in existence any final judgment requiring the Seller or any Subsidiary to take any action of any kind with respect to the Transferred Assets or the operation of the Business, or to which the Seller or any Subsidiary, the Business, the Systems or the Transferred Assets are subject or by which they are bound or affected.

Section 3.9 Employee Plans.

(a) Schedule 3.9 of the Disclosure Schedules sets forth all material Employee Plans.

(b) Except as disclosed on Schedule 3.9 of the Disclosure Schedules, with respect to the Employee Plans: (i) each of the Employee Plans has been operated and administered in all material respects in accordance with applicable Law and administrative or governmental rules and regulations, including ERISA and the Code, except to the extent any noncompliance would not reasonably be expected to result in any liability imposed upon the Buyer, and (ii) neither the Seller nor any ERISA Affiliate has any outstanding liability or could reasonably be expected to incur liability under Section 412(f) or (n) of the Code and/or Title IV of ERISA (other than for the payment of Pension Benefit Guaranty Corporation premiums in the ordinary course).

(c) Each Employee Plan which is intended to be "qualified" within the meaning of Section 401(a) of the Code has received a favorable determination letter from the Internal Revenue Service and, to the Seller's Knowledge, no event has occurred and no condition exists which would reasonably be expected to result in the revocation of any such determination.

(d) Neither the Seller nor any ERISA Affiliate contributes to or is required to contribute to any multiemployer plan.

Section 3.10 Labor and Employment Matters. Except as set forth on Schedule 3.10 of the Disclosure Schedules, as of the date of this Agreement:

(a) no Business Employees are represented by a labor organization or group that was either certified by any labor relations board, including the National Labor Relations Board, or any other Governmental Authority or voluntarily recognized by the Seller or any Subsidiary as the exclusive bargaining representative of a unit of employees and, to the Knowledge of the Seller, no Business Employee is represented by any other labor union or organization. Neither the Seller nor any Subsidiary is a party to or has any obligation under any union contract, or an obligation (other than under any applicable Law) to recognize or deal with any labor union or organization, and there are no such contracts pertaining to or that determine the terms or conditions of employment of any Business Employee;

(b) to the Knowledge of the Seller (i) no representation, election, petition or application for certification has been filed by any Business Employee within the preceding two years or is pending with the National Labor Relations Board or any other Governmental Authority, and (ii) no overt union organization campaign or other overt attempt to organize or establish a labor union, employee organization or labor organization or group involving any Business Employee is in progress, has occurred within the preceding two years or has been threatened; and

(c) no labor dispute, walk out, strike, slowdown, hand billing, picketing, work stoppage (sympathetic or otherwise), or other "concerted action" organized by any Business Employee is in progress, has occurred within the preceding two years or, to the Knowledge of the Seller, has been threatened.

Section 3.11 Real Property.

(a) Schedule 3.11(a) of the Disclosure Schedules lists each parcel of Real Property owned by the Subsidiaries that constitutes a Transferred Asset (the **"Owned Real Property"**) and identifies those parcels that constitute Material Real Property. The Seller has delivered or made available to the Buyer, to the extent it possesses the same, title reports for each parcel of Owned Real Property.

(b) Except as disclosed on Schedule 3.11(b) of the Disclosure Schedules, (i) the Subsidiaries have or as of the Closing Time will have fee simple title to all Owned Real Property, free and clear of all Encumbrances other than Permitted Encumbrances, (ii) neither the Seller nor the Subsidiaries have received written notice from any Governmental Authority that any of the Owned Real Property is not in material compliance with all applicable Laws, except for such failures to comply, if any, which have been remedied, (iii) to the Knowledge of the Seller, there is no pending or written threat of condemnation or similar proceeding affecting the Owned Real Property or any portion thereof, and (iv) there is access to all Owned Real Property either by public roads or by the Easements.

(c) Schedule 3.11(c) of the Disclosure Schedules lists the parcels of Real Property leased by the Subsidiaries that constitute Transferred Assets (the **"Leased Real Property"**) and identifies those parcels that constitute Material Real Property.

(d) Except as disclosed on Schedule 3.11(d) of the Disclosure Schedules (i) the Seller and the Subsidiaries have, or as of the

Closing Time will have, a valid leasehold estate in all Leased Real Property, free and clear of all Encumbrances other than Permitted Encumbrances, (ii) neither the Seller nor the Subsidiaries have received written notice from any Governmental Authority that any of the Leased Real Property is not in material compliance with all applicable Laws, except for such failures to comply, if any, which have been remedied, (iii) all leases in respect of the Leased Real Property are in full force and effect, neither the Seller nor the Subsidiaries have received any written notice of a material breach or default thereunder, and to the Knowledge of the Seller, no event has occurred that, with notice or lapse of time or both, would constitute a breach or default thereunder, (iv) to the Knowledge of the Seller, there is no pending or written threat of condemnation or similar proceeding affecting the Leased Real Property or any portion thereof, (v) the Seller has delivered or made available to the Buyer true and complete copies of the written leases in effect at the date hereof relating to the Leased Real Property; provided, however, that the leases with respect to which copies have not been delivered or made available do not contain obligations material to the Buyer that will be applicable to the Buyer after the Closing and (vi) there has not been any sublease or assignment entered into by the Seller or the Subsidiaries in respect of the leases relating to the Leased Real Property except for those disclosed on Schedule 3.11(d) of the Disclosure Schedules.

(e) Schedule 3.11(e) of the Disclosure Schedules sets forth the material rights to use all other Real Property pursuant to the easements, rights-of-way or other rights necessary to conduct the Business, except for easements or rights-of-way granted pursuant to Permits (collectively, the **"Easements"**). Except as set forth on Schedule 3.11(e) of the Disclosure Schedules and except for easements or rights-of-way granted pursuant to Permits, the Subsidiaries have, or as of the Closing Time will have, the valid and enforceable right to use the Easements, in each case subject only to Permitted Encumbrances.

Section 3.12 Retransmission Consent and Must-Carry; Rate Regulation; Copyright Compliance.

(a) Schedule 3.12(a) of the Disclosure Schedules lists the broadcast stations carried by the Systems and designates whether they are carried pursuant to "must-carry" election or retransmission consent status pursuant to the Cable Act. Except as described on Schedule 3.12(a) of the Disclosure Schedules, each station carried by the Systems is carried pursuant to a retransmission consent agreement, "must-carry" election or other programming agreement.

(b) Neither the Seller nor the Subsidiaries have, since July 1, 2002, received any written notice, and the Seller has no Knowledge that, since July 1, 2002, the Seller, the Subsidiaries or the Business: (i) are not or have not been in compliance in all material respects with the Communications Act and the Cable Act; or (ii) have not made all material filings required to be made by them with the FCC in connection with the Business or provided all notices to customers of the Business required under the Communications Act, other than such filings and notices, the failure of which to be made or provided would not reasonably be expected to have a Material Adverse Effect. To the Knowledge of the Seller, neither the Seller nor the Subsidiaries have, since July 1, 2002, received any notice that any rates are not permitted rates under the rules and regulations of the FCC. Schedule 3.12(b) of the Disclosure Schedules lists, as of the date hereof, all pending rate complaints, to the Knowledge of the Seller, on file at the FCC with respect to the Business.

(c) The Seller and the Subsidiaries have filed with the Copyright Office all required statements of account with respect to the Business that were required to have been filed since July 1, 2002 in accordance with the Copyright Act of 1976 and regulations promulgated pursuant thereto, and the Seller and the Subsidiaries have paid all royalty fees payable with respect to the Business since July 1, 2002. The Seller and the Subsidiaries have made available to the Buyer copies of all statements of account referred to in this Section 3.12(c).

Section 3.13 Taxes. Except as set forth on Schedule 3.13 of the Disclosure Schedules, the Seller and the Subsidiaries have, in a timely manner, filed all material Tax Returns and other reports required of them under all federal, state, local and foreign tax laws. All such Tax Returns and reports are correct and complete in all material respects. The Seller and the Subsidiaries have paid in full all Taxes or other amounts required to be paid by them whether or not such amounts were shown as due on any Tax Returns, including all Taxes that the Seller and the Subsidiaries are obligated to withhold from amounts paid or payable to or benefits conferred upon employees, creditors and third parties. To the Knowledge of the Seller, there are no proposed reassessments of any property owned by any of the Subsidiaries that could reasonably be expected to materially affect the Taxes. Except for Permitted Encumbrances, there are no liens for Taxes on any of the Transferred Assets. Except as set forth on Schedule 3.13 of the Disclosure Schedules, there is no deficiency, assessment or audit from any taxing authority that could materially affect the Seller and the Subsidiaries or that could result in any liability of the Buyer or the imposition of any liens upon the Transferred Assets. No Tax authority in a jurisdiction in which the Seller or any of its Subsidiaries does not file Tax Returns has made a claim, assertion or threat relating to the Business that the Seller or any of the Subsidiaries is or may be subject to Tax in such jurisdictions.

Section 3.14 Environmental Matters.

(a) The Seller and the Subsidiaries are in compliance in all material respects with all applicable Environmental Laws and there are no written claims pursuant to any Environmental Law pending or, to the Knowledge of the Seller, threatened, against the Seller or the Subsidiaries in connection with the conduct or operation of the Business or the ownership or use of the Transferred Assets.

(b) To the Knowledge of the Seller, there are no liabilities under any Environmental Law with respect to the Real Property. To the Knowledge of the Seller, neither the Seller, any Subsidiary nor any other Person has used the Real Property for the manufacture, transportation, treatment, storage or disposal of Hazardous Substances, except for gasoline and diesel fuel, and such use of Hazardous Substances customary in the construction, maintenance and operation of a cable communications system and in amounts or under circumstances that would not reasonably be expected to give rise to material liability for remediation required pursuant to any Environmental Law. Except as set forth on Schedule 3.14(b) of the Disclosure Schedules, to the Knowledge of the Seller, there are no underground or aboveground storage tanks that store or have stored any Hazardous Substance on any of the Real Property. To the Knowledge of the Seller, there have been no releases of any Hazardous

Substances on or from, nor are there any Hazardous Substances on, at, or under any Owned Real Property or, to the Seller's Knowledge, any Leased Real Property that violate any Environmental Law, require notification to any Governmental Authority or require any response action pursuant to any Environmental Law.

(c) The Seller has delivered or made available to the Buyer copies and results of any reports, studies, analyses, tests, or monitoring of which the Seller has Knowledge and which is possessed or initiated by the Seller or any Subsidiary pertaining to Hazardous Substances at, on, about, under or within any Systems, or any Real Property or concerning compliance by the Seller or any Subsidiary or any other Person for whose conduct the Seller and its Affiliates are responsible, with Environmental Laws.

(d) The representations and warranties contained in this Section 3.14 are the only representations and warranties being made with respect to compliance with or liability under Environmental Laws or with respect to any environmental, health or safety matter, including natural resources, related to the Business, the Transferred Assets or the Seller's or the Subsidiaries' ownership or operation thereof.

Section 3.15 Contracts.

(a) Schedule 3.15 of the Disclosure Schedules lists each of the following Contracts (it being understood that Schedule 3.15 of the Disclosure Schedules does not list any agreements with subscribers, including any individually-billed subscribers, multiple dwelling units which serve 200 or less units or commercial establishments for the services provided by the Systems in the ordinary course of business):

(i) any Contract relating to the use of any public utility facilities, including all pole line, joint pole or master contracts for pole attachment rights and the use of conduits (each, a **"Pole Attachment Agreement"**);

(ii) any Contract relating to the use of any microwave or satellite transmission facilities;

(iii) any Contract relating to the sale of cablecast time to third parties for advertising or other purposes;

(iv) any Contract for the purchase, sale or lease of Real Property or any other property or any option to purchase or sell Real Property or any other property, providing for aggregate payments by or to the Seller or the Subsidiaries in an amount in excess of $150,000 or which relate to any Real Property or other property material to the operation of the Business;

(v) any installment sale Contract or liability for the deferred purchase price of property with respect to any of the Transferred Assets involving payments exceeding, an aggregate for any individual Contract of $150,000;

(vi) any other Contract involving aggregate payments under any such Contract, to be made by or to the Seller or any Subsidiary, in excess of $150,000 that are not terminable on 90 days notice or less;

(vii) any agreements with multiple dwelling units which serve more than 200 units; or

(viii) any other contract that is material to the Business, taken as a whole, or that contains any material non-monetary obligation.

The Contracts set forth in clauses (i), (ii), (iv), (v), (vi) and (viii) above and any other agreements designated as "Material Contracts" on Schedule 3.15 of the Disclosure Schedules being **"Material Contracts"**.

(b) Except as set forth on Schedule 3.15 of the Disclosure Schedules, each Material Contract is valid and binding on the Seller or the Subsidiaries, as the case may be, is in full force and effect, and legally enforceable in accordance with its terms upon the Seller or any Subsidiary which is a party thereto and, to the Seller's Knowledge, upon the other parties thereto except as enforcement may be limited by applicable bankruptcy, insolvency, reorganization, moratorium or similar laws affecting creditors' rights generally and by general principles of equity (regardless of whether considered in a proceeding in equity or at law), and to the Seller's Knowledge, upon the other parties thereto. Except as set forth on Schedule 3.15 of the Disclosure Schedules, neither the Seller nor the Subsidiaries, nor, to the Seller's Knowledge, any other Person, are in material breach of, or default under, any Material Contract to which they, or such other Person, are a party.

(c) The Pole Attachment Agreements represent all contracts, permits, privileges and other authorizations necessary to permit the Subsidiaries to install, maintain, operate and use utility poles and conduits and such other facilities as are currently used in the Systems or are necessary for the operation of the Systems and the Transferred Assets as currently operated, other than any such contracts, permits, privileges or other authorizations, the failure of which to be held or of the Seller or a Subsidiary to be a party to that would not, individually or in the aggregate, reasonably be expected to have a Material Adverse Effect. Except as set forth on Schedule 3.15 of the Disclosure Schedules, there are no pending or unresolved or, to the Knowledge of the Seller, threatened audits with respect to any utility attachment or conduit usage relating to the Systems.

(d) Schedule 3.15 of the Disclosure Schedules sets forth a true and complete list of all capital leases related to any of the Transferred Assets.

(e) Schedule 2.2(r) of the Disclosure Schedules lists all contracts, except for those contracts that constitute Excluded Assets pursuant to Sections 2.2(b), 2.2(c), 2.2(d), 2.2(e), 2.2(f), 2.2(g), 2.2(n), 2.2(o), 2.2(p), 2.2(s) and 2.2(t) to which any Subsidiary and/or one or more Affiliates of the Seller are parties that relate to any System as well as one or more cable systems of [ ] and its subsidiaries that are not included in the Systems, including all master contracts for retransmission consent, advertising sales, tower leases, and master multiple dwelling units (other than any subordinate tower lease or multiple dwelling unit contracts that incorporate the terms of such master contracts by reference); in each case, that would, but for the fact that they relate to one or more cable systems of

[ ] and its subsidiaries that are not included in the Systems, be required to be disclosed on Schedule 3.15 of the Disclosure Schedules.

Section 3.16 System Information. Schedule 3.16 of the Disclosure Schedules sets forth, as of the dates set forth in such Schedule, a true and complete statement of the following information with respect to each System: (i) the total number of individual basic subscribers, digital subscribers, equivalent basic units for bulk and commercial subscribers and high speed Internet subscribers served (determined in the same manner as the System Reports); (ii) the bandwidth capacity specified in MHz which each System is capable of passing in accordance with the performance standards set forth in 47 CFR Part 76; (iii) the channel line-up and rate card, (iv) the aerial and underground plant miles, and (v) the approximate number of homes passed (as determined by the Seller in a manner consistent with past practice).

Section 3.17 Brokers. Except for Daniels & Associates and JPMorgan Securities, Inc., the fees of which shall be paid by the Seller, no broker, finder or investment banker is entitled to any brokerage, finder's or other fee or commission in connection with the transactions contemplated hereby based upon arrangements made by or on behalf of the Seller or the Subsidiaries.

Section 3.18 Intellectual Property. To the Seller's Knowledge, except as disclosed on Schedule 3.18 of the Disclosure Schedules, and except with respect to music licensing for which the Seller makes no representation or warranty, the Business has been operated in such a manner so as not to violate or infringe upon the rights of any Person in any copyright, trademark, service mark, patent, license, trade secret or other intellectual property. There are no judgments, proceedings, writs, orders, injunctions, awards or decrees of any court, judge, justice, magistrate or Governmental Authority against the Seller or any Subsidiary that restrict, in any respect, the rights of the Seller or any Subsidiary to use any Intellectual Property. Schedule 3.18 of the Disclosure Schedules lists the software that is physically located at the business offices located within the Systems and material to the operation of the Business.

Section 3.19 Transactions with Affiliates. Except as disclosed on Schedule 3.19 of the Disclosure Schedules and except with respect to customary corporate overhead services provided by the corporate, divisional or regional offices of [ ], neither the Seller nor any Subsidiary is a party to any business arrangement or business relationship with any of its Affiliates with respect to the Transferred Assets or operation of the Systems, and none of their Affiliates owns any property or right, tangible or intangible, that is material to the Seller's or any Subsidiary's operation of the Systems or used primarily in the Seller's or Subsidiary's operation of the Systems.

Section 3.20 Bonds; Letters of Credit. Each franchise, construction, fidelity, performance, or other bond, guaranty in lieu of a bond, letter of credit, indemnity agreement or similar instrument posted by or on behalf of the Seller or any Subsidiary or required to be posted by the Seller or any Subsidiary in connection with its operation or ownership of any of the Systems is set forth on Schedule 3.20 of the Disclosure Schedules, together with the amount thereof.

Section 3.21 Overbuilds. Except as set forth on Schedule 3.21 of the Disclosure Schedules, to the Seller's Knowledge, as of the date of this Agreement, (i) no Person, other than the Seller, the Buyer, or their respective Affiliates, is providing cable television service within the regions in which the Systems operate, (ii) since December 31, 2003, no Person, other than the Seller, the Buyer, or their respective Affiliates, has applied for a franchise to provide cable television service within the regions in which the Systems operate and (iii) since December 31, 2003, no Person, other than the Seller, the Buyer, or their respective Affiliates, has publicly announced an intention to provide cable television service within the regions in which the Systems operate.

Section 3.22 Representations and Warranties Related to the C-Corporations.

(a) Organization and Qualification. The C-Corporation Parent Company and each of the C-Corporations is duly organized, validly existing and in good standing in the state set forth opposite its name on Schedule 3.22(a) of the Disclosure Schedules and has all necessary corporate power and authority to own, lease and operate the Transferred Assets and to carry on the Business as is now being conducted by the C-Corporations. The C-Corporation Parent Company and each C-Corporation is duly qualified or licensed as a foreign corporation to do business, and is in good standing, in each jurisdiction where such qualification or license is necessary or appropriate as set forth opposite its name on Schedule 3.22(a) of the Disclosure Schedules.

(b) Shares. The C-Corporation Parent Company is the record and beneficial owner of the Shares, free and clear of any Encumbrances other than the Encumbrances set forth on Schedule 3.4 of the Disclosure Schedules. The Seller has the right, authority and power to cause the C-Corporation Parent Company to, and the C-Corporation Parent Company has the right, authority and power to, sell, assign and transfer the Shares to the Buyer. Upon delivery to the Buyer of certificates for the Shares at the Closing and the Buyer's payment of the Purchase Price, the Buyer shall acquire good, valid and marketable title to the Shares, free and clear of any Encumbrances, other than Encumbrances created by the Buyer.

(c) Capitalization. Schedule 3.22(c) of the Disclosure Schedules sets forth, for each C-Corporation, the amount of its authorized capital stock, the amount of its outstanding capital stock and the record and beneficial owners of its outstanding capital stock. Except for the Shares and except as set forth in Schedule 3.22(c) of the Disclosure Schedules, the C-Corporations have not issued or agreed to issue any (i) share of capital stock or other equity or ownership interest, (ii) option, warrant or interest convertible into or exchangeable or exercisable for the purchase of shares of capital stock or other equity or ownership interests, (iii) stock appreciation right, phantom stock, interest in the ownership or earnings of any C-Corporation or other equity equivalent or equity-based award or right or (iv) bond, debenture or other indebtedness having the right to vote or convertible or exchangeable for securities having the right to vote. Each Share of each of the C-Corporations is duly authorized, validly issued, fully paid and nonassessable, and each Share is owned by the C-Corporation Parent Company, free and clear of any Encumbrances. All of the Shares have been offered, sold and delivered in compliance with all applicable federal and state securities laws. Except as set forth in Schedule 3.22(c) of the Disclosure Schedules and except for rights granted to the Buyer under this Agreement, there are no outstanding obligations of the C-Corporations to issue, sell or transfer or repurchase, redeem or otherwise acquire, or that relate to the holding, voting or disposition of or that restrict the transfer of, the issued or unissued capital stock or other equity or ownership interests of the C-Corporations. No Shares have been issued in violation of any rights, agreements, arrangements or commitments under any provision of applicable Law, the certificates of incorporation or bylaws or equivalent organizational documents of the C-Corporations or any Contract to which the C-Corporations are a party or by which the C-Corporations are bound. The Seller has delivered to the Buyer true and complete copies of the organizational documents, minutes and other corporate records of each of the C-Corporations as in effect on the date hereof.

(d) Equity Interests. None of the C-Corporations directly or indirectly owns any equity, partnership, membership or similar interest in, or any interest convertible into, exercisable for the purchase of or exchangeable for any such equity, partnership, membership or similar interest, or is under any current or prospective obligation to form or participate in, provide funds to, make any loan, capital contribution or other investment in or assume any liability or obligation of, any Person.

(e) Undisclosed Liabilities. The are no liabilities of the C-Corporations of any nature whether or not required, if known, to be reflected or reserved against on a consolidated balance sheet of the C-Corporations prepared in accordance with GAAP or the notes thereto, other than (i) liabilities that are reflected or reserved against in the Balance Sheet, (ii) liabilities arising since December 31, 2004 in the ordinary course of business consistent with past practice, (iii) liabilities arising in the ordinary course of business pursuant to Contracts disclosed or referred to in the Schedules 3.7(b), 3.11(c) and 3.15 of the Disclosure Schedules or that are not required to be disclosed in the Disclosure Schedules pursuant to the terms of this Agreement, (iv) liabilities expressly set forth in the Disclosure Schedules, and (v) liabilities incurred after the date hereof in accordance with, and not in violation of, Section 5.1.

(f) Transferred Assets; Employees. At the Closing, the C-Corporations will have (x) disposed of any right, title or interest in any asset that is not a Transferred Asset or (y) caused to be assumed or taken subject to, as the case may be, any liability that is not an Assumed Liability, and in each case will have paid all Taxes, if any, imposed by reason of (x) or (y). The C-Corporations do not, and since January 1, 2003, have not had any employees. The C-Corporations do not, and since January 1, 2003, have not maintained any employee benefit plans and do not have any liability in respect of any Affiliate's employee benefit plans.

(g) Taxes.

(i) Except as set forth on Schedule 3.22(g), the C-Corporations have timely filed, or been included in, all Tax Returns required to be filed through the date hereof and will timely file any such Tax Returns required to be filed on or prior to the Closing Date, in each case, subject to any applicable extensions. All such Tax Returns are complete and accurate in all material respects. All Tax Returns required to be filed in respect of the C-Corporations prior to January 1, 2003 relate to periods for which the time for assessment has expired. All tax elections made by or on behalf of the C-Corporations have been timely and properly made;

(ii) All Taxes of the C-Corporations that are payable in respect of taxable periods that end on or before the Closing Date have or will have been timely paid. Taxes that are not yet payable have been fully reserved for on the books and records of the C-Corporations;

(iii) None of the C-Corporations has a Tax deficiency or claim assessed or, to the best of the knowledge of the C-Corporations or the Vice President of Tax of [ ], proposed or threatened (whether orally or in writing) against any C-Corporation;

(iv) None of the C-Corporations (A) has filed a consent under Section 341(f) of the Code concerning collapsible corporations or (B) has been a United States real property holding corporation within the meaning of

Section 897(c)(2) of the Code during the applicable period specified in Section 897(c)(1)(A)(ii) of the Code;

(v) As of the Closing, no C-Corporation shall be a party to, bound by or have any obligation under any Tax allocation or sharing agreement or have any liability thereunder for amounts due in respect of periods prior to the Closing Date;

(vi) None of the C-Corporations (A) has been a member of any affiliated group filing a consolidated federal income Tax Return and (B) has any liability for the Taxes of any other person as defined in Section 7701(a)(1) of the Code or under Treas. Reg. § 1.1502-6 (or any similar provision of state, local, or foreign law), as a transferee or successor, by contract, or otherwise;

(vii) None of the C-Corporations has agreed to or is required to make any adjustment pursuant to Section 481(a) of the Code by reason of a change in accounting method initiated by such C-Corporations and to the knowledge of the C-Corporations or the Vice President of Tax of [ ], the Internal Revenue Service has not proposed any such adjustment or change in accounting method;

(viii) No extension of time has been requested or granted for any C-Corporation to file any Tax Return that has not yet been filed or to pay any Tax that has not yet been paid and no C-Corporation has granted a power of attorney that remains outstanding with regard to any Tax matter;

(ix) Except for Permitted Encumbrances, there are no Tax liens on or pending against any of the C-Corporations or any of the C-Corporations' assets;

(x) There are no presently outstanding waivers or extensions or requests for waiver or extension of time within which a Tax deficiency may be asserted or assessed against a C-Corporation;

(xi) No issue has been raised in any examination, investigation, audit, suit, action, claim or proceeding relating to Taxes of any C-Corporation, by which application of similar principles to any past, present or future period, would result in a Tax deficiency for such period;

(xii) No claim has been made by any Tax authority that any C-Corporation is subject to Tax in a jurisdiction in which a C-Corporation is not then paying Tax of the type asserted; and

(xiii) None of the C-Corporations has participated in a "reportable transaction" or "listed transaction" as defined in Treasury Regulations Section 1.6011-4(b) or any analogous or similar state or local law.

Section 3.23 Contracts Containing Non-Competition Agreements. The Transferred Assets do not include any Contract that contains a non-competition or other similar provision that would be binding on (a) the Buyer and its Affiliates or (b) the Equity Sponsors and their affiliates after the Closing; provided, however, that the representation contained in this Section 3.23 shall be modified by any disclosure made by the Seller pursuant to Section 5.26 hereof.

Section 3.24 No Other Representations or Warranties. Except for the representations and warranties contained in this Agreement or the Ancillary Agreements, neither the Seller, the Subsidiaries nor any other Person makes any other express or implied representation or warranty on behalf of the Seller or the Subsidiaries.

ARTICLE IV

REPRESENTATIONS AND WARRANTIES OF THE BUYER

The Buyer hereby represents and warrants to the Seller that the statements contained in this Article IV are true, correct and complete as of the date of this Agreement and will be true, correct and complete as of the Closing Date, except in each case to the extent that such statements are expressly made only as of a specified date, in which case the Buyer represents and warrants that such statements are true, correct and complete as of such specified date.

Section 4.1 Organization and Qualification. The Buyer is a limited liability company duly organized, validly existing and in good standing under the laws of Delaware and has all necessary limited liability company power and authority to own, lease and operate its properties and to carry on its business as it is now being conducted. The Buyer is duly qualified or licensed as a foreign entity to do business, and is in good standing, in each jurisdiction where the character of the properties owned, leased or operated by it or the nature of its business makes such qualification or licensing necessary, except, in each case, for any such failures that would not, individually or in the aggregate, reasonably be expected to have a Buyer Material Adverse Effect.

Section 4.2 Authority. The Buyer has full limited liability company power and authority to execute and deliver this Agreement and each of the Ancillary Agreements to which it will be a party, to perform its obligations hereunder and thereunder and to consummate the transactions contemplated hereby and thereby. The execution and delivery by the Buyer of this Agreement and each of the Ancillary Agreements to which it will be a party and the consummation by the Buyer of the transactions contemplated hereby and thereby have been duly and validly authorized by all necessary limited liability company action. This Agreement has been, and upon their execution each of the Ancillary Agreements to which the Buyer will be a party will have been, duly and validly executed and delivered by the Buyer. This Agreement constitutes, and upon their execution each of the Ancillary Agreements to which the Buyer will be a party will constitute, the legal, valid and binding obligations of the Buyer, enforceable against the Buyer in accordance with their respective terms, except as enforcement may be limited by applicable bankruptcy, insolvency, reorganization, moratorium or similar laws affecting creditors' rights generally and by general principles of equity (regardless of whether considered in a proceeding in equity or at law).

Section 4.3 No Conflict; Required Filings and Consents.

(a) Except for the execution, delivery and performance by the Buyer of this Agreement, and by the Buyer of each of the Ancillary Agreements to which the Buyer will be a party, and the consummation of the transactions contemplated hereby and thereby, do not and will not:

(i) conflict with or violate the organizational documents (such as the certificates of formation or limited liability company agreements) of the Buyer;

(ii) conflict with or violate any Law applicable to the Buyer or by which any property or asset of the Buyer is bound or affected; or

(iii) conflict with, result in any breach of, constitute a default (or an event that, with notice or lapse of time or both, would become a default) under, require any consent of any Person pursuant to, or give to others any rights of termination, acceleration or cancellation of, any material contract or agreement to which the Buyer is a party;

except, in the case of clause (ii), for any such conflicts or violations that would not, individually or in the aggregate, reasonably be expected to have a Buyer Material Adverse Effect or that arise as a result of any facts or circumstances relating to the Seller or any of its Affiliates.

(b) Assuming the receipt of all Required Consents with respect to the transfer to the Buyer of the Permits, the Buyer is not required to file, seek or obtain any notice, authorization, approval, order, permit or consent of or with any Governmental Authority in connection with the execution, delivery and performance by the Buyer of this Agreement and each of the Ancillary Agreements to which it will be party or the consummation of the transactions contemplated hereby or thereby or in order to prevent the termination of any right, privilege, license or qualification of the Buyer, except (i) for any filings required to be made under the HSR Act or (ii) where failure to obtain such consent, approval, authorization or action, or to make such filing or notification, would not, individually or in the aggregate, reasonably be expected to have a Buyer Material Adverse Effect.

Section 4.4 Financing. The Buyer has received commitments from sources of equity financing (the **"Equity Commitment"**) and debt financing (the **"Debt Commitment"**, together with the Equity Commitment, the **"Financing Commitments"**) in amounts sufficient to enable the Buyer to consummate the transactions contemplated hereby and, subject to the closing of the transactions contemplated by the Financing Commitments on the Closing Date, the Buyer will have available sufficient unrestricted funds to enable it to consummate the transactions contemplated hereby. On the date hereof, the Buyer has delivered true and accurate copies of all Financing Commitments to the Seller.

Section 4.5 Certain Information. The Buyer has provided to the Seller all information reasonably necessary for the completion of the FCC Forms 394 required to be filed in order to obtain the LFA Approvals (including information required by the terms of the Franchises).

Section 4.6 Brokers. No broker, finder or investment banker is entitled to any brokerage, finder's or other fee or commission in connection with the transactions contemplated hereby based upon arrangements made by or on behalf of the Buyer.

Section 4.7 Litigation and Claims. There are no civil, criminal or administrative actions, suits, demands, claims, hearings, proceedings or investigations pending or, to the knowledge of the Buyer, threatened against the Buyer or any of its Affiliates that, individually or in the aggregate, would impair or delay the ability of the Buyer to effect the Closing. Neither the Buyer nor any of its Affiliates is subject to any order, writ, judgment, award, injunction or decree of any Governmental Authority of competent jurisdiction or any arbitrator or arbitrators that, individually or in the aggregate, would impair or delay the ability of the Buyer to effect the Closing.

Section 4.8 No On-Sale Agreements. As of the date of this Agreement, the Buyer and its Affiliates have not entered into any discussions, negotiations, agreements or understandings with any Person (other than the Seller) with respect to a purchase and sale transaction, whether by merger, stock sale, asset sale or otherwise, involving any of the Transferred Assets.

Section 4.9 Investment Intent. The Buyer is acquiring the Shares for its own account for investment purposes only and not with a view to any public distribution thereof or with any intention of selling, distributing or otherwise disposing of the Shares in a manner that would violate the registration requirements of the Securities Act of 1933, as amended (the **"Securities Act"**). The Buyer agrees that the Shares may not be sold, transferred, offered for sale, pledged, hypothecated or otherwise disposed of without registration under the Securities Act and any applicable state securities laws, except pursuant to an exemption from such registration under the Securities Act and such laws.

Section 4.10 Overbuilds. Except as set forth on Schedule 4.10 of the Disclosure Schedules, to the Buyer's Knowledge, as of the date of this Agreement, since December 31, 2003, no Person, other than the Seller, the Buyer, or their respective Affiliates, has publicly announced an intention to provide cable television service within the regions in which the Systems operate.

Section 4.11 No Other Representations or Warranties. Except for the representations and warranties contained in this Agreement or the Ancillary Agreements, neither the Buyer nor any other Person makes any other express or implied representation or warranty on behalf of the Buyer.

ARTICLE V

COVENANTS

Section 5.1 Conduct of Business Prior to the Closing. Between the date of this Agreement and the Closing Date, unless the Buyer shall otherwise agree in writing, the Seller covenants that the Business shall be conducted only in the ordinary course of business consistent with past practices, and the Seller shall cause the Subsidiaries to use their commercially reasonable efforts to preserve the Business, goodwill and relationships with its customers, suppliers, employees, Governmental Authorities and others. Except as provided in Schedule 5.1 of the Disclosure Schedules or otherwise specifically set forth in this Agreement, between the date of this Agreement and the Closing Date, without the prior consent of the Buyer (which consent shall not be unreasonably withheld), neither the Seller nor the Subsidiaries shall, in connection with the Business:

(a) except to the extent prohibited by the Indentures, sell, transfer, encumber or otherwise dispose of any Transferred Assets or any interest therein, other than immaterial dispositions (and where appropriate, corresponding replacements) in the ordinary course of business consistent with past practice;

(b) (i) enter into any contract, agreement or arrangement that would be a Material Contract if entered into prior to the date of this Agreement or modify or amend in any material respect any such existing contract, agreement or arrangement, (ii) enter into any lease for any new parcel of Real Property that is not terminable without penalty on 60 days notice, (iii) modify or amend any lease for (A) any headend, (B) any other property that would be Material Real Property and that serves more than 1,000 individually-billed subscribers, or (C) any other lease other than, for purposes of this clause (C) any immaterial modification or amendment made in the ordinary course of business or (iv) enter into any Franchise or FCC License or modify or amend in any material respect any such existing Franchise or FCC License;

(c) grant or announce any increase in the base salaries payable to any Business Employees, other than as required by Law, pursuant to any Employee Plans or other ordinary increases not inconsistent with the past practices of the Seller and its Affiliates, but in no event shall the aggregate of such increases exceed 5% of the aggregate base salaries payable to all the Business Employees as of the date of this Agreement;

(d) make any material change in any method of accounting or accounting practice or policy, except in accordance with [ ]'s then current practice or as required by GAAP (in which case the Seller will promptly notify the Buyer of such material change);

(e) make or rescind any election relating to Taxes, file any amended Tax Return, settle any Tax claim or assessment or consent to any waiver or extension of the limitation period applicable to any Tax claim or assessment, except for any elections, amendments, settlements or consents of [ ] and its subsidiaries that do not affect the Business or the C-Corporations disproportionately as compared with [ ], taken as a whole (provided that no such election, amendment, settlement or consent shall have any adverse effect on the Business or the C-Corporations after the Closing);

(f) fail to implement procedures for disconnection and discontinuance of service to subscribers whose accounts are delinquent, in accordance with [ ]'s practice in effect during the twelve months preceding the date of this Agreement;

(g) fail to maintain in full force and effect existing policies of insurance with respect to the Business or replacement insurance;

(h) fail to deliver to the Buyer correct and complete copies of monthly System Reports promptly after such statements become available to the Seller;

(i) change the rates charged for Basic Services, Expanded Basic Services, High Speed Internet Services or Pay TV or add, delete, retier or repackage any analog or digital programming services other than annual rate increases and changes to channel positions made in the ordinary course of business and, except to the extent required under any

Law (in which case the Seller will promptly notify the Buyer of any such change);

(j) fail to maintain at least 30 days of inventory of customer premise and customer installation equipment or fail to maintain inventory of any other Equipment in the ordinary course of business consistent with past practice;

(k) incur any liability that would constitute a material Assumed Liability if incurred prior to the date of this Agreement;

(l) dispose of, license or permit to lapse any rights in, to or for the use of any material Intellectual Property included in the Transferred Assets;

(m) fail to make any capital expenditures or repairs in the ordinary course of business consistent with the current budget and past practice of the Seller with respect to the Business;

(n) settle any claims, actions, arbitrations, disputes or other proceedings that would result in the Seller or any Subsidiary being enjoined in any material respect from engaging in the transactions contemplated by this Agreement or materially adversely affecting the System;

(o) engage in any marketing or promotional activities;

(p) waive, release or assign any material right relating to the Systems or the Transferred Assets;

(q) fail to keep any (i) Material Contract or Permit (subject to the expiration of such Material Contract or Permit in accordance with its terms), (ii) lease for (A) any headend or (B) any other Material Real Property that serves more than 1,000 individually-billed subscribers or (iii) retransmission consent included in the Transferred Assets in full force and effect without material default thereunder;

(r) issue or sell, or cause the C-Corporation Parent Company to issue or sell, any shares of capital stock of the C-Corporations, or any of their subsidiaries, or any options, warrants, convertible securities or other rights of any kind to acquire any such shares; or

(s) fail to consider in good faith any requests by the Buyer to dispose of any Real Property included in the Transferred Assets.

This Section 5.1 notwithstanding, prior to the Closing, the Seller shall transfer, sell or otherwise dispose of (1) any assets held by the C-Corporations that are not Transferred Assets and (2) any liabilities of the C-Corporations that are not Assumed Liabilities.

Section 5.2 Covenants Regarding Information.

(a) From the date of this Agreement until the Closing Time, upon reasonable notice, the Seller shall afford the Buyer and its managers, members, general partners, officers, employees, agents, accountants, attorneys, advisors, bankers and other representatives (collectively, **"Representatives"**) reasonable access to the Seller's supervisory employees at the Key Market Area (KMA) level, properties, offices, plants and other facilities, books and records of the Seller and the Subsidiaries to the extent related to the Business, and shall use its commercially reasonable efforts to furnish the Buyer with such financial, operating and other data and information to the extent related to the Business as the Buyer may reasonably request, including: (i) the number of poles currently being billed and rate per pole under each Pole Attachment Agreement and (ii) a list of each Contract that falls within any of the following categories: (A) agreements that provide for annual payments to or by Seller or any Subsidiary in excess of $5,000, (B) any partnership, joint venture or other similar agreement or arrangement of Seller or any Subsidiary, (C) any agreement relating to the acquisition or disposition of any business (whether by merger, sale of stock, sale of assets or otherwise) that has any remaining indemnity obligations, (D) any railroad crossing agreements, (E) any tower lease agreements, (F) any multi-dwelling unit and commercial establishment agreements, (G) any software license not listed on Schedule 3.18 of the Disclosure Schedules and (H) a brief summary of the material terms of any oral Contract that falls into any of the foregoing categories; provided, however, that any such access or furnishing of information shall be conducted during normal business hours, under the supervision of the Seller's or its Affiliates' personnel and in such a manner as does not unreasonably interfere with the normal operations of the Seller, the Subsidiaries or the Business, and the Buyer shall reimburse the Seller promptly for reasonable out-of-pocket expenses it incurs in complying with any such request for access or information by or on behalf of the Buyer. Notwithstanding anything to the contrary in this Agreement, the Seller shall not be required to disclose any information to the Buyer or its Representatives if such disclosure would, as determined in the Seller's sole discretion, (1) jeopardize any attorney-client or other legal privilege, (2) contravene any applicable Laws, fiduciary duty or binding agreement entered into prior to the date hereof, (3) relate to any consolidated, combined or unitary Tax Return filed by the Seller, the Subsidiaries or any Affiliate thereof or any of their respective predecessor entities or (4) relate to any Excluded Asset or Excluded Liability, provided that in the event the Seller shall decline to provide the Buyer with any such information, the Seller shall provide the Buyer with written notice thereof and shall include the reason therefor. If requested by the Buyer and to the extent reasonable under the circumstances, the Seller agrees to seek waivers of any condition or circumstances upon which the Seller relies in denying access to any such information. The Buyer shall reimburse the Seller promptly for reasonable out-of-pocket expenses it incurs in complying with any such request for information by or on behalf of the Buyer. Any access shall be at the risk of the Buyer and its Representatives, and in connection therewith, the Buyer hereby agrees to indemnify and hold harmless the Seller Indemnified Parties with respect to any Losses resulting from or arising out of such access. All requests made pursuant to this Section 5.2(a) shall be directed to one of the Persons identified on Schedule 5.2(a) of the Disclosure Schedules or such other Person or Persons as may be designated by the Seller to the Buyer from time to time. All information received pursuant to this Section 5.2(a) shall be subject to the terms and conditions of Section 5.6.

(b) For a period of seven years after the Closing Date or, if shorter, the applicable period specified in the Buyer's document retention policy, or if such policy does not exist, in accordance with the Buyer's practices, the Buyer shall (i) retain the books and records included in the Transferred Assets relating to the Business relating to periods prior to and including the Closing Date and (ii) upon reasonable notice afford the Representatives of the Seller reasonable access (including the right to make, at the Seller's expense, photocopies), during normal business hours, to such books and records to the extent related to the Business; provided, however, that the Buyer shall notify the Seller in writing at least 30 days in advance of destroying any such books and records prior to the seventh anniversary of the Closing Date in order to provide the Seller the opportunity to copy such books and records in accordance with this Section 5.2(b).

(c) For a period of seven years after the Closing Date or, if shorter, the applicable period specified in the Seller's document retention policy, or if such policy does not exist, in accordance with the Seller's practices, the Seller shall (i) retain the books and records relating to the Business relating to periods prior to and including the Closing Date which shall not otherwise have been delivered to the Buyer and (ii) upon reasonable notice, afford the Representatives of the Buyer reasonable access (including the right to make, at the Buyer's expense, photocopies), during normal business hours, to such books and records to the extent related to the Business; provided, however, that the Seller shall notify the Buyer in writing at least 30 days in advance of destroying any such books and records prior to the seventh anniversary of the Closing Date in order to provide the Buyer the opportunity to copy such books and records in accordance with this Section 5.2(c).

(d) The Seller acknowledges and agrees that, within 45 days of the date of this Agreement, the Buyer may commission, at the Buyer's sole cost and expense, a Phase I environmental site assessment (as such term is described in the American Society of Testing and Materials Standard 1527) of the Real Property (a **"Phase I Assessment"**). The Seller will use its commercially reasonable efforts to comply with any reasonable request for information made by the Buyer or its Representatives in connection with any such investigation, but in no event will the Seller be required under this Section 5.2(d) to disclose any materials constituting attorney-client privileged communications. Upon reasonable request by the Buyer, the Seller will afford the Buyer and its Representatives access to such Real Property at reasonable times and in a reasonable manner in connection with any such investigation; provided, however, that the Buyer shall not unreasonably interfere with the Subsidiaries' use and operation of the Real Property. Should the Buyer commission such an investigation, such investigation will have no effect upon the representations and warranties made by the Seller to the Buyer under this Agreement, except that if any Phase I Assessment documents an environmental condition that would reasonably be construed to be a breach of the Seller's representations or warranties herein and such breach is capable of being cured, the Buyer shall promptly so notify the Seller and the Seller will be deemed not to have breached such representation or warranty if the Seller cures such breach. The Buyer shall reimburse the Seller promptly for reasonable out-of-pocket expenses it incurs in complying with this Section 5.2(d), other than any expense the Seller incurs pursuant to the preceding sentence. Any access to the Real Property shall be at the risk of the Buyer and its Representatives, and in connection therewith, the Buyer hereby agrees to indemnify and hold harmless the Seller Indemnified Parties with respect to any Losses resulting from or arising out of the activities of the Buyer or its representatives undertaken pursuant to this Section 5.2(d). If the environmental firm reasonably determines as a result of any Phase I Assessment that further investigation or testing is necessary, the Buyer may cause to be performed such additional environmental investigations or testing, as appropriate, at the Real Property except to the extent expressly prohibited by the applicable lease, as soon as reasonably practicable by the environmental firm. The Buyer must obtain the Seller's prior written consent to conduct any other environmental investigation, sampling, testing or assessment of any kind at any Real Property, which consent shall not be unreasonably withheld, delayed or conditioned.

(e) All information collected and generated as a result of the environmental due diligence authorized by Section 5.2(d) will be subject to the terms and conditions of Section 5.6 of this Agreement. The Buyer will provide to the Seller copies of all (i) work plans, proposed investigation methodologies and other similar information prepared by the Buyer or the Buyer's environmental consultants no later than 10 days prior to the proposed initiation of any environmental site assessments (other than the Phase I Assessments) and (ii) and draft and final reports, assessments and other information composed or compiled by the Buyer or the Buyer's environmental consultants within 10 days after the Buyer's receipt of copies thereof, but in no event later than 30 days prior to the Closing Date.

(f) Notwithstanding anything to the contrary contained in this Agreement, the Seller and the Subsidiaries shall have the right to retain one copy of all contracts, agreements, books, records, literature, lists (other than customer lists, all of which shall be delivered to the Buyer), and any other written or recorded information constituting Transferred Assets or which otherwise relates to the Business or the Assumed Liabilities (including, without limitation, the Books and Records), in each case to the extent required for (i) the administration by the Seller and the Subsidiaries or their Affiliates of any suit, claim, action, proceeding or investigation relating to the Business, (ii) the administration by the Seller and the Subsidiaries or their Affiliates of any regulatory filing or matter or (iii) any other valid reasonable legal or business purpose of the Seller and the Subsidiaries or their Affiliates.

(g) For a period of 30 days following the Closing Date, the Buyer shall grant to the Seller, the Subsidiaries and each of their respective Representatives access to the hard drives and other electronic information storage devices included in the Transferred Assets for the purpose of obtaining copies thereof. The Buyer shall not erase or otherwise eliminate any information contained on such hard drives and other electronic information storage devices until the expiration of such 30-day period. The parties shall reasonably cooperate in determining the manner and the times of access by the Seller, the Subsidiaries and each of their respective Representatives so as not to interfere with the normal operation of the Buyer's business.

(h) From and after the date hereof, the Seller shall deliver to the Buyer, promptly upon receipt or filing, copies of all pleadings, orders and decisions entered in connection with the litigation described as West Virginia Item 2 in Schedule 3.8 of the Disclosure Schedules.

Section 5.3 Update of Disclosure Schedules; Knowledge of Breach. The Seller shall, promptly after becoming aware of such matter, event or condition, supplement or amend the Disclosure Schedules with respect to any matter, event or condition hereafter arising or discovered which if existing or known at the date of this Agreement would have been required to be set forth or described in such Disclosure Schedules. Any such supplemental or amended disclosure with respect to those matters, events or conditions arising or discovered after the date of this Agreement shall not be deemed to have cured any inaccuracy of any representation or warranty made in this Agreement for purposes of the indemnifications provided for in Article VII hereof and shall not be deemed to have cured any such inaccuracy of representation or warranty for purposes of determining whether the conditions set forth in Article VI have been satisfied. Notwithstanding the foregoing, if the effect of any such supplements or amendments to the Disclosure Schedules is to disclose any one or more additional properties, privileges, rights, interests or claims, in each case acquired after the date of this Agreement (**"New Properties"**) as Transferred Assets that would have been (if owned on the date of this Agreement) required by this Agreement to have been disclosed by the Seller in its original Disclosure Schedules, then the Buyer, at or before Closing, will have the right (to be exercised by written notice delivered to the Seller at least two days prior to the Closing Date, provided that if any supplement or amendment to the Disclosure Schedules occurs less than six days prior to the Closing Date, the Buyer may provide such notice immediately prior to the Closing) to cause any one or more of such New Properties to be designated as and deemed to constitute Excluded Assets for all purposes under this Agreement and any liabilities associated therewith shall be deemed Excluded Liabilities. The failure of the Buyer to designate any New Property as an Excluded Asset prior to the Closing will be deemed an acceptance of such New Property as a Transferred Asset for all purposes under this Agreement as if such New Property were included on the original Disclosure Schedules, and the Buyer will be deemed to have waived, for itself and all Buyer Indemnified Parties, all claims under Article VII arising from the Seller's failure to disclose such New Property in the original Disclosure Schedules.

Section 5.4 Notification of Certain Matters. Until the Closing, (i) each party hereto shall promptly notify the other party in writing of any fact, change, condition, circumstance or occurrence or nonoccurrence of any event related to it of which it is aware that will or is reasonably likely to result in any of the conditions set forth in Article VI of this Agreement becoming incapable of being satisfied, (ii) the Seller will promptly notify the Buyer of any material adverse change relating to the Seller, the Subsidiaries, the Business, the Systems, the Assumed Liabilities or the Transferred Assets and (iii) the Seller will promptly notify the Buyer of any event or change in circumstances that, had it occurred prior to the date of this Agreement, would have resulted in a breach of the representations and warranties set forth in Section 3.10 related to labor and employment matters and Section 3.21 related to overbuilds.

Section 5.5 Employee Benefits.

(a) Continuity of Employment for Business Employees. Upon the execution of this Agreement, the Seller shall provide to the Buyer a list of all Business Employees by work location as of a recent date, showing the original hire date, the then-current positions and rates of compensation, rate type (hourly or salary) and scheduled hours per week, and whether the employee is subject to an employment agreement. The list shall also indicate which of such employees, if any, the Seller intends to retain as its employees (the **"Retained Employees"**). The Seller and the Buyer shall work in good faith to prepare a communication plan to be used in matters related to the Business Employees that shall include the Buyer's right to conduct meetings with the Business Employees (and their supervisors) during the 45 days prior to the Closing. Effective as of the Closing, the Buyer shall make offers of employment to all Business Employees other than Retained Employees and up to 10 additional Business Employees, contingent upon (i) the Closing, (ii) such Business Employees being active employees of the Seller immediately prior to Closing and (iii) the reasonable satisfaction of the Buyer as to any background checks or drug testing it conducts with respect to any Business Employees (each such Business Employee who accepts the Buyer's offer of employment and who becomes an employee of the Buyer effective as of the Closing is referred to in this Agreement as a **"Transferred Employee"**). If the Buyer makes any offers to any employees that are not (A) substantially similar in responsibility, (B) at least the same base compensation as of the Closing and (C) in the same general geographic location as such employee's primary place of employment as of the Closing, then, to the extent such employees do not accept such offers, such employees shall count against the 10 Business Employees to whom the Buyer is not required to make offers (as provided in the previous sentence). The parties agree that the Buyer shall indemnify the Seller for any severance costs (the amount of which shall be calculated in accordance with Schedule 5.5(d) of the Disclosure Schedules) in excess of 10 Business Employees incurred by the Seller pursuant to the previous sentence (for the avoidance of doubt, if the Buyer is required to indemnify the Seller pursuant to this sentence, the

Seller shall be responsible for the severance costs of the 10 lowest paid Business Employees as determined immediately prior to the Closing). The Buyer and the Seller shall cooperate reasonably from and after the date hereof to communicate with Business Employees regarding any offers of employment to be made to them by the Buyer hereunder and otherwise to give effect to this Section 5.5. The Seller and its Affiliates shall retain liability for all obligations and liabilities to the Retained Employees and other Business Employees who do not become Transferred Employees.

(b) Service Credit. The Transferred Employees shall receive credit for all periods of employment and/or service with the Seller or its Affiliates (including service with predecessor employers, where such credit was provided by the Seller or its Affiliates) prior to the Closing Time for purposes of eligibility and vesting (but not for benefit accrual, except for accrual of vacation and severance benefits under the Buyer's relevant plans and policies, and as set forth in this Agreement), including for purposes of satisfying any service requirements for early retirement under any pension plan adopted by the Buyer or its Affiliates with respect to Transferred Employees, to the same extent such employment service was credited for similar purposes under the Employee Plans for at least the six-month period immediately prior to the Closing Time.

(c) Employee Benefits — General. The Buyer shall provide the Transferred Employees with employee benefits that are the same as those generally provided to the similarly-situated employees of the Buyer and its Affiliates. The Seller shall bear the expense of and responsibility for all liabilities arising from claims by the Transferred Employees for benefits attributable to periods prior to the Closing Time under the Employee Plans, and the Buyer shall bear the expense of and responsibility for all liabilities arising from claims by the Transferred Employees for benefits attributable to periods on or after the Closing Time under the benefit plans maintained by the Buyer, including any claims under such plans relating to severance from employment on or after the Closing Time (including any such severance that relates to or results from any failure of the Buyer to comply with the provisions of this Section 5.5). Except as may be specifically required by this Agreement or by applicable Law, the Buyer shall not be obligated to continue to provide any particular employee benefits to any Transferred Employee.

(d) Severance Obligations. If the Buyer discharges any Transferred Employee without cause within 180 days after the Closing, then the Buyer shall pay severance benefits to such Transferred Employee that are at least equal to the severance benefits set forth on Schedule 5.5(d) of the Disclosure Schedules, giving effect to such employee's past service with any Seller or its Affiliate. For purposes of this Section 5.5, for a discharged Transferred Employee, "cause" shall have the meaning set forth in the Buyer's employment policies, procedures or agreements applicable to the Buyer's similarly-situated employees.

(e) Welfare Benefit Plans.

(i) Effective as of the Closing Date, the Buyer shall offer the Transferred Employees and their eligible dependents participation in the medical plans of the Buyer. With respect to any other welfare benefit plans, including dental, life insurance, and short- and long-term disability (all of such welfare plans, including the Buyer's medical plan described in the previous sentence, the **"Buyer Welfare Benefit Plans"**), the Buyer shall offer participation in such other welfare benefit plans to the Transferred Employees as soon as practicable after the Closing Date, but in no event more than 30 days after the Closing Date. All waiting periods and pre-existing condition clauses shall be waived under the Buyer Welfare Benefit Plans for the Transferred Employees and their eligible dependents who were participating in similar welfare benefits plans and programs of the Seller and its Affiliates on the Closing Date. To the extent applicable, the Buyer shall cause the Buyer Welfare Benefit Plans to recognize any out-of-pocket medical and dental expenses incurred by each of the Transferred Employees and their eligible dependents on or prior to the Closing Date and during the calendar year in which the Closing Date occurs for purposes of determining deductibles and out-of-pocket maximums under the Buyer Welfare Benefit Plans (the Seller shall provide such information to the Buyer at or prior to the Closing).

(ii) Effective as of the Closing Date, the Buyer shall assume all responsibilities and obligations for continuation coverage under Sections 601 et seq. of ERISA (the **"COBRA Obligations"**) and any state continuation coverage requirements with respect to the Transferred Employees and their beneficiaries. The Seller agrees that it shall retain responsibility for COBRA Obligations to all qualified beneficiaries of covered employees for whom a "qualifying event" under COBRA occurs prior to the Closing and for any employee, including but not limited to any Business Employee, who is not a Transferred Employee.

(f) Vacation Benefits. After the Closing Date, to the extent permitted by law, the Buyer shall recognize, and permit the Transferred Employees to use, all of the Transferred Employees' accrued and unused vacation (the Seller shall provide such information to the Buyer promptly following the Closing). The Buyer shall recognize service by each Transferred Employee with the Seller and its Affiliates (including service with predecessor employers, where such credit was provided by the Seller and its Affiliates) for purposes of determining entitlement to vacation under the applicable vacation policy of the Buyer.

(g) WARN Act. The Buyer agrees to provide any required notice under the Worker Adjustment Retraining and Notification Act of 1988, as amended (the **"WARN Act"**) and any similar state or non-U.S. statute, and otherwise to comply with any such statute with respect to any "plant closing" or "mass layoff" (as defined in the WARN Act) or group termination or similar event for which the Buyer is responsible affecting Business Employees and occurring after the Closing. The Seller agrees to provide or cause to be provided any required notice and to discharge any liability under the WARN Act, and any similar state or non-U.S. statute, and otherwise to comply with any such statute with respect to any "plant closing" or "mass layoff" (as defined in the WARN Act) or group termination or similar event affecting Business Employees, (including the transactions contemplated by this Agreement) and occurring on or prior to the Closing.

(h) No Third-Party Beneficiaries. Nothing herein express or implied by this Agreement shall confer upon any Business Employee, or legal representative thereof, any rights or remedies, including any right to employment or benefits for any specified period, of any nature or kind whatsoever, under or by reason of this Agreement.

Section 5.6 Confidentiality. Each of the parties shall hold, and shall cause its Representatives to hold, in confidence all documents and information furnished to it by or on behalf of the other party in connection with the transactions contemplated hereby pursuant to the terms of the confidentiality agreement dated March 7, 2005 between the Buyer and the Seller (the **"Confidentiality Agreement"**), which shall continue in full force and effect until the Closing Date, at which time such Confidentiality Agreement and the obligations of the parties under this Section 5.6 shall terminate only in respect of that portion of the documents and materials referenced therein relating to the Transferred Assets. The Confidentiality Agreement shall otherwise continue in full force and effect with respect to all other Confidential Information (as defined in the Confidentiality Agreement), including the terms of this Agreement. If for any reason this Agreement is terminated prior to the Closing Date, the Confidentiality Agreement shall nonetheless continue in full force and effect in accordance with its terms.

Section 5.7 Consents and Filings; Further Assurances.

(a) Each of the parties shall use all commercially reasonable efforts to take, or cause to be taken, all appropriate action to do, or cause to be done, all things necessary, proper or advisable under applicable Law or otherwise to consummate and make effective the transactions contemplated by this Agreement and the Ancillary Agreements as promptly as practicable, including to (i) obtain the Required Consents and (ii) promptly make all necessary filings, and thereafter make any other required submissions, with respect to this Agreement required under applicable Law. All fees to be paid and costs incurred in connection with obtaining the Required Consents and making such filings shall be borne equally by the Seller and the Buyer.

(b) Section 5.7(a) notwithstanding, the Seller and the Buyer shall prepare and file, or cause to be prepared and filed, within 15 Business Days after the date of this Agreement, all applications (including FCC Forms 394 or other appropriate forms required to be filed (i) with the FCC and (ii) with any other Governmental Authority that are necessary for the assignment to the Buyer of the Franchises in connection with the consummation of the transactions contemplated hereby. The Buyer has provided to the Seller all information deemed reasonably necessary by the Seller for the completion of the FCC Forms 394 required to be filed in order to obtain the LFA Approvals (including information reasonably required by the terms of the Franchises and requested by the Seller), and agrees to cooperate reasonably, diligently, and in good faith with the Seller in the preparation of such FCC Forms 394 to permit the filing of such FCC Forms 394 so that they are received no later than March 3, 2006. Following the execution hereof, until the Closing, the Seller shall timely send or cause to be sent all required renewal letters with respect to the Franchises pursuant to Section 626(a) of the Cable Act to the proper Governmental Authority. The Seller shall not, and shall cause the Subsidiaries to not, agree or accede to any material modifications or amendments to, or in connection with, or the imposition of any material condition to the renewal of, any of the Franchises that will impose a material obligation on the Buyer following the Closing. The Seller shall, to the extent reasonably practicable, notify the Buyer of all meetings, hearings and other discussions before or with Governmental Authorities in connection with the renewal or extension of any Franchise or governmental authorization relating to a Franchise or the granting of a Required Consent, such that the Buyer's representatives can participate to the extent reasonably practicable in such proceedings.

(c) (i) The Seller shall deliver with each FCC Form 394 a proposed Franchise transfer resolution substantially in the form of that attached hereto as Exhibit F (each, a **"<u>Franchise Transfer Resolution</u>"**) and which Franchise Transfer Resolution will include a request to extend, for a term of 36 months following the Closing, on substantially the same or on other commercially reasonable terms that are reasonably acceptable to the Buyer, any Franchise that has expired or will expire after the date hereof and prior to the date which is 30 months after the Closing Date in accordance with its terms. From the date of this Agreement until the Closing, the Seller shall seek to obtain any such extension or renewal of any Franchise that has expired or will expire after the date hereof and prior to the date which is 30 months after the Closing Date in accordance with its terms in the ordinary course of business, provided, that, in any event, the Seller will use commercially reasonable efforts to obtain such extension or renewal (A) with a term of 36 months following the Closing and (B) on substantially the same or on other commercially reasonable terms that are reasonably acceptable to the Buyer, and for six months following the Closing, the Seller shall use its commercially reasonable efforts to assist the Buyer in obtaining any such extension or renewal of any such Franchise. The Seller shall request or cause to be requested all other Required Consents not related to Franchises and Leased Real Property by letter substantially in the form of that attached hereto as Exhibit G (each, a **"Seller's Required Consent Letter"**). From the date of this Agreement until the Closing Date, upon the Buyer's request, the Seller shall use commercially reasonable efforts to obtain an extension or renewal of any lease for (I) any headend or (II) any other Material Real Property that serves more than 1,000 individually-billed subscribers that has expired or will expire prior to December 31, 2006, and such extension or renewal shall be for a term of up to 36 months (as so requested by the Buyer) and shall otherwise be on substantially the same or on other commercially reasonable terms that are reasonably acceptable to the Buyer.

(ii) The Buyer agrees that, if in connection with the process of obtaining any Required Consent, a Governmental Authority or other_Person purports to require any condition or any change to a Permit or Contract to which such Required Consent relates that would be applicable to either the Buyer, the Seller or the Subsidiaries as a requirement for granting such Required Consent, which condition or change involves a monetary payment or commitment to such Governmental Authority or other Person, either the Buyer or the Seller may elect, in their sole discretion, to satisfy the full amount of such monetary payment or commitment (notwithstanding the obligation to equally share certain costs set forth in Section 5.7(a)), in which case, the other party shall be deemed to accept such condition or change to the extent so satisfied, provided that if the Seller or any Subsidiary elects to satisfy any such payment or commitment, it shall do so at or before Closing.

(iii) Subject to the terms of subsection (ii) above, neither the Seller nor the Subsidiaries shall agree, without the Buyer's prior written consent, which consent shall not be unreasonably withheld or delayed, to any material change to the terms of any Permit or Contract as a condition to obtaining any Required Consent to the transfer or assignment of such Permit or Contract to the Buyer. If in connection with obtaining any Required Consent, a Governmental Authority or other third party seeks to impose any condition or adverse change to any Permit or Contract to which such Required Consent relates that would be applicable to the Buyer as a requirement for granting such Required Consent, the Seller will promptly notify the Buyer of such fact and the Seller shall not agree to such condition or adverse change unless the Buyer shall, in its reasonably exercised discretion, consent to such condition or change in writing. The Seller is not required to consent to any change to any Permit or Contract that would impose any condition on the Seller following the Closing.

(d) The Buyer shall promptly, but in no event more than 10 days after receipt of such request, furnish to any Governmental Authority or other Person from which a Required Consent is requested such accurate and complete information regarding the Buyer, including financial information relating to the cable and other media operations of the Buyer, as a Governmental Authority or other Person may reasonably require in connection with obtaining such Required Consent.

(e) Notwithstanding the provisions of this Section 5.7, neither the Seller nor the Subsidiaries shall have any further obligation to obtain Required Consents (i) with respect to any Pole Attachment Agreement where the licensing party shall not, after the Seller's exercise of commercially reasonable efforts, consent to an assignment of such Pole Attachment Agreement but requires that the Buyer enter into a new Pole Attachment Agreement with such licensing party on terms that are not materially more burdensome than the existing agreement, in which case the Buyer shall use its commercially reasonable efforts to enter into such agreement prior to the Closing or as soon as practicable thereafter and the Seller shall reasonably cooperate with and assist the Buyer, in obtaining such agreement; (ii) for any business radio license that can reasonably be expected to be obtained within 120 days after the Closing Date and so long as a temporary authorization is available to the Buyer under FCC rules with respect thereto; and (iii) with respect to Leased Real Property, if the Seller obtains and makes operational prior to the Closing substitute Leased Real Property that is reasonably satisfactory to the Buyer as to both use and terms.

(f) Except with respect to the Franchises, which are the subject of Section 2.5(b), if and to the extent that the Seller fails to obtain all Required Consents on or prior to the Closing (regardless of whether the Buyer shall have waived satisfaction of any applicable condition to the Closing), then, for a period of six months following the Closing Date, the Seller shall continue to use commercially reasonable efforts, at the Buyer's request, to obtain such Required Consents in accordance with this Section 5.7.

(g) Section 5.7(a) notwithstanding, the Seller and the Buyer shall, promptly after the execution and delivery of this Agreement, but in no event later than 30 days after the date of this Agreement, complete and file, or cause to be completed and filed, with the FTC and the Antitrust Division any notification and report required to be filed under the HSR Act with respect to the transactions contemplated under this Agreement. Each of the Buyer and the Seller shall coordinate with the other with respect to its filings, shall cooperate to prevent inconsistencies between their respective filings and shall furnish to each other such necessary information and reasonable assistance as the other may reasonably request in connection with its preparation of necessary filings or submissions under the HSR Act. The parties shall use commercially reasonable efforts to respond as promptly as practicable to any requests received from the FTC or the Antitrust Division for additional information or documentation and respond as promptly as practicable to inquiries and requests received from other Governmental Authorities with respect to antitrust matters. The Buyer on the one hand, and the Seller on the other hand, shall share equally the cost of the filing fee required under the HSR Act.

(h) Each of the parties shall promptly notify the other party of any communication it or any of its Affiliates receives from any

Governmental Authority relating to any filing made pursuant to Section 5.7(g). Neither party shall agree to participate in any meeting with any Governmental Authority in respect of any filings, investigation or other inquiry under the HSR Act unless it consults with the other party in advance and, to the extent permitted by such Governmental Authority, gives the other party the opportunity to attend and participate at such meeting. Subject to the Confidentiality Agreement, the parties will coordinate and cooperate fully with each other in exchanging such information and providing such assistance as the other party may reasonably request in connection with the foregoing. Subject to the Confidentiality Agreement, the parties will provide each other with copies of all correspondence, filings or communications between them or any of their Representatives, on the one hand, and any Governmental Authority or members of its staff, on the other hand, with respect to any filings made pursuant to Section 5.7(g).

(i) For purposes of this Section 5.7, subject to subsection (g), above, "commercially reasonable efforts" will not, among other things, be deemed to require a party to undertake extraordinary measures, including the initiation or prosecution of legal proceedings or the payment of amounts in excess of normal and usual filing fees and processing fees, if any.

(j) Prior to Closing, the Seller shall use commercially reasonable efforts to cause the Advertising Purchase and Sale Agreement dated as of October 30, 2003 between the C-Corporation Parent Company and Comcast Advertising Sales, Inc. to be amended to correct the designation of the parties.

Section 5.8 Release of Guarantees. The Seller, the Subsidiaries and their Affiliates that are a party to each of the guarantees, performance bonds, bid bonds, letters of credit and other similar agreements listed in Schedule 3.20 of the Disclosure Schedules and in effect at the Closing (the "**Guarantees**") shall cause such Guarantees to be revoked or terminated effective on the earlier of the replacement thereof by the Buyer and 30 days after Closing. The Buyer shall be responsible for securing replacement guarantees. In the event any of the Guarantees are not released prior to or at the Closing, the Buyer shall indemnify and hold the Seller, the Subsidiaries and their Affiliates harmless for any and all payments required to be made under, and costs and expenses incurred in connection with, such Guarantee by the Seller, the Subsidiaries or their Affiliates until such Guarantee is released.

Section 5.9 Corporate Name. The Buyer acknowledges that, after the Closing Date, the Seller shall have the absolute and exclusive proprietary right to all names, marks, trade names, service marks and trademarks owned by the Seller or any Affiliate and used by the Business (collectively, the **"Names"**), including all trade names incorporating "[ ]" by itself or in combination with any other Name, and that none of the rights thereto or goodwill represented thereby or pertaining thereto are being transferred hereby or in connection herewith. Notwithstanding the foregoing, for a period of 180 days following the Closing, the Buyer may continue to operate the Systems using the Names, including (i) use of any Name affixed to vehicles, signage or other equipment included in the Transferred Assets, (ii) use of any printed literature, sales materials, purchase orders and sales, maintenance or license agreements that bear a Name (as limited by any existing agreements the Seller may have with third parties) until the supplies thereof existing on the Closing Date have been exhausted and (iii) use of any printed billing statements that bear a Name. With respect to the printed purchase orders and sales, maintenance or license agreements referred to in the preceding sentence, after the Closing Date the Buyer shall sticker or otherwise mark such documents as necessary in order to indicate clearly that neither the Seller nor any of its Affiliates are a party to such documents. From and after the expiration of such 180-day period, the Buyer shall cease to use any such literature and sales materials, delete or cover (as by stickering) any such name, phrase or logo from any item included in inventory that bears such name, phrase or logo and take such other actions as may be necessary or advisable clearly and prominently to indicate that neither the Buyer nor any of its Affiliates is affiliated with the Seller, the Subsidiaries or any of their Affiliates. Notwithstanding the foregoing, nothing in this Section 5.9 shall require the Buyer to remove or discontinue using any Name that is affixed as of the Closing Date to converters or other items in or to be used in consumer homes or properties, or as are used in a similar fashion making such removal or discontinuation impracticable.

Section 5.10 Refunds and Remittances. After the Closing: (i) if the Seller, the Subsidiaries or any of their Affiliates receive any refund or other amount that is a Transferred Asset or is otherwise properly due and owing to the Buyer in accordance with the terms of this Agreement, the Seller promptly shall remit, or shall cause to be remitted, such amount to the Buyer and (ii) if the Buyer or any of its Affiliates receive any refund or other amount that is an Excluded Asset or is otherwise properly due and owing to the Seller or any of its Affiliates in accordance with the terms of this Agreement, the Buyer promptly shall remit, or shall cause to be remitted, such amount to the Seller.

Section 5.11 Cooperation on Pending Litigation.

(a) With respect to any defense or prosecution of any litigation or legal proceeding with respect to the Systems that relates to the period prior to the Closing Time and for which the Seller and its Affiliates are responsible pursuant to this Agreement, the Buyer shall cooperate with and assist the Seller and its Affiliates, upon reasonable request at the Seller's expense, by making witnesses available and providing all information in its possession (including access to employees with information regarding such proceedings and access to books and records that may relate to the proceedings) that the Seller and its Affiliates may reasonably require in connection with such litigation or legal proceedings or in response to any complaint, claim, inquiry, order or requirements of any Governmental Authority or other third party.

(b) Without limiting the obligations of the Seller under Section 2.4 and Section 7.2, the Seller shall assume all Losses and other costs related to the litigation described as Item 1 on Schedule 3.8 of the Disclosure Schedules, including reasonable costs incurred by the Buyer to comply with any judgment or settlement arising therefrom, but only to the extent that such costs are necessary to comply with such judgment or settlement.

Section 5.12 Bulk Transfer Laws. The Buyer hereby waives compliance by the Seller with the provisions of any so-called "bulk transfer laws" of any jurisdiction in connection with the sale of the Transferred Assets to the Buyer, provided that this Section 5.12 shall not relieve the

Seller or any Subsidiary from any liability to creditors or for Taxes that they otherwise may have.

Section 5.13 Public Announcements. The Seller and the Buyer shall consult with each other before issuing, and provide each other the opportunity to review and comment upon, any press release or other public statement with respect to the transactions contemplated hereby, and shall not issue any such press release or make any such public statement prior to such consultation, except as may be required by applicable Law.

Section 5.14 Cooperation on Programming Matters.

(a) The Buyer acknowledges that the Systems currently receive some or all of the programming services described on Schedule 5.14(a) of the Disclosure Schedules (the **"Programming Services"**), and that the Seller has discussed with the Buyer the benefits that it may derive from the continued carriage of each of the Programming Services by the Systems, following the Closing. The Buyer further acknowledges that the Seller has recommended that the Buyer continue to carry the Programming Services. The Buyer understands that the Seller is not able to offer the Buyer the same terms that are available to [ ] and its Affiliates, and that the Buyer's rights to carry the Programming Services shall be subject to the Buyer's reaching mutual agreement with each provider of the Programming Services. The Buyer agrees to consider the Seller's recommendation in good faith and that, if the Buyer chooses to negotiate a programming agreement with any programmer, it shall do so in good faith.

(b) No party, in the course of its fulfillment of any of its obligations under this Section 5.14, shall be required to make any payments or otherwise provide any services in respect of the other's obligations to its programmers.

Section 5.15 Transition Planning and Services.

(a) Between the date hereof and the Closing Date, the Seller and the Buyer will reasonably cooperate to transition the services and operations from the Seller and the Subsidiaries to the Buyer, and in connection therewith, the Seller shall provide, and shall cause the

Subsidiaries to provide, and shall use their commercially reasonable efforts to cause the respective officers, employees, representatives and advisors (including legal and accounting advisors) of the Seller and the Subsidiaries to provide, to the Buyer cooperation as reasonably requested by Buyer that is necessary, proper or reasonably advisable in connection with the transitioning at Closing of such services and operations to the Buyer (including with respect to payroll, human resources and benefits administration, financials (general ledger, accounts payable, purchasing and inventory asset management), billing migration, e-commerce (including electronic bill pay and presentment), COM/operational data requests (including, programming information for payments, channel lineups, headend information, service code and work order mapping, subscriber counts by service), e-mail, provisioning, disaster recovery, dispatch system and ticketing system).

(b) Within 60 days of execution of this Agreement, the Seller and the Buyer shall, in good faith, negotiate and execute a transition services agreement in a form reasonably acceptable to each of them (the **"Transition Services Agreement"),** to provide transition services to each other for a period of up to 180 days following the Closing Date to allow for, among other things, the conversion of existing call center, billing system, and all Internet support services, including access to and the right to use its billing system, billing call center, Internet addresses, software, Internet back bone connection, HSI tier 2 support, continued access to reports currently provided to the Systems (unless any such report contains information unrelated to the Systems that the Seller cannot, after exercise of its commercially reasonable efforts, remove), access to existing VOD content (other than VOD programming content), customer access to existing portal and content, e-mail servers, provisioning support for new HSI modems until such time as Buyer begins using its own IP address space and related fixed assets, as well as such other services as are reasonably necessary or appropriate for transitioning the Business and to permit the operation of the Business in the ordinary course (the **"Transition Services"**). Notwithstanding the foregoing, the Seller shall provide customer email transition services for up to an additional 90 days after the termination of the Transition Services Agreement. The Transition Services Agreement shall require the Seller to provide the Transition Services to the Buyer at the Seller's out of pocket cost, including costs arising solely as a result of the transition of the Systems to the Buyer. If and to the extent any System provides services to other cable systems owned by the Seller or any of its Affiliates, the Transition Services Agreement shall require the Buyer to provide Transition Services to such Seller or Affiliate as agreed to by both parties, which Transition Services shall be provided to such Seller or Affiliate at the Buyer's cost, including costs arising solely as a result of the transition of the Systems to the Buyer.

Section 5.16 Cooperation as to Subscriber Reimbursements. If the Seller or the Subsidiaries are required, following the Closing, pursuant to any Law, settlement or otherwise, to reimburse or provide in-kind or another form of consideration to any subscribers of the Systems in respect of any subscriber payments previously made by them, including fees for cable television service, late fees and similar payments, the Buyer agrees that it shall make such reimbursement or provide such in-kind or other form of consideration through the Buyer's billing system on terms specified by the Seller, and the Seller shall reimburse the Buyer, at cost, for all such payments and other consideration made by the Buyer following the Closing and for the Buyer's reasonable out-of-pocket expenses incurred in connection therewith. Such reimbursement shall be reflected in the Pre-Closing Working Capital Statement and Final Working Capital Statement, to the extent then known. For expenses incurred after completion of the Final Working Capital Statement, the Seller shall reimburse the Buyer within 30 days after receipt of a statement therefor. The Buyer shall provide the Seller with all information in the Buyer's possession that is reasonably required by the Seller in connection with such reimbursement.

Section 5.17 Telecommunications Certificates. The Buyer acknowledges and agrees that, following the Closing, the Buyer shall have no right to the Subsidiaries' (other than the C-Corporations', if any) state and federal telecommunications Licenses and authorities for non-cable services, each of which are Excluded Assets, and that the Subsidiaries may terminate some or all of such Licenses and authorities. Following the execution hereof, the Buyer will use commercially reasonable efforts to (i) obtain any Permits related to such Licenses and authorities and (ii) obtain eligible telecommunications provider status from the Universal Service Administration Company, in each case, which the Buyer deems necessary or appropriate, or which are required by any Contract or Permit included in the Transferred Assets, for the offer of services by it. The Buyer will prepare and file, or cause to be prepared and filed, within 30 days after the date hereof, all applications (including any FCC Forms 499) required to be filed in connection with such efforts. The Buyer will pay all fees and expenses incurred by the Buyer with respect to the foregoing. Any liability of the Buyer resulting from the failure to obtain such Licenses or to file such applications shall be an Assumed Liability.

Section 5.18 Leased Vehicles; Other Capital Leases. Prior to the Closing, the Seller will pay, or cause to be paid, the remaining balances on any (i) leases for vehicles or (ii) capital leases for other Equipment or Real Property included in the Transferred Assets and will deliver such vehicles, Real Property and other Equipment free and clear of all Encumbrances (other than Permitted Encumbrances) to the Buyer at the Closing.

Section 5.19 Tax Matters.

(a) All federal, state, local or foreign or other excise, sales, use, value added, transfer (including real property transfer or gains), stamp, documentary, filing, recordation and other similar taxes (but not including any income or corporate franchise taxes, or any Taxes based on, or measured by income, all of which shall be solely the responsibility of the Seller) that may be imposed or assessed as a result of the transactions contemplated hereby, together with any interest, additions or penalties with respect thereto and any interest in respect of such additions or penalties (the "**Transfer Taxes**"), shall be shared equally by the Seller and the Buyer.

(b) Any Tax Returns that must be filed in connection with Transfer Taxes (the "**Transfer Tax Returns**"), other than Transfer Tax Returns relating to Real Property and vehicles that are included in the Transferred Assets (which shall be prepared and filed by the Buyer), shall be prepared and filed by the Seller; provided, however, that the Buyer shall reimburse the Seller for all amounts shown as due and payable on such Transfer Tax Returns for which the Buyer is responsible for payment pursuant to Section 5.19(a), and the Seller shall reimburse the Buyer for amounts shown as due and payable on Transfer Tax Returns prepared and filed by the Buyer for which the Seller is responsible pursuant to Section

5.19(a). The Buyer and the Seller shall provide copies of such items for the other's review at least ten Business Days prior to the due date for such returns to be filed. The Buyer and the Seller shall (and shall cause each of their respective Affiliates to) cooperate in the timely completion and filing of all such Tax Returns, and the Buyer and the Seller shall (and shall cause each of their respective Affiliates to) execute such documents in connection with such filings as shall have been required by Law or reasonably requested by the other party. The Seller or the Buyer, as the case may be, shall furnish to the other party a copy of any Transfer Tax Return (or similar form claiming an applicable exemption from Transfer Taxes) prepared and filed pursuant to this Section 5.19.

(c) The Buyer shall control the conduct of any audit, claim, contest or administrative or judicial proceeding relating to such Transfer Taxes, subject to the Seller's right, at its own expense, to participate in such proceedings. Any additional Transfer Taxes resulting from an adverse determination by a Governmental Authority shall be shared equally by the Buyer and the Seller. If the Buyer, on the one hand, or the Seller, on the other hand, receives any written notice of assessment or other claim from any Governmental Authority with respect to Transfer Taxes for which the other party potentially may be liable, the notified party shall notify the other party of the receipt of such notice of assessment or other claim promptly after the receipt thereof.

(d) Any Transfer Taxes resulting from any subsequent increase in the Purchase Price pursuant to this Agreement shall be borne in accordance with the provisions of this Section 5.19.

(e) All real property taxes, personal property taxes, or ad valorem obligations and similar recurring taxes and fees on the Transferred Assets shall be prorated between the Buyer and the Seller as of the Closing Date. The Seller shall be responsible for all such Taxes and fees on the Transferred Assets to the extent attributable to any period up to and including the Closing Date. The Buyer shall be responsible for all such Taxes and fees on the Transferred Assets to the extent attributable to any period after the Closing Date (including any revaluation or reassessment as a result of this transaction affecting Taxes after the Closing or any subsequent transaction after the Closing Date). With respect to Taxes described in this Section 5.19(e), the Seller shall timely file all Tax Returns due on or before the Closing Date with respect to such Taxes and the Buyer shall prepare and timely file all Tax Returns due after the Closing Date with respect to such Taxes. If one party remits to the appropriate Taxing Authority payment for Taxes, which are subject to proration under this Section 5.19(e), and such payment includes the other party's share of such Taxes, such other party shall promptly reimburse the remitting party for its share of such Taxes.

(f) The Seller shall prepare and file, or cause to be prepared and filed, all Tax Returns of the C-Corporations that are required to be filed for Pre-Closing Tax Periods. The Buyer shall prepare and file all other Tax Returns of the C-Corporations, including Tax Returns, if any, for Straddle Periods. Income Tax Returns relating to Straddle Periods that are prepared by the Buyer shall be prepared and filed in a manner consistent with past practice except (i) as otherwise required by a change in applicable Law, or (ii) as consented to by the Seller, which consent shall not be unreasonably withheld or delayed. Income Tax Returns relating to Straddle Periods that are prepared by the Buyer shall be provided to the Seller for review and comment as soon as possible prior to the final due date for the filing thereof and in any event at least ten days prior to such final due date. The Seller shall be liable for and shall pay any Taxes of the C-Corporations for any Pre-Closing Tax Periods. The Seller shall to the extent permitted by applicable law, elect with the relevant taxing authority to close any Tax period of the C-Corporations as of the day before the Closing Date. If applicable Law does not permit such election to be made, then in the case of any Taxes attributable to a Straddle Period and based upon or related to income, capital or receipts, the portion of such Taxes which relates to a Pre-Closing Tax Period shall equal the amount that would be payable if such taxable period ended on and included the day before the Closing. For purposes of the preceding sentence, any lien, exemption, deduction, credit or other item that is calculated on an annual basis shall be allocated to the portion of the Straddle Period ending on the day before the Closing on a pro rata basis determined by multiplying the total amount of such item allocable to the Straddle Period times the Straddle Period Fraction. In the case of any other Taxes attributable to a Straddle Period and imposed on a periodic basis with respect to the C-Corporations, the portion of any such Taxes which relates to a Pre-Closing Tax Period shall equal the amount of such Taxes for the Straddle Period multiplied by a fraction the numerator of which is the number of days in the portion of the Straddle Period ending on and including the day before the Closing and the denominator of which is the number of days in the entire Straddle Period (the **"Straddle Period Fraction"**). The Seller shall pay to the Buyer the amount of its share of such Taxes within five days prior to the due date for such payments (giving effect to any extensions thereof). Notwithstanding anything else in this Section 5.19(f) to the contrary, the Seller shall be responsible for any Taxes resulting from any transaction undertaken not in the ordinary course of business on the Closing Date but before the Closing (other than the transactions contemplated by this Agreement, the Taxes of which shall be payable as otherwise provided in this Agreement).

(g) The Seller and the Buyer shall cooperate (and shall cause each of their Affiliates to cooperate) fully at such time and to the extent reasonably requested by the other party, in connection with the preparation and filing of any Tax Returns of the C-Corporations or the conduct of any audit, dispute, proceeding, suit or action concerning any Tax of the C-Corporations. Such cooperation shall include, without limitation, (i) the retention and (upon the other party's request) the provision of records, documentation and other information in such party's possession which are reasonably relevant to the preparation of any Tax Return until the expiration of the applicable statutes of limitation (giving effect to any extension, waiver or mitigation thereof); (ii) the provision of additional information in such party's possession and explanation of any material provided hereunder; (iii) the execution of any document that may be necessary or reasonably helpful in connection with the filing of any C-Corporation's Tax Return or in connection with any audit, dispute, proceeding, suit or action respecting any C-Corporation's Tax; and (iv) the use of the parties' commercially reasonable efforts to obtain any documentation from a governmental authority or a third party that may be necessary or helpful in connection with the foregoing.

(h) The Buyer shall control the defense and settlement of any audit or administrative or judicial proceeding involving any asserted liability for Taxes of the C-Corporations for (i) any Straddle Period and (ii) any taxable period beginning on or after the Closing Date; provided, however, that the Buyer shall not settle any proceeding which would give rise to an indemnification obligation under Section 7.2 hereof without prior written consent of the Seller, which consent shall not be unreasonably withheld or delayed.

Section 5.20 Cooperation; Commercially Reasonable Efforts. Without limiting or expanding any of the express obligations of the parties hereunder, the parties shall cooperate with each other and their respective counsel, accountants, agents and other representatives in all commercially reasonable respects in connection with any actions required to be taken as part of their respective obligations under this Agreement, and otherwise use their commercially reasonable efforts to consummate the transactions contemplated hereby and to fulfill their obligations hereunder as expeditiously as practicable.

Section 5.21 Non-Competition; Non-Solicitation.

(a) The Seller shall not, and shall cause the Subsidiaries (other than the C-Corporations), and their respective Affiliates to not, directly or indirectly, whether as principal, agent, consultant, stockholder, investor or otherwise, alone or in association with any Person:

(i) for a period commencing on the Closing Date and expiring on the second anniversary of the Closing Date, manage, operate, finance, participate in, enter into, engage in or own any interest in, any business or Person that engages in the provision of multi-channel video programming service, high speed data service or wireline telephone service (including the ownership or operation of a cable television system, multi-channel multi-point distribution system, direct broadcast satellite system, open video system, master antennae television system or private operational fixed microwave service) in any of the Franchise Areas as of the Closing Date, except (A) the small system digital service (SSD) currently operated by certain Affiliates of the Subsidiaries to the extent provided on the date of this Agreement to cable television systems in any Franchise Area and (B) as a passive investor or shareholder holding less than 5% of the outstanding voting stock or other equity interest of any entity, provided, however, that for so long as [ ] does not, directly or indirectly, control [ ] Communications, Inc. ("[ ]"), no direct or indirect investment by [ ] in [ ] or other participation in the affairs of [ ] will be deemed a breach or violation of this Section 5.21(a);

(ii) from the date of this Agreement to the Closing Date, directly solicit (excluding through any general or public solicitation) for employment after the Closing (including as an independent contractor) any Business Employee (other than the Retained Employees); and

(iii) for a period commencing on the Closing Date and expiring on the first anniversary of the Closing Date, directly solicit (excluding through any general or public solicitation) for employment (including as an independent contractor) any Transferred Employee.

(b) From the date hereof until the Closing (but if a Liquidity Transaction has not occurred by the close of business on May 15, 2006 such that the Seller would have the right to terminate this Agreement pursuant to Section 8.1(e), excluding the period commencing on May 15, 2006 and ending on June 15, 2006) the Seller agrees that it will not, and will cause its Affiliates, or its or its Affiliates respective agents, Representatives, officers, directors, managers and employees not to, directly or indirectly: (A) offer the Transferred Assets, the Systems or the Business for sale, (B) initiate, solicit, encourage, facilitate or entertain offers for the Transferred Assets, Systems or Business, (C) participate in any negotiations or discussions for the possible sale of the Transferred Assets, Systems or Business or (D) make information about the Transferred Assets, Systems or Business available to any Person (other than the Buyer and its Affiliates and Representatives) in connection with the possible sale of the Transferred Assets, Systems or Business. For the period described in the preceding sentence, the Seller shall not enter into any agreement relating to the sale (by merger, exchange or otherwise) of the equity interests of any of the Subsidiaries, or consummate any such transaction, without prior written notice to the Buyer and unless the acquiror of such equity interests agrees in writing on terms and conditions reasonably acceptable to the Buyer to assume the Seller's obligations hereunder and under the Ancillary Agreements; provided, that, unless otherwise agreed in writing by the Buyer, no such assumption shall relieve the Seller of any of its obligations or liabilities hereunder or thereunder; and provided further that in no event may the Seller enter into any agreement relating to the sale (by merger, exchange or otherwise) of the equity interests of any of the C-Corporations, or consummate any such transaction.

(c) If any provision of this Section 5.21 is determined to be unreasonable or unenforceable, such provision and the remainder of this Section 5.21 shall not be declared invalid, but rather shall be modified and enforced to the maximum extent permitted by law.

Section 5.22 Financial and Operational Information.

(a) The Seller shall use commercially reasonable efforts to furnish to the Buyer, the costs of which shall be shared equally by the Buyer and the Seller:

(i) on or before April 1, 2006, a copy of the audited consolidated balance sheet of the Business as of December 31, 2004 and 2005, and the related audited consolidated statements of results of operations, invested equity and cash flows of the Business for the three years ended December 31, 2005, together with all related notes and schedules thereto, accompanied by the reports thereon of KPMG, LLC (which shall contain no "going concern" or other qualification) (collectively referred to as the "**Audited Financial Statements**") which (A) shall have been prepared based on the books and records of the Seller and the Subsidiaries pertaining to the Business (except as may be indicated in any notes thereto), (B) shall have been prepared in accordance with GAAP applied on a consistent basis, (C) will fairly present, in all material respects, the consolidated financial position, results of operations and cash flows of the Business as at the date thereof and for the respective periods indicated therein, (D) will comply in all material respects with the requirements of Regulation S-X promulgated under the Securities Act and (E) shall have been audited by KPMG, LLC; and

(ii) on or before May 15, 2006, a copy of the unaudited consolidated balance sheet with respect to the Business as of March 31, 2006 and 2005, and the related consolidated statements of operations and cash flows for the three months ended March 31, 2006, and 2005, together with all related notes and schedules thereto, which (A) shall have been prepared based on the books and records of the Seller and the Subsidiaries pertaining to the Business, (B) shall have been prepared in accordance with GAAP applied on a consistent basis, (C) will fairly present, in all material respects, the consolidated financial position of the Systems in the aggregate as of March 31, 2006 and 2005, and the consolidated results of their operations for the three months ended March 31, 2006 and 2005, which will include all of the information and footnote disclosure required by GAAP for interim financial information and (D) shall have been reviewed in accordance with SAS 100 by KPMG, LLC. In the event the Closing occurs more than 135 days after any fiscal quarter end, financial information related to the subsequent quarterly period shall be furnished to the Buyer in accordance with this Section 5.22 within 45 days after such subsequent quarter end.

(b) Following the Closing, the Seller shall give the Buyer and its representatives (including the Buyer's accountants) access to the Seller's and the Subsidiaries books and records and any other business and financial data that the Buyer may reasonably request, and the Seller shall, and shall instruct the Subsidiaries, their employees, accountants and other advisors to, at the Buyer's request, cooperate with the Buyer as may be reasonably necessary to enable the Buyer to (i) complete any audit or review in conformity with Regulation S-X promulgated under the Securities

Act, including the preparation and audit of information required for a "black line" presentation with respect to the Systems for the period January 1, 2006 through the Closing Date and for the period beginning the day following the Closing Date through December 31, 2006, and (ii) obtain the relevant information required for the preparation of a Registration Statement on Form S-4 under the Securities Act or any additional information required for filings under the Securities Exchange Act of 1934, as amended, required to be made during or with respect to the 2006 fiscal year. In the event that the Seller or any Subsidiary ceases to exist following the Closing or substantially diminishes its activities, the Seller shall take such actions as are necessary to preserve its books and records and any other business and financial data and shall make arrangements so that such books and records and data are made available to the Buyer upon its reasonable request.

Section 5.23 Risk of Loss. The risk of any loss or damage to the Transferred Assets resulting from fire, theft or any other casualty (except reasonable wear and tear) will be borne by the Seller at all times prior to the Closing. In the event of any such loss or damage to any of the Transferred Assets, Seller shall, at its option, repair or replace such Transferred Assets, as applicable, or pay over to the Buyer at the Closing, cash in the amount necessary to repair or replace such Transferred Assets, as applicable.

Section 5.24 Financing.

(a) The Buyer shall use its commercially reasonable efforts to obtain and effectuate the financing contemplated by the Financing Commitments on the terms set forth therein. The Buyer agrees to notify the Seller promptly and, in any case, within 3 Business Days if, at any time prior to the Closing Date, (i) any Financing Commitment shall expire or be terminated, modified or amended for any reason or (ii) any of the financing sources that is a party to the Debt Commitments notifies the Buyer that such source will not be able to provide financing substantially on the terms set forth in the Debt Commitments. The Buyer shall not, and shall not permit any of its Affiliates to, without the prior written consent of the Seller, take any action or enter into any transaction, including any merger, acquisition, joint venture, disposition, lease, contract or debt or equity financing that would reasonably be expected to materially delay or prevent the financing contemplated by the Financing Commitments. The Buyer shall not amend or alter, or agree to amend or alter, the Financing Commitments in any manner that could reasonably be expected to materially delay or prevent the transactions contemplated hereby without the prior written consent of the Seller, which shall not be unreasonably withheld. Notwithstanding the foregoing, including the first sentence hereof, the Buyer shall not be prohibited from obtaining and effectuating financing on terms other than those contemplated by the Financing Commitments; provided the Buyer's efforts to obtain such alternate financing terms does not materially delay or prevent the financing and consummation of the transactions contemplated by this Agreement.

(b) The Seller shall provide, and shall cause the Subsidiaries to provide, reasonable assistance to the Buyer's efforts to obtain the funds contemplated by the Financing Commitments, including provision of existing financial statements for prior periods, facilitating customary due diligence and arranging for Business Employees to meet with prospective lenders in customary presentations or to participate in customary road shows, in each case upon the Buyer's request with reasonable prior notice and at the Buyer's sole cost and expense. The Seller shall use its commercially reasonable efforts to facilitate the engagement of KPMG, LLC by the Buyer for any purpose relating to the financing of the transactions contemplated hereby (including the provision of an auditors "comfort letter" by April 8, 2006, which, among other things, will relate to the quarterly financial statements for the quarter ending December 31, 2005, provided that such efforts in no way delay the delivery of the Audited Financial Statements) and to cause KPMG, LLC to provide its consent to the inclusion of its reports in any document filed with the Securities and Exchange Commission (it being understood and agreed that the Seller shall not be required to spend any funds, provide any indemnity or make any representations in any manner with respect to such engagement).

Section 5.25 Fiber Audit. The Seller shall use commercially reasonable efforts in the ordinary course of business to continue its audit of the fibers utilized under the agreements with FiberNet, LLC referred to on Schedule 3.15 of the Disclosure Schedules and upon such completion the Seller agrees to promptly deliver the results of such audit to the Buyer.

Section 5.26 Contracts Containing Non-Competition Agreements. No later than 30 days after the date of this Agreement, the Seller shall provide the Buyer with a schedule of those Contracts that contain non-competition or other similar provisions that would be binding on the (a) the Buyer and its Affiliates or (b) the Equity Sponsors and their affiliates after the Closing. Upon receipt of such schedule, the Buyer shall have 15 days to designate any of the Contracts set forth therein as Excluded Assets, which shall not be transferred to the Buyer at the Closing. The previous sentence notwithstanding, if the Seller obtains any waiver or other elimination of such non-competition provision from such Contract with the respect to the (a) the Buyer and its Affiliates and/or (b) the Equity Sponsors and their affiliates, as appropriate, prior to the Closing, such Contract will be transferred to the Buyer as a Transferred Asset.

ARTICLE VI

CONDITIONS TO CLOSING

Section 6.1 General Conditions. The respective obligations of the Buyer and the Seller to consummate the transactions contemplated hereby shall be subject to the fulfillment, at or prior to the Closing, of each of the following conditions, any of which may, to the extent permitted by applicable Law, be waived in writing by either party in its sole discretion (provided that such waiver shall only be effective as to the obligations of such party):

(a) No Governmental Authority shall have enacted, issued, promulgated, enforced or entered any Law (whether temporary, preliminary or permanent) that enjoins, restrains, makes illegal or otherwise prohibits the consummation of the transactions, taken as a whole, contemplated by this Agreement or the Ancillary Agreements.

(b) Any waiting period (and any extension thereof) under the HSR Act applicable to the transactions contemplated by this Agreement and the Ancillary Agreements shall have expired or shall have been terminated.

Section 6.2 Conditions to Obligations of the Seller. The obligations of the Seller to consummate the transactions contemplated hereby shall be subject to the fulfillment, at or prior to the Closing, of each of the following conditions, any of which may be waived in writing by the Seller in its sole discretion:

(a) The representations and warranties of the Buyer contained in this Agreement shall be true and correct both when made and as of the Closing Date, or in the case of representations and warranties that are made as of a specified date, such representations and warranties shall be true and correct as of such specified date, except where the failure to be so true and correct (without giving effect to any limitation or qualification as to "materiality" (including the word "material") or "Buyer Material Adverse Effect" set forth therein) would not, individually or in the aggregate, have a Buyer Material Adverse Effect. The Buyer shall have performed all obligations and agreements and complied with all covenants and conditions required by this Agreement to be performed or complied with by it in all material respects prior to or at the Closing. The Seller shall have received from the Buyer a certificate to the effect set forth in the preceding sentences, signed by an officer thereof.

(b) The Seller shall have received an executed counterpart of each of the Ancillary Agreements, signed by each party other than the Seller or the Subsidiaries that are parties thereto.

(c) The LFA Approvals, consistent with the provisions of Section 5.7, with respect to Franchises that represent, in aggregate, not less than 90% of the individually-billed subscribers of the Systems, (i) shall have been received, or (ii) shall be deemed to have been received in accordance with Section 617 of the Communications Act (47 U.S.C. Section 537), or (iii) shall not be required by applicable Law or under any applicable Franchise; provided, however, if less than 100% of the LFA Approvals have been obtained, all applicable waiting periods (including extensions) shall have expired with respect to the FCC Forms 394 filed in connection with requests for such LFA Approvals that have not been obtained. Solely for purposes of determining the applicable percentage of individually-billed subscriber sunder Section 2.5(b), this Section 6.2(c) and Section 6.3(c), the parties shall use the number of subscribers in the Systems set forth on Schedule 6.3(c) of the Disclosure Schedules.

Section 6.3 Conditions to Obligations of the Buyer. The obligations of the Buyer to consummate the transactions contemplated hereby shall be subject to the fulfillment, at or prior to the Closing, of each of the following conditions, any of which may be waived in writing by the Buyer in its sole discretion:

(a) The representations and warranties of the Seller contained in this Agreement shall be true and correct both when made and as of the Closing Date, or in the case of representations and warranties that are made as of a specified date, such representations and warranties shall be true and correct as of such specified date, except where the failure to be so true and correct (without giving effect to any limitation or qualification as to "materiality" (including the word "material") or "Material Adverse Effect" set forth therein) would not, individually or in the aggregate, reasonably be expected to have a Material Adverse Effect. The Seller shall have performed all obligations and agreements and complied with all covenants and conditions required by this Agreement to be performed or complied with by it in all material respects prior to or at the Closing. The Buyer shall have received from the Seller a certificate to the effect set forth in the preceding sentences, signed by an officer thereof.

(b) The Buyer shall have received an executed counterpart of each of the Ancillary Agreements signed by each party other than the Buyer.

(c) (i) The LFA Approvals, consistent with the provisions of Section 5.7, with respect to Franchises that represent, in aggregate, not less than 65% of the individually-billed subscribers of the Systems, (i) shall have been received, or (ii) shall be deemed to have been received in accordance with Section 617 of the Communications Act (47 U.S.C. Section 537), or (iii) shall not be required by applicable Law or under any applicable Franchise; provided, however, if less than 100% of the LFA Approvals have been obtained, all applicable waiting periods (including extensions) shall have expired with respect to the FCC Forms 394 filed in connection with requests for such LFA Approvals that have not been obtained. Solely for purposes of determining the applicable percentage of individually-billed subscribers under Section 2.5(b), Section 6.2(c) and this Section 6.3(c), the parties shall use the number of subscribers in the Systems set forth on Schedule 6.3(c) of the Disclosure Schedules.

(d) The Required Consents with respect to the assignment of any leases for any Material Real Property serving more than 2,000 individually-billed subscribers shall have been received.

(e) There shall not have occurred any change, event or development that, individually or in the aggregate, has had or is reasonably likely to have a Material Adverse Effect.

(f) The Buyer shall have received (i) the Audited Financial Statements and (ii) the financial statements referred to in Section 5.22(a)(ii) to the extent such financial statements are then due pursuant to the terms of Section 5.22(a)(ii), and the Operating Cash Flow for the year ended December 31, 2005, as derived from the statement of results of operations of the Business in the Audited Financial Statements will not be more than $2,000,000 less than the Operating Cash Flow for the year ended December 31, 2005, as derived from the statement of results of operations of the Business in the Financial Statements.

(g) Forty five days shall have elapsed since delivery of the most recent quarterly financial statements required to be delivered under Section 5.22(a)(ii).

(h) As of the Closing Date, the aggregate number of the RGUs shall be no fewer than 284,537.

(i) The Buyer shall have received the funds in the amount contemplated by the Debt Commitments substantially on the terms and conditions set forth therein.

(j) The Seller shall not have sold, transferred, encumbered or otherwise disposed of any material Transferred Assets or any interest therein, except with the consent of the Buyer (which consent shall not have been unreasonably withheld).

(k) The conditions set forth in Schedule 6.3(i) of the Disclosure Schedules shall have been met.

ARTICLE VII

INDEMNIFICATION

Section 7.1 Survival of Representations and Warranties. The representations and warranties of the Seller and the Buyer contained in this Agreement and the Ancillary Agreements and any certificate delivered pursuant hereto or thereto shall survive the Closing for a period of 12 months after the Closing Date, except representations and warranties relating to authorization of the transactions contemplated by this Agreement, Taxes, the C-Corporations, title to the Real Property and the Transferred Assets, ERISA, environmental matters and brokers, which representations and warranties will survive the Closing for the duration of the applicable statute of limitations.

Section 7.2 Indemnification by the Seller. After the Closing, the Seller shall, and shall cause the Subsidiaries to, save, defend, indemnify and hold harmless the Buyer and its Affiliates, direct and indirect equityholders, owners, general partners, managers and members of the Buyer or its Affiliates, and the respective Representatives, successors and assigns of each of the foregoing (collectively, the **"Buyer Indemnified Parties"**) from and against any and all losses, damages, liabilities, deficiencies, claims, interest, awards, judgments, settlements, penalties, costs and expenses (including reasonable attorneys' fees, costs and other out-of-pocket expenses incurred in investigating, preparing or defending the foregoing) (hereinafter collectively, **"Losses"**) to the extent arising out of or resulting from:

(a) any breach of any representation or warranty made by the Seller contained in this Agreement or the Ancillary Agreements;

(b) any breach of any covenant or agreement by the Seller contained in this Agreement or the Ancillary Agreements;

(c) any Excluded Liability, including any liability arising out of any litigation described on Schedule 3.8 of the Disclosure Schedules as well as any other litigation related to the Business, Transferred Assets or the C-Corporations with respect to any period prior to the Closing; and

(d) any liability that is not an Assumed Liability.

Section 7.3 Indemnification by the Buyer. After the Closing, the Buyer shall save, defend, indemnify and hold harmless the Seller and its Affiliates, direct and indirect shareholders, owners, general partners, managers and members of the Seller or its Affiliates, and the respective Representatives, successors and assigns of each of the foregoing (collectively, the **"Seller Indemnified Parties"**) from and against any and all Losses to the extent arising out of or resulting from:

(a) any breach of any representation or warranty made by the Buyer contained in this Agreement or the Ancillary Agreements;

(b) any breach of any covenant or agreement by the Buyer contained in this Agreement or the Ancillary Agreements; and

(c) any Assumed Liability.

Section 7.4 Procedures.

(a) In order for a Buyer Indemnified Party or Seller Indemnified Party (each an **"Indemnified Party"**) to be entitled to any indemnification provided for under this Agreement or the Ancillary Agreements in respect of, arising out of or involving a Loss or a claim or demand, whether between the parties hereto (a **"Direct Claim"**) or made by any Person against such Indemnified Party (a **"Third Party Claim"**), such Indemnified Party shall deliver notice thereof to the party against whom indemnity is sought (the **"Indemnifying Party"**) describing in reasonable detail the facts giving rise to any Direct Claim or Third Party

Claim for indemnification hereunder, the amount or method of computation of the amount of such Direct Claim or Third Party Claim (if known) (which amount or any computation of such amount shall not in any event limit the amount of indemnification to which an Indemnified Party may be entitled hereunder) and such other information with respect thereto as the Indemnifying Party may reasonably request. If the claim is a Third Party Claim, notice shall be given promptly by the Indemnified Party after receipt by such Indemnified Party of written notice of the Third Party Claim. The failure to provide any such notice of a Direct Claim or Third Party Claim, however, shall not release the Indemnifying Party from any of its obligations under this Article VII except to the extent that the Indemnifying Party is materially prejudiced by such failure.

(b) Following receipt of notice from the Indemnified Party of a Direct Claim or Third Party Claim, the Indemnifying Party shall have 30 days (or such shorter period as is set forth in such notice as may be required in any applicable proceeding, in the event of a litigated matter) to make such investigation of the Direct Claim or Third Party Claim as the Indemnifying Party deems necessary or desirable and, in the case of a Third Party Claim, to notify the Indemnified Party as to whether it intends to assume the defense thereof pursuant to Section 7.4(c). For the purposes of such investigation, the Indemnified Party agrees to make available to the Indemnifying Party and its authorized representative(s) the information relied upon by the Indemnified Party to substantiate the Direct Claim or Third Party Claim. If the Indemnified Party and the Indemnifying Party agree at or prior to the expiration of said 30 day period (or such shorter period, or in either case any mutually agreed upon extension thereof) to the validity and amount of such Direct Claim or Third Party Claim, the Indemnifying Party shall immediately pay to the Indemnified Party the full amount of the Direct Claim or Third Party Claim. If the Indemnified Party and the Indemnifying Party do not agree within said period (or any mutually agreed upon extension thereof), the Indemnified Party may seek appropriate legal remedy.

(c) The Indemnifying Party shall have the right, upon written notice to the Indemnified Party, to assume the defense of any Third Party Claim at the expense of the Indemnifying Party with counsel selected by the Indemnifying Party and reasonably satisfactory to the Indemnified

Party, unless (i) the Third Party Claim relates to or arises in connection with a criminal proceeding, action, indictment, allegation or investigation, (ii) the Indemnifying Party has failed to defend or is failing to defend in good faith the Third Party Claim, (iii) the Indemnifying Party and the Indemnified Party are both named parties to the Third Party Claim, and the Indemnified Party reasonably concludes that representation of both parties by the same counsel would be inappropriate due to actual or potential different interests, (iv) in the case of Losses suffered by a Buyer Indemnified Party, it is reasonably likely that the Losses arising from such Third Party Claim will exceed the amount such Buyer Indemnified Party will be entitled to recover as a result of the limitations set forth in Section 7.5, (v) the Indemnifying Party does not, in the Indemnified Party's reasonable judgment, have sufficient financial resources to satisfy the amount of any adverse judgment that is reasonably likely to result with respect to such Third Party Claim, or (vi) the Indemnifying Party fails to acknowledge in writing that it would have an absolute indemnity obligation for any and all Losses resulting from such Third Party Claim. If the Indemnifying Party assumes the defense of such Third Party Claim, the Indemnified Party shall have the right to employ separate counsel and to participate in the defense thereof, but the fees and expenses of such counsel shall be at the expense of the Indemnified Party; provided, however, that if in the reasonable opinion of counsel for the Indemnified Party, there is a conflict of interest between the Indemnified Party and the Indemnifying Party, the Indemnifying Party shall be responsible for the reasonable fees and expenses of one counsel to such Indemnified Party in connection with such defense. If the Indemnifying Party assumes the defense of any Third Party Claim, the Indemnified Party shall reasonably cooperate with the Indemnifying Party in such defense and use commercially reasonable efforts to make available to the Indemnifying Party all witnesses, pertinent records, materials and information in the Indemnified Party's possession or under the Indemnified Party's control relating thereto as is reasonably required by the Indemnifying Party subject to reimbursement for actual out-of-pocket expenses incurred by the Indemnified Party as the result of a request by the Indemnifying Party. If the Indemnifying Party assumes the defense of a Third Party Claim and continues to diligently defend such claim, the Indemnified Party shall not admit any liability with respect to, or settle, compromise or discharge, or offer to settle, compromise or discharge, such Third Party Claim without the Indemnifying Party's prior written consent, which may be granted or withheld in the Indemnifying Party's sole discretion. The Indemnifying Party shall not, without the prior written consent of the Indemnified Party, which may be granted or withheld in the Indemnified Party's sole discretion, settle, compromise or offer to settle or compromise any Third Party Claim on a basis that would result in (i) the imposition of a consent order, injunction or decree that would restrict the future activity or conduct of, or impose any non-monetary liability, obligation or commitment on, the Indemnified Party or any of its Affiliates, (ii) a finding or admission of a violation of Law or violation of the rights of any Person by the Indemnified Party or any of its Affiliates, (iii) a finding or admission that would have an adverse effect on other claims made or threatened against the Indemnified Party or any of its Affiliates, or (iv) any monetary liability of the Indemnified Party that shall not be promptly paid or reimbursed by the Indemnifying Party. Any such settlement or compromise shall include as an unconditional term thereof the giving by the claimant of a release of the Indemnified Party from all liability with respect to such Third Party Claim.

(d) In the event any Indemnified Party should have a claim against any Indemnifying Party hereunder that does not involve a Third Party Claim being asserted against or sought to be collected from such Indemnified Party, the Indemnified Party shall deliver notice of such claim promptly to the Indemnifying Party, describing in reasonable detail the facts giving rise to any claim for indemnification hereunder, the amount or method of computation of the amount of such claim (if known) and such other information with respect thereto as the Indemnifying Party may reasonably request. The failure to provide such notice, however, shall not release the Indemnifying Party from any of its obligations under this Article VII except to the extent that the Indemnifying Party is materially prejudiced by such failure. The Indemnified Party shall reasonably cooperate and assist the Indemnifying Party in determining the validity of any claim for indemnity by the Indemnified Party and in otherwise resolving such matters. Such assistance and cooperation shall include providing reasonable access to and copies of information, records and documents relating to such matters, furnishing employees to assist in the investigation, defense and resolution of such matters and providing legal and business assistance with respect to such matters.

(e) In the event the Indemnifying Party (i) does not elect to assume control or otherwise participate in the defense of any Third Party Claim, (ii) is not entitled to assume the defense of a Third Party Claim pursuant to Section 7.4(c) or (iii) after assuming the defense of a Third Party Claim, fails to take reasonable steps to defend diligently such Third Party Claim, the Indemnified Party shall have the right, but not the obligation, to assume its own defense with respect to the applicable Third Party Claim (it being understood that the Indemnified Party's right to indemnification for a Third Party Claim shall not be adversely affected by assuming the defense of such Third Party Claim), and the Indemnifying Party shall be bound by the results obtained by the Indemnified Party with respect to such Third Party Claim and shall pay the reasonable fees and expenses of counsel retained by the Indemnified Party; provided, however, that the Indemnified Party shall not have the right to consent or otherwise agree to any non-monetary settlement or relief, including injunctive relief or other equitable remedies, that would reasonably be expected to adversely affect the Indemnifying Party, without the prior written consent of the Indemnifying Party, which consent will not be unreasonably withheld, conditioned or delayed.

Section 7.5 Limits on Indemnification.

(a) No claim may be asserted against either party for breach of any representation or warranty contained in this Agreement or the Ancillary Agreements or any certificate delivered hereto or thereto, unless written notice of such claim is received by such party, describing in reasonable detail the facts and circumstances with respect to the subject matter of such claim on or prior to the date on which the representation or warranty on which such claim is based ceases to survive as set forth in Section 7.1, in which case such representation or warranty shall survive as to such claim until such claim has been finally resolved.

(b) Notwithstanding anything to the contrary contained in this Agreement:

(i) neither party shall be liable to the other party for any claim for indemnification under Section 7.2(a) or 7.3(a), as the case may be, unless and until the aggregate amount of indemnifiable Losses that may be recovered from the Seller or the Buyer under Section 7.2(a) or 7.3(a), as the case may be, equals or exceeds $4,620,000 in which case the Indemnifying Party shall be liable only for the Losses in excess of such amount; provided, however, such limitation shall not apply with respect to representations and warranties relating to title to the Real Property and the Transferred Assets and, in substitute of such limitation, the Seller shall not be liable to the Buyer for any claim for indemnification under Section 7.2(a), in respect of representations and warranties that the Seller is transferring title to the Real Property and the Transferred Assets free and clear of Encumbrances (other than as set forth in this Agreement) unless and until the aggregate amount of indemnifiable Losses that may be recovered from the Seller under Section 7.2(a) in respect of such representations and warranties equals or exceeds $400,000; provided further, however, that such limitations shall not apply to indemnification in respect of representations and warranties relating to authorization of the transactions contemplated by this Agreement, Taxes, C-Corporations as set forth in Section 3.22 and brokers;

(ii) the maximum aggregate amount of indemnifiable Losses that may be recovered by either party under Section 7.2(a) or 7.3(a), as the case may be, shall be an amount equal to $50,000,000; provided, however, that the maximum aggregate amount of indemnifiable Losses that may be recovered by either party under Section 7.2(a) or 7.3(a), as the case may be, with respect to representations and warranties relating to ERISA and environmental matters shall be an amount equal to $154,000,000; provided further, however, that the maximum aggregate amount of indemnifiable Losses that may be recovered by either party under Section 7.2(a) or 7.3(a), as the case may be, with respect to representations and warranties relating to authorization of the transactions contemplated by this Agreement, Taxes, title to the Real

Property and the Transferred Assets, the C-Corporations and brokers shall be the Purchase Price (for the avoidance of doubt, the maximum amounts payable under any clause of this Section 7.5(b)(ii) shall be reduced by any amount previously paid under Section 7.2(a) or 7.3(a));

(iii) no Losses may be claimed by any Indemnified Party or shall be reimbursable by or shall be included in calculating the aggregate Losses set forth in clause (i) above other than Losses in excess of $5,000 resulting from any single claim or aggregated claims arising out of the same facts, events or circumstances;

(iv) the Seller shall not be obligated to indemnify any Buyer Indemnified Party with respect to any Loss to the extent that such Loss was a Current Liability included in the calculation of the Final Net Current Asset Value or to the extent that an accrual or reserve for the amount of such loss was included in the calculation of the Final Net Asset Value (in each case, as finally determined pursuant to Section 2.9); and

(v) no party hereto shall have any liability under any provision of this Agreement for any punitive, incidental, consequential, special or indirect damages, including business interruption, loss of future revenue, profits or income, or loss of business reputation or opportunity relating to the breach or alleged breach of this Agreement, except to the extent awarded by a court or other tribunal of competent jurisdiction to a third party in connection with a Third Party Claim.

(c) For all purposes of this Agreement and the Ancillary Agreements, Losses shall be net of any insurance or other recoveries payable to the Indemnified Party or its Affiliates in connection with the Losses giving rise to the right of indemnification.

(d) The Buyer and the Seller shall reasonably cooperate with each other with respect to resolving any claim or liability with respect to which one party is obligated to indemnify the other party hereunder, including by making commercially reasonably efforts to mitigate or resolve any such claim or liability.

Section 7.6 Assignment of Claims. If any party receives any payment from the other party in respect of any Losses pursuant to Section 7.2 or Section 7.3, as the case may be, and the Indemnified Party could have recovered all or a part of such Losses from a third party (a "**Potential Contributor**") based on the underlying claim asserted against the Seller or the Buyer, as the case may be, the Indemnified Party shall assign, on a non-recourse basis and without any representation or warranty, such of its rights to proceed against the Potential Contributor as are necessary to permit the Seller or the Buyer, as the case may be, to recover from the Potential Contributor the amount of such payment. Any payment received in respect of such claim shall be distributed, (i) first, to the Indemnified Party in the amount of any deductible or similar amount required to be paid by the Indemnified Party prior to the Seller or the Buyer, as the case may be, being required to make any payment to the Indemnified Party, (ii) second, to the Indemnifying Party in an amount equal to the aggregate payments made by the Indemnifying Party to the Indemnified Party in respect of such Loss, plus reasonable costs and expenses (including attorney's costs and expenses) incurred in investigating, defending or otherwise incurred in connection with addressing such claim and (iii) the balance, if any, to the Indemnified Party.

Section 7.7 Payments. The Indemnifying Party shall pay all amounts payable pursuant to this Article VII by wire transfer of immediately available funds, promptly following receipt from an Indemnified Party of a bill, together with all accompanying reasonably detailed back-up documentation, for each Loss that is the subject of indemnification hereunder, except to the extent the Indemnifying Party in good faith disputes the Loss or a portion thereof, in which event it shall so notify the Indemnified Party; provided that the Indemnifying Party shall promptly pay any portion of such Loss not subject to dispute. In any event, the Indemnifying Party shall pay to the Indemnified Party, by wire transfer of immediately available funds, the amount of any Loss for which it is liable hereunder no later than three days following any final determination of such Loss and the Indemnifying Party's liability therefor. A "final determination" shall exist when (i) the parties to the dispute have reached an agreement in writing, or a court of competent jurisdiction shall have entered a final and non-appealable order or judgment.

Section 7.8 Exclusivity. Except as specifically set forth in this Agreement or the Ancillary Agreements, after the Closing, in the absence of fraud on the part of either party in connection with the negotiation, execution or delivery of this Agreement and the Ancillary Agreements or the consummation of the transactions contemplated hereby (to the extent determined by a final judgment by a court of competent jurisdiction), this Article VII shall provide the exclusive remedy of any party against the other party for any breach of any representation or warranty set forth in or made pursuant to this Agreement or the Ancillary Agreements.

Section 7.9 **Disclaimer of Implied Warranties.**

(a) It is the explicit intent and understanding of each party hereto that neither party hereto or any of such party's Affiliates or Representatives is making any representation or warranty whatsoever (including any implied warranty of merchantability or fitness), oral or written, express or implied, as to the accuracy or completeness of any information regarding the Business, the Transferred Assets or the Assumed Liabilities, except as expressly set forth in this Agreement, and neither party hereto is relying on any statement, representation or warranty, oral or written, express or implied, made by the other party hereto or such other party's Affiliates or Representatives, except for the representations and warranties expressly set forth in this Agreement.

(b) In connection with the Buyer's investigation of the Business, the Buyer has received certain estimates, projections and other forecasts regarding the Business and the Transferred Assets, including those set forth in the Confidential Information Memorandum dated October, 2005. The Buyer acknowledges that there are uncertainties inherent in attempting to make such estimates, projections and other forecasts, that the Buyer is familiar with such uncertainties and that the Buyer is taking full responsibility for making its own evaluation of the adequacy and accuracy of all estimates, projections and other forecasts so furnished to it (including the reasonableness of the assumptions underlying such estimates, projections and forecasts). Accordingly, the Seller makes no representation or warranty with respect to such estimates, projections and other forecasts (including the reasonableness of the assumptions underlying such estimates, projections and forecasts).

ARTICLE VIII

TERMINATION, AMENDMENT AND WAIVER

Section 8.1 Termination. This Agreement may be terminated at any time prior to the Closing:

(a) by mutual written consent of the Buyer and the Seller;

(b) (i) by the Seller, if the Buyer breaches or fails to perform in any respect any of its representations, warranties or covenants contained in this Agreement or any Ancillary Agreement and such breach or failure to perform (A) would give rise to the failure of a condition set forth in Section 6.2, (B) cannot be cured or has not been cured within 30 days after written notice thereof is given to the Buyer and (C) has not been waived by the Seller or (ii) by the Buyer, if the Seller breaches or fails to perform in any respect any of its representations, warranties or covenants contained in this Agreement or any Ancillary Agreement and such breach or failure to perform (x) would give rise to the failure of a condition set forth in Section 6.3, (y) cannot be cured or has not been cured within 30 days after written notice thereof is given to the Seller and (z) has not been waived by the Buyer;

(c) by either the Seller or the Buyer if the Closing shall not have occurred by the first anniversary of the date of this Agreement (the **"Termination Date"**); provided, however, that the right to terminate this Agreement under this Section 8.1(c) shall not be available if the failure of the party so requesting termination to fulfill any obligation under this Agreement shall have been the cause of the failure of the Closing to occur on or prior to such date;

(d) by either the Seller or the Buyer in the event that any Governmental Authority shall have issued an order, decree or ruling or taken any other action restraining, enjoining or otherwise prohibiting all of the transactions contemplated hereby, and such order, decree, ruling or other action shall have become final and nonappealable; provided, however, that the right to terminate this Agreement under this Section 8.1(d) shall not be available to a party if such order, decree, ruling or other action was due to such party's failure to perform any of its obligations under this Agreement;

(e) by the Seller, if a Liquidity Transaction has not occurred by the close of business on May 15, 2006; provided, however, that the Seller must elect to terminate this Agreement, if at all, pursuant to this Section 8.1(e) prior to cure by the Buyer and in any event on or prior to June 15, 2006; or

(f) by the Buyer, if the failure of the condition set forth in Section 6.3(j): (i) cannot be cured or has not been cured within 30 days after written notice thereof is given to the Seller and (ii) has not been waived by the Buyer.

The party seeking to terminate this Agreement pursuant to this Section 8.1 (other than Section 8.1(a)) shall give prompt written notice of such termination to the other party.

Section 8.2 Effect of Termination. In the event of termination of this Agreement as provided in Section 8.1, this Agreement shall forthwith become void and there shall be no liability on the part of either party except for the provisions of Sections 3.17 and 4.6 relating to broker's fees and finder's fees, Sections 5.2(a) and (d) relating to expenses and indemnities, Section 5.2(e) relating to confidentiality and sharing of information, Section 5.6 relating to confidentiality, Section 5.13 relating to public announcements, Section 8.3 relating to rights upon termination, Section 9.1 relating to fees and expenses, Section 9.4 relating to notices, Section 9.7 relating to third-party beneficiaries, Section 9.8 relating to governing law, Section 9.9 relating to submission to jurisdiction, Section 9.11 relating to personal liability, Section 9.16 relating to waiver of jury trial and this Section 8.2.

Section 8.3 Rights upon Termination.

(a) In the event of any termination of this Agreement prior to the Closing, the Buyer shall be entitled to the immediate return of the Escrow Fund; provided, however, in the event of a termination of this Agreement by the Seller pursuant to (i) Section 8.1(b)(i), (ii) Section 8.1(c), if the failure of the Closing to occur by the Termination Date was the result of the Buyer's failure to perform any of its obligations under this Agreement, (iii) Section 8.1(d), if the order, decree, ruling or other action referred to in Section 8.1(d) causing the termination was caused by the Buyer's failure to perform any of its obligations under this Agreement, or (iv) Section 8.1(e), then in each case the Seller shall be entitled to receive the Escrow Fund as liquidated damages for the damages suffered by Seller (which amount the parties agree is a reasonable estimate of the actual damages that will be suffered by Seller and does not constitute a penalty).

(b) In the event of a termination of this Agreement by the Buyer pursuant to (i) Section 8.1(b)(ii) (other than as a result of a breach of the non-solicitation covenant contained in Section 5.21(b)), (ii) Section 8.1(c), if the failure of the Closing to occur by the Termination Date was the result of the Seller's failure to perform any of its obligations under this Agreement, (iii) Section 8.1(d), if the order, decree, ruling or other action referred to in Section 8.1(d) causing the termination was caused by the Seller's failure to perform any of its obligations under this Agreement or (iv) Section 8.1(f), the Buyer shall be entitled to damages for breach of contract in an amount equal in value to the amount of the Escrow Fund on the date of termination as liquidated damages for the damages suffered by Buyer (which amount the parties agree is a reasonable estimate of the actual damages that will be suffered by Buyer and does not constitute a penalty).

Section 8.4 Other Termination Provisions.

(a) Notwithstanding the foregoing, a party may not rely on the failure of any condition set forth in Article VI to be satisfied if such failure was caused by such party's breach of or failure to perform any of its representations, warranties, covenants or other obligations in accordance with the terms of this Agreement.

(b) The Seller and the Buyer acknowledge and agree that if the Closing does not occur, the Buyer's maximum liability under this Agreement shall be the amount of the Escrow Fund. The Buyer shall only be liable for such amount if the Closing does not occur and the Seller validly terminates this Agreement and is entitled to the Escrow Fund in accordance with Section 8.3, and such payment is intended to be liquidated damages, it being agreed that said amount shall constitute full payment to the Seller for any claim by Seller for any and all damages suffered by the Seller by reason of any such breach by the Buyer of any of its obligations under this Agreement (other than for attorneys fees provided in Section 8.4(c) below) or by reason of any such termination. The Buyer and the Seller agree in advance that actual damages would be difficult to ascertain and that the amount of the Escrow Fund is a fair and equitable amount to reimburse the Seller for damages sustained due to the Buyer's breach of any of its obligations under this Agreement and that said amount does not constitute a penalty or forfeiture and neither the Seller nor the Buyer will seek to assert that the provisions of this Section 8.4(b) are unenforceable in any way.

(c) Notwithstanding any provision in this Agreement that may limit or qualify a party's remedies, in the event of a breach or default by any party that results in a lawsuit or other proceeding for any remedy available under this Agreement, the prevailing party shall be entitled to reimbursement from the breaching or defaulting party of its reasonable legal fees and out-of-pocket expenses (whether incurred at trial or on appeal).

ARTICLE IX

GENERAL PROVISIONS

Section 9.1 Fees and Expenses. Except as otherwise provided herein, all fees and expenses incurred in connection with or related to this Agreement and the Ancillary Agreements and the transactions contemplated hereby and thereby shall be paid by the party incurring such fees or expenses, whether or not such transactions are consummated. In the event of termination of this Agreement, the obligation of each party to pay its own expenses shall be subject to any rights of such party arising from a breach of this Agreement by the other.

Section 9.2 Amendment and Modification. This Agreement may not be amended, modified or supplemented in any manner, whether by course of conduct or otherwise, except by an instrument in writing signed on behalf of each party and otherwise as expressly set forth herein.

Section 9.3 Waiver. No failure or delay of either party in exercising any right or remedy hereunder shall operate as a waiver thereof, nor shall any single or partial exercise of any such right or power, or any abandonment or discontinuance of steps to enforce such right or power, or any course of conduct, preclude any other or further exercise thereof or the exercise of any other right or power. The rights and remedies of the parties hereunder are cumulative and are not exclusive of any rights or remedies, which they would otherwise have hereunder. Any agreement on the part of either party to any such waiver shall be valid only if set forth in a written instrument executed and delivered by a duly authorized officer on behalf of such party.

Section 9.4 Notices. All notices and other communications hereunder shall be in writing, delivered by personal delivery, facsimile transmission or other electronic means reasonably acceptable to both parties (to be followed promptly by written confirmation mailed by certified mail as provided below) or sent by overnight courier service or certified mail, return receipt requested, and shall be deemed duly given on the earliest of (a) the date of personal delivery, (b) the date of confirmed receipt if delivered utilizing a next day service by a recognized next day courier or (c) the date of recipient's written acknowledgement of receipt of facsimile transmissions or other electronic means. All notices hereunder shall be delivered to the addresses set forth below, or pursuant to such other instructions as may be designated in writing by the party to receive such notice:

(a) if to the Seller, to:

and:

and:

(b) if to the Buyer, to:

and:

With copies (which shall not constitute notice) to:

and:

Rejection or other refusal to accept or inability to deliver because of a change of address of which no notice was given shall be deemed to be receipt of the notice.

Section 9.5 Interpretation. When a reference is made in this Agreement to a Section, Article or Exhibit, such reference shall be to a Section, Article or Exhibit of this Agreement unless otherwise indicated. The table of contents and headings contained in this Agreement or in any Exhibit are for convenience of reference purposes only and shall not affect in any way the meaning or interpretation of this Agreement. All words used in this Agreement shall be construed to be of such gender or number as the circumstances require. Any capitalized terms used in the Disclosure Schedules or any Exhibit but not otherwise defined therein shall have the meaning as defined in this Agreement. All Exhibits annexed hereto or referred to herein are hereby incorporated in and made a part of this Agreement as if set forth herein. The word "including" and words of similar import when used in this Agreement shall mean "including, without limitation", unless otherwise specified.

Section 9.6 Entire Agreement. This Agreement (including the Exhibits and Disclosure Schedules hereto), the Ancillary Agreements and the Confidentiality Agreement constitute the entire agreement, and supersede all prior written agreements, arrangements, communications and understandings and all prior and contemporaneous oral agreements, arrangements, communications and understandings among the parties with respect to the subject matter of this Agreement. Neither this Agreement nor any Ancillary Agreement shall be deemed to contain or imply any restriction, covenant, representation, warranty, agreement or undertaking of any party with respect to the transactions contemplated hereby or thereby other than those expressly set forth herein or therein or in any document required to be delivered hereunder or thereunder, and none shall be deemed to exist or be inferred with respect to the subject matter hereof. Notwithstanding any oral agreement of the parties or their Representatives to the contrary, no party to this Agreement shall be under any legal obligation to enter into or complete the transactions contemplated hereby unless and until this Agreement shall have been executed and delivered by each of the parties.

Section 9.7 No Third-Party Beneficiaries. This Agreement shall be binding upon and inure solely to the benefit of each of the parties and their respective successors and assigns, and nothing in this Agreement, express or implied, is intended to or shall confer upon any other Person any legal or equitable right, benefit or remedy of any nature under or by reason of this Agreement, except as provided in Article VII.

Section 9.8 Governing Law. This Agreement and all disputes or controversies arising out of or relating to this Agreement or the transactions contemplated hereby shall be governed by, and construed in accordance with, the internal laws of the State of Delaware, without regard to the laws of any other jurisdiction that might be applied because of the conflicts of laws principles of the State of Delaware.

Section 9.9 Submission to Jurisdiction. Each of the parties irrevocably agrees that any legal action or proceeding arising out of or relating to this Agreement or for recognition and enforcement of any judgment in respect hereof brought by the other party or its successors or assigns may be brought and determined in federal court sitting in the District of Delaware (or, if such court lacks subject matter jurisdiction, in the Delaware Court of Chancery or the Delaware Superior Court), and each of the parties hereby irrevocably submits to the jurisdiction of the aforesaid courts for itself and with respect to its property, generally and unconditionally, with regard to any such action or proceeding arising out of or relating to this Agreement and the transactions contemplated hereby (and agrees not to commence any action, suit or proceeding relating thereto except in such courts). Each of the parties further agrees to accept service of process in any manner permitted by such courts. Each of the parties hereby irrevocably and unconditionally waives, and agrees not to assert, by way of motion or as a defense, counterclaim or otherwise, in any action or proceeding arising out of or relating to this Agreement or the transactions contemplated hereby, (a) any claim that it is not personally subject to the jurisdiction of the above-named courts for any reason other than the failure lawfully to serve process, (b) that it or its property is exempt or immune from jurisdiction of any such court or from any legal process commenced in such courts (whether through service of notice, attachment prior to judgment, attachment in aid of execution of judgment, execution of judgment or otherwise) and (c) to the fullest extent permitted by law, that (i) the suit, action or proceeding in any such court is brought in an inconvenient forum, (ii) the venue of such suit, action or proceeding is improper or (iii) this Agreement, or the subject matter hereof, may not be enforced in or by such courts.

Section 9.10 Disclosure Generally. Notwithstanding anything to the contrary contained in the Disclosure Schedules or in this Agreement, the information and disclosures contained in any Disclosure Schedule shall be deemed to be disclosed and incorporated by reference in any other Disclosure Schedule as though fully set forth in such Disclosure Schedule to the extent the applicability of such information and disclosure in such other Disclosure Schedule is reasonably apparent on its face. The fact that any item of information is disclosed in any Disclosure Schedule shall not be construed to mean that such information is required to be disclosed by this Agreement. Such information and the dollar thresholds set forth herein shall not be used as a basis for interpreting the terms "material" or "Material Adverse Effect" or other similar terms in this Agreement.

Section 9.11 Personal Liability. Notwithstanding anything to the contrary contained herein or in any Ancillary Agreement, it is expressly understood and the parties expressly agree that nothing contained herein or in any Ancillary Agreement or in any other document contemplated hereby or thereby (whether from a covenant, representation, warranty or other provision herein or therein) shall create or be deemed to create or permit any personal liability or obligation on the part of any direct or indirect equityholder of the Seller (or any of its Affiliates) or the Buyer (or any of its Affiliates) or any officer, director, employee, agent, partner, Affiliate or Representative of such equityholder of either party hereto or such party's Affiliates.

Section 9.12 Assignment; Successors. Neither this Agreement nor any of the rights, interests or obligations under this Agreement may be assigned or delegated, in whole or in part, by operation of law or otherwise, by either party without the prior written consent of the other party, and any such assignment without such prior written consent shall be null and void; provided, however, that (i) the Buyer may assign any of its rights and interests and delegate any of its obligations under this Agreement (in whole or in part) to any Affiliate of [ ] and (ii) at or following the Closing, the Buyer may collaterally assign (in whole or in part) its rights hereunder to any bank or other financing institution in connection with the Buyer's financing arrangements, in each case, without the prior consent of the Seller and; provided further, that the Seller may assign any of their rights under this Agreement, including the right to receive the Purchase Price, to one or more Affiliates of the Seller without the prior consent of the Buyer and; provided still further, that no assignment shall limit the assignor's obligations hereunder. Subject to the preceding sentence, this Agreement shall be binding upon, inure to the benefit of, and be enforceable by, the parties and their respective successors and assigns. In addition, the Seller may assign all or any portion of its rights under this Agreement (but not obligations) to a qualified intermediary within the meaning of Section 1.1031(k)-1(g)(4)(iii) of the Code (**"Qualified Intermediary"**), and the Buyer shall cooperate with the Seller as may be reasonably necessary in connection with such assignment and the deferred tax-free exchange to be accomplished in connection therewith, including acknowledging the execution of a written agreement between the Seller and the Qualified Intermediary, subject to reimbursement by the Seller for actual out-of-pocket expenses incurred by the Buyer as the result of a request by the Seller in connection with the foregoing.

Section 9.13 Enforcement.

(a) The Seller agrees that, prior to the Closing, irreparable damage would occur in the event that any of the provisions of this Agreement were not performed by it in accordance with their specific terms or were otherwise breached. Accordingly, prior to the Closing, the Buyer shall be entitled to specific performance of the terms hereof, including an injunction or injunctions to prevent breaches of this Agreement and to enforce specifically the terms and provisions of this Agreement in federal court sitting in the District of Delaware (or, if such court lacks subject matter jurisdiction, in the Delaware Court of Chancery or the Delaware Superior Court), this being in addition to any other remedy to which they are entitled at law or in equity. The Seller further hereby waives (i) any defense in any action for specific performance that a remedy at law would be adequate and (ii) any requirement under any law to post security as a prerequisite to obtaining equitable relief.

(b) Each of the Seller and the Buyer agree that, after the Closing, irreparable damage would occur in the event that any of the provisions of this Agreement were not performed by it in accordance with their specific terms or were otherwise breached. Accordingly, after the Closing, the Buyer or the Seller, as appropriate, shall be entitled to specific performance of the terms hereof, including an injunction or injunctions to prevent breaches of this Agreement and to enforce specifically the terms and provisions of this Agreement in federal court sitting in the District of Delaware (or, if such court lacks subject matter jurisdiction, in the Delaware Court of Chancery or the Delaware Superior Court), this being in addition to any other remedy to which they are entitled at law or in equity. Each of the Seller and the Buyer further hereby waives (i) any defense in any action for specific performance that a remedy at law would be adequate and (ii) any requirement under any law to post security as a prerequisite to obtaining equitable relief.

Section 9.14 Currency. All references to "dollars" or "$" or "US$" in this Agreement or any Ancillary Agreement refer to United States dollars, which is the currency used for all purposes in this Agreement and any Ancillary Agreement.

Section 9.15 Severability. Whenever possible, each provision or portion of any provision of this Agreement shall be interpreted in such manner as to be effective and valid under applicable Law, but if any provision or portion of any provision of this Agreement is held to be invalid, illegal or unenforceable in any respect by a court of competent jurisdiction under any applicable Law or rule in any jurisdiction, such invalidity, illegality or unenforceability shall not affect any other provision or portion of any provision in such jurisdiction, and this Agreement shall be reformed, construed and enforced in such jurisdiction as if such invalid, illegal or unenforceable provision or portion of any provision had never been contained herein and a suitable and equitable provision shall be substituted therefore in order to carry out, so far as may be valid and enforceable, the intent and purpose of such invalid, illegal or unenforceable provision.

Section 9.16 Waiver of Jury Trial. EACH OF THE PARTIES TO THIS AGREEMENT HEREBY IRREVOCABLY WAIVES ALL RIGHT TO A TRIAL BY JURY IN ANY ACTION, PROCEEDING OR COUNTERCLAIM ARISING OUT OF OR RELATING TO THIS AGREEMENT OR THE TRANSACTIONS CONTEMPLATED HEREBY.

Section 9.17 Counterparts. This Agreement may be executed in two or more counterparts, all of which shall be considered one and the same instrument and shall become effective when one or more counterparts have been signed by each of the parties and delivered to the other party.

Section 9.18 Execution. This Agreement may be executed by delivery of a signature by facsimile or other electronic means reasonably acceptable to both parties and such signature shall constitute an original for all purposes.

Section 9.19 No Presumption Against Drafting Party. Each of the Buyer and the Seller acknowledge that each party to this Agreement has been represented by counsel in connection with this Agreement and the transactions contemplated by this Agreement. Accordingly, any rule of law or any legal decision that would require interpretation of any claimed ambiguities in this Agreement against the drafting party has no application and is expressly waived.

[The remainder of this page is intentionally left blank.]

IN WITNESS WHEREOF, the Seller and the Buyer have caused this Agreement to be executed as of the date first written above by their respective officers thereunto duly authorized.

[ ]

By:____
Name:
Title:

[ ]

By:____
Name:
Title:

Courtesy of Owen D. Kurtin, The Vinland Group LLC

APPENDIX B

CABLE OPERATOR-VOIP PROVIDER OUTSOURCING AGREEMENT

MASTER NETWORK SERVICES AGREEMENT

THIS MASTER NETWORK SERVICES AGREEMENT ("Agreement") made this ____ day of [ ] (the "Effective Date"), by and among "Cable Operator", and "VoIP Provider".

WHEREAS, Cable Operator operates telecommunications equipment and systems (each a "Telecommunications System" and, collectively, the "Telecommunications Systems") serving the markets identified on **Exhibit "A"** to this Agreement, as amended from time to time in accordance with the terms of this Agreement (each a "Designated Market" and, collectively, the "Designated Markets"); and

WHEREAS, Cable Operator and VoIP Provider wish to interconnect their respective networks in certain Designated Markets at certain points for the transport and termination of telecommunications traffic, and to be responsible for maintaining and supporting the interconnection arrangements on their respective sides of these interconnection points; and

WHEREAS, Cable Operator wishes to purchase from VoIP Provider certain telecommunications and related services for use in connection with Cable Operator's business, and VoIP Provider desires to provide said telecommunications and related services to Cable Operator; and

WHEREAS, this Agreement sets forth the rates, terms and conditions for said interconnection, maintenance, support, telecommunications and related services;

NOW, THEREFORE, for and in consideration of the mutual promises contained herein and other good and valuable consideration, the receipt and sufficiency of which are hereby acknowledged, the Parties agree as follows:

1. DEFINITIONS; CONSTRUCTION.

1.1 Definitions. In addition to terms defined elsewhere in this Agreement or in any Service Schedule, the following terms used in this Agreement shall have the following meanings:

Act. "Act" means the Communications Act of 1934, as amended, as interpreted by the rules, orders and decisions of any Regulatory Authority.

Affiliate. "Affiliate" means (a) any Person directly or indirectly controlling, controlled by or under common control with another, where "control" means the power to vote fifty percent (50%) or more of the equity securities or comparable interests of the controlled Person, or (b) with respect to Cable Operator for purposes of Section 16.4 only, any Person in which Cable Operator or any Affiliate of Cable Operator owns, directly or indirectly, at least a twenty percent (20%) interest (as defined below). For purposes of paragraph (b) of this definition, (i) an "interest" shall mean an interest in the capital or profits in such Person or in the management of the operations of such Person or an unconditional right to convert into or acquire, directly or indirectly, an interest equal to at least the required interest, and (ii) an "indirect" interest is an interest resulting from ownership through a series of interests (including corporations, partnerships, limited liability companies, joint ventures, or other forms of business organizations), which shall be quantified in amount by a series of percentage multiplications commencing with Cable Operator's direct interest and multiplying that by the next most proximate interest and then multiplying in turn each succeeding interest in order of its progression away from Cable Operator by the result of the immediately preceding multiplication until the most distant percentage interest is multiplied.

Change of Control. "Change of Control" means (i) the acquisition, directly or indirectly, of assets or businesses that generate more than fifty percent (50%) of the consolidated net revenues or net income of the applicable Party or constitute more than fifty percent (50%) of the consolidated assets of the applicable Party, (ii) the acquisition, directly or indirectly, of beneficial ownership of any class of equity securities of the applicable Party greater than fifty percent (50%) of the number of such securities outstanding before such acquisition, or (iii) any merger, consolidation, business combination, binding share exchange or similar transaction involving the applicable Party pursuant to which any Person or the equity holders of any Person acquire beneficial ownership of greater than fifty percent (50%) of any class of equity securities of such Party or of any resulting parent company of such Party, in each case whether in a single transaction or a series of related transactions; provided, however, that in no event shall any merger, consolidation, business combination or other transfer between a Party and an Affiliate of such Party (other than, with respect to VoIP Provider, a Cable Operator Competitor that after the Effective Date becomes an Affiliate of VoIP Provider) constitute a Change of Control hereunder.

Cable Operator Affiliate. "Cable Operator Affiliate" means, at any particular time, any Affiliate of CC Fiberlink, LLC that (i) is authorized or certificated by a Regulatory Authority to provide telecommunications services, including, without limitation, local exchange services, long distance services and/or competitive access services, or (ii) is a provider of information services, as that term is defined in the Act.

Cable Operator Competitor. "Cable Operator Competitor" means any Person that is a CLEC, an RBOC, an ILEC, a provider of broadband services, or a provider of direct broadcast satellite services.

CLEC. "CLEC" means a competitive local exchange carrier.

Customer Premises. "Customer Premises" means the location or locations occupied by Cable Operator to which Service is delivered.

Customer Requested Date. "Customer Requested Date" or "CRD" means the date that Cable Operator requests delivery of any Service under a particular Service Order (as set forth in the applicable Service Order).

Customer Welcome Letter. "Customer Welcome Letter" means a written communication from VoIP Provider to Cable Operator confirming the details of a particular Service Order.

Facilities. "Facilities" means any property owned, licensed or leased by VoIP Provider or any of its Affiliates and used to deliver Service, including terminal and other equipment, conduit, fiber optic cable, optronics, wires, lines, ports, routers, switches, channel service units, data service units, cabinets, racks, private rooms and the like.

ILEC. "ILEC" means an incumbent local exchange carrier as may be determined from time to time by a Regulatory Authority.

IXC. "IXC" means an interexchange carrier.

Legal Requirement. "Legal Requirement" means any law, rule, ordinance, code, statute, regulation, order, writ, injunction, judgment or decree of any governmental or Regulatory Authority.

Local Traffic. "Local Traffic" means (i) any call, including a call to an information service provider, that is originated by an end user of one Party and is terminated at an end user of the other Party within a given LATA, except for those calls that are Switched Access Traffic, (ii) any call, including a call to an information service provider, that is originated in a given LATA by an end user of one Party that is switched and/or transported by the other Party and delivered to a third party's network for termination in that same LATA, or any call that is originated on a third party's network in a given LATA that is switched and/or transported by a Party and delivered to the other Party's network for termination in that same LATA, except in either case for those calls that are Switched Access Traffic, and (iii) cross-boundary, intrastate intraLATA, intrastate interLATA, interstate interLATA, or any other calls determined to be a local call by a Regulatory Authority.

Network Availability. "Network Availability" has the meaning assigned to such term in any applicable Service Schedule.

<u>Off-Net</u>. "Off-Net" means Service that originates from or terminates to any location that is not on the VoIP Provider network.

<u>On-Net</u>. "On-Net" means Service that originates from and terminates to a location that is on the VoIP Provider network.

<u>Person</u>. "Person" means an individual, partnership, limited liability company or partnership, corporation, business trust, joint stock company, trust, unincorporated association, joint venture, business unit, division or other entity of whatever nature.

<u>Point of Interconnection</u>. "Point of Interconnection" means the telecommunications equipment interface(s) in a Designated Market that perform(s) the interconnection function for Cable Operator, on the one hand, and VoIP Provider, on the other hand.

<u>Regulatory Authority</u>. "Regulatory Authority" means the Federal Communication Commission ("FCC"), the United States Congress, any public service or utility commission, state legislative body, administrative agency, any federal, state or local judicial authority, or any other federal, state or municipal agency (including, without limitation, federal, state and local taxation, health, safety and environmental regulatory authorities) having authority over this Agreement, the Parties, the Services, the tariffs or any matter related thereto.

<u>Request for Service Quotation</u>. "Request for Service Quotation" means a document requesting pricing and Service Term to be delivered or transmitted to VoIP Provider's Program Manager, in substantially the same form as **Exhibit "C"** hereto, the initial form of which shall be mutually agreed by the Parties acting in good faith as soon as practically possible after the Effective Date, which sets forth, at a minimum, (i) the Service(s) which are the subject of such Request for Service Quotation, (ii) the Designated Market in which applicable Service(s) are to be provided, (iii) the Customer Requested Date(s) for Service(s) installation, (iv) the Service Term Cable Operator desires, and (v) any other technical or location-specific information reasonably necessary for VoIP Provider to calculate pricing for such Service. The form of Request for Service Quotation may be modified from time to time upon the mutual agreement of the Parties, and neither Party will unreasonably withhold, delay or condition its agreement to any modifications to the form of Request for Service Quotation reasonably requested by the other Party.

Service. "Service(s)" mean, individually and collectively, those VoIP Provider service(s) described in a Service Schedule and identified on a particular line item of a Service Order.

Service Commencement Date. "Service Commencement Date" means the date of Service Acceptance.

Service Order. "Service Order" means a document delivered or transmitted to VoIP Provider's Program Manager, in the form and media prescribed from time to time by VoIP Provider, which sets forth, at a minimum, (i) the Service(s) which are the subject of such Service Order, (ii) the Designated Market in which such Service(s) are to be provided, (iii) the Customer Requested Date(s) for Service(s) installation, (iv) the non-recurring charges and monthly recurring charges for such Service, (v) the applicable Service Term, and (vi) any other installation-related information reasonably necessary for VoIP Provider to provide the Service.

Service Quotation. "Service Quotation" means a document to be delivered or transmitted to Cable Operator's Program Manager in response to a Request for Service Quotation which sets forth the terms of a Service Order to be issued by Cable Operator if Cable Operator chooses (in its sole discretion) to order the Services specified in such Service Quotation. The Service Quotation shall include, without limitation, (i) the Service(s) which are the subject of such Service Quotation, (ii) the Designated Market in which such Service(s) are to be provided, (iii) the Service Term, and (iv) all charges applicable to such Service (if ordered by Cable Operator pursuant to a valid Service Order).

Service Schedule. "Service Schedule" means a schedule attached hereto, or signed between the Parties from time to time and expressly incorporated into this Agreement, setting forth terms and conditions specific to a particular Service.

Service Term. "Service Term" shall mean the duration of time (measured starting on the Service Commencement Date) for which Service is ordered, as specified in the Service Order. The Service Term shall continue on a month-to-month basis after expiration of the stated Service Term, until terminated by either VoIP Provider or Cable Operator upon thirty (30) days' written notice to the other.

Specifications. "Specifications" shall mean accepted industry and national technical guidelines, including those guidelines issued by nationally recognized governing technical standards bodies, and standard telecommunications industry practices, which shall be mutually agreed by the Parties acting in good faith as soon as practically possible after the Effective Date and in any event prior to the delivery of the initial Service Order by Cable Operator to VoIP Provider.

Switched Access Traffic. "Switched Access Traffic" means (i) any call requiring local transmission or switching services for the origination or termination of telephone toll service, including, but not limited to (and provided that in all cases VoIP Provider shall have the option to choose the applicable termination method), the following types of traffic: Feature Group A, Feature Group B, Feature Group C, Feature Group D, toll-free access (e.g., 8XX), 900 access and their successors, and (ii) any interexchange telecommunications call where the originating and terminating points (i.e., end-to-end points) are in different LATAs, or are in the same LATA and the Parties' switched access services are used for the origination or termination of the call.

Term. "Term" means, collectively, the Initial Term and any Renewal Term.

1.2 List of Additional Definitions. The following is a list of additional terms used in this Agreement and a reference to the Section in which such term is defined:

Term:	Section:
Acceptance Testing Period	2.5
Additional Markets	2.2.3

Agreement	Preamble
ANI	3.1.1
Applicable Taxes	6.3
CDR	3.2.3
Cable Operator	Preamble
Cable Operator Designated Affiliate	16.4
Cable Operator Indemnitees	14.1
Claims	14.1
Damages	14.1
Designated Markets	Whereas Clause
Due Date	6.1
Effective Date	Preamble
Excused Outage	9.2
FCC	1.1
Force Majeure Event	11.1
Initial Term	12.1
Indemnitee	14.3
Indemnitor	14.3
Independent Auditor	6.5.1
Installation Period	2.2
Late Delivery Fee	2.6
VoIP Provider	Preamble
VoIP Provider Authorizations	4.1
VoIP Provider Indemnified Parties	14.2
Market Installation Chart	2.2.1
Negotiated Markets	2.2.2
Notice	17.1
Party/Parties	1.3
Program Manager	8.1.1
Proprietary Information	15.1
Readiness Notice	2.4
Rejection Notice	2.5
Renewal Term	12.1
Service Acceptance	2.5
Service Levels	9.1
Service Level Credit	9.2
Service Level Default	9.2
Service Level Standard	9.1

Telecommunications System(s) Whereas Clause

1.3 Construction. Unless otherwise expressly provided in this Agreement, (a) words used in this Agreement, regardless of gender used, shall be deemed and construed to include any other gender, masculine, feminine, or neuter, as the context requires, (b) the word "including" is not limiting, and the word "or" is not exclusive, (c) the capitalized term "Section" refers to sections of this Agreement, (d) references to a particular Section include all subsections thereof, (e) references to a particular statute or regulation include all amendments thereto, rules and regulations thereunder and any successor statute, rule or regulation, or published clarification or interpretations with respect thereto, in each case as from time to time in effect, (f) references to a Person include such Person's successors and assigns to the extent not prohibited by this Agreement, (g) references to a "day" or number of "days" (without the explicit qualification "business") shall be interpreted as a reference to a calendar day or number of calendar days, (h) as the context requires, Cable Operator shall constitute a "Party" to this Agreement, with VoIP Provider constituting the other "Party" to this Agreement (collectively, the "Parties"), and (i) terms that are neither capitalized nor otherwise defined in this Agreement (or in any Service Schedule) are to be construed in accordance with their customary usage in the telecommunications industry.

2. PROVISION OF SERVICE.

2.1 Provision of Service. During the Term, VoIP Provider shall exercise its best commercially reasonable efforts to provide the Services to Cable Operator for the applicable Service Term, pursuant to the rates, terms and conditions set forth herein. Cable Operator shall pay for the Services in accordance with the provisions of Section 6.

2.2 Designated Markets and Installation Dates. In the event that Cable Operator issues a Service Order for Services in any Designated Market, VoIP Provider agrees to have the Services specified in such Service Order installed in that Designated Market within the timeframe specified on the Market Installation Chart (as defined below) for such Service type in the Designated Market, which shall be either 120 or 180 days as provided in Section 2.2.1 (unless a different Installation Period is otherwise agreed to by the Parties in writing with respect to any Designated Market on the Market Installation Chart) or a negotiated timeframe as provided in Section 2.2.2 (any such period, the "Installation Period"). The Parties acknowledge and agree that (x) the Installation Period shall commence upon VoIP Provider's receipt of a Service Order; and (y) with regard to any Service Order for (3)Link® Fiber Termination Service, Cable Operator shall deliver the requisite cable to the designated delivery point on or before the date occurring sixty (60) days prior to expiration of the Installation Period or such Installation Period shall be extended by each day of delay such that VoIP Provider continues to have sixty (60) days to install and deliver the Services under such Service Order before any Late Delivery Fee shall become due under Section 2.6 hereof. Each of VoIP Provider and Cable Operator agrees to cooperate and work together to develop a mutually agreeable schedule for the rollout of Designated Markets over time.

2.2.1 Agreed Upon Installation Intervals. VoIP Provider has agreed to certain maximum timeframes for installation of Services in certain Designated Markets as of the Effective Date as set forth in **Exhibit "D"** hereto (the "Market Installation Chart"). VoIP Provider shall have the right to deliver a modified Market Installation Chart to Cable Operator's Program Manager (whether by electronic mail or as otherwise permitted hereunder) no more often than every sixty (60) days changing the Installation Period for any Designated Market from 120 days to 180 days or vice versa or eliminating any Designated Market from the Market Installation Chart. The Market Installation Chart will only be modified to increase the Installation Period or eliminate a Designated Market in the event LEC facilities are unavailable.

2.2.2 Negotiated Installation Intervals. With respect to those Designated Markets listed on **Exhibit "A"**, but not listed on the Market Installation Chart, as of the Effective Date, VoIP Provider and Cable Operator have not agreed to a maximum timeframe for installation of Services in those Designated Markets (the "Negotiated Markets"). Upon receipt of a Request for Service Quotation from Cable Operator for a Service in any Negotiated Market, VoIP Provider and Cable Operator shall, in good faith, negotiate and agree upon in writing a commercially reasonable Installation Period.

2.2.3 **Additional Designated Markets**. At any time and from time to time during the Term, Cable Operator may add additional markets in which it operates Telecommunications Systems to the list of Designated Markets set forth at **Exhibit "A"** by providing written notice of such additional markets to VoIP Provider (the "Additional Markets"). Within thirty (30) days after receipt of such notification, VoIP Provider shall, if applicable, notify Cable Operator's Program Manager in writing, by facsimile or by electronic mail of VoIP Provider's updated Market Installation Chart for such Additional Markets and any Additional Markets not included on VoIP Provider's updated Market Installation Chart shall be Negotiated Markets.

2.3 **Ordering**. At any time and from time to time during the Term, Cable Operator may, but is not obligated to, order Service(s) from VoIP Provider by issuing Service Orders. Prior to the issuance of any Service Order, Cable Operator shall submit a Request for Service Quotation. VoIP Provider shall use its best commercially reasonable efforts to deliver a Service Quotation in response to any Request for Service Quotation within (x) for fiber termination, fourteen (14) calendar days and (y) for all other Services, five (5) business days. All Service Quotations shall remain valid for thirty (30) days following the date of issuance irrespective of delivery by VoIP Provider of any revised Market Installation Chart following issuance by VoIP Provider of a Service Quotation. If, upon receipt of such Service Quotation, Cable Operator desires to order the Services described in such Service Quotation, Cable Operator shall issue a Service Order to VoIP Provider. The Parties acknowledge and agree that no Service Order may be issued unless and until VoIP Provider has provided Cable Operator a Service Quotation. VoIP Provider shall use its best commercially reasonable efforts to deliver a Customer Welcome Letter to Cable Operator within ten (10) days of receipt by VoIP Provider of any Service Order.

2.4 **Installation and Support**. VoIP Provider shall complete installation, testing and activation of the Service(s) in a Designated Market before the expiration of the applicable Installation Period. VoIP Provider and Cable Operator shall work cooperatively to complete their individual and jointly required work in a timely manner in order that VoIP Provider may install, test and activate the Service(s) before the expiration of the applicable Installation Period. At no cost to Cable Operator, VoIP Provider or its respective subcontractors or agents shall provide all equipment, facilities and personnel necessary to install, activate and test all Services, including components thereof, and billing systems, databases and equipment supporting the Services. Upon completion of installation, testing and activation of each Service in a Designated Market, VoIP Provider will notify Cable Operator, in writing, that such Service is installed and functioning properly in accordance with all Specifications (the "Readiness Notice"). In no event will VoIP Provider deliver a Readiness Notice prior to the applicable Customer Requested Date.

2.5 <u>Acceptance Testing</u>. Cable Operator may, in its discretion, conduct any reasonable tests of the Service(s) in a Designated Market for seven (7) days (the "Acceptance Testing Period") following the date of Cable Operator's receipt of each Readiness Notice. During the Acceptance Testing Period, Cable Operator may reject the Service(s) in the applicable Designated Market, by providing VoIP Provider with a written, facsimile or electronic notice indicating such rejection ("Rejection Notice"), if the Service(s) or any portion or component thereof are not installed and functioning properly in accordance with the Service Order and Specifications. Upon receipt of a Rejection Notice, VoIP Provider shall correct the deficiencies within five (5) business days, and the Parties shall thereupon repeat the acceptance testing procedure set forth in this Section. Cable Operator shall indicate acceptance of a Service in a Designated Market ("Service Acceptance") by either (x) a written, facsimile or electronic acknowledgement that the Service(s) are installed and functioning properly in accordance with the Service Order and Specifications, or (y) if a Rejection Notice is not received by VoIP Provider prior to the expiration of the Acceptance Testing Period, Cable Operator's Service Acceptance of the Service(s) will be presumed, as of the first calendar day immediately thereafter.

2.6 <u>Failure to Meet Installation Date</u>. VoIP Provider agrees that its obligation to timely install, activate and test Service(s) in a Designated Market that function properly in accordance with the terms of Section 2.5 above before the expiration of the applicable Installation Period is the essence of this Agreement. VoIP Provider's failure to deliver Service within the applicable Installation Period shall be deemed a material breach of its obligation to timely install, activate and test Service(s) in a Designated Market that function properly in accordance with the Service Order and the Specifications and VoIP Provider shall grant to Cable Operator, for each day or portion thereof which elapses from the time of such breach until Service Acceptance, an amount of liquidated damages equal to $5,000 per day for the first ten (10) days of delay following the expiration of the Installation Period and $10,000 per day for each day of delay thereafter in the form of credits against charges for Services hereunder, subject to a cap of $100,000 per Service Order ("Late Delivery Fee"). Unless otherwise specified by Cable Operator, any Late Delivery Fee will be applied by VoIP Provider to reduce Cable Operator's required payment for the Services for the next succeeding month following the month in which the Late Delivery Fee was incurred, and any Late Delivery Fee amount that would exceed Cable Operator's required payment for the Services during such succeeding month will be carried forward and applied against each subsequent payment required by Cable Operator for such Services until used in full; provided, however, that in no event will any Late Delivery Fee be applied to reduce a single month's payment, for either (i) Off-Net Services, or (ii) (3)Voice® Termination Services, by more than thirty percent (30%). VoIP Provider acknowledges and agrees that (i) the injury caused to Cable Operator by VoIP Provider's breach of its obligation to timely install, activate and test Service(s) that function properly in accordance with the Service Order and the Specifications before the expiration of the applicable Installation Period is difficult or impossible of accurate estimation, (ii) the Parties intend that the Late Delivery Fee provides for damages, rather than a penalty, and (iii) the Late Delivery Fee constitutes a reasonable pre-estimate of the probable loss or injury that will be caused to Cable Operator by VoIP Provider's breach. The Late Delivery Fee shall be Cable Operator's sole and exclusive remedy for any failure by VoIP Provider to deliver Service(s) within the applicable Installation Period, subject to Cable Operator's termination rights in Section 12.2.2(a).

2.7 **Customer Premises**. Cable Operator shall allow VoIP Provider access to the Customer Premises to the extent reasonably necessary for the installation, inspection and scheduled or emergency maintenance of Facilities relating to the Service. VoIP Provider shall repair, at its sole expense, to the reasonable satisfaction of Cable Operator, or shall reimburse Cable Operator for the actual and reasonable cost of repairing, any damage to the Customer Premises resulting from VoIP Provider access to the Customer Premises, and VoIP Provider shall indemnify Cable Operator for any Damages resulting from any Claims related to or arising out of VoIP Provider access to the Customer Premises in accordance with Section 14.1. VoIP Provider shall notify Cable Operator as early as is reasonably feasible but in any case at least two (2) business days (unless a shorter time period is otherwise agreed by the Parties) in advance of any regularly scheduled maintenance that will require access to the Customer Premises or that may result in any interruption of Service, provided that VoIP Provider shall exercise commercially reasonable efforts to avoid any interruption of Cable Operator's Service during any such maintenance activity. Cable Operator will be responsible for providing and maintaining, at its own expense, the level of power, heating and air conditioning necessary to maintain the proper environment for the Facilities on the Customer Premises, provided that VoIP Provider has advised Cable Operator in advance as to the characteristics and requirements of such a proper environment. In the event Cable Operator fails to do so, Cable Operator shall reimburse VoIP Provider for the actual and reasonable cost of repairing or replacing any Facilities damaged or destroyed as a result of Cable Operator's failure.

2.8 <u>VoIP Provider Facilities</u>. Except as may otherwise be agreed in writing between the Parties, title to all Facilities shall remain with VoIP Provider. VoIP Provider will provide and maintain the Facilities in good working order. VoIP Provider shall correct or repair any problems or performance deficiencies affecting Cable Operator's Service which may occur in the Facilities or in any Service within a reasonable time. Cable Operator shall not, and shall not permit others (other than VoIP Provider's employees, agents, and representatives) to, rearrange, disconnect, remove, attempt to repair, or otherwise tamper with any Facilities, without the prior written consent of VoIP Provider, which consent shall not be unreasonably withheld, delayed, or conditioned. The Facilities shall not be used for any purpose(s) other than either (i) that for which Cable Operator has indicated in writing to VoIP Provider it intends to use the Facilities or (ii) that for which VoIP Provider provides them. Cable Operator shall not take any action that causes the imposition of any lien or encumbrance by a third party on the Facilities. Except in the case of VoIP Provider's gross negligence or willful misconduct and as otherwise provided hereunder, in no event will VoIP Provider be liable to Cable Operator or any other Person for interruption of Service or for any other loss, cost or damage caused by or related to improper use of the Facilities by Cable Operator or third parties provided access to the Facilities by Cable Operator in violation of this Agreement, and Cable Operator shall reimburse VoIP Provider for any damages incurred as a result thereof. Cable Operator agrees (which agreement shall survive the expiration, termination or cancellation of this Agreement or any Service Order) to allow VoIP Provider to remove the Facilities from the Customer Premises, provided that VoIP Provider shall repair at its sole expense any damage to the Customer Premises caused by such removal:

(A) after termination, expiration or cancellation of the Service Term in connection with which the Facilities were used; or

(B) for repair, replacement or otherwise as VoIP Provider may determine is necessary or desirable, but VoIP Provider shall use reasonable efforts to avoid, if possible, or to minimize disruptions to the Service caused thereby.

2.9 <u>Interoperability Testing</u>. VoIP Provider and Cable Operator shall jointly conduct interoperability testing of all necessary equipment, facilities and applications to ensure Cable Operator's call flows can be supported by the VoIP Provider network. VoIP Provider and Cable Operator shall mutually agree in writing on entrance and exit requirements for such interoperability testing. In the event that the Parties do not complete interoperability testing within thirty (30) days prior to the conclusion of the Installation Period, then the Parties shall immediately commence installation of time division multiplexing (TDM) interfaces for the routing or termination of Cable Operator's telephone calls, unless otherwise agreed by the Parties in writing. Notwithstanding the Parties' installation of TDM interfaces, the Parties will continue to jointly conduct interoperability testing in order to establish Internet Protocol delivery of communications between the Parties.

3. <u>SERVICES</u>. Notwithstanding any contrary term hereof, the Parties acknowledge and agree that all Services hereunder shall be provided in North America only, except long distance service (via the provision of (3)Voice® Termination Services) terminated to international destinations.

3.1 Interconnection. Subject to the terms, conditions and limitations set forth in this Agreement (and execution by each Party of all relevant Service Schedule(s) not attached to this Agreement as of the Effective Date as provided in Section 17.13), VoIP Provider shall provide interconnection in Designated Markets between the Telecommunications Systems of Cable Operator and the network facilities of VoIP Provider in order to provide the Services required under this Agreement, including the transport and termination of Local Traffic and Switched Access Traffic.

3.1.1 Signaling. The Parties shall cooperate to configure their respective interconnection facilities to exchange all appropriate signaling messages, including SS7 signaling and SIP signaling (or SIP-T, if mutually agreed by the Parties), to facilitate full interoperability of all CLASS features and functions generally used in the industry between their respective networks. All SIP or SS7 (or SIP-T, if mutually agreed by the Parties), as applicable, signaling parameters generally used in the industry will be provided, including automatic number identification (ANI), originating line information (OLI), calling company category, and charge number, in conjunction with each Party's interconnection facilities, where and as available in accordance with all Specifications.

3.1.2 Capacity. The Parties shall cooperate to ensure that all interconnection facilities in a Designated Market that interconnect VoIP Provider's network and Cable Operator's Telecommunications System are of sufficient capacity based on the Parties' traffic forecasts and historical traffic utilization measurements, as mutually shared between the Parties from time to time.

3.1.3 Other Calling Services. As applicable to the Service ordered, VoIP Provider shall cooperate with Cable Operator to transport and terminate all types of calls based on routing supplied by Cable Operator on its switch that may be delivered by Cable Operator to VoIP Provider, whether such calls require specialized dialing arrangements or translations, and call information, including, but not limited to, the following: (i) N11 service code calls (i.e., 211, 311, 511, 611, 711 and 811),

(ii) dial around service calls (i.e., 10-10-XXX-XXXX), (iii) calling card and credit card calls, (iv) telecommunications relay service calls, (v) toll-free calls (e.g., 8XX), and (vi) calling name (CNAM) functionality. The Parties acknowledge and agree that the provisioning of the calling services described in this Section is not included in VoIP Provider's rates for any Services and such calling services shall not be a part of the Service provided by VoIP Provider to Cable Operator under this Agreement.

3.2 **Long Distance Service.** Subject to the terms, conditions and limitations set forth in this Agreement, upon Cable Operator's request, VoIP Provider shall provide long distance service (via the provision of (3)Voice® Termination Services) to Cable Operator in Designated Markets for the transport and termination of intrastate, interstate and international long distance calls. VoIP Provider's long distance services will originate over dedicated outbound facilities from a Telecommunications System in a Designated Market and be transported and terminated by VoIP Provider over facilities comprising the VoIP Provider network.

3.2.1 **Long Distance Services.** VoIP Provider shall offer to Cable Operator usage based long distance services. The rates for such products are described on **Exhibit "A"** to the applicable Service Schedule and, unless otherwise provided for herein, shall remain fixed throughout the Term.

3.2.2 **Billing Increments.** VoIP Provider shall rate all long distance calls as follows: (i) domestic United States, Alaska, Hawaii, Puerto Rico, U.S. Virgin Islands and Canada calls in six (6) second increments, subject to a six (6) second minimum charge, (ii) international (except Canada and Mexico) calls in six (6) second increments, subject to a thirty (30) second minimum charge, and (iii) Mexico calls in sixty (60) second increments, subject to a sixty (60) second minimum charge.

3.2.3 **Call Detail Records.** VoIP Provider will provide Cable Operator with call detail records ("CDRs") in a machine-readable format on a monthly, weekly or daily basis, as specified by Cable Operator, which shall include, at a minimum, the originating and terminating numbers, the originating and terminating times, and the duration of the call.

3.3 **Resale of Services.** Cable Operator may resell the Service to third party "end users"; provided that Cable Operator agrees to indemnify, defend and hold VoIP Provider harmless from any claims made against VoIP Provider by such end users arising from their use of the Service, except for claims arising from VoIP Provider's gross negligence or willful misconduct.

3.4 **Acceptable Use Policy**. Cable Operator represents and warrants that the traffic passed to VoIP Provider in its provision of Services hereunder does not transit the public Internet. In the event that the Services change so that such traffic does transit the public Internet, the Parties agree to work in good faith to negotiate and agree to terms regarding Cable Operator's compliance with VoIP Provider's Acceptable Use Policy or agreement on an alternative policy or terms. Notwithstanding the foregoing, VoIP Provider shall have the right to block any traffic from customers that is adversely affecting the VoIP Provider network.

4. VOIP PROVIDER OBLIGATIONS.

4.1 **Certifications.** VoIP Provider shall, or shall cause its designated Affiliates to, obtain and maintain in full force and effect (at VoIP Provider's sole cost and expense) all licenses, authorizations, approvals, permits, tariffs (or in lieu thereof, appropriate price lists) and certifications from all Regulatory Authorities necessary to operate as a CLEC and as an IXC in each Designated Market where VoIP Provider is providing Services in such capacity ("VoIP Provider Authorizations").

4.2 **Legal Requirements.** VoIP Provider shall, or shall cause its designated Affiliates to, comply with all Legal Requirements applicable to the offering of the Services and for operation as a CLEC and as an IXC in each Designated Market where VoIP Provider is providing Services in such capacity, including obtaining and maintaining VoIP Provider Authorizations.

4.3 **Interconnection Agreements.** VoIP Provider represents and warrants that it has, or its designated Affiliates have, entered into all interconnection and related agreements with ILECs and other CLECs serving the Designated Markets where VoIP Provider is providing applicable Services necessary to enable, among other things, the transport and termination of Local Traffic and Switched Access Traffic, consistent with required signaling protocols, and all other required interconnection services in accordance with applicable law and all Specifications.

4.4 Traffic Delivery. VoIP Provider shall support Cable Operator's delivery of Local Traffic, Switched Access Traffic and other telecommunications traffic at a Point of Interconnection using Internet Protocol or time division multiplexing formats. At no cost to Cable Operator, VoIP Provider shall purchase, lease or provide the equipment necessary to receive such traffic.

4.5 Equipment and Related Services. Except as otherwise provided for herein, VoIP Provider shall, at its sole cost and expense, purchase, lease and provide all equipment, facilities and personnel necessary to provide the Services to Cable Operator, and design, configure, deploy, monitor and maintain all components comprising each Service in accordance with applicable Legal Requirements and industry standards.

4.6 Trouble Management/Reporting. VoIP Provider shall provide a trouble management interface permitting Cable Operator to report network impairments, outages, and other Service related problems and deficiencies. VoIP Provider will provide monthly reports to Cable Operator detailing ineffective attempts, blocking and other such measurements mutually agreed upon by the Parties. VoIP Provider shall also provide timely reports to Cable Operator describing network outages and performance problems and deficiencies.

5. RATES AND CHARGES. The Parties acknowledge and agree that VoIP Provider is not purchasing any service or product from Cable Operator under this Agreement.

5.1 Rates.

(a) Cable Operator shall pay VoIP Provider for the Services at the rates set forth on **Exhibit "A"** to the applicable Service Schedule or as set forth in the applicable Service Order. VoIP Provider's charges for any

Services in a Designated Market shall begin to accrue on (and in any event not before) the applicable Service Commencement Date, regardless of whether Cable Operator has procured services from other providers needed to operate the Service, and regardless of whether Cable Operator is otherwise prepared to accept delivery of ordered Service. Except as agreed in writing by the Parties, VoIP Provider shall not assess any charges on Cable Operator for any Services or other telecommunications products, equipment or services not specified on any **Exhibit "A"** to a Service Schedule or in any Service Order.

(b) Unless otherwise expressly specified in the Service Order, any non-recurring charges shall be invoiced by VoIP Provider to Cable Operator upon the Service Commencement Date. However, in the event such Service requires VoIP Provider to install additional infrastructure, cabling, electronics or other materials in the provision of the Service, such Service Order may include (as specified therein) non-recurring charges that are payable by Cable Operator in advance of the Service Commencement Date, as specifically agreed between the Parties in writing. In the event Cable Operator fails to pay such non-recurring charges within the time period specified in the Service Order, (i) the Installation Period for such Service shall be tolled until such time as the non-recurring charges are paid, and (ii) VoIP Provider may suspend installation of the Service until receipt of such non-recurring charges. If Cable Operator requests and VoIP Provider approves (in its sole and reasonable discretion) any changes to the Service Order or Service, additional non-recurring charges and/or monthly recurring charges related to (i) costs already incurred by VoIP Provider in processing the original Service Order and/or Service, and (ii) additional or increased cost structure for the Service ordered under this modified Service Order may apply, as mutually agreed by the Parties.

5.2 **Rate Review.** VoIP Provider shall meet with Cable Operator no more often than every six (6) months to determine whether (and, if so, what) adjustments to the rates and charges for each of the Services are appropriate by virtue of, with respect to Cable Operator, decreases as a result of technological or marketplace developments, and with respect to VoIP Provider, increases as a result of increases in its direct costs to provide (3)Voice® Termination Services. At these meetings the Parties, acting in good faith, will determine by mutual agreement whether (and, if so, what) adjustments to the rates and charges are appropriate by virtue of such developments, in order to preserve for Cable Operator and VoIP Provider the expected benefit of the rates and charges for Services provided in connection with this Agreement. The intent of the Parties is that the rates and charges for Services provided pursuant to the Agreement remain competitive throughout the Term with the rates and charges available in the marketplace for the Services. VoIP Provider may request a rate increase only in the event VoIP Provider experiences an increase in its direct costs (as determined under generally accepted accounting principles) incurred by VoIP Provider (expressly excluding labor costs and costs of capital or borrowed funds) in providing the (3)Voice® Termination Services hereunder, which costs are payable by VoIP Provider to a third party (excluding a VoIP Provider Affiliate), and only to the extent of such increase in direct costs. If, upon completing the rate review, the Parties: (i) agree that Cable Operator's rates and charges for the Services should be adjusted in accordance with this Section, then the Parties shall promptly execute an amendment to this Agreement prospectively adjusting Cable Operator's rates and charges for the Services, or (ii) do not agree on whether Cable Operator's rates and charges for the Services should be adjusted or the amount of such adjustment in accordance with this Section, then if VoIP Provider does not reduce rates as requested by Cable Operator or elects to increase rates in accordance with this Section 5.2 notwithstanding Cable Operator's objection to such increase, then Cable Operator may, upon written notice to VoIP Provider, discontinue any Services subject to such disagreement, without any liability whatsoever other than payment for Services provided through the effective date of discontinuance.

5.3 **Least Cost Routing.** If Cable Operator is purchasing Services from VoIP Provider in any Designated Market where Cable Operator utilizes least cost routing and where there is at least one (1) provider from whom Cable Operator is purchasing services using LATA-tiered pricing, then Cable Operator must purchase (3)Voice ® Termination Services from VoIP Provider on a LATA-tiered pricing basis. In the event VoIP Provider believes Cable Operator has failed to properly implement LATA-tiered pricing for VoIP Provider, VoIP Provider shall provide written notice to Cable Operator that it will implement LATA-tiered pricing within five (5) business days unless Cable Operator provides evidence that it has either implemented LATA-tiered pricing for VoIP Provider or that it is not purchasing on a LATA-tiered basis from another provider of services in the applicable Designated Market. If Cable Operator is purchasing Services from VoIP Provider in any Designated Market where Cable Operator utilizes least cost routing and where there is at least one (1) provider from whom Cable Operator is purchasing services using OCN-based pricing, then VoIP Provider shall have the right to elect either to (i) continue to provide Services to Cable Operator in such Designated Market utilizing the pricing method then in effect under this Agreement, (ii) change to providing Services to Cable Operator in such Designated Market using OCN-based pricing upon thirty (30) days' advance written notice to Cable Operator, which notice shall include VoIP Provider's OCN-based pricing for such Designated Market, or (iii) discontinue providing Services to Cable Operator in such Designated Market effective no less than thirty (30) days after VoIP Provider provides written notice to Cable Operator of VoIP Provider's election to discontinue providing Services in such Designated Market.

6. BILLING AND PAYMENT.

6.1 Monthly Payments. The Parties shall invoice one another for Services on a monthly basis on a Point of Interconnection-by-Point of Interconnection basis (unless otherwise requested by Cable Operator). The Parties shall bill in advance for Service to be provided during the upcoming month, except for charges that are dependent upon usage of Service, which are billed in arrears, and billing for any partial month shall be prorated based on a calendar month. Subject to Section 6.2, each Party shall pay all undisputed amounts set forth on an invoice no later than thirty (30) days after receipt of the other Party's invoice (the "Due Date").

6.2 Disputed Invoices. In the event a Party disputes any portion of the other Party's invoice, the disputing Party shall pay the undisputed portion of the invoice by the Due Date, and shall submit to the other Party a written claim for the disputed amount, which claim shall set forth with specificity the disputing Party's grounds for such dispute. All such claims must be submitted to the non-disputing Party within one (1) year from the date of invoice for those Services. The disputing Party waives the right to dispute any charges not disputed within such one (1) year period. The Parties shall, acting in good faith, attempt to resolve the dispute within forty-five (45) days (or such longer period as may be agreed upon) after the date of receipt of the disputing Party's claim. If the dispute is not resolved within such time period, then the matter shall be escalated to and considered by a team from each Party consisting of an executive-level manager for each Party who has the authority to settle the dispute but who has not been involved in the day-to-day performance under this Agreement. If such dispute has not been settled by the Parties within an additional thirty (30) days (or such longer period as may be agreed upon), then the disputed amounts shall become due and payable, and neither this provision nor the voluntary payment of such amounts shall prevent the disputing Party from pursuing any available legal remedies to obtain a refund or payment of such amounts. During the resolution of disputes under this Section, the Parties shall, in good faith, continue to perform their respective obligations under this Agreement. Any discussions, negotiations or other communications between the Parties with regard to any disputed amounts, including any negotiations conducted pursuant to this Section, shall be deemed and treated as confidential compromise and settlement discussions for purposes of the Federal Rules of Evidence and state rules of evidence.

6.3 **Taxes and Fees.** All charges for Service are net of Applicable Taxes (as defined below). Except for taxes based on VoIP Provider's net income and taxes assessed on VoIP Provider's tangible or intangible property, Cable Operator will be responsible for all applicable taxes that arise in any jurisdiction on the provision, sale or use of the Service and required or permitted by applicable law to be passed through to Cable Operator, including, without limitation, value added, consumption, sales, use, gross receipts, excise, access, bypass, franchise or other taxes, fees, duties, charges or surcharges (collectively, "Applicable Taxes"). If a Party is entitled to an exemption from any Applicable Taxes, such Party shall be responsible for presenting the other Party with a valid exemption certificate. Both Parties will give effect to any such valid exemption certificate to the extent it applies to any Service billed by a Party to the other Party. For clarification purposes, the Parties acknowledge and agree that this Section does not apply to nor shall VoIP Provider have any responsibility for taxes and fees of Cable Operator's end user customers.

6.4 **Interest.** All amounts due from either Party to the other Party under this Agreement that are not paid when due shall bear interest, payable on demand, from and including thirty (30) days after the Due Date up to but excluding the date of payment at an interest rate equal to the lesser of 1.0% per month or the maximum rate permitted by applicable law.

6.5 Audit Rights. From time to time during the Term, but not more often than once during any period of twelve (12) consecutive months, upon not less than thirty (30) days' prior written notice, each Party shall have the right to examine, at its sole cost and expense and during normal business hours, the books and records of the other Party as reasonably necessary to verify such Party's compliance with its obligations under this Agreement; provided, however, that any audit of financial and usage information shall be limited to the period of one (1) year from the date of invoice or Service delivery, as applicable.

6.5.1 Audit Procedure. If any discrepancy is found during an examination made pursuant to Section 6.5 that leads the Party conducting such examination to believe in good faith that the amount owed by the other Party is greater or lesser than the amount that was paid by such Party, then the Parties shall act in good faith to attempt to resolve the payment dispute within forty-five (45) days (or such longer period as may be agreed upon) of completion of such examination. If the payment dispute is not resolved within such time period, then the matter shall be escalated to and considered by a team from each Party consisting of an executive-level manager for each Party who has the authority to settle the dispute but who has not been involved in the day-to-day performance under this Agreement. If such dispute has not been settled by the Parties within an additional thirty (30) days (or such longer period as may be agreed upon), then the payment dispute shall be finally settled by an audit conducted by a nationally recognized firm of certified public accountants ("Independent Auditor") mutually agreed upon by the Parties. All adjustments, if any, due hereunder shall be paid by the Party owing such amount within thirty (30) days of the conclusion of such determination. If the Party who is the subject of the audit is determined to owe an additional amount, the actual and reasonable fees and expenses incurred by the Party who conducted the examination pursuant to Section 6.5 and the actual and reasonable fees of any Independent Auditor shall be borne by such Party, except where the adjustment is less than five percent (5%) of the total payment amount owed (including the additional amount paid based on the results of such audit), in which case the fees and expenses (including the fees of any Independent Auditor) shall be borne by the Party conducting the examination.

6.5.2 Information Disclosed During Audit. Any books and records of a Party that are examined pursuant to Section 6.5 shall constitute Proprietary Information under this Agreement, notwithstanding the lack of restrictive notices or other express communications to the effect that the information in such books or records is proprietary. Any Independent Auditors engaged pursuant to Section 6.5.1 shall be required to execute a confidentiality agreement prior to the commencement of any audit, which agreement shall contain confidentiality provisions at least as protective as those in this Agreement.

6.6 Fraudulent Use of Services. The Parties shall jointly cooperate and work together in good faith to identify fraudulent use of any Service and to take all appropriate and necessary action in response to any such fraudulent use. Cable Operator is responsible for all charges attributable to Cable Operator incurred respecting the Service even if incurred as the result of fraudulent or unauthorized use of Service; except that Cable Operator shall not be responsible for fraudulent or unauthorized use by VoIP Provider or its employees or agents.

7. REPRESENTATIONS AND WARRANTIES.

7.1 Cable Operator's Representations and Warranties. Cable Operator represents and warrants to VoIP Provider as follows:

7.1.1 Organization and Qualification of Cable Operator. Cable Operator is duly organized, validly existing, and in good standing under the laws of the state of its organization, has all requisite power and authority to own and operate the Telecommunications Systems that it owns and operates, and is duly qualified to do business and is in good standing in all jurisdictions in which the ownership of its Telecommunications Systems or the nature of its activities in connection with such Telecommunications Systems makes such qualification necessary, in each case with such exceptions as would not materially and adversely affect the ability of Cable Operator to perform its obligations under this Agreement.

7.1.2 <u>Authority; Binding Effect</u>. Cable Operator has all requisite power and authority to execute, deliver, and perform its obligations under this Agreement. The execution, delivery, and performance of this Agreement on the part of Cable Operator have been duly authorized by all necessary action on the part of Cable Operator. This Agreement has been duly and validly executed and delivered by Cable Operator and is the valid and binding obligation of Cable Operator, enforceable against Cable Operator in accordance with its terms, except as enforceability may be limited by applicable bankruptcy, insolvency, reorganization, moratorium or similar laws affecting creditors' rights generally or by principles governing the availability of equitable remedies.

7.1.3 <u>Non-Contravention; Consents</u>. The execution, delivery, and performance by Cable Operator of this Agreement do not and will not: (a) contravene any provision of the organizational and governing documents of Cable Operator, (b) violate any provision of any Legal Requirements applicable to it, (c) violate, result in a breach of, constitute a default under (without regard to requirements of notice, lapse of time, or elections of any other Person, or any combination thereof), accelerate, or permit the acceleration of the performance required by, any contract, license, lease, indenture, mortgage, loan agreement, note, or other agreement or instrument to which Cable Operator is a party or by which Cable Operator or the assets or properties owned or leased by Cable Operator are bound or affected, (d) result in the creation or imposition of any lien against or upon any of the Telecommunications Systems, or (e) require any consent, approval or authorization of, or filing of any certificate, notice, application, report, or other document with, any Regulatory Authority or other Person (other than those that have been or will be obtained or filed on a timely basis), in each case the effect of which would be to materially and adversely affect the ability of Cable Operator to perform its obligations under this Agreement.

7.1.4 <u>Compliance with Legal Requirements</u>. Cable Operator is in compliance in all material respects with all Legal Requirements applicable to the Telecommunications Systems and their operation, including the rules and regulations of any applicable Regulatory Authority, and holds all franchises, authorizations, certificates, permits, and licenses necessary under applicable Legal Requirements for operation of the Telecommunications Systems as currently conducted.

7.1.5 **Non-Infringement.** The operation of the Telecommunications Systems as currently conducted does not infringe upon, or otherwise violate, the rights of any Person in any U.S. copyright, trade name, trademark right, service mark, service name, patent, patent right, license, or trade secret, and there is not pending or, to the knowledge of Cable Operator, threatened any action with respect to any such infringement or violation that would materially and adversely affect Cable Operator's ability to perform its obligations under this Agreement.

7.2 **VoIP Provider's Representations and Warranties.** VoIP Provider represents and warrants to Cable Operator as follows:

7.2.1 **Organization and Qualification of VoIP Provider.** VoIP Provider is duly organized, validly existing, and in good standing under the laws of the state of its organization, has all requisite power and authority to own and operate the properties and assets that it owns and operates and to conduct its activities related to the provision of the Services, and is duly qualified to do business and is in good standing in all jurisdictions in which the ownership of its properties and the nature of its activities related to the provision of the Services makes such qualification necessary, in each case with such exceptions as would not materially and adversely affect the ability of VoIP Provider to perform its obligations under this Agreement.

7.2.2 **Authority; Binding Effect.** VoIP Provider has all requisite power and authority to execute, deliver, and perform its obligations under this Agreement. The execution, delivery, and performance of this Agreement on the part of VoIP Provider have been duly authorized by all necessary action on the part of VoIP Provider. This Agreement has been duly and validly executed and delivered by VoIP Provider and is the valid and binding obligation of VoIP Provider, enforceable against VoIP Provider in accordance with its terms, except as enforceability may be limited by applicable bankruptcy, insolvency, reorganization, moratorium, or similar laws affecting creditors' rights generally or by principles governing the availability of equitable remedies.

7.2.3 Non-Contravention; Consents. The execution, delivery, and performance by VoIP Provider of this Agreement do not and will not: (a) contravene any provision of the organizational and governing documents of VoIP Provider, (b) violate any provision of any Legal Requirements applicable to VoIP Provider, (c) violate, result in a breach of, constitute a default under (without regard to requirements of notice, lapse of time, or elections of any other Persons, or any combination thereof), accelerate, or permit the acceleration of the performance required by, any contract, license, lease, indenture, mortgage, loan agreement, note, or other agreement or instrument to which VoIP Provider is a party or by which VoIP Provider or the assets or properties owned or leased by VoIP Provider are bound or affected, (d) result in the creation or imposition of any lien against or upon any of the assets or properties owned or leased by VoIP Provider, or (e) require any consent, approval or authorization of, or filing of any certificate, notice, application, report, or other document with, any Regulatory Authority or other Person (other than those that have been or will be obtained or filed on a timely basis), in each case the effect of which would be to materially and adversely affect the ability of VoIP Provider to perform its obligations under this Agreement.

7.2.4 Compliance with Legal Requirements. VoIP Provider is in compliance in all material respects with all Legal Requirements applicable to its operations and the Services to be provided by VoIP Provider hereunder, including the rules and regulations of any applicable Regulatory Authority, and holds all franchises, authorizations, certificates, permits, and licenses necessary under applicable Legal Requirements with respect to the Services to be provided by VoIP Provider hereunder.

7.2.5 Non-Infringement. VoIP Provider's provision of the Services hereunder do not infringe upon, or otherwise violate, the rights of any Person in any U.S. copyright, trade name, trademark right, service mark, service name, patent, patent right, license, or trade secret, and there is not pending or, to the knowledge of VoIP Provider, threatened any action with respect to any such infringement or violation that would materially and adversely affect VoIP Provider's ability to perform its obligations under this Agreement.

7.2.6 Warranty. VoIP Provider warrants that all work performed in connection with the Services to be provided hereunder shall be performed to industry standards and in a workmanlike manner. EXCEPT AS EXPRESSLY SET FORTH IN THIS AGREEMENT, VOIP PROVIDER MAKES NO WARRANTIES OR REPRESENTATIONS, EXPRESS OR IMPLIED, EITHER IN FACT OR BY OPERATION OF LAW, STATUTORY OR OTHERWISE, INCLUDING WARRANTIES OF MERCHANTABILITY OR FITNESS FOR A PARTICULAR USE.

8. ADDITIONAL COVENANTS.

8.1 Program Managers; Technical Cooperation.

8.1.1 Program Managers. Each of Cable Operator and VoIP Provider shall appoint, as appropriate, a full-time program manager (each, a "Program Manager") to manage the implementation of this Agreement and to act as the primary point of contact between the Parties on all operational issues related to this Agreement, other than technical matters as provided in Section 8.1.2. The initial Program Managers are specified on **Exhibit "B"** to this Agreement. Except to the extent either Party otherwise notifies the other Party, each Program Manager shall be authorized to act (but shall not by virtue of being designated as a Program Manager be deemed to have authority to sign any written agreement) on behalf of the Party that appointed the Program Manager in all matters pertaining to the implementation of this Agreement. The Program Managers shall meet frequently (including by teleconference), but not less than weekly, to review the status of the installation and provision of Services in Designated Markets, and other pertinent information regarding performance by the Parties of their respective obligations hereunder. Either Party may name a replacement Program Manager by notifying the other of such replacement.

8.1.2 Technical Cooperation. Cable Operator and VoIP Provider shall consult and cooperate with each other with regard to all technical matters relating to network architecture, interconnection and related matters. Cable Operator and VoIP Provider shall each designate a technical engineering representative to be the primary point of contact under this Agreement with regard to all technical matters. The initial technical engineering representatives are specified on **Exhibit "E"** to this Agreement. With respect to all urgent technical matters, VoIP Provider shall also utilize the contact information for Cable Operator set forth in the Cable Operator NSOC Escalation chart appended to **Exhibit "E"**, and Cable Operator shall use the emergency contact information for VoIP Provider appended to **Exhibit "E"**.

8.2 **Trade Names and Trademarks.** Neither Party shall (a) use the trade names or trademarks of the other Party, (b) represent in any manner that it has any rights in or to any of the other Party's trade names or trademarks, (c) register or attempt to register any trade names or trademarks of the other Party, or (d) do or cause to be done any act or thing impairing the distinctiveness of the trade names or trademarks of the other Party.

8.3 **Notices.** VoIP Provider shall promptly notify Cable Operator of any request by an ILEC for approval from any Regulatory Authority to block traffic from VoIP Provider, and shall promptly provide Cable Operator a copy of any written notice or communication to or from any such ILEC related to any such request. If either Party becomes aware of any other material and adverse event that such Party determines in its reasonable judgment threatens the ability of VoIP Provider to provide the Services hereunder, such Party shall promptly provide written notice of such event to the other Party and the Parties shall meet promptly to discuss such event and appropriate courses of action. Such notice shall include, and such meetings shall be for the purpose of discussion of, the following information: (i) describe the event in reasonable detail, (ii) describe any action taken or threatened to be taken by any ILEC as a result of such event that could materially and adversely affect the Services under this Agreement, and (iii) list any Designated Markets that could potentially be affected by such event.

9. REMEDIES FOR SERVICE LEVEL DEFAULTS.

9.1 **Service Level Standards.** VoIP Provider provides specific remedies regarding performance of Service as set forth in the particular Service Schedule ("Service Levels"). Each Service Level will be measured by VoIP Provider in each Designated Market on a monthly basis and the performance standards for each Service Level (each, a "Service Level Standard") are set forth in the applicable Service Schedule. VoIP Provider shall implement and operate all measurement and monitoring tools and procedures required to measure each Service Level using industry standard methods and shall provide written reports to Cable Operator for each Designated Market on a monthly basis in such format as VoIP Provider and Cable Operator mutually agree. Cable Operator shall be entitled to audit VoIP Provider's measurement, monitoring, and reporting process for each Service Level in any one or more Designated Markets for the period commencing one (1) year prior to the date of such audit through and until the current date. Cable Operator also shall be entitled to conduct its own performance testing in order to confirm VoIP Provider's performance of each Service Level; provided, however, that any testing conducted by Cable Operator shall not interfere with operations of the network. Service Level testing shall commence on the date on which Services become generally available to customers on a commercial basis in any Designated Market.

9.2 **Service Level Defaults.** If VoIP Provider fails to meet any Service Level Standard for reasons other than an Excused Outage in any month in any Designated Market (a "Service Level Default"), VoIP Provider promptly shall (i) perform an analysis to determine the cause of any incident that contributed to such Service Level Default and shall provide a report to Cable Operator, (ii) implement all commercially reasonable remedial actions, and (iii) take all commercially reasonable actions to prevent recurrence of such Service Level Default, in each case at the expense of VoIP Provider. If any Service Level Default occurs, Cable Operator shall receive a credit (a "Service Level Credit") upon request by Cable Operator as described in the applicable Service Schedule for the affected Service. The Parties acknowledge that a failure to meet a Service Level Standard contained in a particular Service Schedule that does not provide for Service Level Credits may cause a Service Level Default under a separate Service Schedule, and, in such event, the Service Level Credits under such separate Service Schedule shall apply. To request a Service Level Credit, Cable Operator must contact VoIP Provider Customer Service or deliver a written request (with sufficient detail necessary to identify the affected Service) within one (1) year of the end of the month for which a credit is requested. VoIP Provider Customer Service may be contacted by calling toll free in the U.S. 1-877-4LEVEL3 (1-877-453-8353) or such other numbers for VoIP Provider Customer Service in other countries as published on www.level3.com. Except for any Late Delivery Fee, in no event shall the total amount of credits issued to Cable Operator per month exceed the non-recurring charges, the monthly recurring charges and usage charges invoiced to Cable Operator for the affected Service for that month. In the event of any damages arising out of VoIP Provider's furnishing or failure to furnish Services under this Agreement, Cable Operator's sole remedies are contained in (a) the Service Levels applicable (if any) to the affected Service, (b) the chronic outage provision (if any) set forth in the Service Schedule applicable to the affected Service, (c) Section 2.6 above, and (d) Cable Operator's right to terminate under Sections 12.2.2(a) and 12.2.2(b). Once issued by VoIP Provider pursuant to the request procedure above, any Service Level Credit shall be applied to reduce Cable Operator's required payments for Services for the next succeeding month following the month in which the Service Level Credit was issued, and any Service Level Credit amount that would exceed Cable Operator's required payment for Services during such succeeding month will be carried forward and applied against each subsequent payment required by Cable Operator until used in full; provided, however, that in no event will any Service Level Credit be applied to reduce a single month's payment, for either (i) Off-Net Services, or (ii) (3)Voice® Termination Services, by more than thirty percent (30%). Notwithstanding the foregoing, VoIP Provider shall not be required to provide any Service Level Credit to Cable Operator (i) if a Service Level Standard is not met during scheduled network maintenance windows; provided, however, that, for the avoidance of doubt, any failure to meet a Service Level Standard during any change in location, configuration or method of any Interconnection or any relocation of a VoIP Provider Facility shall not be deemed to be scheduled network maintenance, (ii) if VoIP Provider notified Cable Operator at least twenty (20) business days prior to the beginning of the month in which the Service Level Default occurred of the need to augment Cable Operator's network and Cable Operator's failure to do so in a timely manner can be definitively shown to be the direct and primary cause of the applicable Service Level Default, (iii) if a Service Level Standard is not met and the direct and primary cause is due to either (x) any action or inaction of Cable Operator or any subscriber or end user of Cable Operator or (y) any Cable Operator provided power or equipment, or (iv) if a Service Level Default occurred as a result of a Force Majeure Event (each such event, an "Excused Outage").

10. CHANGES IN LAW.

10.1 Changes Affecting Enforceability. If any change in Legal Requirements occurs during the Term that results in this Agreement or any material term of this Agreement being determined to be unlawful or unenforceable or that has a material adverse effect on the provision of any Services pursuant to this Agreement (other than any assessment of taxes or fees on the revenues generated or paid pursuant to this Agreement), then this Agreement shall be amended so as to comply with any such change in Legal Requirements. Cable Operator and VoIP Provider shall negotiate in good faith regarding any modifications required to the terms and conditions of this Agreement as a result of any such change in Legal Requirements so as to place the Parties as nearly as possible in the same positions as prior to such change in Legal Requirements.

10.2 Changes Affecting Economics. If any change in Legal Requirements occurs during the Term that materially increases or decreases the costs or other terms of delivery of Service (on an industry-wide basis), VoIP Provider and Cable Operator will negotiate regarding the rates to be charged to Cable Operator to reflect such increase or decrease in cost and, in the event that the Parties are unable to reach agreement respecting new rates within sixty (60) days, or such other period that the Parties may mutually agree to, after either Party's delivery of written notice requesting renegotiation, then (i) VoIP Provider may pass such increased costs through to Cable Operator (if and only if VoIP Provider passes such increased costs through to all of its similarly situated customers); provided, that, in the event of such an increase Cable Operator may terminate the affected Service without termination liability by delivering written notice of termination no later than thirty (30) days after the effective date of the rate increase, or (ii) VoIP Provider shall reduce prices for the affected Service(s) to incorporate such decreased costs. In no event shall Cable Operator be required to pay any increased costs under this Section until such time as VoIP Provider is required to make payment to a third party of the increased costs resulting from the change in Legal Requirements.

11. FORCE MAJEURE.

11.1 Performance Excused. If the performance of this Agreement is delayed or prevented by reason of acts of God or of the public enemy; earthquakes; fires; floods or other catastrophes; epidemics or quarantines; freight embargoes; war; civil strife; insurrection; riot; materials shortages; or labor stoppages or any other action outside the reasonable control of a Party (each, a "Force Majeure Event"), then the Party whose performance is delayed or prevented shall promptly notify the other Party of the Force Majeure Event and shall be excused from performance to the extent delayed or prevented (and the other Party shall be excused from any corresponding performance for the same period); provided, however, that the Party whose performance is delayed or prevented shall take all reasonable steps to avoid or remove such cause of nonperformance and shall continue to perform whenever and to the extent reasonably possible, and provided further that any time for performance set forth in this Agreement shall be extended for a period equal to the period of any such delay. VoIP Provider has in effect, and shall maintain in effect throughout the Initial Term and any Renewal Term, a disaster recovery plan, and VoIP Provider shall provide a copy of its disaster recovery plan in effect from time to time to Cable Operator.

11.2 Termination Right. If it appears that a time for delivery or performance under this Agreement will be extended or interrupted for more than seven (7) consecutive days due to a Force Majeure Event with respect to VoIP Provider, Cable Operator shall have the right to terminate this Agreement with respect to Services in any Designated Market affected by the Force Majeure Event upon notice to VoIP Provider of the Force Majeure Event.

12. TERM AND TERMINATION.

12.1 Term of the Agreement. The initial Term of this Agreement shall commence upon the Effective Date and shall continue until December 31, 2007 (the "Initial Term"). This Agreement shall automatically renew, on the same terms and conditions, for two (2) successive one-year periods (each, a "Renewal Term"), unless Cable Operator provides VoIP Provider with notice to the contrary at least ninety

(90) days prior to the expiration of the Initial Term or any then-effective Renewal Term. To the extent that the Service Term for any Service extends beyond the Term, then this Agreement shall remain in full force and effect for such Service until the expiration or termination of such Service Term.

12.2 Termination of Agreement. This Agreement may be terminated upon any of the following events, effective on the date specified in the notice of termination delivered by the terminating Party:

12.2.1 Termination by Either Party. Either Party may terminate this Agreement in the event of any of the following defaults:

(a) If the other Party applies for or consents to the appointment of a trustee or receiver for any substantial part of its properties; any bankruptcy, reorganization, debt arrangement, dissolution or liquidation proceeding is commenced or consented to by the other Party; or any application for appointment of a receiver or a trustee, or any proceeding for bankruptcy, reorganization, debt management or liquidation is filed for or commenced against the other Party, and is not withdrawn or dismissed within sixty (60) days thereafter;

(b) If the other Party ceases to function as a going concern; or

(c) If the other Party fails to perform in a material respect any of the material provisions of this Agreement (other than provisions for which a specific remedy is provided for in this Agreement) and does not cure such failure within thirty (30) days after receipt of notice from the other Party specifying such failure in reasonable detail and stating such Party's intention to terminate this Agreement if such failure is not cured (or if such failure cannot reasonably be cured with such thirty (30) day period, such Party has not undertaken all commercially reasonable efforts to cure such failure within such thirty (30) day period and does not cure such failure with sixty (60) days).

12.2.2 Termination by Cable Operator. Cable Operator may terminate this Agreement:

(a) If VoIP Provider fails to deliver Service within ten (10) days after the expiration of the applicable Installation Period on four (4) or more occasions during any consecutive twelve (12) month period;

(b) If VoIP Provider is liable under this Agreement for Service Level Credits that, at any given time, exceed an amount equal to ten percent (10%) of the sum of Cable Operator's charges for Services incurred during the shorter of (i) the immediately preceding twelve (12) month period, or (ii) the time period beginning on the Effective Date and continuing through and until the date of termination under this Section 12.2.2(b);

(c) If a Change of Control of VoIP Provider to a Cable Operator Competitor occurs; or

(d) Pursuant to Section 10 or Section 11.2.

12.2.3 Termination by VoIP Provider. VoIP Provider may suspend or terminate a Service if Cable Operator fails to make any payment required hereunder on or before the date occurring thirty (30) days following the Due Date and such failure continues for a period of ten (10) days after written notice of intent to suspend or terminate from VoIP Provider.

12.2.4 Partial Termination As To Designated Markets. A Party shall have the right to exercise any termination rights pursuant to this Section 12 to terminate this Agreement with respect to any one or more Designated Markets rather than terminating the entire Agreement.

12.3 Termination for Convenience. Cable Operator may terminate this Agreement for convenience during the Term at any time upon 180 days' written notice (with sufficient detail necessary to identify the affected Service) to VoIP Provider; provided, however that Cable Operator shall be subject the termination charges in Section 12.4 below.

12.4 Termination Charges.

(a) PREINSTALLATION CANCELLATION: In the event that Cable Operator terminates this Agreement or any Service pursuant to the terms of Section 12.3 above prior to VoIP Provider's installation of the Service, or in the event that the delivery of such Service is terminated by VoIP Provider as the result of an uncured default by Cable Operator pursuant to Section 12.2.1 or 12.2.3 of this Agreement, Cable Operator shall pay VoIP Provider a termination charge equal to the sum of:

(i) any third party cancellation/termination charges related to the installation and/or cancellation of any Off-Net Service;

(ii) the non-recurring charges (including any non-recurring charges that were waived by VoIP Provider at the time of the Service Order; provided that such waived non-recurring charges shall be calculated in an amount proportionate to the remainder of the applicable Service Term for the cancelled Service (e.g., if waived non-recurring charges equal $10,000 with twelve (12) months remaining on a twenty-four (24) month Service Term, the amount owed by Cable Operator for termination under this subsection (ii) would be equal to $5,000)) for the cancelled Service, if not already paid, to the extent actually incurred by VoIP Provider (such as actual out-of-pocket costs paid and a reasonable and appropriate allocation of internal costs); and

(iii) one (1) month's monthly recurring charges for any cancelled On-Net Service.

Cable Operator's right to cancel any particular Service under this Section 12.4(a) shall automatically expire and shall no longer apply upon VoIP Provider's delivery to Cable Operator of a Readiness Notice for such Service.

(b) POST-INSTALLATION TERMINATION: In the event that during any applicable Service Term Cable Operator terminates this Agreement or any Service pursuant to the terms of Section 12.3 above after receipt by Cable Operator of the Readiness Notice for such

Service or in the event that the delivery of Service is terminated by VoIP Provider as a result of an uncured default by Cable Operator pursuant to Section 12.2.1 or Section 12.2.3 of this Agreement, Cable Operator shall pay VoIP Provider a termination charge equal to the sum of:

(i) any third party cancellation/termination charges related to the installation and/or termination of any Off-Net Service;

(ii) the non-recurring charges (including any non-recurring charges that were waived by VoIP Provider at the time of the Service Order; provided that such waived non-recurring charges shall be calculated in an amount proportionate to the remainder of the applicable Service Term for the cancelled Service (e.g., if waived non-recurring charges equal $10,000 with twelve (12) months remaining on a twenty-four (24) month Service Term, the amount owed by Cable Operator for termination under this subsection (ii) would be equal to $5,000)) for the cancelled Service, if not already paid, to the extent actually incurred by VoIP Provider (such as actual out-of-pocket costs paid and a reasonable and appropriate allocation of internal costs); and

(iii) the percentage of the monthly recurring charges for any terminated On-Net Service calculated from the effective date of termination and as applicable to the Service Term that was ordered and delivered, equal to (i) one hundred percent (100%) of the remaining monthly recurring charges that would have been incurred for the Service for months 1-12 of the Service Term, plus (ii) twenty-five percent (25%) of the remaining monthly recurring charges that would have been incurred for the Service for months 13 through the end of the Service Term.

12.5 **Orderly Transition.** Upon the expiration or termination of this Agreement for any reason (other than a termination by VoIP Provider pursuant to Section 12.2.1 or 12.2.3), in whole or with respect to any Designated Market and subject to the then-existing rates and terms under this Agreement, the Parties shall cooperate in good faith to effect an orderly transition of the Services for such period of time as Cable Operator may request up to six (6) months after the expiration or effective date of termination of this Agreement and in compliance with all applicable Legal Requirements; provided, however, that if such transition period serves to extend Cable Operator's Service Term beyond any applicable expiration date, Cable Operator agrees to reimburse VoIP Provider for any documented and actual increases in VoIP Provider's underlying costs for the Services in transition from those costs in existence upon commencement of the original Service Term for such Service. As applicable, the Parties shall use commercially reasonable efforts to develop and implement a plan for the orderly transition of Services as soon as commercially practicable. The Parties shall cooperate fully with each other and with any applicable third party carriers in effecting such transition plan and shall take all reasonable actions requested by any Party in connection therewith.

13. <u>LIMITATION OF LIABILITY; LIQUIDATED DAMAGES</u>.

13.1 <u>Damages Disclaimer</u>. NO PARTY SHALL BE LIABLE TO ANY OTHER PARTY FOR INDIRECT, INCIDENTAL, PUNITIVE, CONSEQUENTIAL, EXEMPLARY, RELIANCE OR SPECIAL DAMAGES SUFFERED BY SUCH OTHER PARTY (INCLUDING DAMAGES FOR HARM TO BUSINESS, LOST PROFITS, LOST REVENUES OR LOST SAVINGS), REGARDLESS OF THE FORM OF ACTION, WHETHER IN CONTRACT, WARRANTY, STRICT LIABILITY, THIRD PARTY CLAIM, TORT (INCLUDING NEGLIGENCE OF ANY KIND), OR ANY OTHER LEGAL THEORY, TO THE EXTENT SUCH DAMAGES ARISE FROM OR IN CONNECTION WITH THE PERFORMANCE OR NONPERFORMANCE OF THIS AGREEMENT OR ANY ACTS OR OMISSIONS ASSOCIATED THEREWITH.

13.2 <u>Exceptions</u>. Notwithstanding the foregoing Section 13.1 to the contrary, each Party's liability to the other Party shall not be limited: (i) for willful or intentional misconduct, or fraud, or (ii) for any loss resulting from injury to or the death of any Person or from the loss of or damage to real or personal property or the environment, in each case when such injury, death, loss or damage is proximately caused by the gross negligence or willful acts or omissions on the part of Cable Operator or VoIP Provider or their respective agents, subcontractors, or employees, or

(iii) with respect to the Parties' respective indemnification obligations undertaken in Section 14 or with respect to any breach thereof, or (iv) with respect to the Parties' respective confidentiality obligations undertaken in Section 15 or with respect to any breach thereof.

13.3 **Liquidated Damages.** If VoIP Provider takes corrective action pursuant to Section 8(C) of the (3)Link® Fiber Termination Service (North America) Service Schedule and it is ultimately determined that neither Cable Operator, its Representatives, nor the Customer Owned Fiber was the cause of the problem (as set forth in such Section of such Service Schedule), VoIP Provider shall pay to Cable Operator in cash as liquidated damages and not as a penalty the sum of $.50 per affected end user of Cable Operator's services for each hour (or fraction of an hour) that Service is unavailable as a result of any suspension of an Interconnection or other action taken by VoIP Provider pursuant to Section 8(C) of such Service Schedule, subject to a cap of $100,000.

14. INDEMNIFICATION.

14.1 **Indemnification by VoIP Provider.** VoIP Provider shall indemnify and hold harmless Cable Operator, its Affiliates, and each of their respective officers, directors, employees, stockholders, partners, members and agents, and the successors and assigns of any of them (collectively, the "Cable Operator Indemnitees"), from and against any and all third party claims, judgments, fines, damages, losses, liabilities, costs, or expenses of any nature (including reasonable attorneys', accountants' and experts' fees and disbursements) (collectively, "Damages"), that any Cable Operator Indemnitee may suffer arising from or out of or relating to:

(a) Any and all third party claims, demands, actions, suits or proceedings, whether civil, criminal, administrative or investigative (collectively, "Claims") of any Person respecting damage to tangible property, personal injury or death resulting from the negligence, willful misconduct, or fraud of VoIP Provider; and

(b) Any Claims of any Person caused by, relating to, or arising out of VoIP Provider's relationships with its employees, agents, and consultants in the course of its performance under this Agreement.

14.2 **<u>Indemnification by Cable Operator</u>.** In addition to the indemnification provision of Section 3.3, Cable Operator shall indemnify and hold harmless VoIP Provider, its Affiliates, and each of their respective officers, directors, employees, stockholders, partners, members, and agents, and the successors and assigns of any of them (collectively, "VoIP Provider Indemnified Parties") from and against any and all Damages arising from or out of or relating to:

(a) Any Claims of any Person relating to any acts or omissions of VoIP Provider in providing the Services to be provided by VoIP Provider pursuant to this Agreement (except to the extent that any Damages result from or relate to any breach by VoIP Provider of its obligations under this Agreement or are attributable to the negligence, willful misconduct, or fraud of VoIP Provider or any VoIP Provider Indemnitee seeking indemnification under this Section 14.2 or to the extent such Damages are covered by insurance maintained by VoIP Provider or such other VoIP Provider Indemnitee);

(b) Any Claims of any Person respecting damage to tangible property, personal injury or death resulting from the negligence, willful misconduct, or fraud of Cable Operator; and

(c) Any Claims of any Person relating to or arising out of Cable Operator's relationships with its employees, agents, and consultants in the course of its performance under this Agreement.

14.3 **<u>Procedures</u>.** Any Person asserting a right to indemnification under this Section 14 (an "Indemnitee") shall so notify the Party from which indemnification is sought (the "Indemnitor") promptly in writing, provided that the failure to give such notice shall not result in the loss of indemnification rights unless and to the extent the Indemnitor is materially prejudiced by such failure. If the facts giving rise to such indemnification involve any actual or threatened Claim by or against a third party, the Indemnitor shall be entitled to control the defense or prosecution of such Claim in the name of the Indemnitee. The Indemnitor shall notify the Indemnitee in writing of its intention to do so within twenty (20) days of the receipt of the notice demanding indemnification from the Indemnitee. The Indemnitee shall have the right, however, to participate in any such proceeding controlled by the Indemnitor through counsel of its own choosing, which participation shall be at its sole expense. If there are one or more legal defenses available to an Indemnitee that conflict with those available to, or that are not available to, the Indemnitor, the Indemnitee shall have the right, at the expense of the Indemnitor, to engage separate counsel reasonably acceptable to the Indemnitor and to participate in any such proceeding. Each Indemnitee shall, to the extent requested by the Indemnitor and at the Indemnitor's expense, cooperate in the prosecution or defense of such Claim and shall furnish such records, information and testimony and attend such conferences, discovery proceedings, hearings, trials and appeals as may be reasonably requested in connection therewith. If the Indemnitor does not undertake to prosecute or defend any Claim within the specified time after receipt of a notice demanding indemnification, the Indemnitee may, but shall have no obligation to, contest any proceeding with respect to such Claim, and the Indemnitor shall be bound by the result obtained with respect thereto by the Indemnitee. The Indemnitee may not settle any proceeding with respect to which the Indemnitee is entitled to indemnification hereunder without the consent of the Indemnitor, which consent shall not be unreasonably withheld, delayed, or conditioned. Any reasonable expenses incurred by any Indemnitee in defending any Claim (or the threat thereof), other than a Claim brought by the Indemnitor, if incurred prior to the assumption by the Indemnitor of the defense thereof, shall be borne and paid by the Indemnitor, in advance of the final disposition of such Claim (or the threat thereof).

14.4 **Settlement.** The Indemnitor shall have the right to settle any Claim for which it is responsible hereunder; provided that the Indemnitor shall not settle any Claim unless the Indemnitee consents in writing to such settlement, which consent shall not be unreasonably withheld, delayed, or conditioned, and which consent shall not be withheld in connection with any such settlement that provides for a general release of the Indemnitee and is for money damages to be paid by the Indemnitor only, that does not (i) admit the fault of the Indemnitee, or (ii) impose injunctive or other equitable relief on the Indemnitee. At any time after the commencement of any proceeding relating to any Claim, the Indemnitor may request the Indemnitee to agree in writing to the abandonment of such Claim or to the payment or compromise by the Indemnitor of such Claim, whereupon such action will be taken unless the Indemnitee determines that the proceeding should be continued and so notifies the Indemnitor within fifteen (15) days of such request from the Indemnitor. Any request from the Indemnitor that any Claim be abandoned shall specify the amount that the other party or parties to the contested Claim have agreed to accept in payment or compromise of the Claim. If the Indemnitee determines that the proceeding should be continued, the Indemnitor shall be liable under this Agreement only to the extent of the lesser of (i) the amount that the other party or parties to the contested Claim had agreed to accept in payment or compromise as of the time the Indemnitor made its request therefor to the Indemnitee, as specified in the Indemnitor's request, or (ii) the amount for which the Indemnitor may be liable with respect to such Claim by reason of the provisions of this Agreement.

14.5 Intellectual Property Indemnification.

14.5.1 Intellectual Property Indemnity. Each Party shall indemnify, defend, and hold harmless the other Party and its Affiliates, and their respective directors, officers, employees, agents, successors and assigns, from and against any and all Damages arising from or out of or relating to any Claim that alleges, in the case of VoIP Provider, that the Cable Operator Telecommunications Systems, and in the case of Cable Operator, that any aspect of the Services provided by VoIP Provider under this Agreement, infringes any patent, trademark, copyright or trade secret, except where and to the extent that the Claim arises out of or results from modifications to the Telecommunications Systems or the Services, as applicable, or combinations of the Telecommunications Systems or the Services, as applicable, with other services or products, by VoIP Provider or Cable Operator, as applicable, other than any such modifications or combinations as may have been mutually agreed by the Parties in writing.

14.5.2 Procedures. Whenever a Party is responsible for indemnification under Section 14.5.1, such Party may, at its option, either procure the right for the other Party to continue performance under this Agreement, or may replace or modify the alleged infringing service or product so that the Services become noninfringing.

15. <u>CONFIDENTIALITY</u>.

15.1 <u>Proprietary Information</u>. Cable Operator and VoIP Provider agree that any information or data (including information or data received by the disclosing Party from a third party and as to which the disclosing Party has confidentiality obligations) (a) fixed in a tangible medium and furnished by one to the other under this Agreement and marked as the confidential or proprietary information of the disclosing Party, including information relating to the Services, (b) otherwise provided or disclosed and stated to be confidential or proprietary at the time the information is provided or in a writing which is provided within thirty (30) days thereafter which generally describes such information, or (c) relating to the terms and conditions of this Agreement (including, without limitation, pricing, Service Levels, and network information or maps) is, in each case, the confidential or proprietary information of the disclosing Party (collectively, the "Proprietary Information"), and shall not be used for any purpose other than the purposes of this Agreement or disclosed to anyone other than to the recipient's employees or agents or consultants rendering services related to the subject matter of this Agreement who need to use the Proprietary Information for the purposes of this Agreement.

15.2 <u>Exceptions Required by Law</u>. Notwithstanding the provisions of Section 15.1, a Party receiving Proprietary Information may disclose such Proprietary Information if required by applicable Legal Requirements or any listing agreement or arrangement to which such Party or any of its Affiliates is a Party with a national securities exchange or association, provided that the disclosing Party has given reasonable notice to the other Party in advance of such disclosure and seeks confidential treatment of such information from the Person to which the disclosure is made.

15.3 <u>Other Exceptions</u>. The restrictions and obligations in Section 15.1 shall not apply with respect to any Proprietary Information that the receiving Party can demonstrate: (a) is or becomes generally available to the public through any means other than a breach by the receiving Party of its obligations under this Agreement, (b) is disclosed to the receiving Party without an obligation of confidentiality by a third party who the receiving Party reasonably believes has the right to make such disclosure, (c) is developed independently by the receiving Party, (d) was in possession of the receiving Party without obligations of confidentiality prior to receipt under this Agreement, or (e) is required to be disclosed to enforce rights under this Agreement.

15.4 **Remedies.** Each Party acknowledges and agrees that the other Party would be irreparably harmed if any of the Proprietary Information of the disclosing Party were to be disclosed to third parties, or if any use were to be made of such Proprietary Information other than that specified in this Agreement, and further agrees that the disclosing Party shall have the right to seek and obtain injunctive relief upon any violation or threatened violation of the terms of this Agreement, in addition to all other rights and remedies available at law or in equity.

15.5 **Return of Proprietary Information.** Upon the termination, cancellation or expiration of this Agreement for any reason or upon the reasonable request of the disclosing Party, all Proprietary Information, together with any copies that may be authorized herein, shall be returned to the disclosing Party (at the expense of the disclosing Party) or, if requested by the disclosing Party, certified destroyed by the receiving Party.

15.6 **Media Releases.** Except for informational releases intended solely for Cable Operator's or VoIP Provider's confidential internal distribution and except for disclosures required by applicable Legal Requirements or any listing agreement or arrangement to which such Party or any of its Affiliates is a party with a national securities exchange or association, all media releases, public announcements or public disclosures by Cable Operator or VoIP Provider or by their respective Affiliates, relating to this Agreement shall be coordinated and approved by the Parties prior to such release. Such approvals shall not be unreasonably withheld, delayed, or conditioned.

16. ASSIGNMENT.

16.1 **Assignment.** No Party shall assign, transfer, delegate, sublease, sublicense or in any other manner dispose of or extend to any other Person, any of its rights, privileges or obligations under this

Agreement without the prior written consent of the other Party, and any attempt to make any such assignment, transfer, delegation, sublease, sublicense or disposition without consent shall be null and void; provided, however, that a Party may, without the consent of the other Party, assign, transfer or delegate all of such rights, privileges and obligations to any Affiliate of such Party or to any successor in the event of such Party's sale of all or substantially all of its assets, sale of stock, merger, consolidation, reorganization or other business combination.

16.2 **<u>Sale or Transfer of Network Assets</u>.** If any Affiliate of Cable Operator sells or otherwise transfers one or more, but not all, of the network assets comprised of cable systems owned and operated by such Person in a Designated Market, VoIP Provider's consent for the assignment, transfer, delegation, sublease, sublicense or disposition of Cable Operator's rights, privileges or obligations under this Agreement with respect to such transferred cable systems shall not be required, provided that Cable Operator notifies VoIP Provider of the sale or transfer of such systems, assigns all of its rights, and such transferee assumes all of Cable Operator's obligations, under this Agreement with respect to the systems included in such transactions, and such transferee's financial condition is reasonably acceptable to VoIP Provider. In such event, if requested by Cable Operator, VoIP Provider will negotiate in good faith with the transferee of such systems to enter into a separate agreement with respect to such cable systems on substantially the same terms and conditions as this Agreement.

16.3 **<u>Addition of Network Assets</u>.** If any Affiliate of Cable Operator acquires network assets that may be used by Cable Operator to deliver Services pursuant to this Agreement, Cable Operator may, but shall not be required to, elect to include such network assets under this Agreement and, upon VoIP Provider's written approval, which shall not be unreasonably withheld, delayed, or conditioned, the Parties shall amend this Agreement as appropriate to reflect such addition.

16.4 **<u>Participation by Affiliates</u>.** Upon Cable Operator's request, VoIP Provider will offer the same terms and conditions of this Agreement to any Affiliate of Cable Operator if and so long as such Person meets the requirements of either paragraph (a) or paragraph (b) of the definition of Affiliate (each, a "Cable Operator Designated Affiliate");

provided, however, that the financial condition of such Cable Operator Designated Affiliate shall be reasonably acceptable to VoIP Provider or VoIP Provider shall be entitled to require a deposit from such Cable Operator Designated Affiliate that is reasonable under the circumstances or to impose such other requirements that may be reasonably required to secure performance by such Cable Operator Designated Affiliate of its financial obligations to VoIP Provider. VoIP Provider agrees to negotiate in good faith with any Cable Operator Designated Affiliate regarding any such additional terms related to securing financial performance by such Cable Operator Designated Affiliate. If any Cable Operator Designated Affiliate ceases to be an Affiliate of Cable Operator during the Term, then Cable Operator shall use its best commercially reasonable efforts to give prompt written notice of such fact to VoIP Provider. In such event, the Service Term for any existing Service ordered by a Cable Operator Designated Affiliate shall continue until its expiration or termination in accordance with its terms, and any new Services (or renewal of existing Services) that may be ordered by any former Cable Operator Designated Affiliate shall not be governed by the terms and conditions of this Agreement and instead shall be governed by such new and separate terms and conditions as VoIP Provider may negotiate with such former Cable Operator Designated Affiliate. For clarification purposes the Parties each acknowledge and agree that from and after the date any Cable Operator Designated Affiliate ceases to be an Affiliate of Cable Operator, VoIP Provider shall have no obligation (a) to provide future Service (whether new Service or a renewal of existing Service), (b) provide any Service Quotation, or (c) accept any Service Order from such Cable Operator Designated Affiliate.

17. MISCELLANEOUS.

17.1 Notices. Any notice, request, approval, authorization, consent or other communication required or permitted to be given or made pursuant to this Agreement (each, a "Notice") shall be in writing and shall be deemed given on the earliest of (a) actual receipt, irrespective of the method of delivery, (b) the delivery day following dispatch if sent by express mail (or similar next-day air courier service), (c) electronic confirmation of receipt, if sent by facsimile transmission, or (d) the third day after mailing by registered or certified United States mail, return receipt requested, postage prepaid and addressed as follows:

To VoIP Provider:	For billing inquiries/disputes, requests for Service Level Credits and/or requests for disconnection of Service (for other than default): VoIP Provider Communications
To Cable Operator:	Cable Operator Communications

or to such substitute addresses and Persons as a Party may designate to the others from time to time by Notice in accordance with this Section; provided, however, that any Notice of a change of address shall be deemed to have been given only upon actual receipt. Notwithstanding the foregoing, any notices delivered by either Party to the other Party pertaining to day to day operations shall be deemed properly given if delivered via any of the methods described above or via electronic mail to the address listed on any Service Order.

17.2 **Relationship of the Parties.** The relationship of Cable Operator and its successors in interest and VoIP Provider and its successors in interest is that of independent contractors, and not one of joint venture or partnership. Neither Cable Operator nor VoIP Provider shall have any authority to create or assume, in the name or on behalf of the other Party, any obligation, express or implied, or to act or purport to act as the agent or the legally empowered representative of the other Party for any purpose whatsoever.

17.3 **Nonexclusivity.** Each Party understands that this Agreement is not exclusive and that the other Party may enter into similar agreements with third parties.

17.4 **<u>Binding Effect</u>.** This Agreement shall be binding on and inure to the benefit of the Parties and their respective successors and permitted assigns.

17.5 **<u>Severability</u>.** If any provision of this Agreement is declared or found to be illegal, unenforceable, or void by a court of law, the Parties shall negotiate in good faith to agree upon a substitute provision that is legal and enforceable and is as nearly as possible consistent with the intentions underlying the original provision. If the remainder of this Agreement is not materially affected by such declaration or finding and is capable of substantial performance, then the remainder shall be enforced to the extent permitted by applicable Legal Requirements.

17.6 **<u>Waiver</u>.** No delay or omission by a Party to exercise any right or power shall impair any such right or power or shall be construed to be a waiver thereof. A waiver by any Party of any of the covenants, conditions, or agreements to be performed by the other Party or any breach thereof shall not be construed to be a waiver of any succeeding breach thereof or of any other covenant, condition, or agreement herein contained. No change, waiver, or discharge hereof shall be valid unless in writing and signed by an authorized representative of the Party against which such change, waiver, or discharge is sought to be enforced.

17.7 **<u>Remedies Cumulative</u>.** Except as expressly provided otherwise in this Agreement, in addition to any remedies provided in this Agreement, the Parties shall have all remedies provided at law or in equity. The rights and remedies provided in this Agreement or otherwise under applicable law shall be cumulative and the exercise of any particular right or remedy shall not preclude the exercise of any other rights or remedies in addition to, or as an alternative of, such right or remedy, except as expressly provided otherwise in this Agreement.

17.8 **<u>No Third-Party Beneficiaries</u>.** Nothing in this Agreement, expressed or implied, is intended or shall be construed to confer upon any Person, other than Cable Operator and VoIP Provider, and their respective successors and permitted assigns, any remedy or claim by reason of this Agreement, and any such remedies or claims shall be for the exclusive benefit of Cable Operator and VoIP Provider.

17.9 Dispute Resolution. Except for any dispute or disagreement related to the effect of a change in any applicable Legal Requirements affecting the regulatory rights and obligations of the Parties for which exclusive jurisdiction resides in a Regulatory Authority, any dispute or disagreement arising between Cable Operator and VoIP Provider relating to or arising out of the interpretation or performance of this Agreement shall be resolved in the following manner: A Party may provide the other with Notice of a dispute which has arisen in connection with this Agreement. Such dispute shall first be considered by the Program Managers designated in this Agreement. If such dispute has not been settled to the satisfaction of the Parties within ten (10) days (or such longer period as may be agreed upon) from the date that a Party provided Notice of the dispute, the matter shall be escalated to and considered by a team from each Party consisting of the designated Program Manager for such Party and an officer of such Party who has the authority to settle the dispute but who has not been involved in the day-to-day management of this Agreement. If such dispute has not been settled to the satisfaction of the Parties within twenty (20) days (or such longer period as may be agreed upon) from the date that a Party provided Notice of the dispute, any Party may pursue its rights and remedies under this Agreement. All discussions conducted by the Parties pursuant to this Section 17.9 shall be confidential and shall be treated as compromise and settlement negotiations for purposes of federal and state rules of evidence.

17.10 Expenses. Except as specifically provided in this Agreement, each of the Parties shall pay its own costs and expenses associated with the negotiation, execution and performance of this Agreement.

17.11 Survival. The rights and obligations of the Parties set forth in this Agreement shall survive the expiration of termination of this Agreement for any reason for the period of the transition contemplated by Section 12.5. In addition, the rights and obligations of the Parties set forth in Sections 13, 14, 15 and 17 shall survive the expiration or termination of this Agreement without limitation.

17.12 Exhibits. Except as expressly provided otherwise in this Agreement, all references herein to Exhibits are to the Exhibits attached hereto, which shall be incorporated in and constitute a part of this Agreement by such reference. If there is any conflict between the terms of this Agreement and the terms of any Exhibit, Service Schedule and/or Service Order, the order of precedence is as follows: (1) this Agreement, (2) the Service Schedule (including any Exhibit thereto), (3) any Exhibit to this Agreement, and (4) the Service Order.

17.13 Entire Agreement. This Agreement, including any Exhibits and documents referred to in this Agreement or attached hereto, constitute the entire and exclusive statement of the Parties' agreement with respect to the subject matter hereof and supersede any and all oral or written representations, understandings, or agreements relating thereto. This Agreement may be modified, supplemented or changed only by an agreement in writing which makes specific reference to this Agreement and which is signed by the Parties. The Service Schedules attached hereto are listed below:

Service Schedule– (3)Link® Private Line Service
Service Schedule– (3)Link® Cross Connect Service and
Mondo Condo Fiber Link Service
Service Schedule– (3)Voice® Termination Service
Service Schedule– (3)Link® Fiber Termination Service

and are integral parts hereof and are hereby made a part of this Agreement. Notwithstanding the foregoing, the Parties acknowledge and agree that the execution or existence of this Agreement shall have no effect on any letter of intent, master agreement or other service contract between VoIP Provider and Cable Operator Communications Holding Company, LLC.

17.14 Specific Performance. The Parties acknowledge that money damages are not an adequate remedy for violations of this Agreement and that any Party may, in its sole discretion, apply to a court of competent jurisdiction for specific performance or injunctive or such other relief as such court may deem just and proper in order to enforce this Agreement or prevent any violation hereof and, to the extent permitted by applicable Legal Requirements, each Party waives any objection to the imposition of such relief.

17.15 **<u>Governing Law; Jurisdiction; Waiver of Jury Trial</u>.** This Agreement shall be interpreted, construed, and governed by the laws, other than choice of law rules, of the State of New York, and each of the Parties hereby submit to in personam jurisdiction in such State and irrevocably waive any objection to jurisdiction such Party may have based on inconvenience of forum. To the fullest extent permitted by applicable Legal Requirements, the Parties further agree that service of any process, summons, notice or document by U.S. certified or registered mail to such Party's address for Notices as set forth in Section 17.1 shall be effective service of process in any action, suit or proceeding with respect to any matters as to which it has submitted to jurisdiction as set forth in the immediately preceding sentence. **Each Party irrevocably waives all right to trial by jury in any action, suit or proceeding brought to enforce or defend any rights or remedies under this Agreement or to interpret or construe any provision of this Agreement or with respect to any dispute arising out of or related to this Agreement.**

17.16 **<u>Attorneys' Fees</u>.** In the event of any action, suit, or proceeding based on or arising out of any alleged breach by any Party of any representation, warranty, covenant, or agreement contained in this Agreement, the prevailing Party will be entitled to recover reasonable attorneys' fees and other actual and reasonable costs associated with such action, suit, or proceeding from any Party determined to have breached any provision of this Agreement.

17.17 **<u>Captions</u>.** The captions and headings contained herein are for purposes of convenience only and are not a part of this Agreement and shall not be used to interpret any provision hereof.

17.18 **<u>Construction</u>.** This Agreement and the Exhibits hereto have been drafted jointly by the Parties and in the event of any ambiguities in the language hereof, there shall be no inference drawn in favor of or against either Party.

17.19 **<u>Counterparts</u>.** This Agreement may be executed in any number of counterparts, each of which shall be deemed an original, but all of which shall constitute one and the same instrument.

17.20 **Time of Essence.** Time is of the essence in each Party's performance under this Agreement. Except as provided otherwise in this Agreement, if the giving of any Notice or the performance of any act required or permitted under this Agreement falls on a day that is not a business day, the time for giving such Notice or performing such act will be extended to the next succeeding business day.

17.21 **Further Assurances.** From and after the Effective Date, each of the Parties shall, from time to time, at the request of another Party and without further consideration, do, execute and deliver, cause to be done, executed and delivered, all such further acts, things and instruments as may be reasonably requested or required to more effectively evidence and give effect to the transactions contemplated by this Agreement.

[Signature Page Follows]

IN WITNESS WHEREOF, the Parties hereto have caused this Agreement to be executed by their duly respective authorized representatives as of the date first written above.

VoIP Provider Communications, LLC
("VoIP Provider")

By: ________________________________
Name: ________________________________
Title: ________________________________

Cable Operator

By: ________________________________
Name: ________________________________
Title: ________________________________

[Signature Page to the Master Network Services Agreement]

EXHIBIT "A"

DESIGNATED MARKETS

(Attached Immediately Behind This Page)

EXHIBIT "B"

PROGRAM MANAGERS

The name, address, telephone number, facsimile number and e-mail address for the initial Program Manager of Cable Operator:

EXHIBIT "C"

REQUEST FOR SERVICE QUOTATION

(To Be Mutually Agreed and Attached Immediately Behind this Page)

EXHIBIT "D"

MARKET INSTALLATION CHART

(Attached Immediately Behind this Page)

APPENDIX TO EXHIBIT "D"

Market Installation Chart (as of the Effective Date)

120/ 180 Day List Description	Address	State	City	Zip	DS3 Circuit Level	Ocn Circuit Level	Notes
This list is dated as of the Effective Date and will be updated on a 60 day rotating basis (subject to the terms of the Agreement)							

EXHIBIT "E"

TECHNICAL ENGINEERING REPRESENTATIVES AND TECHNICAL EMERGENCY ESCALATION CONTACT INFORMATION

The name, address, telephone number, facsimile number and e-mail address for the initial technical engineering representative of Cable Operator:

The name, address, telephone number, facsimile number and e-mail address for the initial technical engineering representative of VoIP Provider:

See technical emergency escalation contact information for Cable Operator and VoIP Provider appended hereto.

APPENDIX TO EXHIBIT "E"

Cable Operator NSOC Escalation

The NSOC is designed to support the national network management efforts for Cable Operator Communications' infrastructure. The NSOC will be responsible for the monitoring of all network equipment, and the escalation of issues either to Cable Operator Tier III or Vendor Support.

The NSOC is staffed 24 hours a day and 7 days a week.

Cable Operator NSOC

Call
Email **Escalation List**

Level	**Name/Title/Email**	**Number**
First Level	Contact	
Escalation		

Notice: Not for use or disclosure outside the Cable Operator Communications family of companies except by written permission.

APPENDIX TO EXHIBIT "E"

VOIP PROVIDER ESCALATION CONTACT INFORMATION

Initial Call

Second Level Hour 2

Switched Services

Transport

Third Level Hour 4 - TCAM Director
IP

Switched Services

Transport

Fourth Level Hour 6 – Global Customer Operations VP
IP

Switched Services

Transport

Fifth Level Hour 8 – Customer Operations SVP
IP

Switched Services

Transport

Courtesy of Owen D. Kurtin, The Vinland Group LLC

APPENDIX C

CELLULAR SERVICE RESALE AGREEMENT

AGREEMENT

THIS AGREEMENT, containing terms and conditions pertinent to reselling service ("Agreement"), effective as of the day of , 199_ is by and between ____________, a __________ Corporation, with its principal place of business at ____________, __________, ___________ on behalf of itself and its current and future affiliates holding licenses to provide non-wireline cellular radio telecommunications service ("Service") within the United States (collectively, the "Company"), and , a corporation organized under the laws of the State of with its principal place of business at _________________ (the "Reseller").

RECITALS

A. Company provides or is authorized to provide "Service" as defined below in certain geographic areas in the United States to "Customers" as defined below. The areas in which the Company is authorized may change from time to time. A list of the areas where the Company is currently licensed to provide Service is set forth in the attached Schedule 1, which Schedule may be revised by Company from time to time.

B. Reseller desires to purchase and resell access to and usage of Company's Service within the areas listed in Schedule 1 designated by Reseller.

AGREEMENTS

In consideration of the mutual covenants and the promises contained herein, the Parties hereto agree as follows:

1. DEFINITIONS

The following terms when used herein shall have the following meanings:

B.1.1 Activation shall mean the initiation of the Service for the account of Reseller.

B.1.2 Affiliate shall mean any person, partnership, corporation, or other business association (hereinafter "person") that directly or indirectly controls, is controlled by, or is under common control with another person. Control shall be defined as (i) ownership of a majority of the voting power of all classes of voting stock, or (ii) ownership of a majority of the beneficial interests in income or capital of an entity other than a corporation.

B.1.3 Area shall mean the areas within the United States, where the Company currently provides Service pursuant to licenses granted by the Federal Communications Commission ("FCC").

B.1.4 Assignment shall mean the assignment of a Number or block of Numbers to Reseller.

B.1.5 Customer shall mean any individual or entity purchasing Service from Company, pursuant to this Agreement.

B.1.6 End User shall mean any person or entity purchasing Service, directly or indirectly, from or through Reseller.

B.1.7 Events of Default shall mean the following:

(a) the execution of any assignment for the benefit of creditors or the filing for relief by either party under any applicable bankruptcy, reorganization, moratorium, or similar debtor relief laws;

(b) the appointment of a receiver for Reseller or Company or for substantially all of their respective assets or properties;

(c) the failure of either party to pay any sum owed to the other hereunder at the time such amount comes due;

(d) the failure of either party to perform or observe any other material term, condition, or covenant to be performed by it under this Agreement;

(e) the commission of any illegal act (excluding misdemeanor traffic offenses and other minor misdemeanors not involving dishonesty or moral turpitude) by Reseller or the filing of any criminal indictment against Reseller, its proprietors, partners, officers, or directors or shareholders controlling the aggregate or individually 10% or more of the voting rights or equity interests of Reseller;

(f) the furnishing within a 12-month period, by Reseller to Company of two or more checks that are not paid when presented due to insufficient funds; and

(g) an unauthorized assignment of this Agreement.
Upon the occurrence of any of these Events of Default, a party shall be deemed to be in default of this Agreement, until such Event of Default is cured.

B.1.8 Home Area shall mean the area served by the Affiliate of the Company holding the FCC license for the MSA or RSA with which the Number is normally associated.

B.1.9 Normal Business Hours shall mean 9:00 a.m. to 5:00 p.m., Monday through Friday, excluding Company observed holidays, except as specifically stated otherwise on Schedule 2, at the office responsible for handling the pertinent interaction between Company and Reseller.

B.1.10 Rate Sheet shall mean the list of services published from time to time by Company which reflects the rates, terms, and conditions at which it makes Service available to Customers under different Service Plans.

B.1.11 Number shall mean the ten-digit (NPA NXX XXXX) number assigned to a cellular telephone unit used to provide access to Service. Roaming user or Roamer shall mean an End User using cellular service outside the Home Area.

B.1.13 Service shall mean Domestic Common Carrier Public Cellular Radio Telecommunications Service provided pursuant to Part 22, subpart K of the Rules of the Federal Communications Commission

("FCC"), as amended, whether provided solely or principally on those frequencies designated in 47 C.F.R. § 22.902, and such other services as may be offered by Company from time to time under this Agreement.

B.1.14 Service Plan shall mean the rates, terms, and conditions under which Reseller purchases Service from Company as set forth in the attached Schedule 2.

B.1.15 Unauthorized Access shall mean any unauthorized use of Service through the modification of the Electronic Serial Number ("ESN") originally installed by the manufacturer in a cellular phone (which shall include the practices generally referred to as "counterfeiting," "cloning fraud," or "tumbling fraud.")

2. ELIGIBILITY, PROVISION OF SERVICE AND RESELLER RELATIONSHIP

B.2.1 Provision of Service. Company shall provide and Reseller agrees to purchase Service from Company within the Area as designated by Reseller, which Service Reseller may resell to End Users. Company shall have the continuing right to market and sell Service to Customers and potential Customers in competition with Reseller.

B.2.2 Failure to Maintain Eligibility Criteria. If Reseller shall at any time fail to meet the eligibility criteria set forth in Schedule 2, Company may provide Reseller with ninety (90) days written notice that Reseller is no longer eligible to receive service under this Agreement. If, Reseller is unable, during the ninety (90) day period after Company's notice is sent, to satisfy the eligibility criteria, Company may terminate this Agreement without further notice. Reseller may continue to receive service by entering into one or more separate agreements with each Affiliate of Company providing service in each portion of the Area in which Reseller wishes to continue to receive cellular service.

3.TERM OF AGREEMENT

Subject to the provisions of Article XIII, the term of this Agreement shall commence on the date set forth above, and shall continue until terminated in accordance with the terms hereof. This Agreement may be canceled at any time by either party without cause upon 90 days prior written notice; provided, however, that neither party may terminate the Agreement without cause prior to the expiration of any term commitment under any Service Plan applicable to any Number. If, however, Reseller does terminate the Agreement or any service without cause prior to the expiration of any such term commitment, Reseller shall be obligated to pay any cancellation fee specified in Schedule 2. A termination shall be deemed to be without cause if it occurs in the absence of an Event of Default. If either party wishes to terminate the Agreement, it shall deliver written notice to the other party, specifying the effective date of termination. Company's obligation to provide additional Numbers to Reseller shall cease: (a) upon receipt by Company of Reseller's written notice of termination; or (b) upon issuance by Company of written notice of termination to Reseller.

4. ASSIGNMENT OF NUMBERS, CONNECTIONS

B.5.1 Provision of Numbers to Reseller. Within thirty (30) days of execution of this Agreement, Company shall assign to Reseller, and Reseller shall accept from Company, an initial order of Numbers for each Area. Reseller may, at any time that it is not in default under this Agreement, and according to procedures (including credit requirements) established by Company, order additional Numbers in such amounts as are set forth in Schedule 3. Subject to the availability of Numbers and the capacity of the Facilities, such additional Numbers will be supplied to Reseller within three business days of Company's receipt of the order. Company shall process orders for Numbers from all Customers, including Customers who are owned or controlled by Company or an Affiliate of Company, in the sequence in which orders for additional Numbers are received. Reseller and Company shall follow reasonable number conservation policies generally accepted by the telecommunications industry and Company may, from time to time change number assignments. If Numbers are unavailable, Company shall follow generally accepted industry standards and/or regulatory requirements, if any, in responding to the shortage of numbers, and shall, by doing so, incur no liability to Reseller.

B.5.2 Restrictions on Numbers. A Number may not be associated with more than one cellular telephone unit at the same time.

B.5.3 Activation of Service. Service shall only be initiated on normal business days, during Normal Business Hours. A Number shall be activated within eight normal business hours following receipt by Company's designated representative for such purpose from an authorized representative of Reseller of written notice and of any deposit required pursuant to Section 7.10. Notwithstanding the foregoing, Company shall use reasonable efforts to activate Numbers as soon as practicable upon its receipt of the notice and the deposit. However, Company shall not be obligated to initiate Service if Reseller is in default.

B.5.4 Remote On-Line Access. Where Company makes a remote on-line access procedure available to Customers, and Reseller elects the remote on-line access option, Reseller will be responsible for ordering, activating, terminating, canceling service, suspending, making features or ESN changes, or other permitted modifications to Numbers. Additions of Numbers to or deletions of Numbers from Number inventory assigned to Reseller may not be made by remote on-line access, but rather are made as set forth in Sections 4.1 and 4.5. Reseller may not use remote on-line access procedure for technical troubleshooting beyond limited inquiry functions. Reseller agrees that it will comply with any procedures developed by Company with respect to this program. Remote on-line access can be accessed Monday through Friday from 7:00 am to 11:00 pm EST, from 7:00 am to 9:00 pm EST on Saturday, and from 12:00 pm to 8:00 pm EST on Sunday.

B.5.5 Modification or Termination of Service. When Reseller desires to modify or terminate Service with respect to one or more Number(s), Reseller shall provide notice to Company. Except as set forth below in Section 11.2 with respect to fraud, such notice shall be provided by an authorized representative of Reseller and shall be given during Company's normal business hours; it shall specify the Number and such additional information as Company may reasonably require. Company shall modify or terminate Service to such Number(s) within four business hours following receipt of such notice from Reseller.

B.5.6 Authorized Representatives. Immediately upon execution of this Agreement, Company and Reseller shall each notify the other of their respective authorized representatives for purposes of giving and receiving the notices provided for under this Article IV and any other Service orders, including those which involve the activation, change, or discontinuance of Service. Each party may appoint no more than three representatives at any time, unless the other party consents to a greater number. The notice of appointment, and the authority of the representative, shall remain effective until the notice is canceled or amended by the party for which such representative is acting. Company will not accept any notice or orders from any End User or other agent of Reseller.

B.5.7 Limitations on Service

B.5.7.1 Limitations on Service within the Home Area. RESELLER ACKNOWLEDGES THAT SERVICE IS MADE AVAILABLE TO CELLULAR TELEPHONE UNITS EQUIPPED FOR SERVICE ONLY WHEN WITHIN OPERATING RANGE OF THE FACILITIES WITHIN THE HOME AREA. SERVICE MAY BE TEMPORARILY REFUSED, INTERRUPTED, OR LIMITED BECAUSE OF: (a) FACILITIES LIMITATIONS; (b) TRANSMISSION LIMITATIONS CAUSED BY ATMOSPHERIC, TERRAIN, OTHER NATURAL OR ARTIFICIAL CONDITIONS ADVERSELY AFFECTING TRANSMISSION, AND OTHER CAUSES REASONABLY OUTSIDE OF COMPANY'S CONTROL; OR (c) EQUIPMENT MODIFICATIONS, UPGRADES, RELOCATIONS, REPAIRS, AND OTHER SIMILAR ACTIVITIES NECESSARY FOR THE PROPER OR IMPROVED OPERATION OF SERVICE INDIVIDUAL CALLS MAY BE "DROPPED" (i.e., INVOLUNTARILY DISCONNECTED) FOR A VARIETY OF REASONS, INCLUDING, WITHOUT LIMITATION ATMOSPHERIC CONDITIONS, TOPOGRAPHY, WEAK BATTERIES, SYSTEM OVERCAPACITY, MOVEMENT OUTSIDE A SERVICE AREA, AND GAPS IN COVERAGE WITHIN A SERVICE AREA. COMPANY SHALL

INCUR NO LIABILITY FOR THEIR INABILITY TO PROVIDE ADEQUATE SERVICES HEREUNDER IF SUCH LIABILITY IS DUE TO A LACK OF NETWORK CAPACITY OR THE CAUSES BEYOND THE REASONABLE CONTROL OF COMPANY, NOR SHALL COMPANY BE RESPONSIBLE FOR ANY ACT OR OMISSION RELATED TO NON-COMPANY EQUIPMENT OR SYSTEMS USED IN CONNECTION WITH THE SERVICE. RESELLER AGREES TO INFORM ITS END USERS OF THE SERVICE LIMITATIONS CONTAINED IN THIS SECTION.

B.5.7.2 Limitations on Roaming Service. COMPANY WILL PROVIDE, AS TO EACH NUMBER ACTIVATED FOR RESELLER, THE SAME ROAMING SERVICE THAT IS AVAILABLE TO COMPANY'S OTHER CUSTOMERS WITH NUMBERS ASSOCIATED WITH THE SAME HOME AREA. IF COMPANY, OR ANOTHER ENTITY WITH WHOM COMPANY HAS A ROAMING AGREEMENT, DISCOVERS OR SUSPECTS FRAUD WITH RESPECT TO CERTAIN NUMBERS, THEN ROAMING PRIVILEGES MAY BE SUSPENDED WITH RESPECT TO SUCH NUMBERS. IT SHALL BE COMPANY'S POLICY TO USE COMMERCIALLY REASONABLE EFFORTS TO PROVIDE RESELLER WITH PRIOR, OR PROMPT SUBSEQUENT, NOTIFICATION OF THE SUSPENSION OF THE ROAMING SERVICE; HOWEVER, COMPANY SHALL HAVE NO LIABILITY ARISING OUT OF ANY FAILURE TO NOTIFY UNLESS SUCH FAILURE RESULTED FROM A DELIBERATE DECISION MADE IN BAD FAITH.

B.5.8 Reassignment of Numbers. RESELLER ACKNOWLEDGES THAT COMPANY MAY BE REQUIRED TO CHANGE OR REASSIGN NUMBERS PREVIOUSLY PROVIDED TO RESELLER FROM TIME TO TIME. COMPANY WILL PROVIDE RESELLER WITH NOTICE OF THE INTENDED CHANGE REASONABLY IN ADVANCE OF MAKING ANY SUCH CHANGE. RESELLER AGREES TO INFORM ITS END USERS OF THE PROVISIONS OF THIS SECTION, AND FURTHER ACKNOWLEDGES AND AGREES THAT NEITHER IT NOT ANY END USER SHALL HAVE OR ACQUIRE ANY PROPRIETARY

RIGHT IN ANY SPECIFIC NUMBER OR BLOCK OF NUMBERS PROVIDED BY COMPANY.

B.5.9 Privacy. Cellular telephone systems use radio channels to transmit voice and data communications over a complex network and privacy cannot be guaranteed. Reseller agrees that Company shall not be liable to Reseller or to End Users for any such lack of privacy.

B.5.10 Notices. Any order, notice, or other communication placed or given pursuant to this Article IV may be delivered by such means as may be permitted from time to time by the general practices of Company. As of the date of this Agreement, facsimile transmission is permitted by Company.

6. PRICES AND TERMS OF PAYMENT

B.6.1 Payment of Charges. Reseller shall pay to Company charges computed as set forth in Schedule 2. All such charges may be modified from time to time in accordance with the provisions of this Article V, Section 5.9.

B.6.2 Minimum Charges. Reseller shall pay Company any minimum charges as set forth in Schedule 2 for each Number assigned to Reseller or for any minimum Number block required by the Service Plan selected by Reseller, regardless whether service has been initiated for such Number or block of Numbers.

B.6.3 Aggregate Volume Reward. Customer may participate in any Aggregate Volume Reward program offered by Company for which Customer is eligible.

B.6.4 Taxes. Except where Reseller provides to Company a valid certificate of resale or such other documentation as would release Company from any liability, levy, or duty, there shall be added to any charges due from Reseller an amount equal to any duty, fee, surcharge, levy or tax, including but not limited to sales, gross receipts, excise, utility, and use taxes, fees or surcharges, imposed by any local, State or Federal government or governmental agency with respect to Reseller, the Service, or transactions contemplated by this Agreement, excepting only taxes on the income of the Company.

B.6.5 Tariffs. In the event that Service provided or charges made therefore are currently subject, or at any time become subject, to any Federal, state, or local regulation or tariff, then the agreed charges set forth in Schedule 2 (as amended from time to time) shall be deemed amended to conform to the rates or any changes in rates or terms and conditions that may occur or be required under such regulation or tariff. Nothing in this Agreement shall be deemed (i) to require or preclude the use of tariff-equivalent or tariff-related charges, or (ii) to provide or imply that such charges are or are not appropriate in the provision of Service provided for this Agreement and in Schedule 2.

B.6.6 Monthly Billing. Company shall bill Reseller for charges incurred for each Number once per calendar month, with the billing date to be the same for that Number each successive month. Company will use reasonable efforts to have all Numbers of Reseller assigned to a single cycle, but any Number may be assigned to any cycle and the cycle to which a Number is assigned may be changed from time to time; provided, however, that Company shall not unreasonably require multiple billing cycles for Reseller. When practicable, Company will provide Reseller with 90-days prior written notice of any change in billing cycles to be used with respect to Numbers assigned to Reseller.

B.6.7 Provision of Magnetic Tapes. Company shall use reasonable efforts to provide to Reseller's billing agent accurate magnetic billing tapes for Service provided pursuant to this Agreement and the associated charges therefor within seven working days of the cut-off date for each billing cycle. Reseller agrees to notify Company immediately if it does not receive a magnetic tape within this time frame. the magnetic tapes provided by Company will include reasonable billing information compiled using standard industry protocols. Reseller Agrees to notify Company within five business days of its receipt of a magnetic tape containing any defects. Reseller must provide Company with written notice of the name, address, and phone number of its billing agent at least 30 days prior to the expected mailing date of the billing tape. Each container within which the magnetic billing tapes are shipped to Reseller's billing agent shall be labeled with Reseller's name, the appropriate Company's name< the applicable Home Area, the name of the Reseller's billing Agent, and the billing period to which the tape pertains. Company shall provide one magnetic billing tape per billing cycle for the charges indicated in Schedule 2, with any additional or lost copies to be provided at Reseller's expense.

B.6.7.1 Provision of Data by Other Means. It is understood and agreed that data related to billing may be transmitted, with Reseller's consent, by means other than magnetic tape, if available, such as by optical disk or by way of wired networks from one computer to another. The substitution of another form of transmission shall not affect the transmission, compliance with standard protocols, timeliness of notice regarding defects, identification of the data by reasonable "labeling," and responsibility for costs of replacing data, nearly as practicable as if magnetic tapes had been used.

B.6.8 Invoices.

B.6.8.1 Itemized Invoices. Reseller shall receive one summary level paper invoice per billing cycle (there may be multiple monthly cycles setting forth the details listed in Schedule 2. Reseller shall be billed in arrears for applicable access, feature, non-usage related charges, airtime, long distance, applicable land line, and other usage related charges at the end of each billing cycle. Reseller agrees to pay all charges incurred, including, but not limited to, long distance, applicable land line, directory listings, custom calling, network service, network, usage, directory assistance, roamer service, and 900 and other Service Access Code service charges (to the extent that Company provides, or is authorized to bill for, these services.)

B.6.8.2 Payment of Invoices. Payment in full for such invoices shall be due in U.S. currency upon the due date set forth in the invoice without any right of offset by Reseller for disputed charges or otherwise -- unless Reseller submits a written explanation of any disputed amounts by the due date together with payment of undisputed amounts and agrees to comply with the following paragraph of this section (5.8.2). Company may at its sole discretion require payment by certified check or money order. Payments are past due if not received by the due date shown on the invoice, or within 30 days after the magnetic tape was mailed, whichever is later. In the event payment is not received within this time period, Reseller agrees to pay a late fee as set forth in Schedule 2. Reseller further agrees that time is of the essence with respect to its payments of invoices. Reseller agrees not to place any condition or restrictive legend, such as "Paid in Full," on any check or instrument used to make a payment. The parties agree that the negotiation of any such check or instrument so inscribed shall not constitute an accord and satisfaction or novation. The resolution of payment disputes, rather, shall be made in accordance with the provisions of section 5.8.3 and Article XV.

If Reseller submits written explanation of any disputed charges by the due date set forth in an invoice, Company and Reseller shall make good faith reasonable efforts to resolve the dispute within 60 days, and will agree to submit any disputes remaining after that 60 day period to arbitration under Section XV below.

B.6.8.4 Disputed Charges.

(a) Reseller shall provide Company with written notice of any disputed charges within 75 days after the date each disputed call occurred. Sending of such notice by Reseller shall not excuse or defer Reseller's obligation to make full payment of the invoice under Section 5.8.2, unless otherwise specifically provided in Schedule 2. Reseller may not thereafter dispute charges. Company shall provide Reseller with its determination with respect to disputed charges within sixty (60) days after receipt of Reseller's notice of dispute and, if appropriate, will credit Reseller's account.

(b) Reseller's failure to provide notice of disputed charges pursuant to Section 5.8.3a. above, shall constitute a waiver by Reseller of the underlying claim, and Reseller shall not, thereafter, make any claim with respect to such disputed charges. This provision shall not shorten the period within which suit must be filed as established by the applicable statute of limitations, but shall constitute a condition precedent to any right of the aggrieved party to contest prior charges. This condition is designed to allow each party the opportunity to preserve important evidence in defense of a claim.

(c) If Reseller claims that certain charges are not payable in full because they are the result of Unauthorized Access by a person with whom Reseller has not dealt, then it is Reseller's obligation to supply Company with clear and convincing evidence of the Unauthorized Access. Company considers the following to be evidence of Unauthorized Access: (i) an affidavit from the appropriate End User stating that s/he or it did not make the call(s) in question; (ii) call detail information for the End User's account; and (iii) a statement by Reseller that it has thoroughly investigated the alleged Unauthorized Access. Such investigation by Reseller should include contacting or attempting to contact a sufficient number of the recipients of calls at issue of each End User so as to establish a reasonable basis for inferring that the remainder of such calls was the result of Unauthorized Access. If Reseller complies with this section within 75 days after the date of each disputed call, charges may be reduced to the extent set forth in Schedule 2.

Notwithstanding the above, the perpetration or claimed perpetration of any fraud or deceit by an End User (i.e., "subscription fraud") does not mitigate the Reseller's obligation to Company.

B.6.8.5 Proration of Charges. Access fees with respect to assigned Numbers for billing periods of less than one month will be prorated based on the actual number of days in such periods. for purposes of such prorations, each monthly billing cycle may be deemed, at Company's discretion, to have 30 days. Company may, at its option, prorate other monthly charges, such as for calling features.

B.6.9 Modification to Schedule 2. The charges set forth in Schedule 2 may be increased to decreased at any time upon 90 days written notice to Reseller, unless Schedule 2 provides otherwise. To the extent that the charges set forth in Schedule 2 are subject to any federal, state, or local regulation or tariff, such charges may be increased or decreased as provided or required by such regulation or tariff. If any modification proposed by Company to Schedule 2 is unacceptable to Reseller, Reseller shall have the right to terminate this Agreement by providing Company with written notice of termination within 30 days of the notice of modification; provided, however, that if Company in turn provides Reseller with written notice rescinding the modification within 15 days thereafter, the Agreement will not terminate but shall continue in full force and effect.

B.6.10 Reseller Right to Select Other Service Plans.

(a) Reseller may, from time to time, change its selection of Service Plan under which Service shall be provided to Reseller's Numbers by providing Company with written notice of the change, provided that Reseller complies with all of the terms and conditions of the new Service Plan. In such event, Schedule 2 shall be deemed to include the Rate Sheet for any Service Plan selected by Reseller and Reseller may be required to sign an addendum to this Agreement to reflect changed terms and conditions applicable for such Service Plan. In such case, except as otherwise provided in the relevant rate sheet, Reseller will not receive a magnetic billing tape. The rates and terms for various Service Plans are available from Company. Any such modification to Schedule 3 pursuant to this Section shall not be deemed a modification for purposes of Section 5.9 above.

(b) In the event Reseller changes Service Plans, Numbers on the Reseller rate plan and Numbers on other rate plans are on different billing cycles. If Reseller selects an annual rate plan, there may be a cancellation fee if Reseller cancels service within the first year.

B.6.12 Loss of Telephones. In the event an End User's cellular telephone is lost, stolen, or otherwise absent from the End User's possession or control in an unauthorized manner, Reseller shall nevertheless be liable for all charges attributable to the access Number assigned to such cellular telephone until it notifies Company during Normal Business Hours of such loss, theft, or unauthorized absence, in which case Reseller's liability therefore shall terminate at the end of four business hours after such notification is received by Company. Company shall use reasonable efforts, taking into account all circumstances which shall include other operational demands placed upon its employees, to deactivate Service to the Number affected as soon as practicable. In instances where a Reseller has selected the Remote On-Line Access option, the Reseller is responsible for terminating the Service of an End user, under the circumstances described in this paragraph, and Reseller shall be liable for all charges incurred on each Number.

B.6.13 Billing Adjustments. In the event of a total service outage ('Outage") within the Home Area or any portion of the Home Area associated with any Number which is not caused by Reseller or End User and which lasts for a period of 24 hours or more, a credit allowance will ne made, at the Reseller's request, in the form of a pro rata adjustment of the fixed charges billed by Company to Reseller with respect to such Number. periods of noncontinuous Outage may not be accumulated in determining if an Outage has continued for at least 24 hours. In order to receive such credit, Reseller must submit a written request to Company, stating the nature and duration of the outage, the Numbers affected, and such other information as Company may reasonably require. Such notice must be received by Company within ten business days following the last day of the period of Outage. Except as provided therein, Company shall incur no liability for outages.

B.6.14 Company's Right to Offset. Company may offset against any deposit, monies, or compensation owed to Reseller by Company any amounts owed by Reseller to Company or its Affiliates pursuant to this Agreement, or otherwise, including without limitation, any expenses and damages that are incurred by Company and are subject to indemnification by Reseller under Section 18.

7. LIMITATIONS OF WARRANTIES AND LIABILITIES

Company supplies a service and not "good(s)" as that term is defined in the Uniform Commercial Code. Notwithstanding and without limitation of the foregoing, to the extent that any portion of Service offered by Company might be construed as a good(s), COMPANY EXPRESSLY DISCLAIMS ANY AND ALL IMPLIED WARRANTIES OF WHATSOEVER NATURE INCLUDING, BUT NOT LIMITED TO, THE WARRANTY OF MERCHANTABILITY AND FITNESS FOR A PARTICULAR USE.

THE LIABILITY OF COMPANY FOR DAMAGES OR COSTS ARISING FROM ERRORS, OUTAGES, OR FAILURES OF SERVICE,

OR DEFECTS OR MALFUNCTIONS OF THE FACILITIES, OCCURRING IN THE COURSE OF PERFORMING UNDER THIS AGREEMENT (INCLUDING THE OBTAINING AND FURNISHING OF INFORMATION WITH RESPECT TO RESELLER, END USERS, OR OTHER USERS OF SERVICE OR FACILITIES), REGARDLESS OF THE LEGAL BASIS FOR SUCH CLAIM SHALL IN ANY EVENT BE LIMITED TO AN AMOUNT EQUAL TO THE PROPORTIONATE CHARGE TO RESELLER FOR THE PERIOD OF SERVICE DURING WHICH SUCH ERRORS, OUTAGES, FAILURES, DEFECTS, OR MALFUNCTIONS OF EQUIPMENT OCCUR.

IN NO EVENT SHALL COMPANY BE LIABLE FOR ANY SPECIAL OR CONSEQUENTIAL DAMAGES.

9. RESELLER'S OBLIGATIONS

B.9.1 Reseller's Charges. Reseller is solely responsible for all charges billed under Article V above, regardless of when billed, with respect to any Number assigned to it.

B.9.3 Equipment.

(a) Reseller is responsible for ensuring that any equipment utilized by it, its agents, or its End Users in connection with Service and each agent's and End User's use thereof shall at all times meet industry standards for compatibility with Service including any Company's requirements for compatibility with upgraded Facilities, and all FCC and other applicable regulatory authorities' requirements. In the event that any of the equipment utilized by an agent or End User does not meet such standards, Reseller shall use its best efforts to ensure that such equipment is no longer used in the reception or transmission of Service and shall, if necessary, terminate Service to such agent or End User.

(b) Company shall not be responsible to Reseller or any End User for the installation, operation, quality of transmission, or testing and maintenance of any cellular telephone unit or cellular terminal equipment, unless Reseller contracts with Company for Company to provide maintenance, warranty, or installation of End User equipment at Company service centers at rates agreeable to Reseller and Company. In that event, the relationship between Company and Reseller as to such matters shall be governed by a separate agreement Company shall hove no obligation to sell or otherwise provide equipment to Reseller or to its End Users.

B.9.5 Obligations to End Users.

(a) With respect to the matters covered by this Agreement, Company shall be obligated only to Reseller, with which it is in privity of contract, and not with End Users with whom Company is not in privity. End Users are not to be deemed to be third-party beneficiaries of this Agreement.

(b) Unless otherwise provided in Schedule 2, Reseller shall provide an adequate and properly trained staff to receive and investigate any complaints from its End Users relating to Service, and will report any trouble with Service to Company only upon reasonable verification that such trouble is due to reasons other than the misuse or malfunctioning of the End User's equipment or the failure of such equipment to meet the technical standards for compatibility with Service.

(c) Unless otherwise provided in Schedule 2, Company is not responsible for sending bills to Reseller's End Users.

B.9.7 Ethical Responsibilities. Reseller shall refrain from doing anything that would tend to discredit, dishonor, reflect adversely upon, or injure, in any manner, the reputation of Company, Reseller, or any other Customers or dealers of Company. Each party shall be governed in all its dealings with respect to this Agreement by the highest standards of honesty, integrity, and fair dealing.

B.9.8 Responsibility for Actions or Omissions. Reseller shall be solely responsible for all risks and expenses incurred in connection with its actions or omissions in the sale of Service or otherwise relating to this Agreement. Reseller shall act in all respects on its own account, and shall be solely responsible for such things as credit verification, deposits, billing, collection, consolidation, rebilling, End User complaints, charges for usage, bad debts, and, except as provided in Schedule 5.8.3 and Schedule 2, fraudulent use of any Number assigned to Reseller, whether by Reseller's employees or agents of Reseller, and End User, or any third party, provided Company has followed Reseller's instructions under this Agreement with respect to any relevant Number.

B.9.9 Responsibility for Agents. Reseller is responsible for the performance of its agents, if any, and shall ensure that its agents are in compliance with any applicable terms of this Agreement, any controlling tariffs, and any other applicable industry standards.

B.9.10 No Rights to Company's Facilities. No provision of this Agreement shall be construed as vesting in the Reseller any control or ownership interest whatsoever in any Facilities or operations of Company.

B.9.11 Notice of End Users.

B.9.11.1 Notice Required. Reseller agrees that it shall file a tariff with the appropriate regulatory authorities containing the following language or that each End User will be given notice containing the information referenced in Sections 4.7 and 4.8 above, together with language similar in all material aspects to the Sections set forth below:

(a) [END USER] HAS NO PROPERTY RIGHT IN THE TELEPHONE ACCESS NUMBER.

(b) [END USER] EXPRESSLY UNDERSTANDS AND AGREES THAT IT HAS NO CONTRACTUAL RELATIONSHIP WHATSOEVER WITH UNDERLYING CELLULAR SERVICE CARRIER AND THAT [END USER] IS NOT A THIRD PARTY BENEFICIARY OF ANY AGREEMENT BETWEEN [RESELLER] AND UNDERLYING CARRIER. IN ADDITION, [END USER] EXPRESSLY UNDERSTANDS AND AGREES THAT UNDERLYING CARRIER SHALL HAVE NO LEGAL, EQUITABLE, OR OTHER LIABILITY OF ANY KIND TO [END USER]. IN ANY EVENT, REGARDLESS OF THE FORM OF THE ACTION, WHETHER FOR BREACH OF

CONTRACT, WARRANTY, NEGLIGENCE, STRICT LIABILITY IN TORT OR OTHERWISE, [END USER'S] EXCLUSIVE REMEDY AND THE TOTAL LIABILITY OF THE UNDERLYING CARRIER ARISING IN ANY WAY IN CONNECTION WITH THIS AGREEMENT, FOR ANY CAUSE WHATSOEVER, INCLUDING BUT NOT LIMITED TO ANY FAILURE OR DISRUPTION OF SERVICE PROVIDED HEREUNDER, IS LIMITED TO PAYMENT OF DAMAGES IN AN AMOUNT EQUAL TO THE PORTION OF THE FIXED MONTHLY CHARGE TO [END USER] FOR THE SERVICES RELATING TO THE PERIOD OF SERVICE DURING WHICH SAID DAMAGES OCCUR.

(c) [END USER] SHALL INDEMNIFY AND HOLD HARMLESS THE UNDERLYING CELLULAR SERVICE CARRIER SUPPLYING SERVICES TO [RESELLER] AND ITS OFFICERS, EMPLOYEES, AND AGENTS AGAINST ANY AND ALL CLAIMS, INCLUDING WITHOUT LIMITATION CLAIMS FOR LIBEL, SLANDER, INFRINGEMENT OF COPYRIGHT, PROPERTY DAMAGE, OR ANY PERSONAL INJURY OR DEATH ARISING IN ANYWAY DIRECTLY OR INDIRECTLY IN CONNECTION WITH THIS AGREEMENT OR THE USE, FAILURE TO USE, OR INABILITY TO USE THE ACCESS TELEPHONE NUMBER, EXCEPT WHERE THE CLAIMS RESULT FROM THE UNDERLYING CARRIER'S NEGLIGENCE OR WILLFUL MISCONDUCT THIS INDEMNITY SHALL SURVIVE THE TERMINATION OF THIS AGREEMENT.

(d) [END USER] HEREBY ACKNOWLEDGES THAT THIS AGREEMENT IS ASSIGNABLE BY RESELLER TO THE UNDERLYING CELLULAR SERVICE CARRIER SUPPLYING SERVICES TO [RESELLER] TO SECURE PERFORMANCE OF [RESELLER] UNDER THE TERMS OF [RESELLER'S] AGREEMENT WITH SUCH CARRIER.

Reseller may, at its option, include such other provisions or modify the foregoing provisions to apply to Reseller as well as to Company, so long as such additions or modifications do not mitigate the effect of the foregoing.

B.9.11.3 Rental Exception. The notification requirement of Section 7.8.1 does not apply in any case: (i) where Reseller provides Service to an End User for a period of less than fourteen (14) days in conjunction with a cellular telephone unit not owned by the End User, and (ii) where it would be impractical for Reseller to enter into contracts with each End User obtaining such short-term rental Service; provided, however, that if Reseller does not obtain contracts with such End Users, or file tariffs in accordance with Section 7.8.1, it must, and does hereby, indemnify Company and hold Company harmless for and from any claims brought by such End Users, and any other damages that may occur and would not have occurred had the End User contracts been in place. Further, if Reseller intends to invoke the exception set forth in this Section, it must notify Company at least four days before doing so, so that Company may determine whether to increase the amount of the security required of Reseller under section 7.10. This Section 7.8.2 is in addition to, and not in place of Section XII regarding indemnification, and does not reduce or mitigate its effect.

B.9.12 Insurance. Reseller shall keep in full force and effect a policy of public liability, personal injury, property damage, and contractual liability insurance with respect to the business operated by Reseller, which insurance shall cover each occurrence in an amount not less than $1 million and shall cover property damage in an amount not less than $500,000. Such policy or policies shall name Company as an additional insured and shall be procured from an insurance carrier reasonably acceptable to Company. Within ten days of execution of this Agreement, Reseller shall furnish Company with a certificate evidencing such insurance. Such insurance shall provide that the insurer will not cancel, alter, or allow such insurance to expire without first giving Company 30 days prior written notice.

B.9.13 Security

(a) Prior to processing any order for Numbers submitted by Reseller, or at any time during the term of this Agreement, Company may require that Reseller deposit cash with Company or provide it with an irrevocable Letter of Credit, issued by a financial institution and having terms and conditions satisfactory to Company, in such amount as is set forth in Schedule 3 hereto or as otherwise required by Company in its sole discretion. A financial institution will generally be satisfactory to Company if it is a bank chartered under the laws of the State of one of the Areas in which Reseller purchases Service or the United States with deposits insured by the Federal Deposit Insurance Corporation ("FDIC") and with an office located within the Area. This security may be required by Company to secure performance of Reseller's obligations under this Agreement, and may be based on its assessment of Reseller's creditworthiness, including Reseller's payment history with Company, and Company may waive the requirement of a deposit or Letter of Credit, or may increase or decrease the amount thereof required from Reseller at any time based on Company's reassessment of Reseller's creditworthiness or an Event of Default under this Agreement by Reseller. All decisions with respect to the necessity for and amount of a deposit or letter of credit shall be made in Company's sole discretion.

(b) In the event Reseller provides Company with a cash deposit, Reseller hereby grants to Company a security interest in such deposit.

(c) If Reseller has fully performed all terms and conditions of this Agreement, any cash deposit without interest (unless payment of interest is required bylaw) shall be returned to Reseller within 30 days following payment of all sums owned by Reseller under this Agreement or within 90 days after termination of this Agreement, whichever is later. If the Postal Service is not able to deliver the funds to Reseller and returns them to Company, and Company is not able upon reasonable inquiry to locate Reseller within 30 days after such return, Company will keep the funds and Reseller shall have no further right thereto.

(d) If Reseller fails to pay all sums owed to Company, all or any part of Reseller's deposit (whether in the form of cash or Letter of Credit) maybe applied by Company, without notice, to pay such sums owed Company under the Agreement. In addition, from time to time Company may apply all or any part of the deposit to sums due hereunder or to cure other breaches by Reseller. This right of offset is in addition to all other rights and remedies available to Company under this Agreement or at law or in equity. Reseller shall restore the deposit to an amount acceptable to Company within ten days of Company's written notice to do so.

(e) In the event Reseller files for bankruptcy protection or an involuntary bankruptcy petition is filed against Reseller, Company and Reseller agree that Company shall be entitled to recoup against the deposit any sums that are owed Company at that time. Should Company seek relief from the automatic stay in order to effect such recoupment, although such relief may not be required under current law, Reseller agrees and stipulates to the entry of relief from the stay to allow Company to recoup the deposit and agrees to raise no defenses thereto. Company and Reseller stipulate that the deposit and the Reseller's obligations under this Agreement arise out of the same transaction.

10. COMPANY'S OBLIGATIONS

B.11.1 Company's Service. Company will provide Service to Reseller subject to the terms and conditions specified in this Agreement. Company's obligations to provide Service is conditioned upon Company's ability to obtain, retain, and maintain, without unreasonable expense, suitable facilities, equipment, licenses, and rights to provide Service. Company's obligation to provide Service is further conditioned upon Reseller's compliance with the terms and conditions of this Agreement.

B.11.3 Informational Material. Company will provide to Reseller, when available, a coverage map of geographic areas where Company's Service is in effect, and a copy of such other pertinent informational material and other assistance reasonable necessary to enable Reseller to acquaint itself and End Users with Company's Service.

B.11.5 Notice of Material Change in Service. Company agrees to provide reasonable notice to Reseller of any material changes in Service of either a permanent or temporary nature.

12. TRADE NAME AND TRADEMARK

B.12.1 Company's Marks. Reseller recognizes the right, title, and/or interest of Company and its Affiliates through ownership or license in and to all service marks, trademarks, and trade names owned by or used in connection with Service by Company (the "Marks"). Company Marks are set forth in Schedule 4. Reseller agrees not to engage in any activities or commit any acts, directly or indirectly, which may contest, dispute, or otherwise impair such right, title, and interest of Company and its Affiliates therein. Reseller has no rights to the Marks, shall not use any Marks, and shall not mention "AT&T" in connection with the Service. Reseller shall not acquire or claim any right, title or interest in or to the Marks through sale of service or otherwise. Reseller is specifically prohibited from incorporating any of the Marks into Reseller Marks or from using any service mark, trademark or trade name which is confusingly similar to any of the Marks.

B.12.2 Reseller's Marks. Company recognizes the right, title, and interest of Reseller and its Affiliates in and to all service marks, trademarks, and trade names owned by Reseller or used in connection with Service by Reseller or its Affiliates (collectively, "Reseller Marks"). The Reseller Marks are set forth in schedule 5. Company agrees not to engage in any activities or commit any acts, directly or indirectly, which may contest, dispute, or otherwise impair such right, title, and interests of Reseller and its Affiliates therein. Company has no rights to the Reseller Marks and shall not use any Reseller Marks in connection with the Service. Company shall not acquire or claim any right, title, or interest in or to the Reseller Marks through sale of Service or otherwise. Company is specifically prohibited from incorporating any Reseller Marks into the Marks or from using any service mark, trademark or trade name confusingly similar to the Reseller Marks.

13. PROPRIETARY INFORMATION; CONFIDENTIALITY

B.14.1 Confidential Information. During the term of this Agreement either party may (but shall not be obligated to) disclose to the other information which is considered proprietary or confidential by the disclosing party. Without the disclosing party's specific prior written consent, disclosure shall not be made to a third party (including but not limited to End Users) of any information which is designated confidential or proprietary and which is supplied by one party to the other party, and which information is not otherwise generally available to the public or is not already known to the other party; provided, however, either party may disclose such information in compliance with a valid order or requirement from a state or federal agency or court of competent jurisdiction, if the other party has been given ten days prior written notice of the proposed disclosure or as much notice as is reasonably possible if the situation dies not permit such ten-day notice.

B.14.2 <u>Additional Protection of Confidential Information</u>. In addition, as a measure to protect each party's confidential business information, each party agrees to notify the other at least five business days prior to employing any person who, during the preceding year, was employed by the other or any of its Affiliates, agents, or dealers, so that such party may take reasonable steps to protect its rights with respect to such information. In addition, each party agrees not to employee any person if such employment would cause such person to be in breach of a non-competition agreement between such person and the other party. Nor may either party otherwise obtain any confidential or proprietary information from the other, its Affiliates, agents, or dealers, or their current or former employees without the other's specific prior written consent.

15. RESTRICTIONS ON USE

B.15.1 <u>Abuse or Fraudulent Use</u>. Service is furnished subject to the condition that there will be no abuse or fraudulent use thereof. Abuse and fraudulent use of Service include, but are not limited to:

(a) Attempting or assisting another to access, alter, or interfere with the communications of and/or information about another cellular Customer;

(b) Tampering with or making an unauthorized connection with any Facilities of Company;

(c) Using or assisting another to use any scheme, false representation, or false credit device, or other fraudulent means or devices in connection with the Service;

(d) Using Service in such a manner so as to interfere unreasonably with the use of Service by one or more other Customers or

End Users or to interfere unreasonably with Company's ability to provide Service; and

(e) Using Service to convey information which is obscene, salacious, prurient, or unlawful.

B.15.2 Cancellation of Service to End User. Company may require Reseller to cancel the right to market or use Service by any of its agents or End Users abusing or fraudulently marketing or using Service. Oral notice may be given by Company in this circumstance, provided that such oral notice is to be confirmed in writing within 24 hours. Reseller shall, within four hours of receipt of notice from Company as to the abuse or fraud, give notice to Company to cancel such Service in accordance with Article IV. If Reseller does not provide this notice in a timely fashion, Company is authorized by Reseller to execute such a notice on behalf of Reseller and to terminate Service to such End User's Number immediately thereafter. For so long as Company act in good faith under this Section, Reseller shall indemnify and hold Company harmless against any claim or liability, including attorneys fees and costs (through any appeals) arising therefrom.

B.15.3 Interference. The parties understood that from time to time one or more End Users may interfere with the System in such a ways to impair the quality of Service provided by Company to their Customers; accordingly, upon discovery of any such abuse by an End User by either of the parties thereto, the party having such knowledge shall promptly notify the other party, and the Reseller shall immediately order the End User to cease from engaging in such act(s) of interference. Company shall have the right to discontinue Service to that End User. Should such acts continue. Reseller shall assist Company in taking all actions reasonably necessary to prevent further interference.

16. INDEMNIFICATION

Reseller and Company each hereby agree to defend, indemnify, and hold harmless each other and each other's Affiliates, and their former, current and future officers, directors, employees, agents, successors, and assigns, from and again any claims, costs, and expenses, including punitive damages, court costs, and reasonable attorneys' and expert witness fees before and at trial and on appeal (collectively, "Claims"), arising from a breach of this Agreement by, or any conduct in connection with this Agreement of, the indemnifying party (including such party's Affiliates, and their officers, directors, employees, agents, and contractors). Reseller further agrees to defend, indemnify, and hold harmless Company, their Affiliates, and former, current, and future officers, directors, employees, agents, successors, and assigns, from and against any Claims of End User; provided, however, that the obligations (of both Reseller and Company) to defend, indemnify, and hold harmless shall not apply to the extent of such Claims results from the other party's negligence or willful misconduct.

Within ten days after being notified of any Claim to which these indemnification obligations may apply, the party receiving such notice shall notify the party from whom the indemnification is sought (the "Indemnifying Party"), and shall give reasonable opportunity to the Indemnifying Party to defend the claims at its own expense and with counsel of its own selection; provided, however, that the party seeking indemnification shall at all time have the right to participate fully (at its own expense) in the defense of and to approve any settlement of the Claim.

If the Indemnifying Party shall, within 30 days after notice, fail to accept defense of the Claim, then the party seeking indemnification shall have the right, but not the obligation, to undertake the defense of, and to compromise or settle (exercising reasonable business judgment), the Claim on behalf, for the account, and at the risk of the Indemnifying Party. If the Claims cannot by their nature be defended solely by one party, the other party shall make available all information and assistance that may be reasonable be requested, regardless of any obligations to indemnify hereunder.

18. DEFAULT AND TERMINATION

i) Default. This Agreement may be terminated upon an Event of Default by either party if such Event of Default is not cured by the defaulting party within 30 days of receipt of written notice of the Event of Default; provided, however, that in the case of (Reseller's Default for failure to pay Company any sums due (including providing any required deposits), or (a violation of Article IX, This Agreement may be terminated if such Event of Default is not cured within ten days of receipt of written notice of Default. If such Event of Default remains uncured, termination shall be effective on the expiration of the cure period without the requirement of additional notice.

B.19.2 Right to Pursue Remedies. If this Agreement is terminated as a result of an Event of Default attributable to Reseller, Company shall have the immediate right, without further notice or proceedings, to deduct any amounts due from the security referenced in Section 7.10 above and to pursue such other actions as Company may deem appropriate.

B.19.3 Survival of Obligations. The obligations undertaken by the parties pursuant to Articles V, except Section 5.10, IX, X, XII, XIII, and XV shall survive termination of this Agreement.

B.19.4 Continuing Obligations. Termination pursuant to the terms of this Agreement, regardless of cause or nature, shall be without prejudice to any other rights or remedies of the Parties, and Reseller shall remain solely responsible for its obligations to its agents and End Users. Termination of this Agreement with or without cause shall not release either party hereto from any liability which at the time of termination has already accrued to the other party or which thereafter may accrue in respect to any act or omission prior to termination, or from any obligation which is expressly stated herein to survive termination; provided, however, that Company may, without liability, cancel any previously accepted orders for Numbers which have not been assigned to End Users on or before the date of termination.

B.19.5 No Company Obligation for Continuing Service to End Users. Upon termination, Company shall have no further obligation to provide Service to Reseller. However, in order to avoid disruption of Service to End Users, upon request of Reseller of End Users, Company may continue Service directly to any End User who meets Company's credit requirements, and enters into a contract for Service with the Company. Upon termination, Company may re-route calls using any Numbers previously assigned to Reseller so that any attempts to access Service will result in connection to Company's personnel, who will advise callers of the termination and describe how they may obtain Service directly from the applicable Company or Companies.

B.19.6 Notice of Reseller's Intended Sale of Its Business or Reseller Lists. In addition, in order to reduce the risk of service disruption to End Users and without reducing the value of Reseller's business, during the term of this Agreement, and any extension thereof, and for 90 days following termination, Reseller shall be obligated to provide Company with reasonable notice of its interest in selling all or a part of its cellular resale business, cellular resale customer lists, or cellular resale End Users' service accounts arising out of this Agreement. Company shall be given a fair opportunity by Reseller to bid for the right to purchase such resale business or assets.

20. ASSIGNMENT

No rights or obligations hereunder shall be assigned or delegated, in whole or in part, by Reseller to any other person, firm, corporation, or other entity, except a parent corporation which owns 100% of the equity securities of Reseller at the time this Agreement is made, without Company's prior written consent, which consent will not be unreasonably withheld. For purposes of this provision, any change in the ultimate control of Reseller, by stock sale, merger, consolidation, or any other means, shall constitute an assignment subject to the consent requirements hereof.

21. ARBITRATION; JURISDICTION; GOVERNING LAW

B.21.1 State Law. The validity, construction, and performance of this Agreement shall be governed by and interpreted in accordance with the laws of the State of Delaware.

B.21.2 Arbitration Required. Except as stated in Section 15.3, all claims and disputes relating in any way to the performance, interpretation, validity, or breach of this Agreement shall be referred to final and binding arbitration under the commercial arbitration rules of the American Arbitration Association. A single neutral arbitrator shall decide claims of less than $100,000. All documents, materials, and information in the possession of each party and in any way relevant to the claims or disputes shall be made available to the other party for review and copying not later than 60 days after the notice of arbitration is served. To the extent that either party would be required to make confidential information available to the other, an agreement or an order shall be entered in the proceeding protecting the confidentiality of and limiting access to such information before either party is required to produce such information. Information produced by either party shall be used exclusively in the arbitration or litigation that may arise, and shall not otherwise be disclosed. In no event shall either party be entitled to punitive damages in any arbitration or judicial proceeding and each party hereby waives its rights to any punitive damages. In the event an arbitration panel or a court concludes that the punitive damages waiver contained in the previous sentence is unenforceable, then the parties agree that the court with subject matter jurisdiction over the confirmation of the award shall have sole and exclusive jurisdiction to determine issues of entitlement and amount of punitive damages. The arbitrators shall NOT have subject matter jurisdiction to decide any issues relating to the statute of limitations or amounts in excess of <u>$100,000, exclusive of interests and costs</u>, and the parties hereby stipulate to stay the arbitration proceeding (without the need of a bond) until any such issues in dispute are resolved.

(a) <u>Court Proceedings/Venue</u>. The parties hereby consent to the sole and exclusive jurisdiction and venue of the State and federal courts located in or covering Bergen County, New Jersey, for the following matters: disputes relating to the statute of limitations; contractual claims where the amount in dispute (excluding interests and costs) exceeds $100,000.00; disputes relating to any "non-contractual" claim (<u>i.e.,</u> those not governed by Section 15.2); and the entry of a judgment confirming an arbitrator's award.

B.21.4 <u>Attorneys' Fees</u>. In the event an action (including an arbitration) is commenced by either party to enforce the terms of this Agreement, the substantially prevailing party in such action shall be entitled to its reasonable costs and attorneys' and expert witness' fees incurred therein through appeal. For purposes of this Section, the efforts of in-house attorneys and their staff shall be valued at rates prevailing in the market for private practitioners.

22. MISCELLANEOUS

B.23.1 Headings. Headings to articles and Sections of this Agreement are to facilitate reference only, do not form part of this Agreement, and shall not in any way affect the interpretation hereof.

B.23.2 Waiver. Except as set forth in Article V above, the waiver, express or implied, by either party of any rights hereunder or of any failure to perform o breach hereof by the other party shall not constitute or be deemed a waiver of any other right hereunder or any other failure to perform or breach hereof by the other party, whether of a similar or dissimilar nature.

B.23.3 No Agency. Neither party is authorized to act as an agent for, or legal representative of, the other party, nor shall either party have authority to assume or create any obligation on behalf of, in the name of, or that shall be binding upon, the other party. Reseller shall not represent itself as an agent of Company in any manner not specifically provided for herein. All sales by Reseller shall be in its own name and for its own account.

i) Notices. Excerpt as otherwise provided in this Agreement, all notices required or permitted to be given hereunder shall be in writing and shall be delivered: (personally; (by certified mail, return receipt requested; (by an overnight courier service having a record of receipt; or (by facsimile, with a confirming copy sent by one of the other three methods described in this sentence. Notices shall be addressed as follows:

(b) If to Reseller:

Corporate Name
ATTENTION:
Street Address
City/State/Zip Code
Phone:
Fax:

(c) If to Company:

with a copy to:

Either party hereto may change its address by a notice given to the other party hereto in the manner set forth above. All notices shall be effective on receipt.

B.23.4 Forms. All notices and communications given by Reseller to Company under this Agreement - including orders, assignments requests, deactivation requests, suspension requests, feature modifications, fraud notices, etc. - shall be submitted by Reseller on forms prescribed by Company. This Section does not apply to any notice of termination of the Agreement. Company may, at its option, approve the use of non-standard forms and may condition any such approval on payment of a reasonable charge for the handling of non-standard forms.

B.23.5 Severability. Should any part of this Agreement for any reason be declared invalid by court order or by any regulatory agency, such order shall not affect the validity of any remaining portion, and the remaining portion of the Agreement shall continue in full force and effect, unless such order materially alters the nature of the obligations of either party hereto. In such event, this Agreement shall immediately terminate.

B.23.6 Force Majeure. Each party's performance under this Agreement shall be excused if such non-performance is due to labor difficulties, governmental orders, equipment failure, inability ro delay in securing equipment, civil commotion, acts of nature, weather disturbances or adverse weather conditions, and other circumstances beyond the party's reasonable control.

B.23.7 Merger/Entire Agreement. With respect to the subject matter hereof, this Agreement represents the entire Agreement between the parties hereto and, except as expressly provided, shall not be affected by reference to any other documents. The attached Schedules are {*text missing - covered up on hardcopy; first half line of p. 24*}. The terms and conditions of this Agreement supersede any other agreements or understandings, including prior or contemporaneous representations of sales representatives or other Company personnel, whether oral or written. Notwithstanding the foregoing, if the parties have previously entered into a written agreement pursuant to which Reseller acquired Service from Company prior to the effectiveness of this Agreement, the provisions of such earlier agreement shall survive to the extent specified herein, except as otherwise provided in a written Termination Agreement executed in conjunction with the making of this Agreement.

B.23.8 Counterparts. This Agreement may be executed in one or more counterparts, each of which shall constitute an original agreement, but all of which together shall constitute one and the same instrument.

B.23.9 Compliance with Laws. Company and Reseller shall at all times comply in all material respects with all laws, rules, and regulations applicable to the performance of this Agreement. If Company, at any time and in its sole discretion, determines that continued performance by Company of one or more provisions under this Agreement would violate applicable law, including any judicial or regulatory decree binding on Company, then, Company may provide Reseller within twenty-four (24) hours notice and, provided that continued performance of the Agreement without such provision(s) is practicable and economically beneficial to Company, terminate performance of such provision(s). If continued performance of the Agreement without such provision(s) is not practicable or economically beneficial to Company, then Company may terminate this Agreement on twenty-four (24) hours notice and, provided that continued performance of the Agreement without such provision(s) is practicable and economically beneficial to Company; terminate performance of such provision(s). If continued performance of the Agreement without such provision(s) is not practicable or economically beneficial to Company, then Company may terminate this Agreement on twenty-four (24) hours notice.

B.23.10 Amendments. Reseller acknowledges that, from time to time, Company may find it necessary to change or update certain procedures set forth in this Agreement in order to more efficiently conduct is business and provide Service to Reseller. Such changes or updates may be accomplished by Company providing 30-days written notice to Reseller. Except as otherwise provided herein, this Agreement may be amended by Company along upon 90 days written notice to Reseller. If Company notifies Reseller of an amendment to this Agreement and such amendment is unacceptable to Reseller, then Reseller has the right to terminate this Agreement upon 30-days prior notice given not more than 60 days after Reseller received notice of the amendment; provided, however, that if Company rescinds the amendment within 20 days after receiving Reseller's notice, this Agreement will not terminate, but shall continue in full force and effect. This Agreement shall be deemed automatically amended to the extent it is inconsistent with any tariff required to be filed by Company.

B.23.11 The Company. This Agreement shall be construed as a separate contract with the entity listed in Schedule 1 and any additional entity which provides Service pursuant to this Agreement in the future. Notwithstanding the foregoing, for so long as any of such entities is affiliated with ______________________ or its successors in interest, the obligations of Reseller with respect to insurance or minimum purchase requirements shall be determined as if all such entities were one entity, and _______, may act on behalf of any of such Affiliates for any purpose arising under this Agreement. If any of such entities shall cease to be affiliated with ___ or its successors in interest, this Agreement may be terminated by such entity at such time as the affiliation shall cease, or at any time thereafter, upon 30-days written notice (which notice may be given prior to or after the disaffiliation). In addition, if any of such entities shall cease to be affiliated with _______, the minimum blocks of Numbers, if any, as may be required by Schedule 2 from time to time, shall be computed only with respect to the markets operated by Affiliates of _____________ within the Areas in which Reseller continues to receive Service pursuant to this Agreement. If the disaffiliation of any entity shall result in Reseller's failure to comply with any of such provisions, Reseller shall be given 30 days within which to attain compliance and Reseller shall have the right to elect during such period to terminate this Agreement by giving 30 days advance notice without being in breach hereof.

B.23.12 Successors and Assigns. This Agreement shall be binding upon, and inure to the benefit of, the parties hereto and their respective successors and permitted assigns.

B.23.13 Preparation of Agreement. This Agreement shall not be construed more strongly against any party regardless of who is responsible for its preparation or drafting.

24. INDEPENDENT INVESTIGATION

COMPANY AND RESELLER ACKNOWLEDGE THEY HAVE READ THIS AGREEMENT AND UNDERSTAND AND ACCEPT THE TERMS, CONDITIONS, AND COVENANTS CONTAINED HEREIN AS BEING REASONABLY NECESSARY TO MAINTAIN COMPANY'S HIGH STANDARDS FRO SERVICE. RESELLER ACKNOWLEDGES AND UNDERSTANDS THAT COMPANY MAY AT ANY TIME ALSO BE ENGAGED DIRECTLY OR INDIRECTLY THROUGH OTHER DEALERS, OR OUTLETS OF ANY KIND, IN SOLICITING POTENTIAL CUSTOMERS FOR THE SERVICE OR OTHER SERVICES OR PRODUCTS OR FOR THE SALE, LEASE, INSTALLATION, REPAIR, OR SERVICING OF EQUIPMENT IN THE AREA. RESELLER ALSO ACKNOWLEDGES AND UNDERSTANDS THAT COMPANY MAY SELL THE SERVICE TO OTHERS WHO MAY RESELL IT. RESELLER HAS INDEPENDENTLY INVESTIGATED THE CELLULAR SERVICE OR EQUIPMENT SALE/LEASING BUSINESS AND THE PROFITABILITY (IF ANY) AND RISKS THEREOF AND IS NOT RELYING ON ANY REPRESENTATION, GUARANTEE, OR STATEMENT OF COMPANY OTHER THAN AS SET FORTH IN THIS AGREEMENT.

(a) IN PARTICULAR, RESELLER ACKNOWLEDGES THAT COMPANY HAS NOT REPRESENTED: RESELLER'S PROSPECTS OR CHANCES FOR SUCCESS SELLING SERVICES UNDER THIS AGREEMENT; THE TOTAL INVESTMENT THAT RESELLER MAY NEED TO MAKE TO OPERATE UNDER THIS AGREEMENT (COMPANY DOES NOT KNOW THE AMOUNT OF THE TOTAL INVESTMENT THAT MAY BE REQUIRED FOR THIS PURPOSE); OR THAT IT WILL LIMIT ITS EFFORTS TO SELL SERVICE OR ESTABLISH OTHER RESELLING CUSTOMERS IN THE AREA.

(b) RESELLER ALSO ACKNOWLEDGES THAT COMPANY HAS NOT REPRESENTED TO IT THAT: COMPANY WILL PROVIDE LOCATIONS OR ASSIST RESELLER TO FIND LOCATIONS TO PROMOTE THE SALE OF SERVICE UNDER THIS AGREEMENT; COMPANY WILL PURCHASE ANY

PRODUCTS MADE BY RESELLER THAT ARE IN ANY WAY ASSOCIATED WITH THE SERVICE SOLD BY RESELLER UNDER THIS AGREEMENT; RESELLER WILL DERIVE INCOME FROM THE SALE OF COMPANY'S SERVICES UNDER THIS AGREEMENT, OR COMPANY WILL REFUND ANY PAYMENTS MADE BY RESELLER TO COMPANY UNDER THIS AGREEMENT; OR COMPANY WILL PROVIDE A SALE OR MARKETING PROGRAM THAT WILL ENABLE RESELLER TO DERIVE INCOME UNDER THIS AGREEMENT.

(c) RESELLER FURTHER ACKNOWLEDGES THAT COMPANY HAS <u>NOT</u> MADE ANY REPRESENTATIONS REGARDING: THE QUANTITY OR QUALITY OF SERVICE TO BE SOLD BY RESELLER; THE PROVISIONS BY COMPANY TO RESELLER OR TRAINING AND MANAGEMENT ASSISTANCE; THE AMOUNT OF PROFITS, NET OR GROSS, THAT RESELLER CAN EXPECT FROM ITS OPERATIONS UNDER THIS AGREEMENT; THE SIZE (OTHER THAN THE GEOGRAPHIC AREA), CHOICE, POTENTIAL, OR DEMOGRAPHIC NATURE OF THE AREA IN WHICH COMPANY'S SERVICE IS AVAILABLE OR THE NUMBER OF OTHER DEALERS OR RESELLING CUSTOMERS THAT ARE OR MAY IN THE FUTURE OPERATE IN THAT AREA; THE TERMINATION, TRANSFER, OR RENEWAL PROVISIONS OF THIS AGREEMENT OTHER THAN ASSET FORTH IN THE AGREEMENT; OR THE SPONSORSHIP OR PARTICIPATION OF A PRIMARY MARKETER OF TRADEMARK PRODUCTS OR SERVICES IN RESELLER'S OPERATIONS UNDER THIS AGREEMENT OTHER THAT AS MAY BE SET FORTH IN THIS AGREEMENT. RESELLER ACKNOWLEDGING THAT IT UNDERSTAND THAT IT WILL <u>NOT</u> OBTAIN ANY EXCLUSIVE RIGHTS UNDER THIS AGREEMENT, EITHER WITH RESPECT TO A TERRITORY OR OTHERWISE, AND UNDERSTANDS THAT COMPANY MAY APPOINT OTHER DEALERS OR CUSTOMERS IN THE AREA AFFECTED BY THIS AGREEMENT. RESELLER ALSO ACKNOWLEDGES THAT COMPANY CANNOT CALCULATE IN ADVANCE THE TOTAL AMOUNT THAT RESELLER MUST PAY TO COMPANY UNDER THIS AGREEMENT AS THAT AMOUNT

DEPENDS ON THE QUANTITY OF SERVICE THAT RESELLER'S END USERS PURCHASE.

IN WITNESS WHEREOF, the parties have caused this Agreement to be executed by their duly authorized officers as of the day and year first above written.

Company:

By: ___________________________

Name: (print)
Title: (print)

RESELLER NAME:

By: ___________________________

Name: (print)
Title: (print)

Courtesy of Owen D. Kurtin, The Vinland Group LLC

APPENDIX D

PUBLIC KNOWLEDGE OPENING BRIEF OF PETITIONERS

SCHEDULED FOR ORAL ARGUMENT ON FEBRUARY 22, 2005
No. 04-1037

United States Court of Appeals
for the District of Columbia Circuit

AMERICAN LIBRARY ASSOCIATION, ET AL.,
Petitioners

- VS. -

FEDERAL COMMUNICATIONS COMMISSION, ET AL.,
Respondents.

OPENING BRIEF OF PETITIONERS

FINAL BRIEF DECEMBER 23, 2004

CERTIFICATE AS TO PARTIES, RULINGS AND RELATED CASES

In accordance with D.C. Circuit R. 28(a)(1), Petitioners American Library Association, Association of Research Libraries, American Association of Law Libraries, Medical Library Association, Special Libraries Association, Consumer Federation of America, Consumers Union, Electronic Frontier Foundation, and Public Knowledge provide the following information:

(A) Parties and Amici

According to Federal Communications Commission records, the parties before the Commission were as follows:

American Antitrust Institute

American Conservative Union, 60 Plus Association, Capital Research Center, Citizens United, The Conservative Party of New York State, The Patrick Henry Center for Individual Liberty, and Shirley & Banister Public Affairs (Joint Commenters)

American Foundation for the Blind

American Library Association, Association of Research Libraries, American Association of Law Libraries, Medical Library Association, Special Libraries Association (Joint Commenters)

American Society of Composers, Authors & Publishers; Broadcast Music, Inc. (Joint Commenters)

Arizona Consumers Council, California Public Interest Research Group, Colorado Public Interest Research Group, Columbia Consumer Education Council, Consumer Assistance Council (MA), Consumer Federation of America, Democratic Processes Center, Florida Consumer Action Network, Massachusetts Consumers' Council, North Carolina Public Interest Research Group, Oregon State Public Interest Research Group, Texas Consumers' Association, The Consumers' Voice, US Action, and Virginia Citizens' Consumer Council (Joint Commenters)

Banks Broadcasting, Inc., LIN Television Corp., Midwest Television, Inc., Post-Week Stations, Inc. and Raycom Media, Inc. (Joint Commenters)

CBS Television Affiliates Association

Center for Democracy and Technology

Computer & Communications Industry Association

Consumer Electronics Association

Corporation for National Research Initiatives

Corporation for Public Broadcasting, The Association of Public Television Stations, and the Public Broadcasting Service (Joint Commenters) Digimarc Corporation and Macrovision Corporation (Joint Commenters) Digital Transmission Licensing Administrator, LLC

Directors Guild of America

DirecTV, Inc.

Electronic Frontier Foundation

Electronic Privacy Information Center

Free Software Foundation

Home Recording Rights Coalition

IBM

Information Technology Association of America

Information Technology Industry Council

International Association of Broadcast Monitors

Internet Commerce Coalition and United States Internet Service Provider Association (Joint Commenters)

IT Coalition (Business Software Alliance and Computer Systems Policy Project) Law Office of Adam Hill

Motion Picture Association of America, ABC, ABC Television Affiliates Association, AFMA, American Association of Advertising Agencies, American Federation of Television and Radio Artists, American Society of Composers, Authors and Publishers, Association for Maximum Service Television, Inc., Association of National Advertisers, Inc., Belo Corp., Broadcast Music, Inc., CBS, Fox Broadcasting Company, International Alliance of Theatrical and Stage Employees, Motion Picture Technicians, Artists and Allied Crafts of the United States, its Territories and Canada, AFL-CIO, CLC, National Association of Broadcasters, Screen Actors Guild, Inc., Writers Guild of America, East, Inc., and Writers Guild of America, West, Inc. (Joint Commenters)

Motorola

National Broadcasting Company

National Cable & Telecommunications Association

National Football League, Office of the Commissioner of Baseball, National Basketball Association, National Hockey League, Women's National Basketball Association, National Collegiate Athletic Association, PGA Tour, Inc., and Ladies Professional Golf Association (Joint Commenters) National Music Publishers' Association

NBC Television Affiliates Association

New Yorkers for Fair Use

North American Broadcasters Association

Philips Electronics North America

Public Knowledge and Consumers Union (Joint Commenters)
Recording Industry Association of America
Thomson Inc.
TiVo Inc.
Veridian Corporation
Verizon Viacom
Walt Disney Company and ABC Television Network (Joint Commenters) Worldcom, Inc.
Thousands of individual consumers also filed comments and reply comments with the FCC.

The parties before this Court are:

American Library Association (Petitioner)
Association of Research Libraries (Petitioner)
American Association of Law Libraries (Petitioner)
Medical Library Association (Petitioner)
Special Libraries Association (Petitioner)
Consumer Federation of America (Petitioner)
Consumers Union (Petitioner)
Electronic Frontier Foundation (Petitioner)
Public Knowledge (Petitioner)
Federal Communications Commission (Respondent)
United States of America (Respondent)
Motion Picture Association of America, Inc. (Intervenor) National Cable & Telecommunications Association (Intervenor)

(B) <u>Ruling Under Review:</u>

<u>In the Matter of Digital Broadcast Content Protection,</u> Report and Order and Further Notice of Proposed Rulemaking, MB Docket No. 02-230, FCC 03-273, 18 F.C.C.R. 23,550, 68 Fed. Reg. 67,599 (2003).

(C) <u>Related Cases:</u>

There are no related cases in any other United States court of appeals or any other court in the District of Columbia.

FED. R. APP. P. 26.1 DISCLOSURE STATEMENT

In accordance with Fed. R. App. P. 28(a)(1), Petitioners American Library Association, Association of Research Libraries, American Association of Law Libraries, Medical Library Association, Special Libraries Association, Consumer Federation of America, Consumers Union, Electronic Frontier Foundation, and Public Knowledge, hereby submit the following Corporate Disclosure Statements:

American Library Association ("ALA") is not publicly traded and has no parent companies, subsidiaries or affiliates that have issued shares to the public. ALA is a nonprofit educational organization of approximately 65,000 librarians, library educators, information specialists, library trustees, and friends of libraries representing public, school, academic, state, and specialized libraries. ALA is dedicated to the improvement of library and information services and the public's right to a free and open information society.

The Association of Research Libraries ("ARL") is not publicly traded and has no parent companies, subsidiaries or affiliates that have issued shares to the public. ARL is a nonprofit association of 123 North American research libraries, including university libraries, public libraries, government and national libraries. Its mission is to shape and influence forces affecting the future of research libraries in the process of scholarly communication, promoting equitable access to and effective uses of recorded knowledge in support of teaching, research, scholarship and community service.

The American Association of Law Libraries ("AALL") is not publicly traded and has no parent companies, subsidiaries or affiliates that have issued shares to the public. AALL is a nonprofit educational organization with over 5000 members nationwide. AALL's mission is to promote and enhance the value of law libraries, to foster law librarianship and to provide leadership and advocacy in the field of legal information and information policy.

The Medical Libraries Association ("MLA") is not publicly traded and has no parent companies, subsidiaries or affiliates that have issued shares to the public. MLA is a nonprofit educational organization of more than 1,100 institutions and 3,600 individual members in the health sciences information field. MLA is committed to educating health information professionals, supporting health information research, promoting access to the world's health information, and working to ensure that the best health information is available to all.

The Special Libraries Association ("SLA") is not publicly traded and has no parent companies, subsidiaries or affiliates that have issued shares to the public. SLA is a nonprofit global organization for innovative information professionals and their strategic partners, serving more than 12,000 members in 83 countries in the information profession, including corporate, academic and government information specialists. SLA promotes and strengthens its members through learning, advocacy, and networking initiatives.

Consumer Federation of America is not publicly traded and has no parent companies, subsidiaries or affiliates that have issued shares to the public. It is a nonprofit association of 300 consumer groups representing more than 50 million Americans, that was established in 1968 to advance the consumer interest through research, education and advocacy.

Consumers Union is not publicly traded and has no parent companies, subsidiaries or affiliates that have issued shares to the public. Publisher of *Consumer Reports,* Consumers Union is an expert, independent nonprofit organization whose mission is to work for a fair, just, and safe marketplace for all consumers and to empower consumers to protect themselves.

Electronic Frontier Foundation ("EFF") is not publicly traded and has no parent companies, subsidiaries or affiliates that have issued shares to the public. EFF is a nonprofit public interest organization dedicated to protecting civil liberties and free expression in the digital world. Founded in 1990, EFF represents the interests of Internet users in court cases and in the broader policy debates surrounding the application of law in the digital age.

Public Knowledge is not publicly traded and has no parent companies, subsidiaries or affiliates that have issued shares to the public. It is a nonprofit advocacy and educational organization that seeks to address the public's stake in the convergence of communications policy and intellectual property law.

ACRA	All Channel Receiver Act
BPDG	Broadcast Protection Discussion Group. A subgroup of the CPTWG, co-chaired by individuals affiliated with the Motion Picture Association of America, and Sony, Hitachi, Intel, Mitsubishi, and Toshiba (the "5C Companies"), that developed the Broadcast Flag proposal.
Broadcast Flag scheme	The framework created by the FCC's Broadcast Flag rules, which operate by allowing broadcasters to add a small amount of data, or "flag," to their DTV transmissions that electronic devices must recognize and obey, prohibiting the transfer of the transmitted digital content over the Internet. Petitioners refer to this conglomeration of technology and regulatory requirements as the "Broadcast Flag scheme," "Broadcast Flag regime," or "Flag regime." Petitioners refer to the data that is added to the DTV broadcast signal simply as the "flag."
CATV	Community Area Television, the precursor to present-day cable television.

CCIA	Computer and Communications Industry Association
CPTWG	Copy Protection Technical Working Group. An inter-industry consortium, founded in 1996, that explores ways to protect digital content from copying.
DMCA	Digital Millennium Copyright Act
DTV	Digital television. DTV is similar to conventional, or analog, television, but is transmitted as digital data that allows more information to be carried in the same amount of electromagnetic spectrum. In this way, DTV allows for enhanced picture and sound quality.
DVD recorder	A consumer electronics device capable of recording video and sound content onto an optical disc-or Digital Versatile Disc ("DVD")-in digital format.
D-VHS	Digital Very High Speed. D-VHS is the format in which digital content may be recorded onto cassette tapes for viewing on digital VCRs. One of the Broadcast Flag-compliant technologies that the FCC recently approved is a D-VHS technology.
Downstream device	Consumer electronics devices-such as DVD recorders, third-generation cellular telephones, personal video recorders, iPods, and digital VCRs-that can access and manipulate digital content from a DTV or other device capable of capturing DTV broadcast signals, such as a personal computer

	equipped with a digital tuner card. Under the Broadcast Flag rules, downstream or "peripheral" devices may not access flagged content unless they will keep the content's protection secure and "robust."
EFF	Electronic Frontier Foundation
EPIC	Electronic Privacy Information Center
FCC	Federal Communications Commission
HDCP	High-bandwidth Digital Content Protection. One of the copy protection methods that the FCC recently approved as "compliant" with the Broadcast Flag regime.
HDTV	High Definition ("HD") Television. A type of digital television that has significantly enhanced picture and sound detail and quality, through the use of several times the number of pixels per frame than in standard digital television.
iPod	A handheld consumer electronics device equipped with varying amounts of computer storage, allowing consumers to store files containing digital entertainment content.
Legacy DTV tuners	Digital television tuners manufactured prior to promulgation of the Broadcast Flag rules that do not contain flag circuitry. Legacy DTV tuners are fully capable of receiving, translating, and passing on digital broadcasts marked

	with the flag, but will not give effect to the Broadcast Flag scheme's restrictions on distribution of content. Legacy tuners thus render the Broadcast Flag regime ineffective at preventing redistribution of DTV content over the Internet.
MPAA	Motion Picture Association of America
PC	Personal Computer
PDNE	Personal Digital Network Environment. PDNE is defined as the loose "network" of computers, televisions, and other electronics devices that a single consumer might use to access digital broadcast or entertainment content. The FCC declined in the Broadcast Flag order to resolve how flagged content could be used within a PDNE.
PVR	Personal Video Recorder. A consumer electronic device that can be connected to a television or other device equipped with a television tuner. PVRs, such as the name-brand TiVo, contain digital storage capacity that allows consumers to time-shift viewing of television programs, in much the same way as traditional VCRs but without the need for VCR cassette tapes and with the advantage of superior viewer maneuverability back and forth through the stored program.
Table A	An appendix to the BPDG Co-Chairs' Report intended to serve as a list of "approved" technologies under the

Broadcast Flag proposal. Initially left blank, the Co-Chairs' Report anticipated that technologies approved as compliant with the Broadcast Flag regime would be listed on Table A. It was expected that technologies created by the 5C Companies would be included.

JURISDICTIONAL STATEMENT

In this petition, nine not-for-profit organizations representing consumer, research, educational, and library interests seek the Court's review of a final Order issued on November 4, 2003 by the Federal Communications Commission ("FCC"). *In re Digital Broadcast Content Protection,* 18 F.C.C.R. 23,550, 68 Fed. Reg. 67,599 (2003) *("Order"),* J.A. 1254. The FCC asserted authority to promulgate the regulations pursuant to its "ancillary" jurisdiction, citing 47 U.S.C. §§ 151, 152, 154(i)-(j), 303, 307, 309(j), 336, 337, 396(k), 403, 521, 534(b), and 544a. Each of the petitioners participated in the rulemaking proceeding below and has members whose right to make use of copyrighted information will be adversely affected, and who will very likely have to pay higher prices for certain consumer electronics equipment, as a result of the Commission's *Order.* Petitioners timely filed a petition for review on January 30, 2004.

This Court has jurisdiction pursuant to 28 U.S.C. §§ 2342(1) & 2344, and 47 U.S.C. § 405. Venue properly lies pursuant to 28 U.S.C. § 2343.

QUESTIONS PRESENTED

1. Whether the FCC exceeded its statutory authority by requiring Broadcast Flag technology to be included in digital television ("DTV") receivers and other consumer electronic devices, despite the fact that this technology operates entirely outside interstate radio communications and Congress has specifically withheld authority from the FCC to control television receiver designs.

2. Whether the FCC acted outside its statutory authority by attempting to protect copyright holders through a mandate similar to that previously rejected by Congress in the Digital Millennium Copyright Act

("DMCA"), and by usurping the prerogative of Congress to create and define the scope of copyright.

3. Whether the FCC arbitrarily and capriciously promulgated the Broadcast Flag rule in the absence of substantial evidence that it is needed, and where the technology will not resolve the problem it is intended to address.

STANDARD OF REVIEW

The Court grants no deference to agency statutory interpretations that are outside the agency's delegated authority. *Adams Fruit Co. v. Barrett,* 494 U.S. 638, 649-50 (1990); *Motion Picture Ass 'n of Am. v. FCC,* 309 F.3d 796, 801 (D.C. Cir. 2002) ("MPAA"). *"To* determine whether the agency's action is contrary to law, we look first to determine whether Congress has delegated to the agency the legal authority to take the action that is under dispute." *Michigan v. EPA,* 268 F.3d 1075, 1081 (D.C. Cir. 2001). Thus, deference under *Chevron USA, Inc. v. Natural Resources Defense Council, Inc.,* 467 U.S. 837 (1984), applies only if (1) the agency's interpretations "have the force of law," *Christensen v. Harris County,* 529 U.S. 576, 587 (2000), and (2) they are reasonable interpretations of ambiguous provisions whose effect cannot be determined by their plain "language, structure, and purpose." *Dole v. United Steelworkers of Am.,* 494 U.S. 26, 35-43 (1990). If the agency interpretation is outside its delegation, it does not have the force of law, and the agency may claim only "respect according to its persuasiveness." *United States v. Mead Corp., 533* U.S. 218, 221 *(2001).*

STATEMENT OF THE CASE

This case involves the FCC's assertion of power-without any express statutory grant to require electronics manufacturers to add a governmentally-approved technological scheme into a wide array of consumer products. The technological scheme at issue-the Broadcast Flag-was conceived by a consortium of movie studios and others that seek to benefit from its use. The asserted aim of the technology is to prevent "indiscriminate redistribution" of "high value" DTV programs over the Internet. *Order ¶ 6, J.A. 1257.*

The FCC, however, mandated the technology without any proof that DTV programs have ever been placed on the Internet, and in the face of undisputed evidence that the Broadcast Flag regime will be entirely ineffective at stopping any pirate armed with an existing ("legacy") DTV tuner that does not recognize the flag. The FCC equivocated from the beginning over whether Congress had empowered it to promulgate such a rule, but nevertheless decided that it could dictate, for "the first time," how consumer electronics used in millions of American homes should be designed. *Order* ¶ *33*, J.A. *1270.*

STATEMENT OF FACTS

I. DIGITAL TELEVISION AND THE BROADCAST FLAG

The Broadcast Flag rule creates a regulatory and technological framework for controlling the redistribution of DTV broadcasts received over the air by consumers. DTV works in essentially the same way as traditional analog broadcasting, but because digital signals can be compressed more tightly on the electromagnetic spectrum, DTV allows for more information to be transmitted at a higher quality and resolution. As a consequence, DTV allows the broadcast of high definition television ("HDTV"). Recognizing this potential, Congress required that television broadcast licensees switch their signals to DTV by December 31, 2006, a deadline that may be extended depending on the penetration of DTV sets among consumers at that time. *See 47* U.S.C. § 309(j)(14).

What is the Broadcast Flag scheme?[1] Essentially, it is a mechanism for expanding the copyright protection that parties such as movie studios and broadcasters enjoy for DTV broadcasts. It achieves this by acting like an invisible tattoo on a DTV signal that requires special glasses to reveal its presence. The "flag" itself is simply a small amount of data added to the DTV signal that cannot be seen, but that with the appropriate technology can provide commands to the receiving device. *Order* ¶ 13, J.A. 1260. Thus, if a DTV signal tattooed with this "flag" is received by a television equipped to recognize its presence, the

[1] The "Broadcast Flag regime," "scheme," or "rule" includes both the actual data, or "flag," that is tattooed onto the DTV signal, as well as the FCC rules requiring use of technology to recognize this flag.

television will read the flag and obey whatever command its data carry. *Id.* ¶ *40*, J.A. 1274. On the other hand, if the same "flagged" signal is received by a DTV that is not equipped with flag-recognition technology, the set will display the accompanying video content, ignoring the flag. *See id.* Accordingly, the flag embedded in the signal cannot do anything unless the device receiving the broadcast signal is equipped with flag-recognition technology. *Id.* ¶¶ 13, 39, J.A. 1260, 1273.

The FCC *Order* requires all DTV tuners, personal computers, digital VCRs, DVD recorders, and personal video recorders that are capable of directly receiving DTV signals and that have digital outputs to incorporate into their architecture the flag-recognition technology by July 1, 2005. J.A. 1294-95. The rule prohibits these devices from sending flagged digital content to any other downstream device that is not "compliant": Once a television equipped to read the flag recognizes its presence, the television becomes unable to send the content outside its walls unless it does so through approved protection technology. *Id.* ¶ 13, J.A. 1260.

As a practical matter, this means that the flagged digital content is thereafter blocked from distribution over the Internet, over any other managed network outside the consumer's home system, and to any other electronic device such as a cell phone, personal computer ("PC"), digital VCR, or DVD recorder unless that device is itself equipped to preserve the "robustness" of the flag. *Id.* ¶ *5*, J.A. 1256-57, 1275-77.

The Broadcast Flag thus has a wide sweep. It creates a whole new regime of technical and copyright-related regulation in one stroke: design regulation of electronic consumer equipment, including PCs; restrictions on use of the Internet; licensing requirements for downstream devices; and rules that will impede consumers from engaging in lawful uses of broadcast material. *See, e.g.*, Reply Comments of Philips Electronics North America Corp. ("Philips"), J.A. 1020; Comments of Electronic Privacy Information Center ("EPIC"), J.A. 734; Comments of Verizon, J.A. 936-37.

The effects of the scheme are equally forbidding. It increases the cost of DTV sets and downstream devices alike. While the FCC characterized the cost of the Flag regime as "minimal," *Order* ¶ *20,* J.A. 1263, and the record lacked conclusive quantitative data, one thing is clear: The Flag regime costs something, and the added cost will likely be borne by consumers, if it has not been passed through already by manufacturers anticipating the rule's onset.[22] Comments of Public Knowledge and Consumers Union ("Consumers"), J.A. 908; Comments of Veridian Corp. ("Veridian"), J.A. 648-49. The encryption required to preserve the flag's "robustness" in connection with downstream devices further compounds these costs. Comments of Electronic Frontier Foundation ("EFF"), J.A. 722-24. Indeed, the FCC acknowledged that "[t]here may be additional cost[s] to implement the flag to the extent manufacturers cannot or do not rely on existing content protection technologies." *Order* ¶ *14* n.29, J.A. 1261.

The Flag requirement also increases the complexity and diminishes the functionality of a broad range of consumer electronics devices. EFF Comments, J.A. 718-21; Consumers Comments, J.A. 917. Consumers buying DTVs in the future will have to determine whether their existing peripheral devices will be compatible with flag-equipped devices, whether flag-compliant devices from different manufacturers are interoperable, and what uses of flagged content will be permitted. For instance, any flagged broadcast material that is recorded onto a DVD will not be viewable on existing non-flag-compliant DVD players. *Order* ¶ 21 n.47, J.A. 1263-64; *see also* EFF Comments, J.A. 721.

Equally important, the Flag scheme affects consumers by indiscriminately restricting uses of broadcast programming, and does so regardless of whether these programs are entitled to copyright protection, or are even copyrightable. EFF Comments, J.A. 721; Comments of Computer & Communications Industry Association ("CCIA"), J.A. 688. For example, if the Flag rules stay in place, consumers will not be able to:

- Send any portion of a flagged DTV broadcast over the Internet for any reason;
- E-mail a DTV broadcast to an office, second home, or traveling family member;
- Use uncopyrighted or newsworthy materials, such

[2] *See Order* ¶ *19 n.45, J.A.* 1263.

as the State of the Union Address, that have been marked with the flag to make, illustrate, or rebut an argument in an Internet discussion group, website, or "blog";

- Share a clip of a DTV broadcast with a virtual classroom during a distance learning lesson; or
- Create original works using the DTV broadcasts in ways that have not yet been conceived. No one may be able to fully assess the extent of this loss, since the new rule will halt creativity and innovation before it can blossom.

II. DIGITAL CONTENT PROTECTION AND DEVELOPMENT OF THE BROADCAST FLAG PROPOSAL

The FCC Broadcast Flag rule is an outgrowth of a broader entertainment industry effort to expand copyright protection by controlling technology design. The broadscale emergence of the digital age and the Internet in the 1990s set the stage for a new phase in the historical debate of whether additional copy protection mechanisms should be adopted to address new technologies. Industry interests in particular sought to expand their rights under the existing copyright statute through technological mandates.

In 1998, Congress spoke on the matter in the Digital Millennium Copyright Act. Lobbied heavily by content owners to ban technologies designed to circumvent encryption and other methods of protecting content from copying,[3] Congress adopted a ban on such technologies. 17 U.S.C. § 1201(a). However, Congress specifically declined to mandate digital copy protection technologies, directing that:

> Nothing in . . . section [1201] shall require that the design of, or design and selection of parts and

[3] *See* Pamela Samuelson, *Intellectual Property and the Digital Economy: Why the Anti-Circumvention Regulations Need to be Revised,* 14 Berkeley Tech. L.J. 519, 523, 538-39 (1999).

> components for, a consumer electronics, telecommunications, or computing product provide for a response to any particular technological measure.

17 U.S.C. § 1201(c)(3).[4]

Following the DMCA's adoption, content owners shifted their efforts to other forums. In 1996, they helped form the Copy Protection Technical Working Group ("CPTWG"), an inter-industry consortium composed primarily of representatives from the motion picture, electronics, information technology, cable, and broadcast industries, to explore ways to control the copying of DVDs and digital cable and satellite signals. In November 2001, CPTWG expanded its focus to consider the protection of DTV programs broadcast over the air. *See* Final Report of the Co-Chairs of the Broadcast Protection Discussion Subgroup to the Copy Protection Technical Working Group, at 2 (June 3, 2002) *("BPDG Report")*, J.A. 593; *see also Digital Broadcast Copy Protection*, Notice of Proposed Rulemaking, 17 F.C.C.R. 16,027, ¶ 2 (2003) ("NP"), J.A. 629-30.

To this end, CPTWG formed a subgroup, known as the Broadcast Protection Discussion Group ("BPDG"), that was charged with evaluating technical DTV copy control proposals. *BPDG Report*, J.A. 595. On June 3, 2002, the BPDG's co-chairs, along with the MPAA and the "5C Companies,"[5] issued a final report recommending a "proposed solution" to protect DTV transmissions from "unauthorized redistribution" by flagging content and protecting it with approved technologies to be included on a list it dubbed "Table A." *BPDG Report*, J.A. 609-12.

---

[4] The DMCA contains one narrow exception to this policy, which requires that analog VCRs conform to certain copy control technologies. 17 U.S.C. § 1201(k). "[T]his particular provision [was] included in the bill in order to deal with a very specific situation." H.R. Conf. Rep. No. 105-796, at 68 (1998); *see also* 17 U.S.C. § 1002 (1992 technology mandate for digital audio recorders). These narrow mandates demonstrate that Congress knew well how to impose such mandates if it so desired.

[5] "5C" is a group of companies including Sony, Hitachi, Intel, Mitsubishi, and Toshiba that had developed technologies that would give effect to the Broadcast Flag

This report was not a consensus effort. A number of the BPDG's members vociferously complained that the process had been hijacked by the 5C Companies and MPAA. In the words of one: "The BPDG approach has been marred by repeated and credible claims of back-room dealing by a small number of parties who have excluded most participants from real decision making.[6] In fact, the proposal offered by the BPDG co-chairs arose directly out of 14-plus hours of *exclusive* negotiations among the MPAA and the 5C Companies-negotiations that began *the day after* the BPDG held a member-wide "two hour status meeting." Thus, despite the fact that most of the BPDG's "meaningful negotiations occurred behind closed doors," the FCC's rulemaking here adopted for the entire nation a regulatory regime that was drafted by essentially nine corporations, with only slight changes. Philips Comments, J.A. 892.[7]

III. THE NOTICE OF PROPOSED RULEMAKING

Two months after the BPDG released its final report, the FCC issued a five-page Notice of Proposed Rulemaking that requested comment on "whether a regulatory copy protection regime is needed within the limited sphere of digital broadcast television." *NPRM¶ 3, J.A.* 630. The NPRM asked "whether quality digital programming is now being withheld because of concerns over the lack of digital broadcast copy protection," and "[t]o what extent ... the absence of a digital broadcast copy protection scheme [would] . . . delay or prevent the DTV transition." *Id.*

It is clear that the Commission planned from the outset to draw heavily on the *BPDG Report.* The NPRM cited a "consensus" in the co-chairs' report "on the use of a `broadcast flag' standard for digital broadcast copy protection," *id.* ¶ *2,* J.A. 629, and recognized that it was motivated not by any activity expressly within the FCC's statutory authority, but by *"the importance placed upon digital broadcast copy protection by some industry participants." Id.* ¶ *3,* J.A. 630 (emphasis added). While highlighting the *BPDG Report,* however, the NPRM did not actually

---

[6] CCIA Comments on BPDG Report, J.A. 628; *see also* CCIA Comments, J.A. 687; Consumers Comments, J.A. 915-16; Comments of National Cable & Telecommunications Association, J.A. 857.

[7] Comments of Zenith, Thomson, and Philips Electronics on BPDG Report, J.A. 613.

propose adopting the Broadcast Flag. It read more like a preliminary Notice of Inquiry, seeking suggestions regarding the different types of copy protection. *Id.* IT 3-5, J.A. 630. And unsurprisingly, in light of the absence of any specific congressional authorization, the NPRM also sought comment regarding a more fundamental question-whether there even was a "jurisdictional basis for Commission rules dealing with digital broadcast television copy protection." *Id.* ¶ 10, J.A. 631.

The NPRM stirred a groundswell of opposition. Literally thousands of comments were filed, the vast majority of which expressed the concerns of consumers from across the country that any Commission-mandated copy protection regulations would affect their ability to lawfully copy, redistribute, and manipulate DTV programming.[8]

Many commenters, including Petitioners here, pointed out that the Communications Act ("Act") gives the FCC no power to control how entertainment content (digital or otherwise) is treated after it has already been received in consumers' homes, and that Congress had expressly withheld from the Commission plenary authority over television design. E.g., Consumers Comments, J.A. 926-30; *see also* Philips Comments, J.A. 896-98.

For their part, the MPAA and a conglomerate of entertainment companies-who were bold enough to attach to their comments *draft Broadcast Flag regulations* built on the BPDG proposal[9]-insisted that the Commission did have jurisdiction to impose the Flag under Section 336(b)(4) and its ancillary jurisdiction. *See* Joint Comments of the Motion Picture Association of America *et al. ("MPAA")*, J.A. 795, 799 (citing 47 U.S.C. § 336(b)(4)).

---

[8] *See, e.g.*, Comment of Sally Jarvis (Centreville, Va.), J.A. 645 ("I believe that the broadcast flag would interfere with legitimate use of content."); Comment of Bryce Verdier (Sonoma, Cal.), J.A. 932-33 ("[The Broadcast Flag p]uts too much power into the companies to decide what [I] can and cannot save to watch later."); Comment of Brian Ristuccia (Tewksbury, Mass.), J.A. 1249 (Broadcast Flag will create "unnecessarily complex and expensive equipment").

[9] *See* MPAA Comments Aft. B, J.A. 821.

In letters filed with the FCC, a few members of Congress supported the Commission's jurisdiction to impose the Flag regime. These views were based primarily on Section 336 of the Act, even though that section contemplates regulations exclusively for ancillary or supplementary services.[10] But a number of other members of Congress disagreed, warning that "[w]hile Title 47 grants authorities to the FCC in respect of broadcasting, *no express authority is provided to address the complex issues of intellectual property matters in general or digital broadcast copy protection in particular.*" Letter from Sen. Patrick J. Leahy, Chairman, Senate Judiciary Committee and Rep. F. James Sensenbrenner, Jr., Chairman, House Committee on the Judiciary, *et al.* to Michael K. Powell, Chairman, FCC (Sept. 9, 2002) (emphasis added); *see also* Letter from Sen. John McCain to Michael K. Powell, Chairman, FCC (Oct. 16, 2003).[11] Likewise, in hearings before the House Judiciary Committee, Representative Howard Berman stated: "The FCC doesn't have expertise in this particular area, and so I am opposed to the FCC attempting to interpret, regulate, or otherwise limit the exclusive rights of copyright owners in the course of its broadcast flag rulemaking." *Hearing before the Subcommittee on Courts, the Internet, and Intellectual Property*, 108th Cong. Serial No. 5, at 12 (Mar. 6, 2003).

With respect to the facts, the content owners failed to answer the essential question posed by the NPRM-whether there was a problem that needed to be solved. None of the movie studios, television producers, or networks came forward with any proof that they had withheld one single program from digital broadcasting because of a lack of protection, or of a single instance of Internet redistribution of HDTV programming. In fact, each of the major networks recognized that substantial amounts of digital broadcast content are already available absent any protection whatsoever.[12] Instead, to substantiate their claim that the Broadcast Flag was needed, the

---

[10] *See* Letter from W.J. `Billy" Tauzin, Chairman, House Committee on Energy and Commerce, to Michael K. Powell, Chairman, FCC (July 19, 2002).at http://energycommerce.house.gov/107/Letters/07192002_684print.htm; Letter from Senator Ernest F. Hollings, Chairman, Senate Committee on Commerce, Science, and Transportation, to Michael K. Powell, Chairman, FCC (July 19, 2002), *at* http://hollings.senate.gov/materials/ ltr.broadcastflag.pdf.

[11] Available at
http://pl1foss2.fcc.gov/pro&ecfs/reeve.cgi?nativeoddf&id document=6513293947 (Leahy); http://www.eff.org/IP/Video/HDTV/bflag_letter.php (McCain).

[12] *See* Comments of National Broadcasting Co. ("NBC"), J.A. 851; Comments of the Walt Disney Co. and the ABC Television Network ("Disney"), J.A. 956; Comments of Viacom ("Viacom"), J.A. 942.

networks resorted to tendering threats about what they *would* do, as if DTV broadcasts were still a thing of the future. CBS owner Viacom was most blatant in its effort to coerce FCC action:

> [I]f a broadcast flag is not implemented and enforced by Summer 2003, Viacom's CBS Television Network will not provide *any* programming in high definition for the 2003-2004 television season.

Viacom Comments, J.A. *942; see also* Disney Comments, J.A. 955; NBC Comments, J.A. 851. That threat, however, was not carried out.[13]

With respect to the Flag's effectiveness, commenters, including Petitioners, pointed to the primary ways pirates can circumvent it, leaving only law-abiding consumers inhibited: using "legacy" DTV tuners not equipped with flag recognition technology, and converting broadcasts from digital to analog and then back to digital (the "analog hole"). Consumers Comments, J.A. 917-19; EFF Comments, J.A. 717-18; EPIC Comments, J.A. 733; Comments of the IT Coalition, J.A. 757. The content owners recognized these vulnerabilities. In the words of the Fox Entertainment Group, the Broadcast Flag scheme alone "doesn't really ring any bells, because there are so many work-arounds." Consumers Comments, J.A. 916 n.41 (quoting Fox). As the MPAA conceded, the Broadcast Flag is powerless to stop redistribution of DTV content, and can merely make it "more difficult." Reply Comments of MPAA, J.A. 1093, 1098; *see also* EFF Comments, J.A. 714-18.

IV. THE BROADCAST FLAG ORDER

In November 2003, the FCC issued its final Order. Pushing aside all criticism, the Commission adopted the MPAA's proposed regulations essentially

[13] Indeed, the CBS website reveals that it continues to broadcast the vast majority of its primetime programming in high definition, *see* http://www.cbs.com/info/hdty/index.php, even as DTVs have continued to be added to American households. Viacom Comments, J.A. 949.

wholesale,[14] and required inclusion of Broadcast Flag technology in all covered electronics equipment no later than July 1, 2005. J.A. 1295.

In announcing this rule, the Commission rejected the MPAA's argument that it had express authority to require the Broadcast Flag under Section 336-the one provision of the Communications Act that directly addresses DTV rulemaking and instead claimed that it had the power to dictate equipment design under its implicit "ancillary jurisdiction." *Order* ¶¶ 27-29, J.A. 1266-67. Specifically, the Commission asserted that even though the Broadcast Flag scheme plays no part in the actual reception of a DTV signal, televisions and similar devices fall generally within the FCC's statutory grasp because they are part of "radio" or "wire communications" as defined by Section 152(a) of the Communications Act. *Id.* ¶ 29, J.A. 1267-68.

Based on this conclusion, the FCC declared that it could use its ancillary jurisdiction as an overarching power to regulate televisions irrespective of other congressional pronouncements, so long as the FCC finds the rule "necessary" to "lead the nation into a new era of free, over-the-air digital broadcasting." *Id.* ¶ 31, J.A. 1268-70. Thus, instead of finding any specific authorization by Congress, the Commission boldly claimed that the *failure* of Congress to expressly withhold power gave the agency the authority to promulgate the Flag rules:

> Congress [has never] indicate[d] any intent to limit the Commission's ability to exercise its ancillary jurisdiction over manufacturers except, and only by implication, in the context of regulating manufacturers with respect to their activities that Congress specifically addressed by statute.

Id. ¶ 32, J.A. 1270.

The Commission consequently explained away statutory statements limiting its authority over manufacturers on the curious premise that they did not circumscribe the implicit authorization that the Commission now discovered:

---

[14] The only portion of the MPAA proposal not enacted by the Commission was the MPAA's criteria for selecting "approved" technologies. *See Order* IT 36, 59, J.A. 1272-73, 1281.

> *Accordingly, Congressional admonitions and past Commission assurances of a narrow exercise of authority over manufacturers ... are properly limited to the context of those explicit authorizations.*
>
> *Id.* (emphasis added).

The FCC also glossed over the question of whether the Broadcast Flag was even needed. The Commission explicitly recognized that current technology "inhibit[s] the redistribution of HDTV over the Internet," but nevertheless decided that a Broadcast Flag regime is necessary now because "indiscriminate" DTV redistribution would be possible at an undisclosed point "in the future," forcing "high value" content off broadcast television and onto cable and satellite. *Order* ¶ 8, J.A. 1258. The FCC then brusquely discounted all claims that the Broadcast Flag would be ineffective at protecting digital content from unlawful copying on the Internet. It concluded that the Broadcast Flag was necessary as a "speed bump" to decrease the number of individuals who can share broadcast material online. *Order* ¶ *20,* J.A. 1263.

Commissioners Copps and Adelstein dissented in part from the final rule. They stated that the FCC rules reach too far in blocking consumers' right to lawfully use broadcast material. The Broadcast Flag, Commissioner Adelstein explained, has an "unlimited" and "boundless" scope that upsets the balance of current copyright law by "mandating a technological protection regime that can be used to restrict the flow of content that is in the public domain, or is not subject to copyright protection for other reasons." J.A. 1324-25; *see also* J.A. 1320-21 (Copps).

The FCC declined in its final *Order* to adopt any definite standards and procedures for approving "compliant" technologies,[15] instead initiating a Further Notice of Proposed Rulemaking. *Order* ¶¶ 59-65, J.A. 1281-83. At the same time, the FCC announced that it would consider proposals under an interim "appropriate for use" standard. *Id.* ¶ 52, J.A. 1279. Recently, the FCC approved thirteen flag "compliant" technologies

[15] Another important unresolved issue was the definition of a personal digital network environment ("PDNE"), and what consumers will be able to do with flagged content within their PDNEs. *See Order* ¶¶ *61, 63, J.A.* 1282.

under these interim proceedings. *See In re Digital Output Protection Technology & Recording Method Certifications et al.*, FCC Order 04-193 (Aug. 12, 2004) *("Approved Technologies Order")*. The FCC's action in that proceeding underscores the harm that can be done now that the Commission has asserted general jurisdiction over electronic devices based on copyright principles. Although the FCC repeatedly claimed in its final rule that the Broadcast Flag scheme would not interfere with consumers' ability to copy flagged programs for personal use, e.g., *Order* ¶ 18, J.A. 1262, many of the technologies approved do exactly that.

SUMMARY OF ARGUMENT

The FCC has asserted jurisdiction it does not have. Bowing to a group of copyright holders led by the MPAA, the FCC promulgated a rule drafted by those corporate interests that will dictate design aspects of a vast array of consumer electronics-televisions, DVD recorders, PCs, TiVos, digital VCRs, iPods, and cell phones-for years to come. The FCC claims no specific statutory authority allowing it to meddle so radically in the nation's processes of technological innovation, but instead cites to its latent "ancillary" jurisdiction, which the FCC astonishingly contends is boundless unless Congress specifically acts to limit it.

In fact, the FCC's rules here flout multiple explicit limits on its jurisdiction. In the All Channel Receiver Act ("ACRA"), Congress went out of its way to ensure that the FCC would not regulate broadly in issues of television receiver design, a pattern it has repeated throughout the Communications Act. Now, however, the FCC has claimed that the Communications Act is precisely what the ACRA says it is not-"a general precedent for regulation of manufactured products." In any case, in no circumstance can the FCC regulate an activity that is not an interstate "communication" by radio or wire, and the Broadcast Flag rules regulate neither. The Broadcast Flag does not dictate how DTV transmissions are made, but simply controls how the transmitted content can be treated *after* it is received. Likewise, the Communications Act is clear that, unless specified elsewhere, it gives the FCC authority over receipt "services," not the receipt "apparatuses" the agency now attempts to regulate.

The FCC has not only transcended its own authority, it has also trespassed on a domain clearly not its own-copyright law. The Constitution exclusively reserves for Congress the power to create and regulate copyrights and balance the interests of copyright holders with the interest of the public in making "fair use" of copyrighted, or freely using uncopyrighted, works. Yet the FCC has taken it upon itself to legislate a new protection mechanism for digital works, notwithstanding the Supreme Court's admonition in *Sony Corp. v. Universal City Studios, 464* U.S. *417, 429-31* (1984):

> Sound policy, as well as history, supports our consistent deference to Congress when major technological innovations alter the market for copyrighted materials. Congress has the constitutional authority and the institutional ability to accommodate fully the varied permutations of competing interests that are inevitably implicated by such new technology.

Had the FCC required changes to the design of VCRs in the early *1980s* to protect copyright holders, the Supreme Court might never have had the opportunity to decide that home video recording constitutes fair use. The FCC's *Order* would likewise preempt that debate here, giving movie studios, television networks, and broadcasters unfettered discretion to stop redistribution of their works through a technological mandate, effectively foreclosing many fair uses of those works in the process. Indeed, the Broadcast Flag upsets a specific congressional balance between copyright protection and public use. It requires the inclusion of a governmentally-approved technological scheme in consumer electronics when Congress already expressly declined to adopt such a mandate in the DMCA.

Nor are the Broadcast Flag rules reasonable or supported by substantial evidence, even putting aside their serious jurisdictional flaws. They were adopted without any proof that the problem they purport to address even exists, there being no record that HDTV was or could be unlawfully distributed via the Internet. Rather, the FCC relied entirely on the self-serving statements of the Flag proponents to "conclude" that without the regime in place, undefined "high value" content would migrate from broadcast television to cable and satellite. The FCC thus engaged in the height of unreasoned decisionmaking by putting in place expansive rules that burden consumers and, by the Commission's own admission, are not effective in stopping piracy of DTV broadcasts.

ARGUMENT

I. THE FCC LACKS STATUTORY AUTHORITY TO IMPOSE A BROADCAST FLAG MANDATE

Agencies only have the powers that Congress gives them. *Lyng v. Payne*, 476 U.S. 926, 937 (1986); *Atlantic City Elec. Co. v. FERC, 295* F.3d 1, 8 (D.C. Cir. 2002). Accordingly, it is "treacherous" to find a delegation of administrative power in "congressional silence." *Girouard v. United States,* 328 U.S. 61, 69 (1946). "[W]e will not presume a delegation of power based solely on the fact that there is not an express withholding of such power." *Am. Petroleum Inst. v. EPA,* 52 F.3d 1113, 1120 (D.C. Cir. 1995). The FCC, as a "creature of statute," *Michigan,* 268 F.3d at 1081, is bound by this rule: It "literally has no power to act ... unless and until Congress confers power upon it." *Louisiana Pub. Serv. Comm 'n v. FCC,* 476 U.S. 355, 374 (1986).

Here, the FCC concedes that it lacks specific statutory authority to require the Broadcast Flag scheme. Instead, the FCC appeals to its "ancillary authority to regulate equipment manufacturers," which it claims arises from its "general jurisdictional grant in Title I of the Communications Act" over interstate "radio communications." *Order* ¶ *29,* J.A. 1267. The FCC's retreat to its so-called ancillary jurisdiction is conspicuous, not only because this is "the first time" the FCC has attempted to exercise ancillary authority over electronics manufacturers, *id.* ¶ 33, J.A. 1270, but because courts have consistently construed this authority as "limited" to television broadcasting-not as a nebulous expansion of its powers generally. *Bldg. Owners & Managers Ass 'n Int'l v. FCC,* 254 F.2d 89, 95 n.7 (D.C. Cir. 2001); *accord California v. FCC,* 905 F.2d 1217, 1240 n.35 (9th Cir. 1990). In marked contrast, the Commission now reads its ancillary authority as extending into every area that involves a television receiver, if Congress has not sounded a clear "intent to limit the Commission's ability to exercise its ancillary jurisdiction" in the area. *Order* ¶ 32, J.A. 1270.

The FCC's characterization of its authority rides dangerously close to a claim that "because Congress has not expressly forbidden this assertion of federal jurisdiction, the agency may assert it." *Michigan,* 268 F.3d at 1085. The fact, however, is that Congress has spoken in the area the FCC seeks to regulate. Even assuming that the FCC could properly rely on Title I alone,[16] the Broadcast Flag rules do not regulate interstate "radio communications" as defined by Title I, because the Flag is not needed to make a DTV transmission, does not change whether DTV signals can be received, and has no effect until after the DTV transmission is complete. Equally crucial, Congress has explicitly delineated the FCC's authority to regulate television receivers-rejecting the possibility that the agency should have "involvement in questions of receiver design." *Elec. Indus. Ass 'n Consumer Electronics Group v. FCC,* 636 F.2d 689, 694 (D.C. Cir. 1980) ("EIA").

A. The FCC Does Not Have Ancillary Jurisdiction, Because the Broadcast Flag Operates Outside the Scope of Title I

The FCC erred in determining that it had ancillary jurisdiction. On its face, the Communications Act sets forth the unambiguous boundaries of FCC jurisdiction. *See Connecticut Nat'l Bank v. Germain,* 503 U.S. 249, 253-54 (1992).

Specifically, Section 152(a) gives the FCC authority over "all interstate and foreign communication by wire or radio."[17] 47 U.S.C. § 152(a). Section 153 defines "radio" and "wire communications" as

---

[16] It is questionable whether Title I gives the FCC autonomous rulemaking authority in the first place. The Title I rulemaking provision, Section 154(i), has been characterized simply as a housekeeping provision limited to procedural rulemaking. *See North American Telecomm. Ass 'n v. FCC,* 772 F.2d 1282, 1292 (7th Cir. 1985). Thus, for the FCC to properly engage in substantive rulemaking, it must do so under Title II (common carriers), Title III (broadcasting), or another substantive grant of authority. But the Broadcast Flag rules do not properly fall within any of these substantive grants.

[17] The statutes discussed by Petitioners are reproduced in the Addendum appended hereto.

> The transmission [by radio or wire] of writing, signs, signals, pictures, and sounds of all kinds [by aid of wire, cable, or other like connection between the points of origin and reception of such transmission,] including all instrumentalities, facilities, apparatus, and services (among other things, the receipt, forwarding, and delivery of communications) incidental to such transmission.

Id. §§ 153(33), (52). Thus, the FCC has jurisdiction over a subject only if it is (1) a transmission or a person engaging in a transmission, (2) by radio, wire, cable, or similar connection, (3) between two or more states.

The law is clear that unless a subject falls within the scope of the FCC's general statutory authority, it cannot assert ancillary jurisdiction to regulate in the area. As this Court has explained: "[T]here are limits to [the FCC's] powers. No case has ever permitted, and the Commission has never, to our knowledge, asserted jurisdiction over an entity not engaged in `communication by wire or radio.' *Accuracy in Media, Inc. v. FCC,* 521 F.2d 288, 293 (D.C. Cir. 1975).

The recent *MPAA* case illustrates the principle. There, this Court rejected the FCC's claim of plenary authority under Sections 151, 152(a), 154(i), and 303(r)-the same general jurisdictional and rulemaking provisions the Commission relies on in this proceeding-to require the use of "video description" of television programs. 309 F.3d at 798. The court ruled, however, that "program content was at the core" of these rules, and that Section 151 did not allow the FCC "to regulate program content." *Id.* at 804, 807. Consequently, the FCC's reliance on its ancillary rulemaking authority under Section 303(r) was unlawful: "The FCC cannot act in the `public interest' if the agency does not otherwise have the authority to promulgate the regulations at issue." *Id.* at 806.

Likewise, in *Illinois Citizens Committee for Broadcasting v. FCC,* 467 F.2d 1397 (7th Cir. 1972), the Seventh Circuit held that the FCC lacked ancillary authority over objects that interfere with television transmissions. The plaintiffs in *Illinois Citizens* asserted that FCC jurisdiction over construction of the Sears Tower in Chicago was "`necessary to protect . . . an adequate signal,'" because otherwise, the tower would create "multiple ghost images" on area televisions. *Id.* at 1398, 1399. The Seventh Circuit rejected plaintiffs' claim. When courts have allowed the FCC to assert ancillary jurisdiction, the court explained, they have "tread[ed] lightly even where the activity at issue easily falls within sections 151, 152(a), 153(a) and (b), as being `communication by wire or radio.' Accordingly:

> [W]e do not understand how the limited extension of the Commission's jurisdiction to a hybrid activity like CATV, *but one nevertheless within the category of a signal-transmitting facility*, justifies regulation of any and all activities that "substantially affect communications."

Id. at 1400, 1401 (emphasis added); *Building Owners*, 254 F.3d at 95-96; *see also Accuracy in Media*, 521 F.2d at 293-94 (no FCC jurisdiction over Corporation for Public Broadcasting because not engaged in actual radio communications).

Even in the case that first recognized the FCC's ancillary jurisdiction, which the FCC relies upon here, *United States v. Southwestern Cable Co.*, 392 U.S. 157 (1968), the Supreme Court ruled that the FCC had rightly asserted jurisdiction over community area television ("CATV") networks only after determining that the industry was directly engaged in "interstate . . . communication by wire or radio" as defined in Section 152. *Id.* at 168. Therefore, the six-member majority held, the FCC's assertion of jurisdiction was *"reasonably ancillary* to the effective performance of [its] . . . responsibilities for the *regulation of television broadcasting." Id.* at 157, 169, 178 (emphasis added).

For two reasons, the Broadcast Flag rules fall outside the definition of interstate "radio" or "wire communications" as used by the *Southwestern* court and defined in Section 153. First, no transmission is involved; and second, while "interstate communications" covers "incidental" apparatus, it does not extend to apparatus that are used for the receipt of a transmission.

First, the FCC's assumption of ancillary jurisdiction here improperly asserts control over the digital "signals, pictures, and sounds" in a way that does not regulate interstate "radio communication." This is because, by definition, the Broadcast Flag scheme does not require televisions, computers, and other devices to "give effect to the redistribution control descriptor" until *after* the DTV broadcast has been completed. *Order* ¶ 39, J.A. 1273. The FCC rules thus do not compel broadcasters to use the flag, and a DTV broadcast does not need to contain the flag for a television viewer to receive the broadcast. *Id.* ¶ 37, J.A 1272. Similarly, a DTV set does not need to include a flag to improve reception or avoid electrical interference from other devices. *See id.* ¶ *21, J.A.* 1263-64. Nor do the rules regulate communications occurring by wire over the Internet: The Flag restricts the use of all *content-even* if it is only within a consumer's home-*before* that content can be transferred to *any other* digital device, including the Internet. *Id.* ¶¶ 37-38, 40, J.A. 1272-73, 1274. As the rule's title indicates, the Broadcast Flag scheme is a "Digital Broadcast Television *Redistribution* Control"-not a "Digital *Broadcast* Control." J.A. 1288.

In this respect, the Broadcast Flag resembles an assertion of FCC jurisdiction over an entire automobile simply because the car contains a satellite radio receiver. By the FCC's reasoning here, because that device can receive an over-the-air signal, the agency should have the authority to control not just the radio's outputs, speakers, and volume, but also the vehicle's doors, windows, and sunroof in order to prevent "redistribution" of the transmitted program outside the car in a way that could incentivize the broadcaster to shift its "high value" content to a more secure type of vehicle. The Broadcast Flag works in precisely this fashion. It forces both the receiving device and any other DVD recorder, TiVo, or other downstream equipment to "lock up" the digital content through encryption so that it cannot be "redistributed" outside those devices' walls absent FCC approval.

Granting the FCC such wide latitude as part of its purview over interstate "communication by radio" would render meaningless the boundaries established by the Act. *See, e.g., Southwestern Bell Tel. Co. v. FCC,* 19 F.3d 1475, 1481 (D.C. Cir. 1994); *Radio Station WOW, Inc. v. Johnson,* 326 U.S. 120, 131 (1945). If the FCC can mandate technology in DTV sets and downstream devices, what stops it from dictating the copies a fax machine can make once connected to a consumer's communications system? *Cf. California Indep. Sys. Operator v. FERC*, 372 F.3d 395, 398 (D.C. Cir. 2004). And if the FCC can compel the lockdown of digital content after transmission simply because it was once in radiowave form, then it can order broadcasters to use video descriptions because their broadcasts involve radio transmissions.

But the FCC did not have that authority in *MPAA* or *Illinois Citizens* just as it does not here. Indeed, if the Commission can require "downstream" and "peripheral" electronics devices located within someone's home-devices that undisputedly are not engaged in interstate communication-to obey the Flag, then the FCC's jurisdiction would know almost no bounds. Section 153's use of the term "instrumentalities, facilities, apparatus, and services . . . *incidental to such transmission*" would become superfluous, because the FCC could assert authority over any electronic device, skyscraper, mountain, or tree that can impact, alter, or influence radio communications. 47 U.S.C. § 153 (emphasis added). It is a fundamental canon of statutory construction that courts must give effect to every word in a statute, not disregard them. E.g., *Kilburn v. Socialist People's Libyan Arab Jamahiriya*, 376 F.3d 1123, 1127 (D.C. Cir. 2004). The FCC's imposition of the Broadcast Flag breaches this rule.

Thus, notwithstanding the FCC's claim that its imposition of a technological mandate here is "narrow," *Order* ¶ 48, *J.A.* 1277, the Broadcast Flag rules are the very type of measure the Seventh Circuit warned would make the FCC's implied jurisdiction "far too broad." *Illinois Citizens*, 467 F.2d at 1400. Now, as the FCC again grasps to regulate outside the Communication Act's bounds, this Court's warning from *MPAA* controls once more: "Contrary to the FCC's arguments suggesting otherwise, [Section 151] does not give the FCC unlimited authority to act as it sees fit with respect to all aspects of television transmissions." 309 F.3d at 798.

Second, the Broadcast Flag rules fall outside the definition of "radio communications" for another reason. The FCC entirely premised the Broadcast Flag scheme on the ground that "`radio communication' and `wire communication' are defined broadly to include not merely the transmission of the communication over the air or by wire, but also all incidental ... `apparatus'... that are *used for the `receipt . . .'* of such transmissions." *Order* ¶ *29,* J.A. 1267 (emphasis added). The Communications Act does not say this.

The text of the provision makes clear that the words "receipt, forwarding, and delivery of communications" are included in a parenthetical that defines transmission "services," not transmission "apparatus." Therefore, for the FCC to have jurisdiction over some apparatus, it must be incidental to *"transmission"-not* to "receipt." 47 U.S.C. § 153 (emphasis added). Section 153's legislative history leaves no doubt as to this reading. The relevant portion of Section 153 was added as part of the 1934 Communications Act. In connection with this new language, the Interstate Commerce Commission ("ICC") submitted a report explaining that the word "receipt" modifies only "services." The ICC wrote:

> [P]erhaps the word "services" is in itself sufficient to connote `receipt, forwarding, and delivery of massages' [sic] etc. *It seems preferable, however, that matters of such importance should not be left to the necessity for construction, but should be as definitely stated in the bill as they are now in the act.*

Hearings of Senate Interstate Commerce Committee, S. 2910, 73d Congress, at 201 (1934) (emphasis added).

In its quest to expand its own powers, the *Order* adopts a reading of the statute that ignores Section 153's plain language and clear legislative history, as well as the interpretive rule against boundless authority-as almost everything in this area can be said to be incidental to the receipt of communication. To meet its own ends, the FCC does precisely what the Act's legislative history says it should not. The Broadcast Flag rules improperly assert jurisdiction over television receivers generally when the Commission does not have that authority.

B. The Broadcast Flag Violates Congress' Express Decision to Limit FCC Jurisdiction Over TV Receiver Design

The FCC's rules also contravene Congressional intent by regulating in an area that the legislature has specifically marked off-limits. The courts have repeatedly struck down FCC regulations announced under its ancillary jurisdiction if the rules infringe on other provisions in the Communications Act, run contrary to the intent of Congress, or claim jurisdiction that the legislature has withheld. *See, e.g., FCC v. Midwest Video Corp.*, 440 U.S. 689, 701 (1979) *("Midwest II")* (no ancillary authority to "impose common-carrier obligations" on cable operators because Act precludes such regulation of broadcasters); *AT&T v. FCC*, 487 F.2d 865, 872 (2d Cir. 1973) (no ancillary authority to regulate "private line" rates where ratemaking authority is "specific"); *AT&T v. Iowa Utils. Bd.*, 525 U.S. 366, 381 n.8 (1999) (no ancillary jurisdiction over intrastate communications); *see also New York v. FCC*, 267 F.3d 91 (2d Cir. 2001); *Illinois Bell Tel. Co. v. FCC*, 883 F.2d 104 (D.C. Cir. 1989).

Accordingly, in *MPAA*, this Court rejected the FCC's reliance on its ancillary rulemaking authority under Section 303(r) in part because Congress had "originally entertain[ed]"-but declined-giving the Commission the authority to promulgate video description rules. 309 F.3d at 806. Simply because a regulation purports to benefit the public, the *MPAA* court ruled, does not mean that it is lawful. "The FCC must act pursuant to delegated authority *before* *<u>any</u>* `public interest' inquiry is made under § 303(r)." *Id.* (emphasis added); *see also, e.g., Southwestern Bell*, 19 F.3d at 1481; *NARUC v. FCC, 525* F.2d 630, 644 (D.C. Cir. 1976). "[I]n our anxiety to effectuate the congressional purpose of protecting the public," the Supreme Court has explained, "we must take care not to `extend the scope of the statute beyond the point where Congress indicated it would stop.' *United States v. Article of DrugBacto-Unidisk*, 394 U.S. 784, 800 (1969) (citation omitted).

In this case, Congress has not only indicated where the FCC's authority "should stop," it has expressly declined to extend the agency's powers into the field the Broadcast Flag rules now seek to occupy-television receiver design.

1. <u>Congress Has Withheld Authority from the FCC to Regulate Television Design</u>

Congress carefully circumscribed the Commission's authority over television receivers in the ACRA, 47 U.S.C. §§ 303(s), 330(a). Enacted in 1962, the ACRA gave the FCC authority to require that televisions sold in interstate commerce are "capable of adequately receiving all frequencies allocated by the Commission to television broadcasting." *Id.* § 303(s). This specific delegation thus confined the FCC's jurisdiction over television design to the ACRA's narrow grant of authority. By giving the FCC this specific limited power, Congress denied the Commission any authority to exert general control over television receiver design. *API,* 52 F.3d at 1119 ("[An agency cannot] rely on its general authority to make rules necessary to carry out its functions when a specific statutory directive defines the relevant functions.").[18] As the Senate Report accompanying the ACRA unequivocally explained:

> It has been argued that [the ACRA] would be a dangerous precedent which might lead to congressional control of all types of manufactured products. [But i]t must be remembered that this [Act] involves a unique situation which *would not in any way constitute a general precedent for such congressional regulation of manufactured products.*

S. Rep. 1526, 87th Cong., 2d Sess. 1, 7 (1962), *reprinted* 1962 U.S.C.C.A.N. 1873, 1876 (emphasis added).

Indeed, in *EIA,* the leading case on the ACRA, this Court adopted exactly this reading. At issue was an FCC requirement that all television receivers achieve a 12 decibel "noise figure," a technical improvement of UHF television reception over present levels that was not necessary for the sets to receive UHF channels. 636 F.2d at 693. This Court struck down the FCC's regulations as "`in excess' of its regulatory jurisdiction. *Id.* at 696 n.13. The court held that while the ACRA bestowed the Commission with "limited . . . authority to ensur[e] that all sets `be capable of adequately receiving' all television

[18] *See also, e.g., Sierra Club v. EPA,* 311 F.3d 853, 861 (7th Cir. 2002); *Am. Bus Ass'n v. Slater,* 231 F.3d 1, 4 (D.C. Cir. 2000); *Nat'l Min. Ass 'n v. Dep 't of the Interior,* 105 F.3d 691, 694 (D.C. Cir. 1997); *Martello v. Superior Court,* 261 P. 476, 478 (Cal. 1927) ("In the grants (of powers) ... no other than the expressly granted power passes by the grant.").

frequencies," Congress had intentionally restricted this jurisdictional grant to preclude broad-ranging FCC "receiver design regulation." *Id.* at 695, 696.

Last year, this Court reaffirmed the rule of *EIA* by upholding the Commission's authority to reach TV sets within the narrow confines of the ACRA. *Consumer Electronics Ass 'n v. FCC,* 347 F.3d 291 (D.C. Cir. 2003), considered regulations requiring all televisions of a certain size to include DTV reception by 2007. In establishing these requirements, the FCC did not invoke its ancillary jurisdiction, even though the rule that TV sets must be equipped to receive DTV transmissions is much more closely related to the DTV transition than the rule at issue here. Indeed, the FCC did not cite its ancillary jurisdiction even as a subsidiary ground, but relied exclusively on the ACRA, and was upheld by the Court in that reliance. The Court noted that while the *EIA* case rightly found the FCC's authority over televisions to preclude mandates "for enhanced reception," the DTV receiver rule fit squarely within its statutory power to require that televisions "adequately receive" all channels-including digital ones. *Id.* at 298 & n.3.

The ACRA's limits on FCC authority to regulate television design are made even more clear by the decision of Congress to reject a broader grant of authority. Originally, Congress had proposed to give the FCC the authority "to set `minimum performance standards' for all television receivers shipped in interstate commerce." *EIA,* 636 F.2d at 694 (citation omitted). However, when this proposal came under "considerable criticism" for "allowing the Commission too great . . . an involvement in questions of receiver design," Congress modified the language to the form in which it was enacted. *Id.* Consequently, the ACRA was adopted on twin promises: Congress' directive that it was not "open[ing] the door to regulation of the design of television receivers extending far beyond the objective of all-channel tuners," *id.* at 694 (quoting ACRA hearings), and the FCC's assurance that it would not use this new power to reach beyond achieving adequate channel reception:

> The FCC has assured us that the practical need for procuring authority which would permit effective enforcement of this legislation *would*

> *not involve the Commission broadly in the dealings of television set manufacturers.*

Id. at 645 (emphasis added).

Congress' decision in the ACRA that it did not want the FCC "broadly [involved] in the dealings of television set manufacturers" forecloses the Commission's assertion of ancillary jurisdiction here. *Id.* at 695. The FCC's new rules impose the very type of controls on television manufacturers that Congress sought to avoid. The Flag rules require manufacturers to modify their reception devices so that once a signal is received, the device cannot function as it otherwise would unless its architecture includes FCC-approved technology. *Order* It 39-47, J.A. 1273-77. Manufacturers thus lose control over at least two significant aspects of equipment design. They are forced to install content redistribution control mechanisms regardless of whether they would have done so absent FCC action, and they are divested of any meaningful choice over what type of control mechanism to use.

These constraints on manufacturer choice are exactly why Congress determined it does not want the FCC invoking "unbridled authority" over television design. *EIA*, 636 F.2d at 694. If the FCC can use its ancillary jurisdiction to compel electronics manufacturers to use Flag technology, it can also impose agency-approved standards for other technical measures. But as the *EIA* court recognized, Congress "carefully limited the Commission's authority" over television design specifically because it did not want to give the FCC the "`power to require that all sets be color sets, or have a certain size of picture tube or be made with a certain size speaker and so forth.' *Id.* at 694, 696 (quoting *All-Channel Television Receivers: Hearings on S.2109 Before the Subcomm. on Communications of the Senate Comm. on Commerce*, 87th Cong., 2d Sess. 59 (1962) (testimony of Rep. Kenneth A. Roberts)).

Accordingly, the Commission was wrong when it determined that Congress has not "limit[ed] the Commission's ability to exercise its ancillary jurisdiction over manufacturers." *Order* ¶ *32*, J.A. 1270. It is hornbook law that "`Congress does not intend *sub silentio* to enact statutory language that it has earlier discarded in favor of other language.'" *INS v. Cardoza-Fonseca*, 480 U.S. 421, 442-43 (1987) (citation omitted); *Russello v. United States*, 464 U.S. 16, 23-24 (1983) ("Where Congress includes limiting language in an earlier version of a bill but deletes it prior to enactment, it may be presumed that the limitation was not intended."); *FDA v. Brown & Williamson Tobacco Corp.*, 529 U.S. 120, 144 (2000). Here, just as in *MPAA*, after "originally entertaining the possibility of providing the FCC with authority to [regulate television receiver designs], Congress declined to do so." 309 F.3d at 806. Thus, by expressly abandoning language in the ACRA that would have given the FCC the type of authority it now claims, Congress cannot be deemed to have delegated these powers through the Commission's residual "ancillary" authority. Congress made a "conscious choice" not to allow the FCC to regulate television receivers broadly-and that choice must be obeyed. *North Haven Bd. of Educ. v. Bell*, 456 U.S. 512, 527-28 (1982).

2. Section 303 Reinforces Congress' Decision to Restrict FCC Authority Over Television Design

Reading the FCC's ancillary jurisdiction to curb, rather than expand, the agency's powers over television equipment design also comports with the overarching statutory scheme. Congress' decision to limit the FCC's authority in the ACRA was not confined to that Act alone. Rather, in *every case* where Congress has given the FCC authority to regulate television design, it has been "scrupulously clear," giving the FCC unambiguous, specific statutory power. *MPAA*, 309 F.3d at 805. The FCC concedes: "We recognize that the Commission's assertion of jurisdiction over manufacturers of equipment in the past has typically been tied to specific statutory provisions." *Order* ¶ *32*, J.A. 1270.

The FCC's jurisdictional grant to regulate television receivers appears in Section 303 of the Communications Act, which is appropriately entitled "Powers and Duties of Commission." 47 U.S.C. § 303. Subdivision (s) of this provision is the ACRA. *Id.* § 303(s). Subdivision (u) directs the FCC to require that televisions be equipped with closed captioning for the hearing impaired. *Id.* § 303(u). And subdivision (x) mandates that the FCC ensure all televisions 13 inches or larger are equipped with the "V-chip," which allows parents to "block" the "display" of programs they deem inappropriate. *Id.* § 303(x).

Together, these provisions establish a clear rule for FCC jurisdiction over television design. They create a regulatory mosaic under which Congress has declined to leave television design within the FCC's ancillary authority, and will allow the FCC to regulate televisions only after giving it a specific conveyance of power to do so. Section 303(e) undergirds the point. The FCC's "control ... over all the channels of radio transmission" is its core Title III duty. 47 U.S.C. § 301. But even when it comes to governing transmission apparatuses that use these channels, Section 303(e) grants the FCC authority only to regulate "the kind of apparatus to be used *with respect to its external effects and the purity and sharpness of the emissions." Id.* 303(e) (emphasis added). The fact that Congress delimited even FCC regulation of radio transmitters shows just how far from controlling the radio spectrum the FCC has strayed with these rules on copy protection.

Indeed, Congress has repeated this pattern of specific authorizations throughout the Act for other consumer electronics devices: When the FCC regulates household devices to ensure they can withstand radio interference, it does so under Section 302a. 47 U.S.C. § 302a. When the FCC promulgates regulations on cable and satellite "set-top boxes," which consumers use to view these services, it does so under Section 549. *Id. § 549.* And when the FCC requires making televisions "cable ready," it does so in accordance with Section 544A. *Id.* § 544A.

Thus, the FCC's authority over television design fits neatly within the "familiar maxim of statutory construction" *expressio unius est exclusio alterius,* or the "`mention of one thing implies exclusion of another thing.' *Ethyl Corp. v. EPA,* 51 F.3d 1053, 1061 (D.C. Cir. 1995) (citation omitted). Repeatedly, where Congress has wanted the Commission to have this regulatory authority, it has said so explicitly-necessarily "implying the exclusion" of any other jurisdiction over television design. *See, e.g., MPAA,* 309 F.3d at 805.

In fact, in a recent case highly analogous to this one, *Independent Insurance Agents of America, Inc. v. Hawke,* 211 F.3d 638 (D.C. Cir. 2000), this Court ruled, on this very basis of *expressio unius,* that the Comptroller of the Currency improperly determined that all national banks could act as crop insurance agents. Under the National Bank Act, all of the banks at issue enjoyed broad authority to exercise "`all such incidental powers as shall be necessary to carry on the business of b a n g . ' *Id.* at 640. Because, however, Congress had given only banks in certain-sized towns authority to sell insurance, the panel unanimously ruled that *expressio unius* invalidated the Comptroller's decision. "Because § 92 ... grants [some banks] the general power to sell insurance as an agent, reading § 24 (Seventh) to authorize the sale of insurance by all national banks transgresses .. . common sense." *Id.* at 643.

Similarly here, while the FCC may claim broad authority over interstate broadcasting, Congress has always given the FCC power to dictate television design in the specific measures like Sections 303(s), (u), and (x). Under *Hawke,* this is "inarguabl[e]" evidence that the Commission's authority has been constrained. *Id.* at 644. Indeed, Congress has not just limited the FCC's television design authority under the Act, it has established this authority in a very careful way. Section 303 does not stand alone. This provision works in conjunction with Section 330, which bolsters Section 303's structure. Specifically, Section 330 creates a uniform national television market by generally banning the interstate sale of televisions that do not comply with FCC rules adopted under three enumerated statutory provisions-Sections 303(s), (u), and (x). *Id.* As a result, there can be no doubt that the FCC has violated *expressio unius* here. Congress has prescribed a specific method for the FCC to carry out each one of its statutory grants on television design, and the agency has now erected a regulatory scheme that perfectly parallels the statute-both dictating television receiver design and banning sales of televisions that do not comply, *see Order* ¶ *32, J.A.* 1270-without any statutory authorization to do so. E.g., *Int'l Bhd. of Teamsters v. ICC,* 801 F.2d 1423, 1430 (D.C. Cir. 1986) ("[I]t will not do for an agency to invoke the broad purposes of an entire act in order to contravene Congress' intent embodied in a specific provision."); *In re Permanent Surface Mining Regulation Litig., 653* F.2d 514, 523 (D.C. Cir. 1981) (en bane).

Nevertheless, the Commission intimates that *expressio unius* does not apply because the rule is "inappropriate in the administrative context."

Order ¶ 32 n.85, J.A. 1270. This argument proves too much. Not only have courts used *expressio unius* in myriad disputes over agency authority,[19] but it is well-settled that this tool is at its "zenith" when it applies "in tandem" with the rule "that the Congress cannot be presumed to do a futile thing." *Hawke,* 211 F.3d at 645; *Halverson v. Slater,* 129 F.3d 180, 185 (D.C. Cir. 1997). In this case, the FCC's assertion that it has ancillary jurisdiction to require the flag irrespective of Section 303 violates this "no futility" rule. If the FCC already had the authority to regulate television design in any way it wanted under its ancillary jurisdiction, then Congress' subsequent awarding of this same type of design authority under Sections 303(s), (u), and (x) "would have been completely useless." *Hawke,* 211 F.3d at 644; *see also Halverson,* 129 F.3d at 185; *Qi-Zhuo v. Meissner,* 70 F.3d 136, 139 (D.C. Cir. 1995).

In fact, what may be most striking about the FCC's rulemaking here is that, despite the vehement urging of the MPAA, other commenters, and members of Congress, the FCC does *not* rely on the one statutory provision that could possibly be construed to give it authority to promulgate these regulations. *See Order* ¶ 66, J.A. 1283. The only provision in the statute giving the FCC express DTV rulemaking authority is Section 336(a). That provision, however, is limited to the regulation of "ancillary and supplemental services" p a y services that broadcasters can provide through "multicasting" several digital channels at once. 47 U.S.C. § 336(a). For instance, Section 336(b)(4) gives the FCC authority to "adopt such technical and other requirements as may be necessary" to "assure the quality" of the ancillary signal, and Section 336(b)(2) allows the FCC to ensure "such services [are] consistent with the technology or method designated by the Commission for the provision of advanced television services." *Id.* §§ 336(b)(1), (4). This is plainly the closest provision in the Act to giving the agency power broad enough to require the Broadcast Flag, albeit with respect to a subset of DTV broadcasts-those most likely to include premium programming. However, the FCC

[19] E.g., *Tennessee Valley Auth. v. Hill,* 437 U.S. 153, 188 (1978); *Next Wave Personal Communications, Inc. v. FCC,* 254 F.3d 130, 152-53 P.C. Cir. 2001); *Shook v. District of Columbia,* 132 F.3d 775, 782 P.C. Cir. 1998); *Michigan Citizens for an Indep. Press v. Thornburgh,* 868 F.2d 1285, 1292-93 (D.C. Cir. 1992); *see also* 2A Norman J. Singer, *Statutes and Statutory Construction* § 47:24, at 321-22 (6th ed. 2000) *("[Expressio unius]* has been found useful in the interpretation of all types of statutes, including legislation on . . . administrative bodies.").

never relied on Section 336(a), presumably because it would limit the Flag solely to ancillary services and could not reach DTV sets generally. *See id.* § 336(a).[20]

Indeed, Congress' reason for doling out in small portions the power to regulate televisions and similar devices makes both historical and common sense. Consumer electronics are a significant sector in the nation's economy, and it is a sector that thrives on entrepreneurship and invention. Disrupting the innovation that drives such an important part of our national economy is not something Congress should be presumed to do blithely. Rather, the courts have long construed the Communications Act under a presumption that Congress does not act lightly where it might stifle competitive aims: "It is highly unlikely that Congress would leave the determination of whether an industry will be entirely, or even substantially, []regulated to agency discretion." *MCI Telecomm. Corp. v. AT&T, 512* U.S. *218,* 231 (1994); *Brown & Williamson, 529* U.S. at 147. *As* Congress itself reminded the nation in enacting the ACRA, this narrow authority must not "in any way" be considered a "general precedent for congressional regulation of manufactured products." 1962 U.S.C.C.A.N. at 1876.

So too here, the FCC should not be permitted to keep in place its expansive Broadcast Flag rules, which threaten to dictate not just how television manufacturers make their products-but also how computer companies, DVD manufacturers, and all other manner of electronic equipment firms operate-on an unfounded claim that it has always had this authority but has simply kept it innovation at the time," and so granting the FCC flexibility might have been considered appropriate. *Accuracy in Media,* 521 F.2d at 294 n.22. With DTV, however, Congress

[20] Nor is Section 303(g) a refuge. *See Order* ¶ 30, J.A. 1268-69. The FCC has never claimed that the Broadcast Flag is a "new use" of radio, or is only "experimental." Nor is this the same situation as *Southwestern.* "Cable television was an unforeseen technological secretly, silently hidden away. *See Order* ¶ 33, J.A. 1270. "Congress does not alter the fundamental details of a regulatory scheme in vague terms or ancillary provisions-it does not, one might say, hide elephants in mouseholes." *Whitman v. Am. TruckingAss'ns,* 531 U.S. 457, 468 (2001). Nor has Congress done so for television design. Congress has spoken, and it specifically withheld the authority the Commission asserts.

has already specified how the FCC should facilitate the transition: through licensing.

II. THE BROADCAST FLAG REGIME IMPERMISSIBLY CONFLICTS WITH COPYRIGHT LAW

The Supreme Court instructed in *Sony* that it is Congress that has the authority to define the scope of copyright and "fashion[] the new rules that new technology [makes] necessary." *Sony,* 464 U.S. at 429-31; *accord Metro-Goldwyn-Mayer Studios v. Grokster, Ltd.,* 380 F.3d 1154, 1167 (9th Cir. 2004). Had the FCC done in the 1980s what it now claims the power to do, the Supreme Court might never have had the opportunity to pass on the legality of copying by VCRs in *Sony.* Thus, the Broadcast Flag rule cannot stand for an additional reason: It contravenes Congress' intent in enacting the copyright laws and Congress' prerogative to determine the appropriate scope of copyright protection. *Midwest II,* 440 U.S. at 708 (ancillary jurisdiction improper because rules thwarted congressional goal of broadcaster editorial discretion); *see also NARUC v. FCC,* 533 F.2d 601 (D.C. Cir. 1976).

A. The FCC's Action Contravenes Congress' Decision Not to Impose Copy Protection Mandates in the DMCA

While Congress enacted the DMCA to enhance copyright protection in the digital era, it refused to do so by requiring consumer electronics devices to respond to any particular protection measure. 17 U.S.C. § 1201(c)(3).

The legislative history of the DMCA explains that there is no "affirmative mandate requiring manufacturers of consumer electronics, telecommunications, and computing products to design their products . . . to affirmatively respond to any particular technological protection measure employed to protect a copyrighted work." H.R. Rep. No. 105-551, pt. 2, at 41 (1998); *see also* S. Rep. No. 105-190, at 30-31 (1998). The import of this policy, legislators explained, was that "[t]echnology and engineers-not lawyers-should dictate product design." 144 Cong. Rec. S9936 (daily ed. Sept. 3, 1998) (remarks of Sen. Ashcroft); *see also* 144 Cong. Rec. H7100 (daily ed. Aug. 4, 1998) (remarks of Rep. Mug). Not surprisingly, when copy protection mandate proposals were discussed by Congress subsequently, they were criticized as inconsistent with DMCA.[21]

The Broadcast Flag rules ignore all of this, however, concluding that the no-mandates provision applies only to circumvention devices. *See* Order ¶ 41, J.A. 1274. But there can be little question that, just as Congress determined in the ACRA not to meddle with television receiver design, it made clear in the DMCA its intention not to require equipment design to respond to any particular technological copy protection measure.

B. The FCC's Action Upsets the Balance Between Copyrights and Fair Use

Congress has provided copyright owners with a variety of exclusive rights in their copyrighted work, including the right to reproduce, prepare derivative works, distribute copies, perform, and publicly display those works. 17 U.S.C. § 106. However, those exclusive rights "do[ ] not give a copyright holder control over all uses." *Fortnightly Corp. v. United Artists,* 392 U.S. 390, 393 (1968). They are subject to certain limitations, including the public's ability to make "fair use" of the work. *Id.* § 107; *see Campbell v. Acuff-Rose Music, Inc.,* 510 U.S. 569, 577 (1994) (citation omitted). The principle of "fair use" thus balances the exclusive rights of copyright owners with the competing needs of the users of that information so as "not [to] put manacles upon science." *Id.* at *575* (citation omitted).

The DMCA was not intended to alter the balance between copyright owners' exclusive rights and the public's ability to make fair use of copyrighted works. Rather, it explicitly retained the existing "fair use" regime in the digital context. 17 U.S.C. § 1201(c)(1); *see also* H.R. Conf. Rep. No. 105-796, at 75 (1998). Indeed, in the DMCA, Congress specifically sought to foster one of the very objectives the FCC now defeats. As the Senate Report put it, the DMCA strikes a balance that

---

[21] *See, e.g., Copyright Piracy Prevention and the Broadcast Flag: Hearing Before the House Judiciary Subcommittee on Courts, Internet and Intellectual Property* (Mar. 6, 2003) (testimony of Edward J. Black, President and CEO, Computer & Communications Industry Association), *at* www.house.gov/judiciary/courtsO30603.htm.

aims to "make available via the Internet the movies, music, software, and literary works that are the fruit of American creative genius." S. Rep. No. 105-190, at 2 (1998). Recently, the Federal Circuit recognized the continued vitality of the fair use doctrine in the digital realm, explaining that the DMCA does not "allow any copyright owner, through a combination of contractual terms and technological measures, to repeal the fair use doctrine." *Chamberlain Group, Inc. v. Skylink Technologies, Inc.*, 381 F.3d 1178, 1202 (Fed. Cir. 2004).

Now the FCC has arrogated unto itself power to protect the copyright holders that solicited its help-a power that Congress never intended it to have, and a kind of protection that Congress in the DMCA specifically sought to prevent. The very nature of the Commission's Broadcast Flag mandate contradicts its insouciant assertion that "the scope of our decision does not reach existing copyright law." *Order* ¶¶ 9, 18, J.A. 1259, 1262. The basis for the Commission's view is its assertion that the rule has nothing to do with copying, but involves redistribution control. *Order*, J.A. 1254 n.1. This is a distinction without a difference.

To be sure, the Commission took great pains to distance the Broadcast Flag from the idea of copyright, going so far as to rename the proceeding, which was based on the work of the *Copy* Protection Technology Working Group and had initially been captioned "Digital Broadcast *Copy* Protection." Indeed, it was only after commenters cried foul at the FCC's attempt to regulate copyright that the Commission effected a cosmetic name change of the rule, replacing "copy" with "content," and "copy protection" with "redistribution control." *Id.*

To no avail. Protections against redistribution are no less a trespass of copyright than protections against copying. Copyright law protects copyright owners from unauthorized redistribution as well as from copying, and exempts fair uses whether they involve redistribution or copying. It is this protection that the Commission has decided to expand, and this delicate balance between the interests of copyright-holders and those of the public that it has stepped in to tilt. Unquestionably, the rules will constrain further use of DTV broadcasts, to the benefit of the copyright holders and detriment of all other would-be users. That is the rule's purpose, and its proponents concede as much. E.g., MPAA Comments, *J.A.* 772-74.

Nor is the Commission's distinction between copying and redistribution even accurate, since the technologies for implementing the Broadcast Flag can rely on copy control, and many do. In the *Approved Technologies Order,* the FCC granted requests by several applicants for approval of content protection technologies that specifically achieved the goal of "content protection" by stopping copying. The D-VHS technology, for example, limits broadcast content to one generation of copies. *Approved Technologies Order* ¶ *75.* The approved "HDCP" product explicitly prohibits copying. *Id.* Even the TiVoGuard technology, approved over fierce opposition by the MPAA, limits the number of devices that may receive protected DTV content. *Id.* ¶ *20.* The Commission itself conceded:

> We continue to believe that . . . a redistribution control content protection system for digital broadcast television will not interfere with or preclude consumers from copying, using or redistributing digital broadcast television content as consistent with copyright law. *We recognize, however, that certain of the above-referenced content protection technologies and recording methods are unable to effectuate redistribution control through means other than copy restraints.*

Id. ¶¶ *75-77* (emphasis added). The FCC protests too much.

Because the Commission has promulgated its rule in phases, there are several unknowns. The extent to which copying of DTV broadcasts will be permitted, and how consumers will be able to use the broadcasts, is unclear. What *is* clear is that the Commission, by virtue of its Broadcast Flag rulemaking, has granted copyright holders an irrebuttable presumption that certain uses of DTV broadcasts are not "fair use" under the copyright laws.

Perhaps the best way to illustrate how far the FCC has gone is to return to *Sony,* where the Supreme Court determined that the noncommercial home use of VCRs for "time-shifting" the viewing of over-the-air broadcasts was a "fair use." Congress set forth a series of four factors to be weighed on a case-by-case basis to determine whether a use is "fair." *Sony*, 464 U.S. at 476. The Broadcast Flag rule, however, usurps any court's case-by-case analysis of whether a particular use is "fair" by preventing many uses from ever occurring.

We may never know whether it would be a "fair use" for consumers to transfer DTV broadcasts via the Internet from their homes to other locations for later viewing, or whether it is "fair use" for one to manipulate such a broadcast to create and distribute a parody, or to annotate a political commentary in one's "blog." Many of these uses would not merely be made more difficult or less optimal by the Commission's rule-they would be foreclosed altogether. Because broadcasters are entitled to tattoo the Broadcast Flag onto DTV signals without oversight, it is also possible that uncopyrighted works, which the Constitution intended to live on in the public domain, will nevertheless be foreclosed to the public.

Indeed, even the simple "time shifting" use approved in *Sony* within a consumer's own home is jeopardized if the only "approved" technology is HDCP or similar regimes that allow no copying. Of course, the FCC will likely respond that it has approved other less limiting technologies. But that is true only for now. If the authority to adopt the Flag is upheld, there is no guarantee that this Commission or a later one would not exercise that authority to preclude all uses.

The warning signs are already apparent in the Commission's consideration of the TiVoGuard technology.[22] One Commissioner expressed concerns with TiVoGuard's lack of "proximity controls" over redistribution of broadcasts. *See Approved Technologies Order* at 51 (separate statement of Martin, C.). The jurisdictional finding underlying the decision below allows the Commission to reconsider and nix TiVoGuard and directly interfere with any number of consumer-friendly technologies for copying and disseminating content,

[22] The more popular TiVo digital recorder itself has not yet been considered for approval by the Commission.

thereby preempting a debate over the legality of these technologies in the domain in which it properly belongs-Congress.

III. THE FCC'S CONCLUSIONS THAT THERE WAS A PROBLEM, AND THAT THE BROADCAST FLAG WOULD SOLVE IT, ARE ARBITRARY AND CAPRICIOUS

A. Standard of Review

The Court must set aside any of the FCC's factual findings, reasoning and conclusions that are "arbitrary, capricious, . . . or otherwise not in accordance with law." 5 U.S.C. § 706(2)(A). Findings that are "devoid of needed factual support," *Ass 'n of Data Processing Service Orgs., Inc. v. Bd. of Governors of the Federal Reserve Sys.*, 745 F.2d 677, 683-84 (D.C. Cir. 1984), or "`not supported by substantial evidence,'" *Pac. Legal Foundation v. Dep 't of Transp.*, 593 F.2d 1338, 1343 (D.C. Cir. 1979) (citation omitted), are arbitrary by definition. "Substantial evidence" is more than "some" evidence; it means sufficient evidence that a reasonable mind would find adequate to support a conclusion. *Consolidated Edison Co. v. NLRB*, 305 U.S. 197, 229 (1938). The Court accordingly conducts a "`searching and careful' review, *Home Box Office, Inc. v. FCC*, 567 F.2d 9, 35 (D.C. Cir. 1977) ("HBO") (citations omitted), "ensur[ing] that the [agency] engaged in reasoned decisionmaking." *Farmers Union Central Exchange, Inc. v. FERC*, 734 F.2d 1486, 1500 (D.C. Cir. 1984) (citations omitted).

B. The Problem That the Rule Is Supposed to Resolve Has Not Been Adequately Shown to Exist

There was not substantial evidence in the record to establish the existence of the problem the flag was adopted to remedy. A regulation that is "`perfectly reasonable in the face of a problem' is "`highly capricious if that problem does not exist.' *HBO*, 567 F.2d at 36 (quoting *City of Chicago v. FPC*, 458 F.2d 731, 742 (D.C. Cir. 1972)). The problem here, according to the FCC, is that the potential threat of indiscriminate redistribution of DTV broadcasts will cause "diversion of high quality digital programming," causing the "success of the DTV transition" to be threatened by the deterioration of "free, over-the-air broadcast television." *Order* ¶ 31, J.A. 1270.

In the record below, however, there was no more evidence to support these views than in *HBO*, where the Commission made rules based on a now-familiar refrain-that "high-value" programming would be "siphoned off" from broadcast television to cable. *HBO*, 567 F.2d at 32-33. The anti-siphoning measure in *HBO* lacked a reasoned basis because its underlying premise-that siphoning was a "problem" that was likely to lead to the loss of broadcast programming-was not substantiated by the record. The FCC committed the same error here.

There was no evidence below of even a single instance where a high definition broadcast was redistributed over the Internet, or where "high-value" content was withheld because of possible redistribution. Instead, the Commission's scant three-paragraph explanation relied exclusively on self-serving statements by the Flag proponents about what would happen in the future, ignoring that DTV broadcasts have already commenced.

Nor were the forward-looking jeremiads offered by the content holders concrete. Rather, the Commission relied on bald assertions that HD programming would be diverted from broadcast television if there was no Broadcast Flag and that content owners' distribution channels would be threatened. *See Order* ¶ *6*, J.A. 1257. The one prediction that appeared to be more tangible was Viacom's indecorous threat to pull its HD service if the Broadcast Flag was not adopted. Comments of Viacom, J.A. 940, 951. Viacom soon recanted, however, leaving the Commission unable to invoke even this hollow ultimatum in adopting the flag.

The Commission also did not review any of the self-interested content owners' claims with anything approaching a critical eye. *See Archenar Broadcasting Co. v. FCC, 62* F.3d 1441 (D.C. Cir. 1995). There was no examination of how the content owners' distribution models function;[23] no analysis of how these models might be affected if redistribution became possible on the Internet; and no explanation even of the Commission's definition of "high value" content. In short, the only

[23] Petitioners pointed out, for example, that consumers' present ability to record analog versions of first-run television series had not prevented record sales of the same programs in boxed DVD sets. *See* Memorandum from Consumers Groups to Media Bureau, J.A. 1202-03. The Commission did not respond to these comments.

basis for the Commission's conclusion that programming would migrate was a mere assumption.

The Commission also relied on assumptions in deciding that there would be "mass trading" of broadcast DTV programs on the Internet. Indeed, the broadcast flag proponents conceded that there is not presently an Internet redistribution problem, especially considering the practical constraints of downloading massive HD files,[24] and the Commission acknowledged that these constraints "will inhibit" Internet redistribution "for the immediate future." *Order* ¶ *8, J.A.* 1258. Commenters similarly debunked the speculation about faster download capability in the future. *See* Letter from Mike Godwin, Public Knowledge, to Marlene Dortch, Secretary, FCC, att. (May *23, 2003).*[25] The Flag proponents' rejoinder was not to offer proof, but merely to urge the Commission to hurry up before the DTV transition reached a "tipping point" and the Broadcast Flag was "too late." *See, e.g.*, MPAA Reply Comments, *J.A.* 1092; Viacom Comments, J.A. *950.*

In the absence of any evidence of past redistribution, the Commission again resorted exclusively to prediction, forecasting that redistribution would become a problem at some future point. Its basis? A conclusory statement that *analog* broadcast content is present today on the Internet, and two press releases about Internet speed improvements. *Order* ¶ *8* & n.20, J.A. 1258. Such predictive judgments are not entitled to deference where, as here, they are not adequately substantiated. *See, e.g.*, *Prometheus Radio Project v. FCC,* 373 F.3d 372, 409 (3d Cir. 2004) ("[T]he Commission needs to undergird its predictive judgment . . . to survive arbitrary and capricious review."); *Fox Television Stations, Inc. v. FCC,* 280 F.3d 1027, 1051 (D.C. Cir. 2002) (same). Substantiation cannot be adequate where the thing predicted for the future has undeniably not happened in the past. The record shows that the future is now-much of the major broadcast networks' programming is transmitted in HD

[24] *See, e.g.*, Consumers Reply Comments, J.A. 1051-54; Philips Comments, J.A. 889-90; Raffi Krikorian Reply Comments, J.A. 977-77a.

[25] *See* http://svartifoss2.fcc.gov/prod/ecfs/retrieve.cgi?native; *see also* MPAA Reply Comments, J.A. 1090-93 ("There is not yet a sufficient combination of receivers, broadband connections, and pirates to create a critical mass for the widespread unauthorized redistribution of broadcast DTV content."); Disney Comments, J.A. 957 (same).

already. The Commission cannot reasonably hang everything on predictive judgment when solid record evidence contradicts its position. E.g., *Bechtel v. FCC, 10* F.3d 875, 880-81 (D.C. Cir. 1993).

C. The Decision to Mandate the Broadcast Flag as a Solution Was Unreasoned

Nor did the record show that the Broadcast Flag is rationally connected to the alleged problem. *HBO,* 567 F.2d at 35 (agency must "demonstrate[] `a rational connection between the facts found and the choice made'). The Flag regime is fraught with flaws that allow easy circumvention by pirates, even as regular consumers remain inhibited by its constraints. For example, the Flag has no effect whatsoever on those sophisticated enough to preserve legacy DTV tuners not equipped to recognize it, nor will it prevent the redistribution of content converted from digital to analog, and then back to digital. *See Order* ¶ 17, J.A. 1261-62.

Yet, despite the content owners' recognition of these vulnerabilities, the FCC summarily dismissed indisputably more effective alternatives to the Flag such as source encryption for premium services,[26] blithely acknowledging that the Flag is a mere "speed bump" discouraging redistribution. *Id.* ¶¶ 14, 21, J.A. 1260, 1263-64. But there is no rational basis for a solution that hampers so many to create a "speed bump" (if that) for the few.

The Commission also impermissibly disregarded the burdens created by the Flag. The tangible and intangible costs of the Broadcast Flag-to ordinary consumers who must pay more for flag-equipped devices while suffering the loss of current and potential future fair uses, and to society because of the mandate's chilling effect on innovation-were barely addressed or vastly understated. In contrast, the Flag's unquestionable inadequacy means this burden cannot rationally be characterized as "minimal." *Order* ¶ 21, *J.A.* 1263. Imposing a rule whose benefit will be almost zero and whose cost is more substantial than estimated does not constitute reasoned decision making. *Farmers Union,* 734 F.2d at 1500.

---

[26] *See id. at* IT 23-24, J.A. 1264-65 ("[C]ontent owners do not question the technical effectiveness of an encryption system.").

CONCLUSION

For the foregoing reasons, the. Court should vacate the Commission's Broadcast Flag rule as arbitrary and capricious and unauthorized by law.

Respectfully submitted,

Gigi B. Sohn, *President*
Mike Godwin, *Legal Director*
Public Knowledge
1875 Connecticut Ave., NW
Washington, D.C. 20009
(202) 518-0020
Attorneys for Petitioners American Library Association, Association of Research Libraries, American Association of Law Libraries, Medical Library Association, Special Libraries Association, Consumer Federation of America, Consumers Union, and Electronic Frontier Foundation

Pantelis Michalopoulos
Cynthia L. Quarterman
Rhonda M. Bolton
Lincoln L. Davies
Steptoe & Johnson LLP
1330 Connecticut Ave., NW
Washington, D.C. 20036
(202) 429-3000
Attorneys for Petitioner Public Knowledge

CERTIFICATE OF COMPLIANCE WITH TYPE-VOLUME LIMITATION, TYPEFACE REQUIREMENTS, AND TYPE-STYLE REQUIREMENTS

1. This brief complies with the type-volume limitation of Fed. R. App. P. 32(a)(7)(B) because it contains 13,942 words, excluding the parts of the brief exempted by Fed. R. App. P. 32(a)(7)(B)(iii) and D.C. Cir. R. 32(a)(2).

2. This brief complies with the typeface requirements of Fed. R. App. P. 32(a)(5) and the type style requirement of Fed. R. App. P. 32(a)(6) because it has been prepared using proportionally spaced

typeface using Microsoft Word 2002 in 14 point Times New Roman type.

Respectfully submitted,

Pantelis Michalopoulos
Cynthia L. Quarterman
Rhonda M. Bolton
Lincoln L. Davies
Steptoe & Johnson, LLP
1330 Connecticut Avenue NW
Washington, DC 20036
(202) 429-3000

Counsel for Petitioner Public Knowledge

Dated: December 23, 2004

CERTIFICATE OF SERVICE

I hereby certify that on December 23, 2004 I caused true and correct copies of the foregoing Petitioners' Final Opening Brief to be served via U.S. mail, first-class postage prepaid, upon the following:

Courtesy of Pantelis Michalopoulos, Steptoe & Johnson LLP

APPENDIX E

ECHOSTAR CONSOLIDATED APPLICATION FOR AUTHORITY TO TRANSFER CONTROL

Before the
FEDERAL COMMUNICATIONS COMMISSION
Washington, D.C. 20554

	)
Application of	)
	)
ECHOSTAR COMMUNICATIONS CORPORATION	)
GENERAL MOTORS CORPORATION	)
HUGHES ELECTRONICS CORPORATION,	)
	)
Transferors,	File Nos.________
	)
and	)
	)
ECHOSTAR COMMUNICATIONS CORPORATION,	)
	)
Transferee,	)
	)
For Authority to Transfer Control.	)
	)

CONSOLIDATED APPLICATION FOR AUTHORITY TO TRANSFER CONTROL

EchoStar Communications Corporation ("ECC"), General Motors Corporation ("GM") and Hughes Electronics Corporation ("Hughes"), a subsidiary of GM (collectively, the "Merger Parties" or "Applicants"), have agreed to a merger and series of related transactions that will create an integrated, full-service satellite company better able to compete effectively with dominant cable operators in the multichannel video programming distribution ("MVPD") market. The Merger Parties hereby request the Commission's consent, in accordance with Sections 214 and 310 of the Communications Act of 1934, as amended,[1] to transfer control of the satellite, earth station, and other related authorizations held by their wholly- or majority-owned subsidiaries to Hughes (or a newly formed holding company above Hughes that will hold all of the capital stock of Hughes, also referred to as "Hughes").[2] The merged entity will have a new ownership structure and will be renamed EchoStar Communications Corporation ("New EchoStar").[3] The proposed license transfers will result from the split-off of Hughes from GM, the merger of ECC into Hughes, and the transfer of Hughes' indirect majority equity stake in PanAmSat Corporation ("PanAmSat"), either to New EchoStar through the merger, or to ECC through a separate purchase of Hughes' indirect stake in PanAmSat in the event the merger agreement is terminated under certain circumstances (the "PanAmSat Purchase").[4] The Merger Parties request that approval of these transfers be granted expeditiously.

---

[1]47 U.S.C. §§ 214, 310 (1994 & Supp. V 1999).

[2]Although the Implementation Agreement and Merger Agreement (as defined below) call for ECC to merge with and into Hughes Electronics Corporation and for Hughes Electronics Corporation (renamed EchoStar Communications Corporation) to be the top level entity in the post-merger ownership structure, GM has the ability under those agreements to (and the Merger Parties currently expect that GM will) form a new subsidiary (which is expected to be a Delaware Corporation named HEC Holdings, Inc.) and contribute all of the capital stock of Hughes Electronics Corporation to HEC Holdings, Inc. prior to the split-off and the merger. The effect of this transaction would be to insert an additional corporation above Hughes Electronics Corporation in the post-split-off and post-merger ownership structure, to substitute HEC Holdings, Inc. for Hughes Electronics Corporation as the merger partner with ECC and to substitute HEC Holdings, Inc. (renamed EchoStar Communications Corporation) for Hughes Electronics Corporation as the top level entity in the post-merger ownership structure. However, this transaction would have no practical impact on the rights of the parties or the Commission's review of the transaction because HEC Holdings, Inc. would have a governance structure identical to that described herein for the merged entity and the post-merger, and because relative percentage holdings of the capital stock of HEC Holdings, Inc. by the current ECC shareholders, the GM Class H shareholders and GM would remain the same.

[3]Attachment C hereto provides a consolidated list of authorizations to be transferred and the entities that currently hold them.

[4]These transactions are the subject of a definitive Agreement and Plan of Merger dated October 28, 2001 between ECC and Hughes ("Merger Agreement"), a Stock Purchase Agreement between ECC, Hughes, and several Hughes entities regarding Hughes' stake in PanAmSat ("PanAmSat Stock Purchase Agreement"), and several related agreements executed on the same date. The Merger Agreement and the PanAmSat Stock Purchase Agreement are conditioned, among other things, on approval of the transfers proposed herein. *See* Volume II of the Application for copies of each of these merger-related agreements and the PanAmSat Stock Purchase Agreement.

INTRODUCTION

When measured against various components of the Commission's public interest standard, the proposed merger of ECC and Hughes is consistent with all relevant Commission rules and policies, and will result in extraordinary, affirmative public interest benefits. It will advance the Commission's core policies in favor of a more competitive video marketplace, efficient use of scarce spectrum and satellite resources, and the provision of advanced broadband services to all Americans.

Unfortunately for consumers, today's MVPD market remains dominated by cable operators, which hold a share of about 80%. As described in the attached Declaration of Dr. Robert D. Willig,[5] New EchoStar will become an integrated, full-service satellite company that can contend with cable systems and create the kind of vigorous competition that will benefit all Americans. In the process, the merger will allow the combined company to provide many other public benefits that Congress and the Commission have been striving for years to achieve.

One of the most compelling efficiencies of the ECC-Hughes merger will be the elimination of a major restraint on the ability of Direct Broadcast Satellite ("DBS") operators to compete with cable systems in the MVPD market – duplicative use of the radio spectrum that the Commission has allocated for DBS service. Currently, ECC and Hughes' subsidiary DIRECTV, Inc. ("DIRECTV") use different portions of the DBS spectrum, each with its own expensive satellite fleet, each to provide overlapping programming services – the same HBO channels, the same CNN channels, in most cases the same local network channels to the same local metropolitan areas and, starting in January 2002, even many of the same home shopping local channels in the same local areas.[6]

---

[5]Declaration of Dr. Robert D. Willig on Behalf of EchoStar Communications Corporation, General Motors Corporation, and Hughes Electronics Corporation ("Willig Decl.") (appended hereto as Attachment A). The Willig Declaration, among other matters, sets forth an analysis of the relevant market for this transaction, *see id.* at ¶¶ 7-18.

[6]*See* Joint Engineering Statement in Support of Transfer of Control Application, at 8-9 (Attachment B hereto) ("Joint Engineering Statement").

Today, like never before, this spectrum inefficiency has become a potentially debilitating competitive impediment for DBS providers due to a combination of factors, including the imposition of satellite mandatory carriage obligations, the advent of digital cable services and the new bandwidth that "going-digital" gives to cable operators. The merger will eliminate the inefficient duplicative use of the DBS spectrum and liberate DBS capacity that will be used to facilitate the offering of new and expanded programming choices to consumers, ultimately introducing more meaningful competition to cable systems.

One dramatic example of this effect will be the addition of more satellite-delivered local broadcast channels to more local metropolitan areas. New EchoStar will provide local broadcast programming to far more metropolitan areas – 100 or more – compared to the 36 and 41 metropolitan areas (with an overlap of 35) served respectively by ECC and DIRECTV now.[7] This dramatic expansion of the number of local channels that can be carried on a DBS system will allow New EchoStar to compete more vigorously against the cable industry's carriage of local broadcast television channels in more U.S. metropolitan areas and also help achieve Congress's goal of broad-based local television service by satellite, as reflected in the Satellite Home Viewer Improvement Act of 1999 ("SHVIA").[8]

There will be other significant consumer benefits resulting from the expanded programming choices delivered by New EchoStar, as well. The merged entity will provide consumers with many more programming choices than each company is able to offer standing alone, including the bandwidth-intensive high definition programming that will encourage consumer adoption of digital television equipment. The merger also will bring significantly more programming and a better quality DBS service to Americans living in rural areas, as well as in the states of Alaska and Hawaii, than would be achievable by each company operating independently.[9]

[7] *Id.* at 9.
[8] Act of Nov. 29, 1999, Pub. L. No. 106-113, § 1008, 113 Stat. 1501, Appendix I (1999) (codified in scattered sections of 47 U.S.C. and 17 U.S.C.).
[9] Joint Engineering Statement at 10.

Moreover, there will be no anticompetitive MVPD market effects associated with the proposed transaction. As Dr. Willig observes, the characteristics of the MVPD market in general and of DBS firms in particular "make it very unlikely that . . . [this merger] will result in higher prices and lower output through either coordinated behavior among participants in the MVPD market or unilateral behavior by the merged firm."[10] And in response to concerns regarding the merger's possible effects on rural consumers, Dr. Willig notes that the expansion of programming and new services that will be made available to these consumers, combined with New EchoStar's commitment to maintain uniform national pricing for DBS services, renders it "more likely that the merger would be of distinct benefit to rural TV households than that it would diminish competition available to them."[11]

The proposed merger also will have positive effects in the programming market. Unlike most large cable operators, ECC has no ownership stake in any programming producer, and the Merger Parties do not intend to pursue a strategy of vertical integration with programmers post-merger. With the spectrum that would be freed up by this transaction, New EchoStar will have both the ability and the incentive to serve as an important outlet for promoting the development of new independent programming services. Furthermore, as Dr. Willig observes, the approximately 15 million subscribers of the combined entity "should provide an attractive platform for launching new programs, providing an interested programmer with a large percentage of the subscribers it would need to create a viable network."[12]

The merger will also dramatically aid New EchoStar in its efforts to introduce nationwide competition to broadband products and bring true broadband services to rural and underserved areas – another respect in which the effect of this transaction is aligned with Congress's and the Commission's objectives and the public interest. The bandwidth advantage of digital cable systems has allowed cable operators to bundle

[10] Willig Decl. at ¶ 6.
[11] *Id.* at ¶ 40.
[12] *Id.* at ¶ 42. This estimate of the combined subscriber base of New EchoStar excludes the subscribers of the National Rural Telecommunications Cooperative and its affiliate entities who receive DIRECTV programming.

their traditional video offerings with high-speed Internet access, a package that consumers increasingly demand. The current transitional broadband products of ECC and Hughes are struggling to achieve a critical mass of subscribers using Ku-band satellite platforms that are not optimized for broadband services. The next-generation Ka-band broadband satellite systems will be optimized for very high speed Internet services, but are also highly capital-intensive, being the first generation of commercial spacecraft to operate in these frequencies.

The proposed combination will allow New EchoStar to proceed with prompt and robust broadband deployment in the Ka-band by spreading the high fixed costs of deployment over a critical mass of broadband subscribers and achieving an offering that combines a competitive price and a reasonably short time to market. Each company standing alone would face significantly greater challenges in accomplishing those objectives within the time frame that is necessary to effectively compete with cable's bundled broadband offering of high speed Internet access products. The creation of New EchoStar will resolve the inefficiencies and uncertainties that would arise if both companies were faced with replicating investments in satellite platforms and will eliminate the spectrum inefficiencies that would exist if each company, in its own right, conducts duplicative multicasting and broadcast-type IP services. New EchoStar, by contrast, will have the significantly greater wherewithal to construct the type of advanced, high-capacity, cost-effective space platform to offer competitive, next generation high-speed Internet access nationwide – including to areas served neither by cable nor other broadband offerings – that are essential if the satellite technology is to have any chance of competing with the bundled video/IP services offered by cable companies.[13]

The potential consumer benefits of maximizing New EchoStar's prospects in the Ka-band are extremely significant for rural areas as well. In those areas, the New EchoStar Ka-band system will be an important element in bridging the "digital divide" because it can provide the same high-quality advanced Internet and IP services to rural subscribers and to subscribers in urban and suburban areas.

[13]Joint Engineering Statement at 14-16.

The acquisition of PanAmSat either by New EchoStar or ECC[14] is in the public interest as well. Significant benefits to consumers will result from combining the Fixed-Satellite Service ("FSS") resources of ECC and Hughes to bring broadband satellite services to market faster. The transaction will not create any significant overlap in the provision of FSS services in the same product and geographic markets that should raise any concern, as ECC does not currently provide any telecommunications services of the same type as PanAmSat in the United States or elsewhere.

The proposed merger marks the conclusion of a long and careful search on the part of GM and Hughes for the optimal merger partner for Hughes. GM and Hughes have chosen ECC as that partner, in large part due to the extraordinary spectrum efficiencies and cost and revenue synergies promised by the proposed merger. These benefits cannot be realized unless and until this proposed transaction is consummated. Accordingly, the Applicants respectfully request that this consolidated Application be granted as expeditiously as possible.

This consolidated Application consists of a narrative description of the parties and the transaction, including a discussion of the public interest benefits of the transaction, along with several attachments containing the completed FCC forms and other materials. Each FCC form and its associated exhibits and filing fee have been filed separately in accordance with the Commission's Rules. Following the closing of the transactions, the Applicants will supplement all pending applications under the Commission's Rules, 47 C.F.R. § 1.65 (2000), to reflect the new party in interest. To the extent that any pending applications, or any other applications for new facilities or for renewal or modification of existing facilities, are granted prior to the closing of this transaction, the Merger Parties request a determination by the Commission that the grant of this Application includes authority for New EchoStar to acquire control of any subsequently granted authorizations.

---

[14]As noted above, Hughes' interest in PanAmSat will either be transferred to New EchoStar through the merger or transferred through a separate purchase by ECC of Hughes' interest in the event the merger agreement is terminated under certain circumstances.

A. Description of the Parties

1. ECC and its Present Affiliates

ECC was started more than twenty years ago when its Chairman and CEO, Charles W. Ergen, entered the satellite television business as a distributor of C-band television satellite systems under the name Echosphere. Since its founding, ECC has earned a reputation as an innovator in the satellite television business by achieving a number of significant firsts, including: development of the first UHF remote control; the first nationwide installation network dedicated solely to satellite television systems; and the first company to offer an Integrated Receiver Descrambler for C-band satellite television.

ECC was granted authorization to use the 119° W.L. orbital location in 1992.[15] ECC launched its first satellite to that location in December 1995,[16] and has provided continuous DBS service to customers throughout the continental United States since early 1996. Also in 1995, the Commission approved ECC's acquisition of control over Directsat Corporation, which launched its first satellite to the 119° W.L. orbital location in September 1996. The combination allowed ECC, upon acquiring Directsat, to integrate the two satellites into an offering of about 125 video channels.[17] Since that time, ECC has deployed four additional satellites, including one to the 110° W.L. orbital slot after the Commission's 1999 approval of ECC's acquisition of the authorization held jointly by MCI Telecommunications Corp. and The News Corporation Limited ("News Corp.").[18] ECC's subsidiaries hold several DBS authorizations and own and operate six operational DBS satellites located at the 61.5° W.L., 110° W.L., 119° W.L., and 148° W.L. orbital positions.[19] Through its

---

[15] *See EchoStar Satellite Corporation,* 7 FCC Rcd. 1765 (1992).

[16] *See EchoStar Satellite Corporation,* 11 FCC Rcd. 3015, 3015 (Int'l Bur. 1996).

[17] *See Directsat Corporation,* 11 FCC Rcd. 10575, 10577 (1996); *see also Directsat Corporation and EchoStar Communications Corp., Application for Commission Consent to Transfer of Control,* 10 FCC Rcd. 88 (1995).

[18] *In re Application of MCI Telecommunications Corp. and EchoStar 110 Corp., For Consent to Assignment of Authorization to Construct, Launch and Operate a Direct Broadcast Satellite System Using 28 Frequency Channels at the 110° W.L. Orbital Location,* FCC 99-109, 15 Communications Reg. (P&F) 1038 (1999) ("*MCIT*").

[19] *See* Attachment C for a list of ECC authorizations.

DISH Network brand, ECC is now a provider of DBS television services in the United States to more than 6 million subscribers. ECC is also an international supplier of digital satellite receiver systems and a provider of other satellite services.

ECC continues to upgrade its fleet of satellites. EchoStar 7, its seventh DBS satellite, equipped with state-of-the-art spot-beam technology, is scheduled to launch soon. ECC plans to launch an additional spot beam satellite, EchoStar 8, in the year 2002. ECC also has Commission authorizations for Ku-band and Ka-band FSS systems. ECC's first FSS satellite, a hybrid Ku-band/Ka-band satellite, is expected to be launched in 2002.

In addition, ECC currently holds an approximate 32% percent interest in StarBand Communications, which began offering consumers a two-way, "always-on," high-speed Internet access service along with DISH Network programming in November 2000. ECC also holds less than 20 percent interests in Wildblue Communications, Inc. and Celsat America, Inc., both of which hope to offer a similar high-speed Internet service from Ka-band satellites in the future. The Commission recently approved the acquisition by an ECC subsidiary of a controlling interest in VisionStar, Inc., another Ka-band licensee.[20] This transaction is expected to close shortly.

Attachment D contains a chart summarizing the relevant ECC ownership structure prior to the proposed transaction.

2. The GM and Hughes Parties

Hughes, a Delaware corporation, is a wholly-owned subsidiary of GM, which is also a Delaware corporation.[21] Hughes is the corporate parent of several other companies that provide specialized

---

[20] *In the Matter of Application of VisionStar, Inc. and EchoStar VisionStar Corp. for Consent to Transfer of Control Over Authorization to Construct, Launch and Operate a Ka-band Satellite System in the Fixed-Satellite Service at the 113° W.L. Orbital Location*, File No. SAT-T/C-20001215-00163, DA 01-2481 (Int'l Bur. rel. Oct. 30, 2001).

[21] As discussed herein, GM has created a publicly-traded tracking stock of GM (GM Class H common stock) designed to provide holders with financial returns based on the financial performance of GM's wholly-owned Hughes subsidiary.

communications services to a wide range of end users. Hughes directly owns all of the issued and outstanding stock of DIRECTV Enterprises, Inc., a Commission DBS licensee.[22] In addition, Hughes controls various Commission licenses and authorizations through various other subsidiaries that are directly or indirectly wholly owned, including Hughes Communications, Inc.; Hughes Communications Galaxy, Inc.; Hughes Communications Satellite Services, Inc.; Hughes Global Services, Inc.; HOT Telecommunications, Ltd.; and USSB II, Inc.[23] Hughes indirectly holds an approximately 81% economic and voting interest in PanAmSat,[24] a publicly-traded Delaware corporation and Commission licensee.[25] Attachment E includes a chart summarizing the relevant GM/Hughes ownership structure prior to the proposed transaction.

DIRECTV launched the United States' first DBS satellite in December 1993 and a second DBS satellite in August 1994.[26] In June 1995, DIRECTV launched a third high-power DBS satellite and in April

---

[22]DIRECTV Enterprises, Inc. ("DTVE, Inc.") is filing contemporaneously with this Application several applications for consent, *inter alia*, to the *pro forma* assignment of certain Commission licenses held by DTVE, Inc. and certain of its subsidiaries to a new Delaware limited liability company, DIRECTV Enterprises, LLC. Those applications are intended to obtain Commission consent to the conversion of DTVE, Inc. from the corporate form of organization to the limited liability company form of organization under Delaware law. It is anticipated that this *pro forma* assignment to DIRECTV Enterprises LLC will occur, upon Commission consent, well in advance of, and without regard to, the transactions contemplated by this Application. Thus, the attached organizational chart and the attached Form 312s reflect the consummation of that *pro forma* assignment.

[23] Hughes Network Systems, Inc. ("New HNS"), a new Delaware corporation wholly owned by Hughes, is filing contemporaneously with this Application several applications for consent, *inter alia*, to the *pro forma* assignment of certain Commission licenses held by Hughes and certain Hughes subsidiaries to New HNS. It is anticipated that this *pro forma* assignment to New HNS will occur, upon Commission consent, well in advance of, and without regard to, the transactions contemplated by this Application. Thus, the attached organizational chart and the attached Form 312s reflect the consummation of that *pro forma* assignment.

[24] PanAmSat has recently filed, an application for consent to the *pro forma* assignment of certain Commission licenses held by PanAmSat Corporation to its indirect wholly owned subsidiary, PanAmSat Licensee Corp. It is anticipated that this *pro forma* assignment to PanAmSat Licensee Corp. will occur, upon Commission consent, well in advance of, and without regard to, the transactions contemplated by this Application. Thus, the attached Form 312s reflect the consummation of that *pro forma* assignment.

[25] *Hughes Communications, Inc.*, 12 FCC Rcd. 7534 (1997).

[26] *United States Satellite Broadcasting Co.*, 7 FCC Rcd. 7247 (1992).

and May 1999, the Commission authorized the transfer to DIRECTV of DBS assets and related authorizations held by United States Satellite Broadcasting Company, Inc. ("USSB")[27] and Tempo Satellite, Inc., respectively.[28] As a result of these transactions, DIRECTV currently provides service to U.S. consumers from five DBS satellites using 32 channels at 101° W.L., 3 channels at 110° W.L., and 11 channels at 119° W.L.[29] DIRECTV, together with certain independent distributors, now have approximately 10.3 million subscribers in the United States.[30]

Hughes Network Systems ("HNS"), a division of Hughes, provides broadband satellite network solutions for businesses and consumers around the world. HNS's high-speed, satellite-based Internet access service is marketed globally under the DirecPC® and DIRECWAY® brands. The current satellite broadband services are provided using leased Ku-band transponders. HNS supplies mobile satellite networks and user terminals and manufactures DIRECTV™ satellite television receivers and set-top boxes. HNS is also responsible for designing and managing the development, deployment and operation of the Hughes SPACEWAY system, a next generation, Ka-band satellite platform that will provide new and advanced services for DIRECWAY customers, consumer and business alike. SPACEWAY is currently scheduled to begin North American service in 2003. DIRECTV Broadband, Inc. (formerly known as Telocity, Inc.) offers terrestrial high-speed DSL service across the country where DSL is available.

Directly and through its subsidiaries, PanAmSat owns and operates a fleet of 21 satellites around the world that operate in the FSS bands and a comprehensive system of teleports and terrestrial resources. PanAmSat carries programming for broadcasters and programmers to millions of households worldwide, provides Internet backbone support to Internet service providers, supports private business communications

[27] *United States Satellite Broadcasting Co.*, 14 FCC Rcd. 4585 (Int'l Bur. 1999).
[28] *Tempo Satellite, Inc.*, 14 FCC Rcd. 7946 (Int'l Bur. 1999).
[29] DIRECTV voluntarily surrendered the DBS channels previously allocated to it at the 157° W.L. orbital location in May 1998. *See* Public Notice, Rep. No. SPB-127 (rel. June 10, 1998).
[30] Hughes also has interests in direct-to-home ("DTH") satellite services in several other countries. For example, it holds a 74.7% interest in DIRECTV Latin America LLC, which provides DTH pay television services throughout Latin America. The licenses for the services provided in foreign countries are not part of this Application.

networks to corporations, and provides essential pipelines worldwide for telecommunications providers. PanAmSat and its subsidiaries hold various FCC satellite earth station licenses as well as Section 214 authorizations for the provision of international services.

3. New EchoStar

As described in more detail in Section B below, the transferee, New EchoStar, is Hughes Electronics Corporation (or a newly formed holding company above Hughes Electronics Corporation)[31] with a new ownership structure that will result from the merger of ECC with and into Hughes after Hughes is split off from GM. New EchoStar will control indirectly the interests in all of the FCC licensees that are the subject of this Application, including Hughes' indirect interest in PanAmSat that is proposed to be transferred pursuant to the Merger Agreement. The new company will be renamed EchoStar Communications Corporation (for clarity, referred to herein as "New EchoStar"). After closing, New EchoStar will use the DIRECTV™ brand for all of its Direct-to-Home ("DTH") consumer offerings. New EchoStar will have three classes of common stock. As of the closing of this transaction, Mr. Charles W. Ergen, ECC's controlling shareholder and a U.S. citizen, will be the Chairman and Chief Executive Officer of New EchoStar, and through a family trust, will be New EchoStar's largest individual shareholder, holding all of the outstanding shares of Class B common stock of New EchoStar, which would represent approximately 16.7% of the total shares of outstanding common stock (and an approximate 39% voting interest) in New EchoStar.[32] The other ECC public shareholders at the time of the closing will receive shares of Class A common stock representing approximately 24.3% of the economic interest (and approximately 5.7% of the voting interest) in New EchoStar (including newly issued shares and convertibles). GM potentially would retain (after giving effect to the Debt/Equity Exchange, (as defined below)) shares of Class C common stock representing an approximate 4.9% economic interest (and an approximate 4.6% voting interest) in New EchoStar while the GM Class H shareholders would own shares of Class C common stock representing an

[31]*See* n. 2 above.

[32]Certain matters will also require a separate class vote of the holders of the shares of Class B common stock of New EchoStar.

approximate 54.1% economic interest (and an approximate 50.7 % voting interest) in New EchoStar.[33] Attachment F summarizes the relevant New EchoStar ownership structure post-merger.

B. Description of the Transactions

ECC and Hughes plan to merge their businesses in accordance with the Merger Agreement. This agreement, as well as an Implementation Agreement and a Separation Agreement (and various ancillary agreements contemplated thereby), set forth the transactions contemplated by the parties to effect the business combination. The PanAmSat Stock Purchase Agreement sets forth the terms under which ECC would purchase Hughes' approximately 81% indirect interest in PanAmSat in the event the Merger Agreement is terminated under certain circumstances. The transactions will be accomplished in a series of interrelated steps, as follows.

The Recapitalization and Split-off of Hughes. At present a "tracking stock" GM security related to Hughes' operations is available to the public and is traded on the New York Stock Exchange and on other exchanges as GM Class H common stock. While this tracking stock is designed to provide holders with financial returns based on the financial performance of Hughes, actual ownership of all Hughes' capital stock remains with GM. Accordingly, to accomplish the proposed business combination with ECC, prior to the merger, Hughes must be recapitalized and its stock distributed to GM's stockholders in order to separate Hughes from GM.

To accomplish the recapitalization and split-off, the Separation Agreement calls for Hughes to pay a dividend of up to $4.2 billion to GM (or to a wholly-owned limited liability subsidiary company of GM)[34] and for GM's deemed retained economic interest in Hughes to be

---

[33]All of the economic and voting interest percentages above are estimated, as of the consummation of the merger, based on the recent trading prices of ECC common stock, and certain assumptions regarding the pre-merger issuance of new ECC equity securities, conversion of currently outstanding preference shares and other convertible securities, as well as the treatment of certain shares for federal income tax purposes.

[34]GM has the ability under the Merger and Implementation Agreements to create a new wholly-owned limited liability company and insert that company into the ownership structure between GM and Hughes (or HEC Holdings, Inc., as the case may be) prior to the split-off and merger.

reduced by an amount commensurate with the dividend. In addition to the dividend to GM, Hughes will issue to GM shares of new Hughes Class C common stock pursuant to the Separation Agreement. Next, GM will split off Hughes by distributing to GM Class H common stockholders one share of new Hughes Class C common stock in redemption of and in exchange for each share of GM Class H common stock that they hold. GM will either retain or distribute to holders of its $1-2/3 common stock all or a portion of the remaining shares of Hughes Class C common stock representing its deemed retained economic interest in Hughes. In connection with the split-off, the GM Class H common stock will be cancelled. Upon completion of these transactions, Hughes will be an independent, publicly-owned company.

The Merger. Immediately following the re-capitalization and split-off, ECC will merge with and into Hughes or a newly-formed holding company above Hughes. Hughes will be the surviving corporation, and the merged entity will be renamed EchoStar Communications Corporation ("New EchoStar"). As a result of the merger: (i) the holders of ECC Class A common stock before the merger will receive shares of the Class A Common Stock of New EchoStar, (ii) the holders of ECC Class B common stock before the merger will receive shares of the Class B Common Stock of New EchoStar, and (iii) the holders of Class C Common Stock of Hughes before the merger (the former GM Class H shareholders and GM and/or the holders of GM's $1-2/3 common stock who obtained their Class C shares in connection with the split-off) will retain their Class C Common Stock, now in New EchoStar. The Class A, Class B and Class C classes of stock will exercise the voting percentages described above with respect to New EchoStar immediately after the merger.

Debt for Equity Exchange. GM has the option, at any time up until the date that is six months after the closing of the merger, to satisfy certain of its outstanding debt obligations by issuing or distributing GM Class H common stock or New EchoStar Class C common stock, respectively, to creditors in exchange for such debt obligations pursuant to one or more transactions (each a "Debt/Equity Exchange"). Prior to the merger, GM would effect the Debt/Equity Exchanges using newly issued shares of GM Class H common stock. After the merger, the Debt/Equity Exchanges would be effected using shares of New EchoStar Class C common stock retained by GM after the split-off. The transaction documents allow GM to distribute up to 100 million shares of GM Class H common stock or New EchoStar Class C common stock pursuant to Debt/Equity Exchanges.

The PanAmSat Purchase. GM and Hughes currently own indirectly through various Hughes subsidiaries an approximate 81% controlling interest in PanAmSat. These subsidiaries would become subsidiaries of New EchoStar pursuant to the merger. However, in the event the merger transaction is not consummated under certain circumstances, the GM and Hughes interest in PanAmSat (currently held through subsidiaries of Hughes) will be transferred, upon Commission consent and upon satisfaction of other conditions, in its entirety to ECC pursuant to the PanAmSat Stock Purchase Agreement.

II. PUBLIC INTEREST STATEMENT

To approve the transfer of the Hughes and ECC licenses to New EchoStar, the Commission must find that the proposed transfer serves the public interest, convenience, and necessity.[35] To make this finding, the Commission has traditionally weighed the public interest benefits of the proposed transaction against any potential public interest harms to determine whether, on balance, the benefits outweigh any harms.

The Commission's public interest analysis generally has included an examination of the following fundamental questions: (i) whether the transaction would result in a violation of the Communications Act or the Commission's rules; (ii) whether the transaction would substantially frustrate or impair the Commission's implementation or enforcement of the Communications Act or other related statutes or interfere with the Act's objectives; and (iii) whether the transaction promises to yield affirmative public interest benefits.[36]

The analysis also includes an evaluation of the likely competitive effects of the transaction and whether the proposed transfer

---

[35] 47 U.S.C. §§ 214(a), 310(d).

[36] *See, e.g., Time Warner Inc. and America Online, Inc.*, 16 FCC Rcd. 6547 ¶ 1 (2001)("*AOL/Time Warner*"); *MCIT,* 15 Comm. Reg. (P&F) 1038, ¶ 7.

creates a significant likelihood of competitive harm.[37] On this issue, more than mere speculation is required.[38] At the same time, Chairman Powell has stated his intention that the Commission subject proposed mergers to careful "rules-based" scrutiny and otherwise focus its inquiry in a manner that limits duplication of effort between its own review and the work of the agencies charged with evaluating such transactions under the antitrust laws.[39]

Each of the fundamental questions considered by the Commission as part of its analysis is addressed below. The unavoidable conclusion is that the proposed merger of ECC and Hughes is manifestly in the public interest. The synergies created by the combination will create substantial public interest benefits with respect to MVPD competition,[40] new programming and other content, and improved broadband services for millions of Americans. The transaction will create an integrated, spectrally efficient, full-service satellite competitor that is truly equipped to combat the dominance of incumbent cable Multiple System Operators ("MSOs"), and to provide new and expanded services, including state-of-the-art broadband services, to consumers in both urban areas as well as underserved and rural areas. At the same time, the structure of the market in which the combined entity will compete, as well as the combined entity's commitment to non-discriminatory pricing and service, prevent the merger from posing any risk of harm to the public interest. Accordingly, the Commission should not only grant this application – it should do so expeditiously.

A. *The Transaction Will Comply With the Requirements of the Communications Act, All Other Applicable Statutes, and With the Commission's Rules.*

---

[37] *Id.*

[38] *See, e.g., United States v. Citizens & S. Nat'l Bank*, 422 U.S. 86, 122 (1975) ("The Clayton Act is concerned with 'probable' effects on competition, not with 'ephemeral possibilities.'") (quoting *Brown Shoe Co. v. United States*, 370 U.S. 294, 323 (1962)); *see also United States v. Baker Hughes, Inc.*, 908 F.2d 981, 984 (D.C. Cir. 1990).

[39] *See* "Powell Offers Views on CLEC Woes, Spectrum Policy," Communications Daily, May 23, 2001, at 5. "Powell Urges Restraint in FCC Merger Reviews," Communications Daily, Dec. 11, 1998, at 1; *cf. AOL/Time Warner*, 16 FCC Rcd. at 6555 (concurring statements).

[40] *See* Willig Decl. at ¶¶ 21-25.

The proposed transaction does not implicate any foreign ownership, aggregation, cross-ownership, or any other restrictions imposed by the Communications Act, Commission regulation or applicable statute. Both ECC and Hughes are currently shareholders of a number of companies that are Commission licensees, and New EchoStar's Chief Executive Officer will be Mr. Charles W. Ergen, now Chief Executive Officer of ECC. The qualifications of all relevant parties are therefore a matter of record before the Commission. The combined entity will not have alien ownership that even approaches the benchmark of any applicable foreign ownership rule. [41] Nor does the proposed merger implicate any Commission rule or policy governing cross-ownership or MVPD programming relationships.[42]

B. The Transaction Will Not Impair Any Statutory Objectives and Will Yield Substantial Affirmative Public Interest Benefits

Far from impairing any statutory policies or objectives, the proposed transaction will in fact further the important Commission policies in favor of vigorous competition, the efficient use of spectrum and satellite resources, and the provision of advanced broadband communication services to all Americans. In doing so, the merger will yield a number of significant affirmative benefits to the public interest. The Commission is well-suited to recognize and weigh these benefits in light of its statutory responsibilities.

1. The Transaction Will Promote Competition With Cable by Allowing Increased Spectrum and Satellite Resource Efficiency

For almost a decade now, both Congress and the Commission have made concerted efforts to open up the MVPD market to effective competition – Congress with the enactment of the Cable Television Consumer Protection

---

[41] While ECC has received from the Commission a waiver of certain foreign ownership rules (to the extent applicable) to allow an investment from an Australian corporation, News Corp., that investment is now well below 5% and nowhere near the 25% limit of these rules to the extent they apply. *See In re Application of MCI Telecommunications Corp.*, File No. 73-SAT-P/L-96, FCC 99-110 (rel. May 19, 1999).

[42] AOL Time Warner Inc. has an indirect ownership interest in DIRECTV, which would represent less than a five percent interest in the combined company.

and Competition Act of 1992 and the Satellite Home Viewer Improvement Act of 1999, and the Commission with its rules implementing these laws. Nothwithstanding these efforts, however, the MVPD market is still dominated by cable operators.[43] Both Congress and the Commission have noted this competitive problem on a myriad of occasions.[44] Moreover, policy makers and regulators alike have envisioned DBS as the most promising alternative MVPD technology that could help alleviate this problem and ultimately cure it.[45]

DBS, however, remains fundamentally constrained by its dependence upon the radio spectrum for operations. DBS providers must use limited bandwidth from orbital locations that were not originally optimized for digital transmissions. The problem of finite bandwidth is seriously exacerbated by the currently duplicative use of the DBS spectrum. To help accomplish the Commission's vision of promoting DBS as a complete substitute for cable, DBS providers have had to offer subscribers programming services similar to those provided by cable systems, resulting

---

[43]*See* Willig Decl. at ¶¶ 7-18, and below at 37-41, for an analysis of the relevant market.
[44]*See, e.g.*, S. Rep. No. 102-92, at 1 (1992) (explaining that Congress enacted the Cable Television Consumer Protection and Competition Act of 1992 ("1992 Cable Act") "to promote competition in the multichannel video marketplace and to provide protection for consumers against monopoly rates and poor service.*"); In the Matter of Implementation of Section 19 of the Cable Television Consumer Protection and Competition Act of 1992: Annual Assessment of the Status of Competition in the Market for Delivery of Video Programming*, First Report, 9 FCC Rcd. 7442 (1994) ("*First Competition Report*"), at ¶ 5 (observing that "Congress . . . found that without competition, there was 'undue market power for the cable operator as compared to that of consumers and video programmers,' and that 'the cable television industry has become a dominant nationwide video medium.'" (citing 1992 Cable Act, §§ 2(a)(2-3), 106 Stat. 1460)); *In the Matter of Implementation of the Satellite Home Viewer Improvement Act of 1999; Retransmission Consent Issues: Good Faith Negotiation and Exclusivity*, CS Docket No. 99-363 (rel. Mar. 16, 2000) (promulgating rules under SHVIA designed "to place satellite carriers on an equal footing with local cable operators when it comes to the availability of broadcast programming, and thus give consumers more and better choices in selecting a multichannel video program distributor.").
[45]Congress noted in 1999 that "with the development of high-powered satellite service, or DSS, which delivers programming to a satellite dish as small as 18 inches in diameter, the satellite industry now serves homes nationwide with a wide range of high quality programming. . . . it offers an attractive alternative to other providers of multichannel video programming; in particular, cable television." H.R. Conf. Rep. No. 106-464, at 91 (1999); *see also First Competition Report,* 9 FCC Rcd. 7442, at ¶ 62 (noting the Commission's expectation in 1990 that DBS "had the potential to 'readily compete with cable.'") (citing *Rate Deregulation & the Commission's Policies Relating to the Provision of Cable Television Service*, Report on Competition, 5 FCC Rcd. 4962 (1990)).

in the use of each provider's spectrum for largely overlapping programming services. [46] For example, currently, ECC and DIRECTV use portions of the same DBS spectrum, each with its own expensive satellite fleet, each to provide the same HBO channels, the same CNN channels, and in most cases the same local network channels to the same metropolitan areas.[47] DBS operators have attempted to mitigate this inefficient duplicative use of DBS spectrum by relying on upgrades in digital compression and other technologies to "squeeze" as many digital programming channels as possible in their licensed bandwidth, and indeed, to offer more channels and superior picture and sound quality relative to analog cable systems. In addition, DBS providers historically had no need to allocate channel capacity for the provision of local network signals because they were legally hampered from retransmitting them in most instances.

Today, however, DBS spectrum inefficiency has become progressively a more debilitating problem owing to a number of factors, including satellite mandatory carriage obligations and the increased competitive threat posed by the enhanced capabilities of digital cable. While the enactment of the SHVIA alleviated some of the disparity between DBS and cable program offerings by giving DBS providers a limited legal ability to retransmit local broadcast signals starting in November 1999, it did so at a significant cost – the unprecedented spectrum requirements associated with satellite mandatory carriage obligations. Without the merger, must-carry obligations will effectively preclude the potential of effective competition with cable in all but the largest metropolitan areas now served by each DBS provider – DIRECTV now serves 41 local areas and ECC serves 36 local areas, for a total of 42

[46]In fact, the current duplicative use of this spectrum was not always the model for DTH satellite services. In the 1980s, when the Commission first authorized the DBS service, DTH satellite services were analog, meaning that each provider could not deliver much more than a handful of channels. Indeed, DBS itself was first contemplated as an analog service. The DTH satellite providers therefore planned to use their limited capacity to provide programming services that generally complemented, rather than duplicated, one another. It was in that environment that the Commission decided to fragment the DBS spectrum into a patchwork of small channel assignments – issuing separate permits for 11, 3 or even 1 DBS channel at each orbital location. The emergence of digital DBS in the early 1990s and the desire to introduce price competition to cable systems made that paradigm completely obsolete, and led to the current problem of duplicative use of the DBS spectrum.

[47]*See* Joint Engineering Statement at 8-10.

areas and with an overlap of 35 areas. All in all, each of ECC and DIRECTV expects to have to carry upwards of 300-400 local must-carry stations starting in January 2002, and most of these stations will be the same from one DBS provider to the other.[48] Must-carry is expected to bring the total of overlapping programs (both national and local) transmitted by the two companies to over 500.

Moreover, cable operators have aggressively upgraded the capacity of their systems to allow for the digital retransmission of video programming.[49] Although DBS's digital quality and former capacity superiority have allowed it initially to make inroads into cable's dominant market position, the roll-out of upgraded, digital cable facilities has compounded cable's incumbency advantages. A fully upgraded digital cable system now utilizes up to 750 MHz or 850 MHz of equivalent bandwidth, with no theoretical limitation on the ability to increase its bandwidth utilization by upgrading its physical plant.[50]

Digital cable also allows MSOs to offer a bundle of video and high-speed Internet access offerings, which has significantly and negatively affected the willingness of cable subscribers to switch to DBS, as well as other interactive broadband services. For example, many of the MSOs are now running trials of their Video on Demand ("VOD") products in test markets,

---

[48]For example, as of January 1, 2002, ECC expects that it will be required to transmit numerous local home shopping channels because of the satellite must-carry obligations imposed under the SHVIA. *See* 47 U.S.C. § 338 (Supp. V 1999) (as a condition of using the compulsory license made available by SHVIA for retransmission of local broadcast stations into their "home" market, DBS providers must carry, on request, the signals of *all* television broadcast stations located within the same local market, subject only to certain limited exceptions).
[49]*See* Comments of National Cable & Telecommunications Association responding to Notice of Inquiry, *In the Matter of Annual Assessment of the Status of Competition in the Market for the Delivery of Video Programming*, Notice of Inquiry, CS Docket No. 01-129, CS Docket No. 01-129 (dated Aug. 2, 2001), at 25-29 (describing cable companies' $50 billion investment in upgraded infrastructure over the past five years to facilitate "a broad range of video, voice and high-speed data possibilities, as well as improved signal reliability, improved pictures and two-way transmission capability."); *see also Annual Assessment of the Status of Competition in the Market for the Delivery of Video Programming*, Seventh Annual Report, 16 FCC Rcd. 6005, 6009 (2001) ("*Seventh MVPD Competition Report*") (Commission observation that "[v]irtually all the major MSOs offer Internet access via cable modems in portions of their nationwide service areas. . . . Many cable operators also are planning to integrate telephony and high-speed data access.").
[50]The information capacity per MHz of a digital cable system is not limited by the signal propagation constraints inherent in DBS systems.

and some have already commercially launched this service. One observer has noted that "VOD has emerged as the silver-bullet to DBS, and the MSOs are stockpiling for a 2002 showdown."[51] Even before that showdown, the impact of the video/Internet access/broadband bundle offered by cable has been acutely felt by the DBS providers. As a result of these developments, cable dominance persists and may yet be augmented.[52] Indeed, in its most recent annual cable competition report, the Commission notes that the cable industry continues to maintain a dominant position in the MVPD market, providing service to about 80% of the national MVPD subscribership.[53]

Combining the satellite and spectrum resources of ECC and Hughes will eliminate the duplicative use of the limited amount of available DBS spectrum to deliver the same programming,[54] and allow DBS to compete more effectively against cable's recent offerings. Elimination of this duplication is an enormous efficiency resulting from the merger. The Commission is uniquely equipped to evaluate this benefit because the increased spectrum efficiency resulting from the merger would promote directly its long-standing policy in favor of efficient and non-duplicative use of the spectrum.[55]

---

[51]Morgan Stanley, *Notes from NCTA 2001* (June 15, 2001); *see also* Deutsche Banc Alex. Brown, *Cable Industry Outlook*, Apr. 16, 2001, at 19, 38 (VOD is cable's "killer app" that will highlight cable's technological advances over DBS).

[52]Brigitte Greenberg, "VOD, High-Speed Data, Voice Keys to Cable Future, Operators Say," Communications Daily (Nov. 29, 2001) at 7 (noting cable operators' "optimism that services satellite couldn't deliver – video-on-demand ("VOD"), subscription VOD, interactivity, high-speed data and telephony – would solidify cable's relationship with current customers and bring many defectors to satellite back into fold.").

[53]*See Seventh MVPD Competition Report*, 16 FCC Rcd. at 6008. Cable claimed more than a 77% share of the MVPD market in August 2001. *See* Comments of National Cable & Telecommunications Association responding to Notice of Inquiry, *In the Matter of Annual Assessment of the Status of Competition in the Market for the Delivery of Video Programming*, CS Docket No. 01-129, at 7.

[54]*See* Joint Engineering Statement at 8-9.

[55]*See, e.g., In the Matter of Implementation of the Cable Television Consumer Protection and Competition Act of 1992*, 10 FCC Rcd. 3105, 3120 (1994), at 3120 ¶ 39 (1994) (recognizing the public interest in avoiding "duplication of programming" in the DBS service, which leads to "more diversity in programming for the consumer"); *cf. Hughes Communications Galaxy, Inc.*, 3 FCC Rcd. 7015 ¶ 2 (1988) (noting that use of the INTELSAT system "to duplicate programming already available on domestic satellites would be an inefficient use of the available radio spectrum"); *In re Revision of Radio Rules & Policies*, 7 FCC Rcd. 2755, 2783 (1992) (explaining that the Commission restricts duplicative use of spectrum utilized by commercial AM and FM radio stations with overlapping service areas because "[t]he limited amount of available spectrum could be used more efficiently by other parties to serve competition and diversity goals.").

The proposed transaction will do much more, however, than serve the Commission's spectrum policies in the abstract. Increased spectrum efficiency will translate into concrete benefits for customers, each recognized specifically by Congress or the Commission as important in its own right: more local channels to more markets; more high definition television ("HDTV") channels; better service to rural areas, Alaska and Hawaii; more diverse and educational programming; and broader availability of satellite-based Internet access services. These benefits will in turn spur the incumbent cable operators to greater efforts for the benefit of cable as well as cable consumers.[56] In short, DBS spectrum efficiency will serve as a means to the all-important end: more vigorous competition in the MVPD market.

(a) More Local Channels to More Areas

New EchoStar will provide local broadcast programming to far more communities – 100 or more, including at least one city in each state, compared to the 36 and 41 metropolitan areas that ECC and DIRECTV each respectively serve now.[57] The inability to provide local programming has been recognized by Congress and the Commission as a significant impediment to DBS becoming fully competitive with cable.[58] The legal constraints that

---

[56]*See, e.g., Merger Impact on Cable: A Wall Street View,* skyreport.com (Nov. 26, 2001) *available at* http://www.skyreport.com/skyreport/nov2001/112601.htm#one (noting financial analysts' prediction that the advantages resulting from "a combination of DBS assets" would prompt cable to "convert their systems to 100 percent digital, ... become more aggressive in developing and distributing both broadband content and communications in order to drive the penetration of broadband connectivity," and to "bundle aggressively," with the end result being that "[c]osts to the consumer will come down through bundled pricing."); Valerie Milano, "Cable Sees PVRs as Serious Threat, SvoD the Answer," Communications Daily (Nov. 29, 2001) at 8 (pending merger will spur cable toward more innovation).

[57]*See* Joint Engineering Statement at 9. The total number of metropolitan areas now served by either DIRECTV or ECC is 42, with 35 of these areas served by both companies.

[58]In the Conference Report accompanying SHVIA, Congress declared that enabling DBS operators to offer local channels would "allow satellite carriers for the first time to provide their subscribers with the television signals they want most: their local stations," and "create parity and enhanced competition between the satellite and cable industries in the provision of local television broadcast stations." H.R. Conf. Rep. No. 106-464, at 93; *see also Seventh MVPD Competition Report*, 16 FCC Rcd. at 6010 ¶ 13 (observing that "[c]onsumers historically reported that their inability to receive local signals from DBS operators negatively affected their decision as to whether to subscribe to DBS . . . . Under

contributed to the competitive imbalance were alleviated somewhat by the passage of SHVIA. The limited channel capacity of DBS providers, however, as well as the burdens to be soon imposed upon that capacity in the form of satellite must carry, continue to limit DBS's ability – even with the implementation of spot-beam satellites and other new technologies – to offer local programming to many consumers. As a result, local-into-local service has for now been confined only to the relatively larger metropolitan areas.[59] The merger will dramatically expand the number of areas that can receive local broadcast station signals and will result in more vigorous competition to cable in these areas.

(b) More Programming Choices, Including HDTV Channels and More Pay-Per-View

New EchoStar also will have the ability to provide consumers with many more national programming choices than each company is able to provide standing alone. Just as the merger will eliminate the need to duplicate carriage of local channels, it will also eliminate the duplication of national channels, thereby freeing spectrum for more diverse programming choices. This includes more high definition programming that will encourage consumer adoption of digital equipment – another explicit Commission objective.[60] Currently, ECC and DIRECTV each offer a limited number of HDTV channels – 2 for DIRECTV and 3 full-time HDTV channels for ECC. The combined entity will be able to devote several times that number of channels to HDTV content,[61] driving demand for both HDTV content and equipment, and breaking the vicious circle of too little HDTV content to drive

SHVIA, DBS operators can offer a programming package more comparable to and competitive with the services offered by cable operators.")

[59]*See* Joint Engineering Statement at Exhibit 2.

[60]*See, e.g., In the Matter of Review of the Commission's Rules and Policies Affecting the Conversion to Digital Television*, Report and Order and Further Notice of Proposed Rulemaking, 16 FCC Rcd. 5946 (2001) (stressing the Commission's desire for a "rapid" conversion to digital television ("DTV")); *id.* at 5950 ¶ 11 (Commission expressing its "agree[ment] that the wide availability of digital programming . . . will help speed the transition to DTV.").

[61]*See* Joint Engineering Statement at 10.

consumers to purchase HDTV equipment and too little equipment to justify investment in more content.

The savings in spectrum that will result from the merger will also enable New EchoStar to offer greatly expanded pay-per-view ("PPV") and VOD-like[62] services – services that are very important to the economics and competitiveness of MVPD providers. For example, capacity can be devoted to caching (*i.e.*, saving for future viewing) on Personal Video Recorders, allowing users to play PPV movies or have access to specialty programming virtually on demand.[63]

(c) Expanded Product Offerings to Meet Competition from Digital Cable

The merger will enhance competition by enabling New EchoStar to compete better with new MSO product offerings made possible by the advent of digital cable. As mentioned above, the digital cable roll-out has allowed cable MSOs to offer consumers a broadband bundle, packaging the conventional video services with high-speed Internet access, VOD and other interactive services, and Internet telephony. These packages are increasingly popular with MVPD subscribers.[64] DBS, on the other hand, is competitively disadvantaged in this regard. The DBS spectrum to a consumer's home is now only one-way via satellite and needs to be supplemented by the use of different frequencies and satellites or by using terrestrial technologies to allow a broadband two-way offering. Both ECC and Hughes have attempted to create such broadband packages, ECC with its

---

[62] *See* discussion in B(1)(c) below.

[63] *See* Joint Engineering Statement at 11.

[64] As early in the digital cable roll-out as 1998, the Commission recognized that "[m]ulti-service offerings and bundling services for sale seem to enhance subscription to alternative services offered by cable companies. . . . Indications are that customers value receiving these services through 'one-stop-shopping.' . . . For example, many large MSO's have found that bundling increases penetration of video and of new services." *In the Matter of Annual Assessment of the Status of Competition in the Market for the Delivery of Video Programming*, Fifth Annual Report, 13 FCC Rcd. 24284, 24322 ¶ 60 (1998) (footnotes omitted).

StarBand investment, and Hughes with its HNS DirecPC and DIRECWAY offerings. However, during the first year of service, subscription rates have been low, with only one percent of total DBS subscribers, less than 200,000, subscribing to these data services nationwide.[65] As will be seen below, next-generation satellite broadband services require significant investment and will be dramatically improved by combining the resources of both companies.

As mentioned above, the deployment of digital cable has also provided cable operators with the ability to offer new interactive services. These services include video-on-demand, information-on-demand (*e.g.*, sports scores, financial market information, electronic yellow pages, etc.) and electronic shopping services. These services are typically enabled through two-way interaction between the digital cable set-top and server equipment located at the cable operator's headend.

Even though the "one-way via satellite" architecture of a DBS operator does not allow for the same type of headend to set-top connectivity as exists in a digital cable system, a DBS service can provide many of the same types of interactive offerings as the digital cable operator *provided sufficient bandwidth for content distribution is available to the satellite operator.*[66] The latency of this type of service (*i.e.*, how quickly the information is presented to the viewer) and depth of the service (*i.e.*, how much information is available to the viewer) is directly proportional to the amount of satellite bandwidth allocated to the content carousel associated with the

[65] *See* Joint Engineering Statement at 14.

[66] In contrast to cable operators, a DBS provider enables its interactive services by the continuous broadcast of content "carousels" to its set-top boxes. Under the direction of either the operator or the consumer, each set-top box selects and presents or stores information from the content carousel transmitted by the satellite. For example, in the case of an interactive financial information service, the consumer would identify the particular stock symbols of interest and the set-top box would wait for the relevant information to be transmitted over the carousel, "grab" it and display it to the consumer. If the content is transmitted frequently enough, this interaction appears to be instantaneous to the viewer. This content carousel approach applies not only to information-on-demand services but to almost any satellite-delivered interactive service, including video-on-demand services and electronic shopping services.

service. Simply put, the more bandwidth that is applied to a service, the more interactive and robust (and consequently the more competitive) the consumer experience.

Thus the DBS spectrum efficiencies created through the merger will allow New EchoStar to offer satellite-based interactive services that can compete favorably against increasingly sophisticated digital cable offerings and at the same time provide rural consumers with access to interactive services they might otherwise not be able to obtain.

The merger also will enable New EchoStar to compete more effectively against cable companies (and the telephone companies) as a possible third line for a bundle of video/data/Internet services into the home. Cable companies with digital infrastructure can now offer consumers the attractive bundles of video, high-speed Internet access and other interactive services, and Internet telephony. As will be seen below, the merger will allow New EchoStar to provide a truly competitive broadband service, as the new entity will be able to combine the spectrum available to each company for broadband services and use the combined potential subscriber base to achieve more competitive price points and sustain the extraordinary high up-front capital investment that is required to launch quickly an advanced satellite broadband network.

New EchoStar will thus be able to establish a viable satellite-based Internet/data service that would compete with cable modem access and telephone lines as a third line into the home. This efficiency will confer significant consumer benefits by creating an effective competitive alternative in a line of business that is increasingly important to consumers – and in which consumer options currently are limited.[67]

[67]The necessity and importance of spreading the huge costs of pure broadband satellite services across the required critical mass of broadband subscribers is discussed in greater detail below.

(d) Better Service to Rural Areas, Alaska and Hawaii

Another major benefit of the newly-freed spectrum will be New EchoStar's ability to provide Americans living in rural areas, Alaska and Hawaii with more national programming networks and a better signal. [68] As explained above, by not duplicating each other's programming over the same spectrum, the combined entity will be able to offer a much greater variety of national networks than rural and remote areas can receive today.

This means that New EchoStar will be better able to provide subscribers in Alaska and Hawaii with a programming package more akin to what is available to their fellow citizens on the mainland today. Moreover, the combination of assets, including uplink facilities, will make more feasible the redeployment of finite satellite assets to non-CONUS western orbital slots, portending further improvements to service in Alaska and Hawaii.

The same spectrum and satellite efficiency that will facilitate a greater variety of programming also will provide for a more reliable signal in all rural and remote areas. This could translate into any number of benefits, including potentially smaller dish sizes for some subscribers in remote areas such as Alaska and Hawaii.[69]

In addition, as discussed further below, citizens in rural America will also benefit from the extent to which the combination of ECC and Hughes will improve competition with cable incumbents in numerous metropolitan areas. National pricing is the most practicable and efficient method of DBS pricing, and New EchoStar will commit to continued uniform and non-discriminatory pricing and service throughout the country. As a result of national pricing, rural DBS customers will reap many of the benefits that enhanced competition with cable will provide to customers in non-rural areas. In effect, the national price will act as a conduit that allows the competitive dynamic

[68] *See* Joint Engineering Statement at 10.
[69] *See* Joint Engineering Statement at 11.

in such important, highly competitive regions to have a beneficial impact on consumers throughout the nation, including in rural areas where cable does not exist.[70]

Finally, perhaps one of the largest benefits promised by the transaction for rural areas is that the merger will help make seamless satellite broadband a reality for all Americans – deploying faster to all regions, with greater applications and service offerings. Broadband deployment is discussed in more detail below.

(e) More Ethnic, Foreign Language and Niche Programming

The same principle of spectrum efficiency will apply to iche programming such as ethnic, foreign language, or other programs that appeal to specialized audiences. These audiences would have greatly expanded viewing opportunities with the additional programming available as a result of the merger. For example, the merged entity could provide several more channels of Spanish-language programming than the companies' combined current offerings, as well as increased exposure for foreign language programming with smaller followings – a very important benefit for audiences that desire this programming.

(f) More Educational Programming

The spectrum efficiencies resulting from the merger will allow the provision of additional educational programming, another area in which the benefits from the transaction serve explicit statutory goals. Congress has required DBS providers to set aside a percentage of their capacity for such programming,[71] but the qualified programmers using ECC's and DIRECTV's set-aside channels overlap. For example, DIRECTV and ECC now use different portions of the spectrum to provide the same C-SPAN

[70]*See* Willig Decl. at ¶¶ 38-39.
[71]*See* 47 U.S.C. § 335(b) (1994) (DBS providers are required to set aside four to seven percent of channel capacity "exclusively for noncommercial programming of an educational or informational nature.").

and C-SPAN II feeds. Eliminating this overlap would free spectrum for additional public interest programming.

(g) Other Efficiencies That Will Result From the Merger

The combination will also allow the rationalization of the two companies' satellite fleets. These satellites are now inefficiently deployed due to the fragmentation of DBS spectrum assignments, which was in turn based on the now-discarded model of analog DBS. The deployment of satellites at 110° W.L. is a good example of this inefficiency. DIRECTV has a satellite at that location for the purpose of using its assignment of only 3 DBS channels, even as EchoStar's EchoStar 5 satellite now located at that slot and the EchoStar 8 satellite to be launched to that slot are each equipped with 32 transponders and stand ready to use all of the spectrum at that location. The result is that the two DBS companies are constrained in their ability to compete by outdated requirements that are the equivalent of an airline being required to fly its planes only half-full. The merger will allow the companies to align their combined satellite fleet to the dictates of market efficiency.[72]

In addition, New EchoStar will achieve greater economies of scale and substantial cost synergies as a result of the integration of the ECC and DIRECTV satellite platforms. For example, the proposed merger will allow New EchoStar to offer a common service platform to new customers; to combine and improve each company's distribution networks; and to use the satellite uplink centers for new, rather than redundant, services. The resulting cost synergies resulting from such steps will include: reduced subscriber acquisition costs; reduced customer turnover, or "churn"; improved signal security as a result of moving to a standardized DBS service platform; reduced programming costs as a result of having a larger subscriber base; and the elimination of duplicative overhead.[73] All of these synergies will contribute to the creation of

---

72 *See* Joint Engineering Statement at 4-7.

73 *See* Joint Engineering Statement at 2-3, 7-8, 12.

a dramatically stronger competitor to cable's dominance of the MVPD marketplace and will be manifested to the DBS consumer.

2. The Merger Will Have Other Significant Pro-Competitive Effects and Will Not Have An Anti-Competitive Impact In any of the Relevant Markets

MVPD Market. The merger will have significant pro-competitive effects – increased competition to cable operators – and will not have an anticompetitive impact in the relevant product market – the MVPD market. Recent technological and regulatory developments have left no doubt that the relevant market for purposes of analyzing this transaction, as previously defined by the Department of Justice ("DOJ"), is now "the delivery of multiple channels of video programming to the home . . . via . . . cable, satellite, or wireless technologies."[74] As Dr. Willig testifies, definition of a "relevant market" for the purpose of competition analysis of mergers depends crucially on demand substitution considerations – the degree to which consumers view the products as substitutable.[75] This ability to raise prices profitably is a function of the degree to which consumers view two products as providing similar services or benefits. If one firm came to become the only provider of one of the products, but not the other, and if consumers found the products to be good substitutes, then the presence of

---

[74] *See* Willig Decl. at ¶¶ 12-13 (discussing the relevant market determination made by the Department of Justice in the *Primestar* case.) In 1998, Primestar, a joint venture of large cable companies, sought to acquire rights to an orbital slot for nationwide DBS service that were held jointly by News Corp. and MCI Telecommunications Corp. DOJ sued to enjoin that acquisition, alleging that allowing cable operators through Primestar to control those DBS assets would eliminate the possibility that those assets could be used to compete against cable. In its complaint, DOJ alleged that the MVPD market was the relevant product market for the purpose of evaluating Primestar's proposed purchase of the DBS assets. *See United States v. Primestar, Inc.*, Civ. No. 1:98CV01193 (JLG) (D.D.C. May 12, 1998).

[75] *See* Willig Decl. at ¶ 8. In particular, the U.S. Department of Justice and Federal Trade Commission define a market "as a product or group of products and a geographic area in which it is produced or sold such that a hypothetical profit-maximizing firm, not subject to price regulation, that was the only present and future producer or seller of those products in that area likely would impose at least a 'small but significant and nontransitory' increase in price, assuming the terms of sale of all other products are held constant." *Id.* (citing Department of Justice and Federal Trade Commission, Horizontal Merger Guidelines, *available at* http://www.usdoj.gov.atr.public/guidelines/horiz_book/toc.html).

the second product would prevent the firm from realizing an increase in profits by significantly raising its price. Therefore, the second product would directly constrain the price of the first product, and the relevant market would include the second product.

Dr. Willig has concluded, based on the business behavior of the DBS industry, federal government cases and studies, the views of the cable industry, and the views of independent analysts, that DBS prices are directly constrained by cable prices. Therefore, the relevant market for evaluating the merger of ECC and DIRECTV includes cable providers.[76]

For example, Dr. Willig observes, DBS pricing decisions appear to be driven by competition with cable companies, as the stated primary objective of both companies is to gain market share by luring consumers away from the leading cable providers, and the firms accordingly price their DBS programming services at levels based primarily on the prices charged by cable providers. Additionally, Dr. Willig observes that each company has laid claim to success in luring subscribers away from cable, which is corroborated by public statements of cable companies attributing DBS subscriber growth to aggressive efforts by DBS to target cable customers, the fact that the cable industry itself views DBS as a significant competitor, and the acknowledgement by cable companies that their pricing and advertising strategies are influenced by competition from DBS.

Dr. Willig also notes that a number of cases and studies by the federal government confirm that cable firms are part of the relevant market. The DOJ, for example, found that the MVPD market was the relevant market in the *Primestar* case, discussed above. And in its annual analysis of competition in video programming, the FCC groups the cable industry and the DBS industry in the MVPD market.[77] The FCC has also concluded that DBS and cable

[76]Indeed, Dr. Willig explains that the market is dynamic and the boundary of the market in which DBS providers compete may well expand. As bundled packages with digital television, high-speed Internet access, and video-on-demand become relatively more important in the MVPD market, the participants in the relevant market may grow beyond the historical MVPD participants to include DSL providers, incumbent phone companies, and cellular phone providers. *See id.* at ¶ 17.
[77]*See Seventh MVPD Competition Report*, 16 FCC Rcd. 6037, at ¶ 61.

services are substitutes.[78] In sum, Dr. Willig concludes, the relevant market for analyzing a merger between ECC and DIRECTV is the MVPD market.[79]

As previously noted by the Commission, over 96 percent of all television households in the United States are passed by cable television systems and these cable operators continue to be the dominant distributors in the national MVPD market.[80] Indeed, cable television operators maintain nearly an 80 percent share of the total MVPD market.[81] DBS also competes with a number of other MVPD distributors using different transmission media, such as wireless cable, SMATV, open video systems, direct-to-home analog and digital satellite offerings, cable overbuilds and electric utilities.[82] In addition, there may soon be a number of new providers using technologies and frequency bands that will compete in this market, including terrestrial point-to-multipoint services in several fixed service bands and potential new satellite entrants.[83]

---

[78]In its 2000 *Report on Cable Industry Prices*, the FCC concluded that DBS puts statistically significant downward pressure on demand for cable services. The report continues to state that "DBS is a substitute for cable services. This result is different from our earlier finding reported in the *1999 Price Survey Report*, which showed DBS exerting only a modest influence on the demand for cable service. One explanation for the increased importance of DBS as a competitor of cable is the passage of . . . [SHVIA] in November 1999, which eliminated the prohibition on DBS delivery of local network signals into their local television markets. The two DBS operators have begun offering local signals in many major television markets thus more closely matching services provided by cable operators." *See In the Matter of Implementation of Section 3 of the Cable Television Consumer Protection and Competition Act of 1992; Statistical Report on Average Rates for Basic Service, Cable Programming Services, and Equipment*, Report on Cable Industry Prices, 16 FCC Rcd. 4346, 4364 (2001), ¶ 53.

[79]Dr. Willig also explains that, for the purposes of evaluating the competitive impact of the proposed merger, the national pricing for monthly subscription and programming fees by both EchoStar and DIRECTV suggest that a national-level analysis is the most appropriate. *See* Willig Decl. at ¶ 18.

[80]*See Seventh MVPD Competition Report*, 16 FCC Rcd. 6005, at App. B, Table B-1 (noting that approximately 96.6 percent of U.S. households with at least one television were passed by cable at the end of 1999); *MCIT*, 15 Comm. Reg. (P&F) 1038, at ¶ 16.

[81]*Seventh MVPD Competition Report*, 16 FCC Rcd. 6005 at ¶ 15.

[82]*Id.*

[83]*See, e.g.*, OpTel, Inc.'s Request for Action, *In the Matter of Petition for Rulemaking To Amend 47 C.F.R. § 101.603 and Related Rules – To Allow the use of 12 GHz OFS Frequencies for the Delivery of Video Programming Material*, CS Docket No. 99-250, RM-9257 (dated Nov. 6, 2001).

Evaluated in this market, the proposed merger will have decidedly pro-competitive effects. The effect on competition is not adequately measured by the number of competitors, but rather by their effectiveness. As the DOJ and the Commission have recognized, increasing the effectiveness of DBS competition (and thus ensuring adequate MVPD competition) may only be achievable by foregoing additional DBS competitors.[84] As described above and by Dr. Willig, the transaction will result in improved and expanded programming choices for consumers, as well as the provision of innovative new services, which will make New EchoStar a better competitor to cable.[85] Indeed, as all cable firms roll out their digital upgrades, DBS has a narrow window of opportunity to ignite full-scale competition as cable customers transition to digital service, before consumer inertia and the high switching costs from cable to DBS leave consumers locked in, and cable further entrenched. Moreover, as Dr. Willig discusses, the characteristics of the MVPD market in general and of DBS firms in particular "make it very unlikely that a merger of EchoStar and DirecTV would result in higher prices and lower output through either coordinated behavior among participants in the MVPD market or unilateral behavior by the merged firm."[86]

As outlined above, this transaction will produce enormous benefits for all Americans, including the small percentage of U.S. households that are not currently passed by cable operators. These sparsely populated areas already are being served by a number of C-band providers that are beginning to roll out new digital offerings (*e.g.*, 4DTV products) and offer

[84]For example, when the Commission considered the application of an ECC subsidiary to acquire additional DBS licenses, the Department of Justice commented that "MVPD competition is best served by the emergence of a strong high-power DBS competitor with enough capacity to compete effectively with cable." Comments of the United States Department of Justice, *In the Matter of the Application of MCI Telecommunications Corp. and EchoStar 110 Corp.*, File No. SAT-ASG-19981202-00093, at 8 (Jan. 14, 1999). The Commission agreed: "[W]e view the potential competitive benefits of allowing EchoStar to become a stronger competitor in MVPD markets as outweighing the potential competitive costs of reduced entry into the DBS industry." *MCIT*, 15 Comm. Reg. (P&F) 1038, at ¶ 21.
[85]Willig Decl. at ¶¶ 23-24 (discussing merger specific efficiencies that will lead to benefits such as greater geographic coverage of local channels, more specialty, ethnic and foreign language programming, interactive television services, and video-on-demand).
[86]*Id.* at ¶ 6.

over 500 programming channels.[87] These products remain very attractive, particularly in areas where dish size is not a significant deterrent.

In addition, recognizing the concerns of consumers in the 3.4% of U.S. television households not passed by cable,[88] New EchoStar is committed to pricing its DBS services on a uniform, nationwide basis. This means that, after the merger, the few consumers in areas not served by cable will in fact benefit from the intensified MVPD competition that will exist in all other areas where New EchoStar will compete with cable. In this way, these rural customers will obtain the benefits of competition between and among DBS, different cable MSOs, as well as the newer cable overbuilders and other emerging competitors offering other solutions throughout the country that increasingly are promoting and comparing their digital offerings to DBS. In other words, those consumers located in sparsely populated areas not currently served by cable will obtain DBS service at prices developed as a result of the more vigorous competition among New EchoStar and the 8 or 9 largest cable operators and other new entrants providing overbuild and other solutions in the rest of the country. In short, not only will the merger not have an anti-competitive impact in rural areas, it will produce tangible competitive benefits for consumers in those areas, too.

Programming. The programming market also will benefit from the proposed merger as a result of the more efficient use of spectrum and the creation of a much stronger alternative distribution outlet for programmers not affiliated with cable MSOs. In this regard, the proposed merger will not create the types of vertical relationships that raised concern in other transactions. The DOJ and the Federal Trade Commission have brought a number of cases addressing the vertical relationships between cable MSOs and competition in programming that were settled by consent decree.[89] In

---

[87] *Satellite Today*, C-Band Subscribers on Motorola's Front Burner, April 13, 2001. *See also*, www.4DTV.com.

[88] *See* note 81, *supra*. The Commission noted that there were approximately 100.8 million television households during the 1999-2000 television season. *See Seventh MVPD Competition Report*, 16 FCC Rcd. 6005, at ¶ 18. Based on this total, it may be estimated that roughly 3.4 million are not passed by cable.

[89] *See, e.g.*, Time Warner Inc., et al.; Prohibited Trade Practices, and Affirmative Corrective Actions, 62 Fed. Reg. 11202 (Federal Trade Comm'n Mar. 11, 1997) (consent order).

contrast, the Merger Parties do not intend to pursue a strategy of vertical integration with programmers post merger. Combined with the amount of available spectrum that will be freed up, this absence of vertical integration will help create a significant outlet for existing and new non-affiliated cable programmers, which now find it difficult to obtain carriage on the platforms of vertically integrated cable operators.[90]

3. The Merger Will Promote Deployment of Advanced Broadband Services to All Americans

The merger of ECC and Hughes will have a profoundly positive effect on the deployment of facilities-based, advanced, two-way, broadband services via satellite to all Americans, especially in rural areas outside the reach of other broadband alternatives such as DSL and cable modem services. The combined resources of ECC and Hughes will enable the merged company to accelerate and better promote the deployment of such services to both rural and urban markets.[91] This will support the Congressional and Commission policy objectives of providing affordable, high-speed Internet access to all Americans, particularly those living in rural areas.

The Telecommunications Act of 1996 specifically directs the Commission to "encourage the deployment on a reasonable and timely basis of advanced telecommunications capability to all Americans . . ."[92] In its most recent annual report on advanced broadband services, the Commission emphatically stated its commitment "to ensuring that advanced services become available to all Americans."[93] The Commission

---

[90]Gary Thorne, President of Moviewatch, a programming service expected to premiere next year, underscored this potential benefit, observing that with the proposed merger "the additional spectrum at least gives us opportunities to place networks. Because if there was – if there is – one place where spectrum eventually does get used up, it's on the satellite side of the world." Linda Moss, *New Nets Squeeze Into Consolidated Market*, Multichannel News, Nov. 26, 2001.

[91]*See* Joint Engineering Statement at 14-16.

[92]*See* Telecommunications Act of 1996, Tit. VII, § 706(a), Pub. L. No. 104-104, 110 Stat. 153 (1996), *reproduced in* the notes following 47 U.S.C. § 157 (Supp. 2001).

[93]*See In the Matter of Inquiry Concerning the Deployment of Advanced Telecommunications Capability to All Americans in a Reasonable and Timely Fashion, and Possible Steps to Accelerate Such Deployment Pursuant to Section 706 of the Telecommunications Act of 1996*, Second Report, 15 FCC Rcd. 20913, 20917 ¶ 8 (2000)

went on to note, however, that certain consumers (*e.g.*, those in rural areas) are "particularly vulnerable" to not receiving such services.[94]

Satellite systems are especially well-suited for the provision of broadband services in rural and other underserved areas and for providing a critical competitive alternative in suburban and urban environments. Satellite systems have nationwide coverage areas and are able to offer high-quality, ubiquitous service as soon as the satellite system is launched and operational. As such, satellite systems offer instantaneous deployment to low-population density and low-income areas that may not have enough demand to justify a terrestrial build-out.[95]

In spite of this potential, however true, satellite broadband deployment to date has been minimal. According to the *Second Report*, high speed services over satellite as of 1999 accounted for less than 50,000 lines, with none of these lines satisfying the Commission's definition of advanced services due to the limited upstream capabilities of these facilities.[96] ECC and Hughes have made reasonable progress compared to that baseline with early-entry interactive Ku-band broadband products. However, to date, only one percent of DBS subscribers has purchased high-speed satellite data services. The current consumer costs for these products, including equipment and monthly fees, given the low market penetration and lack of economies of scale, place them out of reach for many consumers, and make them less competitive with terrestrial offerings that offer bundled video and IP services in one package.[97]

As the Commission has recognized, the future of truly seamless satellite broadband communications lies with the deployment of next-generation systems in the Ka-band. The Commission has licensed these

("*Second Report*").

[94]*Id.* at 20918.

[95]In addition, satellites offer ubiquitous service at prices that are distance insensitive, in contrast to the distance-based prices that are characteristic of many terrestrial networks. These advantages allow satellite operators to provide first- and last-mile connectivity more cost-effectively than terrestrial systems, which have historically focused their deployment on high-density urban areas. *See Extending Wireless Telecommunications Services to Tribal Lands*, Notice of Proposed Rulemaking, FCC 99-205, WT Docket No. 99-266, ¶ 24 (rel. Aug. 18, 1999).

[96]*Id.* ¶ 111.

[97]*See* Joint Engineering Statement at 14-16.

systems in the hope that they would usher in "a new age in satellite communications" by providing "a wide variety of broadband interactive digital services in the United States and around the world."[98] The reality, however, is that deployment of these new satellite systems is taking longer and requiring more capital than many companies/licensees have been able to sustain. In the more than four years that have elapsed since the Commission's May 1997 authorization of the construction, launch and operation of Ka-band satellites in the first round of Ka-band licensing, certain licensees have encountered serious obstacles in their attempts to marshal the enormous capital and infrastructure required to construct, launch and operate satellite systems.[99] Even well-established satellite companies such as Lockheed Martin Corporation have backed away from the challenge of developing a Ka-band system, with its recent announcement that it will not invest further in its Ka-band venture, Astrolink.[100]

Each of ECC and Hughes has already made significant broadband investments and plans future deployment of additional high-speed Internet access services, but there are tremendous economic and technological hurdles that must be overcome to do so using satellites.[101] For example, in view partly of the financing community's reluctance to finance such projects, ECC's first Ka-band satellite, EchoStar 9 (to be launched in 2002), is a cautiously modest project, equipped with only a limited number of spot beams designed to serve only a few geographical areas in the United States. And while Hughes will invest approximately $1.5 billion and has already spent nearly $1 billion to begin deploying SPACEWAY system spacecraft in early 2003,[102] Hughes is not immune to downturns in the capital markets that could affect the timing of its deployment or its ability to offer competitively priced offerings. Current investments, divided between the

---

[98]*See In the Matter of Rulemaking to Amend Parts 1, 2, 21 and 25 of the Commission's Rules to Redesignate the 27.5-29.5 GHz Frequency Band, to Reallocate the 29.5-30.0 GHz Frequency Band, and to Establish Rules and Policies for Local Multipoint Distribution Service and for Fixed Satellite Services*, 12 FCC Rcd. 22310, 22310 (1997).
[99]Global Wireless, *Pie in the Sky*, September 1, 2001.
[100]*Decision Near on Astrolink as Lockheed Ends Funding*, Communications Daily, November 1, 2001.
[101]*See* Joint Engineering Statement at 14-16.
[102]The first phase of the SPACEWAY system will consist of two satellites and one spare to serve North America.

firms, may lack the economies of scale to compete with terrestrial services, thus implying higher prices to rural communities and less competition in non-rural areas.[103]

The merger will promote exponentially the efforts of both companies to implement truly competitive next-generation broadband systems in a fashion that, absent the merger, would likely be significantly less beneficial to the public. The parties expect that the proposed transaction will allow the two companies to develop a combined critical mass of broadband subscribers to spread the tremendous fixed costs that, as noted above, have deterred other satellite companies from proceeding with broadband satellite systems. The merger will speed broadband service availability, significantly improve subscriber growth, and therefore substantially enhance the competitive position of broadband satellite services vis-à-vis cable operators that can and do offer fully bundled Internet Protocol/video packages.[104] Cross-technology competition always benefits the public. The lower prices resulting from "intermodal" competition in urban areas will also benefit rural and underserved users with lower prices.

Second, a greater breadth of service will be implemented by the combined company more rapidly than would be possible absent the combination, and thereby will reach the consuming public more quickly. Time to market is of the essence. If next-generation satellite broadband services reach the market only after cable and DSL have commanded 60% of potential broadband customers, it is not clear whether any late-coming service would be able to attract enough of the remaining customers to become viable. This consideration highlights the more general point, noted above, that only a narrow window of opportunity is presented for imposing heightened competitive pressure on cable before cable is able to lock in its dominant position. The fact that effective competition occurs on the basis of bundles of offerings, and that broadband is a critical element of the bundle, reinforces the point further.

---

[103] *See* Joint Engineering Statement at 14-16.
[104] *Id.*

The merger will also boost broadband deployment by combining the Ka-band spectrum resources available to each entity. To be competitive with cable high-speed access, a satellite broadband platform needs to be capable of supporting several million U.S. subscribers. Each of ECC and Hughes (including PanAmSat) now has access to Ka-band spectrum at 3 orbital locations (in ECC's case, only two of these slots can support a one-dish solution), but Ka-band spectrum is limited in its ability to provide ubiquitous broadband services as a result of the Commission's satellite-terrestrial sharing decisions in the 18 GHz band. Even with the most advanced technology, each orbital location can only serve a finite number of customers. The number of customers that can be served is directly proportional to the amount of spectrum that is available. By combining resources in a merged entity, ECC and Hughes will be better positioned to create a Ka-band system capable of serving the nation's broadband service requirements while effectively and competitively challenging cable modem and DSL services.[105]

In short, commercialization of the Ka-band has been a cornerstone in the Commission's laudable effort to promote rapid deployment and competition in the provision of advanced broadband services and to promote the efficient use of spectrum by using the Ka-band to provide a new class of service that is simply not possible in the crowded Ku- and C-bands used for traditional Fixed-Satellite Service.[106] Approval of the proposed transaction will pave the way for the rapid deployment of a Ka-band satellite system capable of providing competitive broadband and other advanced services to all Americans, including those in rural areas, consistent with the Commission's goals and the public interest.

4. The PanAmSat Purchase Is In The Public Interest

The ECC-Hughes combination will result in a transfer of control of Hughes' controlling interest in PanAmSat, either to New EchoStar as a consequence of the merger, or through a separate purchase by ECC of Hughes' indirect interest in PanAmSat in the event the merger agreement is terminated under certain circumstances. In either event, the transfer of

---

105 Id.

106 See *Rulemaking to Amend Parts 1, 2, 21, and 25 of the Commission's Rules, 12 FCC Rcd. at 22312.*

control of Hughes' interest in PanAmSat is in the public interest and should be approved.

As outlined above, significant benefits to consumers will result from combining the FSS resources of ECC and Hughes to bring broadband satellite services to market faster. The merger will not create any significant overlap in the provision of FSS services in the same product and geographic markets that should be of any concern to the Commission.[107] ECC does not currently provide any telecommunications services of the type provided by PanAmSat in the United States or elsewhere. While Hughes and PanAmSat own and operate a fleet of FSS satellites and associated earth stations that are utilized primarily to provide domestic and international satellite services, respectively, the Commission has already determined that the consolidation of their businesses and operations under the control of Hughes serves the public interest.[108] Moreover, the combined FSS authorizations held by all three companies do not create market power in any one company in light of the large number of FSS satellite licenses held by other non-affiliated companies.[109]

III. WAIVER REQUESTS: APPLICATION CUT-OFF RULES AND ADDITIONAL APPLICATIONS

In connection with the approval of this transaction, the parties respectfully request that the Commission waive the application of its "cut-off" rules with respect to all pending applications filed by Hughes or its subsidiaries (including PanAmSat) and by ECC for additional space station authorizations, to the extent that those applications have been the subject of an FCC cut-off notice prior to the closing date.[110]

---

107 While ECC is a potential competitor in the FSS market, there are a number of other existing domestic and international FSS service providers (*e.g.* Loral/Orion, GE/SES, New Skies, etc.) as well as new entrants.

108 *See Hughes Comm., Inc., and Anselmo Group Voting Trust/PanAmSat Licensee Corp.*, 12 FCC Rcd. 7534 (1997).

109 *See, e.g., TRW, Inc.*, 16 FCC Rcd. 14407 (Int'l Bur. rel. Aug. 3, 1999); *CAI Data Systems, Inc.*, 16 FCC Rcd. 14269 (Int'l Bur. rel. Aug. 3, 1999);

110 Attachment G appended hereto provides a consolidated list of pending applications filed by Hughes and its subsidiaries and by ECC.

Section 25.116 of the Commission's rules provides that any pending application will be considered "newly filed" and therefore may lose its place in a processing round if it is modified by a "major amendment" – including an amendment that specifies a substantial change in beneficial ownership or control of the applicant.[111] An amendment will not be deemed a major amendment, however, if it reflects a change in ownership or control that the Commission determines is in the public interest and the Commission grants an exemption from the cut-off date.[112] The Commission has traditionally granted such exemptions where the proposed transaction will serve a legitimate business purpose and will serve the public interest.[113]

As described throughout this application, the proposed transaction serves a legitimate business purpose. By combining their satellite assets and operational resources, the transaction will enhance the combined enterprise's U.S. and global service capabilities, allowing it to compete more effectively and efficiently with dominant cable and other MVPD service providers. The transaction involves – indeed, it is primarily focused upon – operational satellites. Moreover, the applications currently pending are an integral part of Hughes' and ECC's expansion plans that were announced well before this proposed transaction and are essential to the continued competitiveness of their respective businesses. Under these circumstances, there can be no question that the transaction serves an independent business purpose and was not entered into for the purpose of acquiring the pending applications.[114] For these reasons, the Commission should exempt all currently pending applications filed by Hughes and its subsidiaries and by ECC from any applicable cut-off rules.

IV. SECTION 304 WAIVER

In accordance with Section 304 of the Communications Act of 1934, 47 U.S.C. § 304, the Applicants hereby waive any claim to the use of

---

[111] *See* 47 C.F.R. § 25.116(b) (2000).
[112] See 47 *C.F.R.* at § 25.116(c)(2) (2000).
[113] *See, e.g., DirectCom Networks, Inc.*, DA 01-1683 ¶ 16 (Int'l Bur. rel. Aug. 3, 2001); *Loral Space & Comm. & Orion Network Syst.*, 13 FCC Rcd. 4592, 4599, ¶ 17 (1998); *Hughes Comm., Inc. & Anselmo Group Voting Trust/PanAmSat Licensee Corp.*, 12 FCC Rcd. 7534 (1997); *AT&T Corp. & Loral SpaceCom Corp.*, 12 FCC Rcd. 925 (1997).
[114] *GE/SES*, DA 01-2100 at ¶ 56; *Loral/Orion*, 13 FCC Rcd. at 4599.

any particular frequency or of the electromagnetic spectrum because of previous use of the same, whether by license or otherwise.

V. CONCLUSION

For the foregoing reasons, the Applicants respectfully request that the Commission grant this application promptly and provide for any other authority that the Commission finds necessary or appropriate to enable the Applicants to consummate the proposed transactions.

Respectfully submitted,

GENERAL MOTORS CORPORATION

By: ______________________________

[name]
[title]

HUGHES ELECTRONICS CORPORATION

By: ______________________________

[name]
[title]

ECHOSTAR COMMUNICATIONS CORPORATION

By: ______________________________

Courtesy of Pantelis Michalopoulos, Steptoe & Johnson LLP

APPENDIX F

FORM OF CONFIDENTIALITY AGREEMENT

[LETTERHEAD]

[DATE]

[NAME OF COMPANY]

[ADDRESS]

[ADDRESS]

Ladies and Gentlemen:

In connection with a possible transaction (the "Transaction") between you and [NAME OF COMPANY] (the "Company"), the Company will be disclosing to you certain information relating to the Company, its direct and indirect subsidiaries, and its affiliates for the purpose of enabling you to evaluate the Company. As a condition to furnishing you with such information, the Company requires that you agree, as set forth below, to treat confidentially such information and any other information relating to the Company, its subsidiaries, and its affiliates, whether furnished to you before or after the date hereof and regardless of the form in which it is communicated or maintained (collectively, the "Evaluation Material"), which the Company or any of its advisors, representatives (including attorneys, accountants and financial advisors) or agents (collectively, "Company Representatives") furnishes to you or your agents, advisors, representatives (including attorneys, accountants and financial advisors), directors, officers, members, partners or employees (collectively, your "Representatives"). The term "Evaluation Material" also includes all reports, analyses, compilations, studies, notes or other documents prepared by you or your Representatives containing or based in whole or in part on any information furnished by the Company or the Company Representatives ("Analyses"). The term "Evaluation Material" does not include information which (i) is or becomes generally available to the public through no fault of you or your Representatives, (ii) was available to you on a non-confidential basis prior to its disclosure to you by the

Company, or (iii) becomes available to you from a source other than the Company or the Company Representatives, provided that such source is not bound by a confidentiality obligation of any kind to the Company.

You agree that the Evaluation Material will be kept strictly confidential by you and your Representatives, and shall not, except as hereinafter provided, without the Company's prior written consent, be disclosed by you or your Representatives. You agree that the Evaluation Material will be used by you and your Representatives solely and exclusively in connection with the Transaction. Moreover, you further agree to transmit Evaluation Material only to those of your Representatives who need to know such information for the purpose of the Transaction and who shall (i) be advised by you of this Confidentiality Agreement, and (ii) agree with you to be bound by the provisions hereof. You shall be responsible for any breach of this Confidentiality Agreement by your Representatives.

Without our prior written consent, you will not, and will direct your Representatives not to, disclose to any person (other than your Representatives who need to know) the fact that the Evaluation Material has been made available to you, that discussions or negotiations between you and the Company are taking place or any of the terms, conditions or other facts with respect to the Company or the Transaction.

In the event that you or your Representatives are requested or become legally compelled (by court order, interrogatories, subpoenas for the production of documents, or civil investigative demand) to disclose any of the Evaluation Material or the fact that the Evaluation Material has been made available to you, that discussions between you and the Company are taking place, or any of the terms, conditions or other facts with respect to the Transaction, it is agreed that you or your Representatives, as the case may be, will provide the Company with prompt written notice of each such request so that the Company may seek a protective order or other appropriate remedy and/or waive compliance with the provisions of this Confidentiality Agreement. In the event that such protective order or other remedy is not obtained, or that compliance with the provisions of this Confidentiality Agreement is waived, you agree that you will furnish only that portion of the Evaluation Material and other information which in the opinion of your legal counsel is legally required, and you further agree to use best efforts to obtain reliable assurance that confidential treatment will be accorded to that portion of the Evaluation Material and other information which is being disclosed; provided, that you will immediately provide the Company with written notice listing the Evaluation Material disclosed by you and/or your Representatives.

Upon notice from the Company to you, you and your Representatives will promptly deliver to the Company, or destroy, as instructed by the Company in the sole discretion of the Company, all Evaluation Material supplied by the Company or the Company Representatives to you and/or your Representatives and all copies thereof, and will destroy and erase all other Evaluation Material in your possession or under your control, including but not limited to your Analyses.

The Company does not make any representation or warranty as to the accuracy or completeness of the Evaluation Material. You agree that neither the Company nor any of the Company Representatives shall have any liability whatsoever under this Confidentiality Agreement to you and your Representatives resulting from the use of the Evaluation Material by you or your Representatives pursuant to the terms of this Confidentiality Agreement or otherwise.

For a period of two (2) years from the date hereof, you will not (and will not assist or encourage others to) solicit the services, as employees, consultants or otherwise, of any person who is an employee of the Company, or any of its direct or indirect subsidiaries or affiliates, at the time of such solicitation and about whom you learned in connection with your evaluation of the Transaction; provided, that you will be permitted to pursue employment of, and employ any such person who submits a resume to you either on an unsolicited basis or in response to a general employment solicitation.

It is further understood and agreed that no failure or delay by the Company in exercising any right, power or privilege hereunder shall operate as a waiver thereof, nor shall any single or partial exercise thereof preclude any other or further exercise thereof or the exercise of any right, power or privilege hereunder. Also, you understand and agree that money damages may not be a sufficient remedy for the breach of this Confidentiality Agreement by you or your Representatives, and that the Company and the Company Representatives shall be entitled to seek equitable relief, including injunction and specific performance, in the event of any breach of the provisions of this Confidentiality Agreement, in addition to all other remedies available at law.

In the event of litigation arising out of this Confidentiality Agreement, if a court of competent jurisdiction issues a final, non-appealable judgment, the non-prevailing party in such litigation agrees to reimburse the prevailing party for its costs and expenses (including, without limitation, reasonable attorneys' fees and expenses incurred by the prevailing party in obtaining such judgment).

You hereby agree to indemnify and hold harmless the Company and the Company Representatives from any damage, loss, cost or liability (including legal fees and the cost of enforcing this indemnity) arising out of or resulting from any unauthorized use or disclosure of the Evaluation Material.

The invalidity or unenforceability of any provision of this Confidentiality Agreement shall not affect the validity or enforceability of any other provisions of this Confidentiality Agreement, which shall remain in full force and effect.

This Confidentiality Agreement may be executed in counterparts, each of which shall be deemed an original and all of which shall constitute one and the same instrument. This Confidentiality Agreement shall inure to the benefit of the parties and their respective successors and permitted assigns.

This Confidentiality Agreement shall be governed by the laws of the State of [STATE].

The obligations set forth in this Confidentiality Agreement shall expire on the Second (2nd) anniversary of the return of all Evaluation Material to the Company.

[Signature Page Follows]

If you are in agreement with the foregoing, please sign and complete and return one copy of this Confidentiality Agreement to the Company, which will constitute the entire agreement with respect to the subject matter hereof.

[NAME OF COMPANY]

By: ______________________________

Name:
Title:

ACKNOWLEDGED, CONFIRMED AND AGREED TO:

[NAME OF COMPANY]

By: ______________________________

Name:
Title:

Date: ______________________________

[Signature Page to Confidentiality Agreement]

Courtesy of Barry A. Friedman and Rachel Gagnebin Talay, Thompson Hine LLP

APPENDIX G

TERM SHEET

[FORM OF LETTER AGREEMENT WITH SUMMARY OF NON-BINDING TERMS]

[LETTERHEAD]

[DATE]

[NAME OF COMPANY]
[ADDRESS]
[ADDRESS]

Ladies and Gentlemen:

[NAME OF COMPANY] ("Buyer") and [NAME OF COMPANY] ("Seller") wish to engage in negotiations regarding the potential [DESCRIBE TRANSACTION] (the "Transaction"). In order to induce Buyer (and in recognition of the time and effort that Buyer may expend, and the expenses that Buyer may incur in pursuing these negotiations and in investigating Seller's business) to enter into negotiations with Seller regarding the Transaction on the general terms and conditions of the Non-binding Terms attached to this Letter Agreement as Appendix A, Seller agrees as follows:

1. The parties hereto shall immediately proceed with the negotiation, preparation and execution of a definitive agreement for the Transaction (the "Definitive Agreement"). The parties will execute the Definitive Agreement on or before [DATE].

2. The parties hereto shall also negotiate, prepare and execute a confidentiality agreement within five (5) business days of the date of execution hereof.

3. Seller acknowledges and agrees that, until the earlier of [DATE] or the date on which Buyer advises Seller in writing that Buyer is terminating all negotiations regarding the Transaction, neither Seller nor any of its Representatives (as defined below) will, directly or indirectly:

(a) solicit or encourage the initiation or submission of any expression of interest, inquiry, proposal or offer from any person or entity (other than Buyer) relating to any Potential Deal (as defined below);

(b) participate in any discussions or negotiations or enter into any agreement with, or provide any non-public information to, any person or entity (other than Buyer) relating to, or in connection with, any Potential Deal; or

(c) entertain, consider or accept any proposal or offer from any person or entity (other than Buyer) relating to any Potential Deal.

Seller shall, and shall cause each of its Representatives to, immediately discontinue any ongoing discussions or negotiations (other than any ongoing discussions with Buyer) relating to any Potential Deal, and shall promptly provide Buyer with an oral and a written description of any expression of interest, inquiry, proposal or offer relating to any Potential Deal that is received by Seller or by any of its Representatives from any person or entity (other than Buyer) on or prior to [DATE].

4. Seller acknowledges and agrees that neither this Letter Agreement nor any action taken in connection with this Letter Agreement will give rise to any obligation on the part of Buyer to: (a) continue any discussions or negotiations with Seller; or (b) pursue or enter into any transaction or relationship of any nature with Seller.

5. Until the earlier of date on which the Definitive Agreement is executed or the date on which Buyer advises Seller in writing that Buyer is terminating all negotiations regarding the Transaction, Seller shall afford to Buyer, through its Representatives, free and full access to the properties, books and records of Seller during normal business hours in order to permit Buyer to make such investigation of the business, properties and operations of Seller as Buyer may deem appropriate.

6. Unless otherwise required by law, neither party hereto, nor any of its Representatives, shall make or permit any disclosure to any person or entity regarding (a) the existence or terms of this Letter Agreement, (b) the existence of discussions or negotiations between Seller and Buyer, or (c) the existence or terms of any proposal regarding the Transaction.

7. Seller acknowledges and agrees that, in addition to all other remedies available (at law or otherwise) to Buyer, Buyer shall be entitled to equitable relief (including injunction and specific performance) as a remedy for any breach or threatened breach of any provision of this Letter Agreement. Seller further acknowledges and agrees that Buyer shall not be required to obtain, furnish or post any bond or similar instrument in connection with or as a condition to obtaining any remedy referred to in this Paragraph 7, and Seller waives any right it may have to require that Buyer obtain, furnish or post any such bond or similar instrument.

8. Each party shall be responsible for the fees, costs and expenses incurred by it in connection with the Transaction.

9. In addition to the terms in Appendix A to this Letter Agreement, the Transaction would be contingent on:

[INSERT CONDITIONS]

10. This Letter Agreement shall be governed by and construed and enforced in accordance with the internal laws of the State of [STATE] (without regard to principles of conflict of laws), and shall be binding upon the parties hereto in the United States and worldwide. Each party: (a) irrevocably and unconditionally consents and submits to the jurisdiction of the state and federal courts located in the State of [STATE] for purposes of any action, suit or proceeding arising out of or relating to this Letter Agreement; (b) agrees that service of any process, summons, notice or document by U.S. registered mail to the addresses set forth on the signature pages to this Letter Agreement shall be effective service of process for any action, suit or proceeding brought against such party; (c) irrevocably and unconditionally waives any objection to the laying of venue of any action, suit or proceeding arising out of or relating to this Letter Agreement in any state or federal court located in the State of [STATE]; and (d) irrevocably and unconditionally waives the right to plead or claim, and irrevocably and unconditionally agree not to plead or claim, that any action, suit

or proceeding arising out of or relating to this Letter Agreement that is brought in any state or federal court located in the State of [STATE] has been brought in an inconvenient forum.

11. For purposes of this Letter Agreement:

(a) "Representatives" shall mean with respect to any party to this Letter Agreement, such party's officers, directors, members, partners, employees, subsidiaries and other affiliates, attorneys, advisors, accountants, agents and representatives.

(b) "Potential Deal" shall mean any transaction involving:

(i) the sale, license, disposition or acquisition of all or a material portion of the business or assets of Seller or any direct or indirect subsidiary or division of Seller;

(ii) the issuance, grant, disposition or acquisition of (A) any capital stock or other equity security of Seller or any direct or indirect subsidiary of Seller, (B) any option, call, warrant or right (whether or not immediately exercisable) to acquire any capital stock or other equity security of Seller or any direct or indirect subsidiary of Seller, or (C) any security, instrument or obligation that is or may become convertible into or exchangeable for any capital stock or other equity security of Seller or any direct or indirect subsidiary of Seller; or

(iii) any merger, consolidation, business combination, tender offer, share exchange, reorganization or similar transaction involving Seller or any direct or indirect subsidiary of Seller;

8. This Letter Agreement shall be binding on the parties hereto in accordance with the terms hereof; provided, that it is expressly understood that neither party hereto intends to be legally bound by the Non-Binding Terms set forth in Appendix A to this Letter Agreement.

[Signature Page Follows]

This Letter Agreement shall not become effective and shall be null and void if not executed by Seller and delivered to Buyer by [TIME], on [DATE].

Very truly yours,

[NAME OF COMPANY]

By:

Name:
Title:
Address:

ACKNOWLEDGED, CONFIRMED AND AGREED TO:
[NAME OF COMPANY]
By:
Name:
Title:
Address:
Date:

[Signature Page to Letter Agreement with Summary of Non-Binding Terms]

EXHIBIT A

Summary of Non-binding Terms

This preliminary Summary of Non-binding Terms sets forth certain key terms of the Transaction involving Buyer and Seller. Neither this Summary of Non-binding Terms nor any action taken in connection with matters referred to in this Summary of Non-binding Terms will give rise to any obligation on the part of Buyer or Seller to continue any discussions or negotiations or to pursue or enter into any transaction or relationship of any nature.

Structure of Transaction:	
Consideration:	
Stock Options and Warrants:	
Employment Agreements:	
Customary Deal Protection Measures:	
Pre-Closing Covenants:	
Conditions to Closing:	
Due Diligence:	
Governing Law:	
Dispute Resolution:	

Courtesy of Barry A. Friedman and Rachel Gagnebin Talay, Thompson Hine LLP

ASPATORE